A TRAILS BOOKS GUIDE

THE GREAT IOWA TOURING BOOK

27 SPECTACULAR AUTO TOURS

Mike Whye

TRAILS BOOKS
Black Earth, Wisconsin

Library of Congress Control Number: 2003115109
ISBN: 1-931599-35-1

Editor: Stan Stoga
Photos: Mike Whye
Graphic Designer: Emily Culp
Cover Photo: Mike Whye

Printed in the United States of America.

09 08 07 06 05 04   6 5 4 3 2 1

Trails Books, a division of Trails Media Group, Inc.
P.O. Box 317 • Black Earth, WI 53515
(800) 236-8088 • e-mail: info@wistrails.com
www.trailsbooks.com

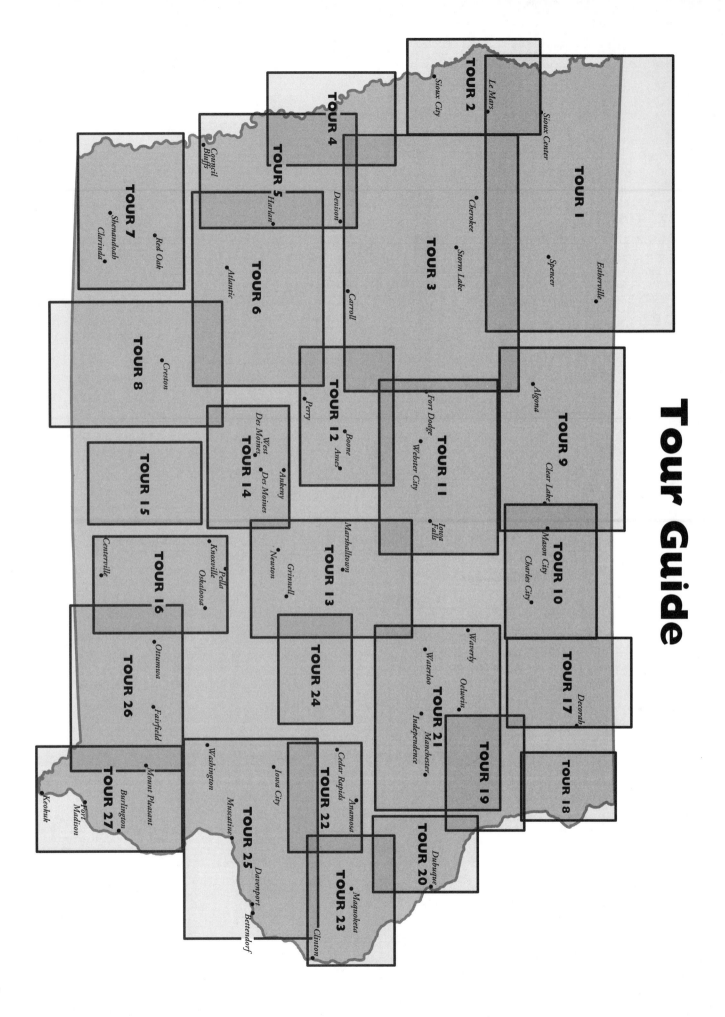

Tour Guide

TOUR 1
Estherville
Spencer

TOUR 2
Sioux City
Le Mars
Sioux Center

TOUR 3
Cherokee
Storm Lake
Carroll

TOUR 4
Denison

TOUR 5
Harlan

TOUR 6
Atlantic

TOUR 7
Red Oak
Shenandoah
Clarinda

TOUR 8
Creston

TOUR 9
Algona
Clear Lake

TOUR 10
Mason City
Charles City

TOUR 11
Fort Dodge
Webster City
Iowa Falls

TOUR 12
Perry
Boone
Ames

TOUR 13
Marshalltown

TOUR 14
West Des Moines
Des Moines
Ankeny

TOUR 15

TOUR 16
Pella
Knoxville
Oskaloosa
Centerville

TOUR 17
Decorah

TOUR 18

TOUR 19

TOUR 20
Dubuque

TOUR 21
Waverly
Waterloo
Oelwein
Manchester
Independence

TOUR 22
Cedar Rapids
Anamosa
Iowa City

TOUR 23
Maquoketa
Clinton

TOUR 24

TOUR 25
Muscatine
Davenport
Bettendorf

TOUR 26
Ottumwa
Fairfield
Washington

TOUR 27
Keokuk
Fort Madison
Burlington
Mount Pleasant

Grinnell
Newton

Contents

Introduction

Iowa: A Land of Surprises and Wonderful People

Fields create an attractive pattern near Hull, a scene repeated all over Iowa.

When settlers first arrived in Iowa, some wrote in their journals about their experiences. At first they remarked about how the land appeared to roll on forever without any change. Then, as they continued their travels, they described how they suddenly encountered steep cliffs that plunged down to rivers meandering below. Prairie soils would give way to rocks, some of which still held the outlines of creatures that vanished eons ago; and, for no apparent reason, a boulder would sit by itself on a landscape that was featureless except for tall prairie grasses and wildflowers bobbing in the breeze. Lakes would appear almost out of nowhere.

Times have changed. The prairie is nearly all gone, replaced by farm fields more than anything else. But the reaction of many people encountering Iowa for the first time is similar to those who first saw the endless prairie years ago: "Ah, there's not much to see."

Without suggesting that people take to their feet and walk across Iowa like the settlers and Native Americans did as they came upon one surprise after another, there are still ways to find the surprises that abound in modern Iowa. This is best done by getting off the major highways and taking the less-traveled roads that bring travelers much closer to the charms that exist in the long stretches between the big cities.

Sure, big cities feature many attractions such as museums, art galleries, entertainment centers, concert facilities, sports complexes, shopping areas, and the like; but while this guidebook will cover those too, its emphasis is on Iowa's smaller communities and the vast countryside where the pleasures are simpler and life moves along at a slower pace. This is where one finds the country church with doors that are open to anyone who stops there. Mazes made of corn rise up in different patterns each year. Soda fountains established decades ago still pump cold treats in the business districts of small towns. Some out-of-the-way museums have one-of-a-kind collections that can amaze visitors and make them shake their heads and smile.

Meeting friendly people is part of the charm of traveling in Iowa. Here, the soda fountain at Penn Drug in Sidney is a popular gathering spot for visitors and local folks.

Of course, as one travels across Iowa, there's no way its people can be overlooked. Some of the nicest folks you will ever meet are here. You will encounter many at museums, stores, restaurants, and lodging places. Some will be travelers just like you, out to have a good time visiting the state's many attractions. You might exchange pleasantries with one another, perhaps along the lines of "Hey, this is something, isn't it?"

You will also see them when you're in your vehicle. Watch as you drive the back roads in particular and you may see "the wave." Most often it's a little shake of the hand in the air, a quiet "hello there" hand signal even though they don't know you. At other times, it's a driver raising a couple of fingers in a salute as you pass one another. Occasionally, it's a nod of the head, and if that's combined with a wave of the hand, you're really doing well. Of course, if you get a wave, a nod, and a smile, you've hit a home run and you can't help but smile in return, can you?

That's the kind of feeling that makes visiting Iowa so special and the reason why I have enjoyed traveling across Iowa all these years. This guidebook is my attempt to distill that experience into a form that travelers will find useful and informative. I hope the book en-hances your enjoyment of discovering Iowa. It's a wonderful state.

Practicalities

Even though people use four-lane highways and interstates to zip along from here to there, that's not the purpose of this book. Instead, you're going to be directed onto the lesser known highways, the two-lane roads (including many county roads),

most of which are paved and well maintained and lie across Iowa in a way few other states can match. These are your best bet to reach many of Iowa's treasures that are not seen by the people who sail along on the four-lane highways. Still, the book occasionally advises you to take a four-lane highway now and then, usually for a short distance. Conversely, there will be times when good gravel roads will be the best way to reach a particular place, and this book does not shy away from suggesting them. But in those rare cases, paved routes are always presented as an option.

Besides this book, it's recommended that you pick up three more items: the Iowa Travel Guide, the Iowa Calendar of Events, and the Iowa Transportation Map, all of which are available free from the Iowa Tourism Office (see below) and at any of the Iowa Welcome Centers (the maps are also found at all rest areas).

This book was written so that it relates to the annually published Iowa Travel Guide in that the chapters are arranged from north to south in the western third, central third, and eastern third of the state. The travel guide has a brief listing of attractions with their Web sites, addresses, and phone numbers, plus listings for hotels, bed and breakfasts, inns, and campgrounds, as well as a listing of some of the state's annual events and festivals. A complete listing of events, celebrations, and festivals is found in the Iowa Calendar of Events.

Finally, it is recommended that you obtain an Iowa Transportation Map, which is also available from the Iowa Department of Transportation (see below). This statewide map also has maps for

15 urban areas in Iowa, a locator of all communities and counties, contact information and phone numbers, a mileage chart, and a listing of all welcome centers.

Tourist Information: The Iowa Tourism Office, (515) 242-4705, and toll-free, (800) 345-IOWA, 200 East Grand Avenue, Des Moines, IA 50309. Its Web site is www.traveliowa.com, and its e-mail is tourism@ided.state.ia.us

State Parks, Preserves, and Forests (including fishing, hunting, trails, and outdoor recreation): Iowa Department of Natural Resources, (515) 281-5145, Wallace State Office Building, Des Moines, IA 50319-0034. Its Web site is www.state.ia.us/dnr

Transportation: Iowa Department of Transportation, (515) 239-1372, 800 Lincoln Way, Ames, IA 50010. Its Web site is www.state.ia.us/government/dot

Emergencies and 911: The 911 system is in effect across Iowa, in urban and rural areas, and is toll-free from any phone. It is to be used only for emergency calls to law enforcement authorities, fire departments, or medical personnel. To contact the Iowa State Patrol on a non-emergency basis, call toll-free, (800) 525-5555.

Road Conditions and 511: The Department of Transportation maintains a phone number, 511, that is offered statewide in Iowa and covers the interstate highways, U.S. routes, and some state highways. The service does not cover all county roads or city streets at the time of this writing, although it may be expanded to cover all of those other roads in the future. Besides providing road conditions in inclement weather, it also warns of accidents and road closings that may cause travelers to change their route.

There is no charge for dialing 511, although a regular local charge may apply at a pay phone. The 511 service can also be reached by calling, toll-free, (800) 288-1047. More information about the 511 system within Iowa can be found at www.dot.state.ia.us/511

Seat Belt/Child Restraints: All passengers in the front seats of vehicles are required to wear seat belts, and children under six years of age must be in proper child restraints.

Motorcycle Helmets: Not required.

Radar Detectors: Permitted but not in commercial vehicles.

Population: Approximately 3,000,000.

Capital: Des Moines.

Area: 55,875 square miles.

Admitted to Union: December 28, 1846, as the 29th state.

Nickname: The Hawkeye State.

Motto: Our Liberties We Prize and Our Rights We Will Maintain.

Time Zone: Central Time Zone.

Highest Point: 1,670 feet above sea level at Hawkeye Point, north of Sibley in Osceola County.

Lowest Point: 480 feet above sea level at Keokuk.

Holidays: January 1; Martin Luther King Jr. Day (third Monday in January); Memorial Day (last Monday in May); July 4; Labor Day (first Monday in September); Veterans Day (November 11); Thanksgiving; Friday after Thanksgiving; Christmas (December 25).

Sales Tax: The state rate is five percent, with local options totaling a maximum of two percent; no sales tax on groceries.

A car cruises past fall foliage in the Loess Hills east of Mondamin.

27 SPECTACULAR AUTO TRIPS

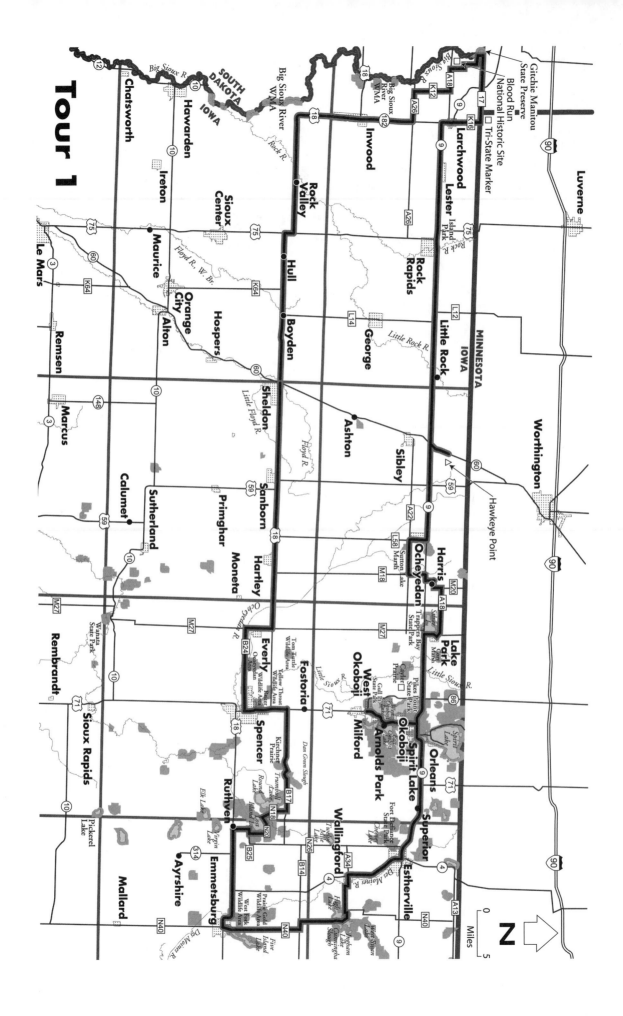

Tour 1

Tour 1
Iowa's Greatest Northwest

Okoboji—Rock Rapids—Blood Run—Hull—Sheldon—Spencer—Emmetsburg—Estherville—Okoboji

Distance: approximately 275 miles

Way up in northwest Iowa, the Great Plains seem to roll on forever—that's a given. But there are also unexpected attractions that will surprise and delight you. First, you'll encounter the Great Lakes—Iowa's Great Lakes, that is. These are a series of large natural lakes that form the state's prime recreation spot, which includes the oldest amusement park west of the Mississippi River. Later on, you'll come upon Iowa's highest points (both past and present), its oldest rocks, the site of an ancient encampment where more than 10,000 Indians lived in the seventeenth century, the Irish capital of Iowa, and the town that was almost hit by the largest stony-iron meteorite to fall in the recorded history of North America.

Mention Okoboji to Iowans and they'll respond that it's a fun place to go with great lakes, fantastic restaurants, fabulous resorts, entertainment parks, state parks, sandy beaches, sailing, boating, fishing, and more. In short, it's been Iowa's playland since the late nineteenth century.

In case you're wondering, there is no Lake Okoboji . . . there are two: East Lake Okoboji (the smaller, shallow one) and West Lake Okoboji (the larger, deeper one). Actually, there are many others near here but most of the fun is around West Lake Okoboji, especially in the summer. This tour includes a few trips on gravel roads.

Start your tour on U.S. Highway 71 at the south end of West Lake Okoboji and drive north. On some summer days, the traffic can be a bit heavy, by Okoboji standards. Coming up from Milford, travelers encounter *Boji Bay*, located at Highway 71 and State Highway 86, (712) 338-2473, admission, a large water park with a wave pool, water slides, kiddy pool, tube rides, and volleyball courts. A short distance to the north is *Arnolds Park*, located in the community of the same name, the oldest amusement park west of the Mississippi. Built in 1889, the park's highlights include a 63-foot-high Ferris wheel, a wooden roller coaster that continues to generate screams, and a new log ride. There are also plenty of kiddy rides.

Docking near the park is the excursion boat *Queen II*, (712) 332-5159. Although modern, the

The excursion boat *Queen II* pulls up to the dock at Arnolds Park.

The Spirit of the Lakes, an excursion train, passes through northwest Iowa between Spirit Lake and Harris.

Iowa's Greatest Lakes

West Lake Okoboji is Iowa's deepest lake at 136 feet; East Lake Okoboji is the state's longest natural lake at 16 miles and Spirit Lake is Iowa's largest glacial lake.

Queen II resembles its forerunner, the *Queen*, which took visitors around West Lake Okoboji about a century ago. A series of 90-minute narrated cruises start at noon each day and cover 18 miles.

In the same area is the *Okoboji Spirit Center*, (712) 332-2107 or (800) 270-2574, free. Inside are an *Iowa Welcome Center* featuring information about area attractions, events, lodging, and restaurants; a gift shop with items from the Iowa Navy; and the *Iowa Great Lakes Maritime Museum*, which tells about the region's water-based recreation over the years and has a marvelous collection of classic boats.

Also in the same region is the *Roof Garden Ballroom*, (800) 270-2574, where each day during the summer you can listen to live rock, jazz, and blues from 11 a.m. to 4 p.m. while enjoying great food. Listening in the evenings to nationally known performers requires admission, though. In the same building is the *Iowa Rock "N" Roll Music Association Hall of Fame*, (712) 332-6540, admission, honoring all facets of the days when rock and roll ruled the radio raves (pun intended): performers, producers, songwriters, radio DJs, radio stations, dance pavilions, and recording studios. Artifacts on display include guitars and organs used by famous performers and beautiful stereo consoles used by listeners at home. Gold records, posters, and photographs adorn the walls. Within a few steps of the Roof Garden is a public beach.

A few blocks to the west, the *Abbie Gardner Cabin State Historic Site*, 34 Monument Drive, (712) 332-7248 and (712) 352-2643, free, memorializes the 1857 Spirit Lake Massacre. Although the incident was called the Spirit Lake Massacre, most of the action occurred at other places. Somehow, though, Spirit Lake's name was used to title the slaughter.

Inkpaduta, of the Wahpektue Santee (a small division of the Santee Sioux), is generally painted as the villain of the Spirit Lake Massacre, but things aren't as simple as they seem. During the early 1850s, Inkpaduta and some other Santee were already upset about European-Americans moving into their lands, when a white horse thief named Henry Lott killed a Santee who may have been a relative of Inkpaduta. Lott disappeared before he could be punished by an American court, angering the Santee. Next, the winter of 1856–1857 was hard, and supplies promised by the federal government failed to show. Disgruntled, Inkpaduta and his group arrived at the Gardner family cabin near West Lake Okoboji on the morning of March 8, 1857. At first they were given food and ammunition but long-burning hatreds ignited, and by day's end 35 settlers in the area lay dead and Ink-paduta's group was on the move with four white women as captives. After three months, 13-year-old Abbie Gardner was the last captive to be released to Yankton Sioux, who were friendly with whites; only one of the three other women survived the ordeal. Never captured, Inkpaduta reportedly joined the Sioux led by Sitting Bull, was at the Battle of the Little Big Horn in 1876, and died in Canada in 1881.

Continue north on Highway 71, crossing the bridge that spans the channel connecting East Lake Okoboji and West Lake Okoboji, and enter the town of Okoboji. The town boasts a year-round population of about 800 residents, and considerably more in the summer. There, the *Higgins Museum*, 1507 Sanborn Avenue, (712) 332-5859, has one of the best collections of bank notes made between 1863 and 1935 with an emphasis on banks in Iowa, Minnesota, South Dakota, and Nebraska, as well as nearly 20,000 photo postcards of Iowa scenes. North of the museum on the highway is *Ranch Amusement Park*, (712) 332-2159, which has kiddy rides, arcade games, bumper boats, an ice cream parlor, a skee-ball alley, and the state's longest go-cart track. Also nearby is the *Lakes Art Center*, 2201 Highway 71, (712) 332-7013, which hosts showings of its permanent collection as well as traveling exhibits, and foreign films, concerts, and recitals. Farther up Highway 71, the *Okoboji Summer Theater*, (712) 332-7773, features melodramas and musicals that have long been popular with the summertime crowds.

From Okoboji, continue north on Highway 71 for about 4 miles to the T intersection with State Highway 9 and turn left (west).

Continue west on Highway 9 for approximately 11 miles until you reach County Road M27; turn right (north) and drive into Lake Park. This small community rests alongside *Silver Lake*, making for an atmosphere that is quieter than the hubbub that often occurs around Okoboji.

Quick Trip Option 1: From the intersection of Highways 71 and 9, go west on 9 for 3 miles to State Highway 86; turn left (south) and go about 3 miles to 180th Street, where you turn left (east). Watch for signs to *Lakeside Laboratory*, (712) 338-4238, a part of Iowa State University. Established in 1909, the lab is where lectures about wetlands, mammals, birds, trees, and more are given throughout the summer on Sundays, Wednesdays, and Thursday evenings. Nearby are resorts and *Gull Point State Park* (712) 337-3211, which has 112 campsites (60 with electricity), boat ramps, swimming, and fishing.

Return west to Highway 86, cross it, and continue on 180th Street (which is now gravel) for 3.5 miles to 170th Avenue (also called County Road M38). Turn right (north) and go until you see the sign for *Caylor Prairie*, near 170th Street, and park on the right. *Caylor Prairie* is a restored prairie similar to what once covered more than three quarters of Iowa. Even if you have been here before, come back to see the various wildflowers that bloom at different times of the year.

To return to Highway 9, go north on 170th Avenue for just under 2.5 miles. Turn left (west) on 9 and drive about 4 miles to County Road M27; turn right (north) and proceed into Lake Park.

From Lake Park, turn west on County Road A18 and go about 5.5 miles until it intersects with County Road M20. Turn left (south) and, a mile later, turn right (west) into tiny Harris. On the south side of the town's east-west main street is a grotto billed as the world's smallest, so don't blink.

From Harris, continue to take M20 for one mile to the south and rejoin Highway 9. Head west on Highway 9 for barely a mile until you see County Road M18 on the left (south); take that for 2 miles to County Road A22 where you turn to the right (west) and drive for about 5 miles. You'll soon notice a substantial hill (substantial for this area, that is) rising on the right side of the road. Pull into the parking area that's near the hill. You're at the

The Spirit of the Lakes

Turn right (east) at Highway 9 and, after nearly 1 mile, you will see a HyVee grocery on your left (north); turn left at the very next street beyond the HyVee, Memphis Avenue. Just after crossing the railroad tracks, park in the lot on the right (east) side of the road and wait for your train to come in. Specifically, it's the *Spirit of the Lakes*, (712) 366-9600 and (866) 621-9600, fee, a tour train with open-air and air-conditioned passenger cars. It also has dessert trains and dinner trains with five-course meals, Friday to Sunday in the summer months. The train runs to Harris and back while the meals on steel wheels versions go just to Lake Park and back at an easier pace for dining comfort; both trips last two hours and pass open fields, farms, wetlands, pristine glacial lakes, and some stretches of woods near the tracks.

Ocheyedan Mound and in case you're wondering, it's pronounced "oh-shee-dan" or "oh-chee-dan." Rising more than 100 feet above the surrounding plains, it may not look all that lofty compared to other high points; but for years it was thought to be the highest spot in Iowa, topping out at 1,655 feet above sea level (for those who want to know about Iowa's lowest point, see Tour 27). However, precise measurements made in 1971 dropped the mound a few notches in the ratings as some higher points were found elsewhere . . . a bit more on that in a moment.

From Ocheyedan Mound, continue west on A22, then turn right (north) onto County Road L58, which leads into the town of Ocheyedan. On the other side of town, you will meet Highway 9 again; turn left (west) and drive about 11 miles to State Highway 60. Turn right on 60, which runs northeast at this point. Two miles from the 9/60 intersection, turn right (east) onto 130th Street, a gravel road, and go about an eighth of a mile. You are now at the farm of Merrill and Donna Sterler. Enter the second drive, park, and walk up a gentle rise to the end of what once was a feed trough where a sign states that you're at *Hawkeye Point*. At 1,670 feet above sea level, this is Iowa's highest point. Okay, having caught your breath, sign the register . . . it's in the metal box . . . to add your name to those left by others who have come from as far away as Japan, Europe, and South America. The Sterlers appreciate being called, (712) 754-2045, before you visit.

From Hawkeye Point, return to Highway 60, turn left, and return to Highway 9.

Quick Trip Option 2: You can venture into Sibley, which is on Highway 60 about 2 miles south of Highway 9, to view the *McCallum Museum* and *Brunson Heritage House* at 5th Street and

8th Avenue, (712) 754-3882. The facilities are open on summer Sunday afternoons and contain Civil War and pioneer artifacts, horse-drawn vehicles, and an automobile sold by Sears in 1908.

On Highway 9, head west again for 22 miles to Rock Rapids. Along the way are signs for George and Edna—towns named after the children of a railroad executive when the railroad first came through here. As you enter Rock Rapids, the county seat of Lyon County, you will see the large water tower on the left (south). Note the small concrete bridge near its base in a city park. Although moved from its original site, the *Melan Bridge* was the first steel-reinforced concrete bridge in the world when built in 1893.

Blood Run

Despite the sanguinary name, Blood Run was actually a peaceful place and was occupied mainly between 1650 and 1705 when up to 10,000 people lived here. Blood Run is the largest site known to be connected with the Oneota culture. These prehistoric Indians raised corn, beans, and squash, hunted elk, deer, and bison, and fished. Artifacts show that the Oneota Indians used shell-tempered pottery in the form of bowls, jars, and other containers. The high content of gravel in the area provided good drainage, permitting Indians to create storage pits. Once those pits were emptied of the good items, they became garbage pits. Before quarrying and modern farming practices altered the land, Blood Run had at least 176 mounds, of which 80 are visible today. Originally the creek ran between two bluffs; the one near the parking lot was used later as a quarry while the far plateau was farmed for a while. Gathering artifacts is forbidden.

As for the name Blood Run, it came from the rust-colored water that would sometimes appear in the creek, stained by iron-laden minerals in the soil.

As soon as you cross the Rock River, take a right (north) onto Marshall Street and continue for about a block, then turning down a short slope. Now you've done it—you're in *Island Park*, not a bad place to be by the way, with camping, picnic facilities, a playground, and a small zoo. You can also fish along the shaded banks and near the base of the dam. When you come to a fork in the park road, take a right and cross to another area of the park via a low-lying concrete bridge, which is sometimes a bit underwater when the water is high. Or you can veer left and exit the park past the mini-zoo.

Just past the mini-zoo, the park drive exits onto North 4th Avenue. Take a left (east) for a few car lengths and turn right (south) onto North Story Street. In a moment you will pass the town's swimming pool, *Heritage House,* and the *Rock Island Depot,* 110-1/2 North Story Street, (712) 472-3101, admission, which now houses the *Lyon County Historical Society*. In another block you're at the main

intersection of downtown Rock Rapids. The Lyon County Courthouse is another block south on Story Street.

At Highway 9, head west for 14 miles until you reach a stop sign at a T intersection. There the highway turns to the north for 1.2 miles, and as it begins to resume going west, keep heading straight north into the town of Larchwood on Chestnut Street. As it heads out of town, Chestnut becomes County Road K16. Take that for 3 miles to Cherry Avenue, also called County 17. Notice the change in the road designation; that's because you're at Iowa's northern border and are about to enter Minnesota. Hence, the different county road designation. Now, if being where two states meet thrills you, hang on . . . things get better.

Turn left (west) onto County 17 and go 1 mile. A small white marker on the northwest corner of the T intersection there marks the juncture of Iowa, Minnesota, and South Dakota. Now you can stand where *three* states come together!

From the tristate marker, keep going west. In a little more than 3 miles, you'll meet Highway 9 again. Cross that and drive 4 more miles to County Road K10. Turn left (south). You'll soon come to a parking area at *Gitchie Manitou State Preserve*, (712) 336-3524, free, on the right (west). A 15-minute walk on a mown trail leads through prairie grasses to outcroppings of Sioux quartzite on the 91-acre preserve. Said to be 1.6 billion years old, these pink-colored rocks are Iowa's oldest. Beware of prickly pear cactus in the area.

Continue south on County K10. A mile south of Gitchie Manitou is the entry to *Blood Run National Historic Site*, (712) 472-2217, free, on the right (west). A gravel road leads back to the main portion of the site, which is about 650 acres and has an information kiosk and a parking area. Tours are self-guided. A small stream cuts through the site and if you want to get to the far side, be prepared to take off your shoes and socks for a shallow wade. During the summer, the gate to the property is usually open, but in the fall the Lyon County Conservation Board allows hunting on the grounds at certain times and for safety reasons everyone else is kept out then.

From Blood Run, continue south and east on County K10 for less than 2 miles to County A18. Turn left (east). Go 3 miles to County Road K12 and turn right (south). About 4 miles later, turn left onto County Road A26 and in about 2 miles you will reach

Named after the creek that runs through it, Blood Run National Historic Site was a large Indian settlement in Iowa's northwest corner.

Lake Pahoja County Park, (712) 472-2217. The park is sited around a 69-acre lake that hosts fishing and boating and has a one-room school and a teacher's house, both furnished as they had been about a century ago. The lake is stocked with largemouth bass, bluegill, channel catfish, black crappie, and bullheads.

From the park, head east on County A26 until you reach State Highway 182, where you turn right (south). Just south of Inwood, you'll meet U.S. Highway 18. Continue south, then east, on 18 for about 20 miles to U.S. Highway 75, passing south of Rock Valley on the way. Follow Highway 18 as it jogs briefly to the south and goes east once more toward Hull. On the near edge of this town of almost 2,000, you will see the *Foreign Candy Company*, (712) 439-1496 or (800) 831-8541, which is a wholesale distributor of . . . yup, you guessed it . . . foreign-made candies. Although you can't stop here, mercifully, the company has an outlet in town at 910 Main, (712) 439-2691, so follow the signs over there

and enjoy some candy you don't normally find in America, such as Pierrot Gourmand lollipops from France, sour revitas from Spain, and Hitschler SoftiChew Sticks from Germany.

From Hull, continue east on Highway 18 for 14 miles until you roll into Sheldon. At the intersection of Highway 18 and State Highway 60 is an original *A&W Restaurant*, 101 Park Street, (712) 324-3368, and the carhops there still bring frosty mugs of root beer to your vehicle. In the former Carnegie Library is the *Prairie Queen Museum*, 4th Avenue and 10th Street, (712) 324-4482, which has a large display of military items, especially those related to the National Guard troops of northwest Iowa, along with early fire-fighting equipment and a model of the Prairie Queen Milling Company's mill. On the east side of town on Highway 18 is a complex housing the *Wansink Art Gallery, Prairie Schoolhouse*, and *Pioneer Home*, (712) 324-3371. Besides hosting fine art shows, the schoolhouse holds art classes, and the home has also been a hotel and a church.

Head east on Highway 18 for about 33 miles to County Road M27, passing through Sanborn and Hartley along the way. Turn right (south) onto M27 and go through Everly; about a mile south of town, turn left (east) onto County Road B24. Take this for less than 10 miles into Spencer. As you enter town, the road becomes West 4th Street, which goes into the downtown area. Some nice stores are there, including *Arts on Grand*, 408 North Grand Avenue, (712) 262-4307, a local art gallery featuring a gift shop and exhibits by artists from within and beyond the Midwest, and the *Parker Historical Museum of Clay County*, 300 East 3rd Street, (712) 262-3304. Housed in a 1916 Arts-and-Crafts-style house and other buildings, the museum has vintage clothing, a one-room schoolhouse, agricultural implements, an antique fire truck, and a general store.

North of downtown and west of Grand Avenue are the grounds of the *Clay County Fair*, (712) 262-4740. Held for a full week each September, this is the largest county fair in Iowa, and it's said to be larger than some state fairs. Its agricultural equipment display is North America's largest.

The Estherville Meteorite

About 5 p.m. on May 10, 1879, people in and around Estherville heard a tremendous set of thunderous booms that shook the ground so hard that windows vibrated and the china rattled on the shelves. An earthquake? No. From the sky flashed a series of fireballs that thudded into the ground two to three miles north of town. Within hours people were recovering thousands of pieces, totaling more than 744 pounds, of the largest stony-iron meteorite recorded to fall in North America. The largest piece weighed 437 pounds and was recovered from where it lay, 14 feet underground. Although the majority of the meteorite is elsewhere now, an eight-and-a-half-pound piece is at the Estherville Public Library, (712) 262-2187. In 2003, a small cube-shaped piece of the meteorite was sold for $12,000.

If you're into canoeing, go south on Grand Avenue and on the far side of the Little Sioux River at West Leach Park, ease a canoe into the river to travel the *Inkpaduta Canoe Trail*, (712) 262-2187. With about 30 access points on the river, canoeists can paddle 134 miles south to Smithland (see Tour 4).

From Spencer, go north on Grand Avenue, which is also U.S. Highway 71. Two miles past Highway 18, turn right (east) on County Road B17; drive for about 5 miles to *Dan Green Slough*. The highway here jigs and jogs a bit, providing a nice contrast to Iowa's usual straight-as-an-arrow roads. *Dan Green Slough* is one of several pothole lakes created in this part of Iowa by glaciers. A number of waterfowl are here throughout the year, particularly during the fall when flocks of geese, duck, and

pelican are migrating. County Road B17 curves around the south side of the slough and straightens to head east for 4 more miles before meeting County Road N18.

Turn right (south) on County Road N18. On the right (west) you'll see *Trumbull Lake* as you pass through more state-owned wetland areas. *Mud Lake* will soon appear on the left, followed by *Lost Island Lake*, then County Road N20.

Turn left (east) onto County Road N20. This leads around the lake's north side to *Lost Island Prairie Wetland Nature Center*, (712) 837-4866, free. In a county park on the lake's northeast corner, the center's main focus is on the glacial pothole lakes that dot northwest Iowa. The park offers nature trails, picnic facilities, boating, campgrounds, and fishing.

From the Lost Island Nature Center, go south on County N20 until you meet County Road B25. Turn right (west) and drive for less than a mile to a paved road. Turn left (south) and drive less than 2 miles into Ruthven. On the town's south side, turn left (east) onto Highway 18 and proceed to Emmetsburg 12 miles away. Well, it might be expected that a town named after Irish orator and patriot Robert Emmet might have a lot to do with the Irish and this one certainly does, especially when it claims that it's Iowa's Irish capital and has Dublin as a sister city. An *Iowa Welcome Center*, 1121 Broadway, (712) 852-2283, helps to orient visitors and lead them to local attractions. Almost across the street from the welcome center is the *Palo Alto County Courthouse*, 1010 Broadway, and on its front lawn are a bronze statue of Emmet and a rock that is called—what else—the *Blarney Stone*. The *Victorian Muse-um on Main*, 1703 East Main, (712) 852-3781, is preserved in all its splendor as an 1883 wedding gift from a prominent businessman to his daughter. Jutting into town from the north, *Five Island Lake* has swimming, boating, and camping.

In Emmetsburg, take Lake Street north, along the west shore of Five Island Lake. At the intersection with Lawler Street, turn right (north) and drive a short distance until Lawler intersects with College Drive, which is also County Road N40. Turn right (east), then follow the road as it jogs north. Go for about 8 miles to County Road B14. Turn left (west) and drive for 1 mile; turn right to resume going north on N40. In a few minutes, you will be on a narrow strip of land between two pothole lakes: *High Lake* on the left (west) and *Ingham Lake* on the right.

Follow N40 as it curves left, crosses High Lake, and meets a T intersection. Turn left (south) and follow the road as it soon turns

west and becomes County Road A34. In about 3 miles, it turns to the right (north). At the very next left, turn left (west) as A34 leads you across the Des Moines River and into tiny Wallingford. On the west side of town, turn right (north) on State Highway 4 and proceed for about 6 miles into Estherville. Upon approaching this town of over 6,600 people, you will see on the left, of all things, the *Riverside Hills Ski Area*, (712) 362-5376, one of the few ski venues in the state. Further evidence that Estherville takes its winters seriously is the fact that the word *blizzard* was created when a newspaper writer here used it to describe a local 1870 snowstorm.

Quick Trip Option 3: Southwest of Estherville is *Fort Defiance State Park*, (712) 337-3211, the site of a sod-and-log fort built after Minnesota's 1862 Sioux Uprising. The 191-acre park is set alongside School Creek and has trails and 16 campsites, eight with electricity. To reach the park from Highway 9, turn south at West South 1st Street, which turns into Park Road and leads to Fort Defiance 1 mile away.

Near the park on County Road A22 (which is Central Avenue on Estherville's west side) is *Heartland Hills Golf Course* (formerly Estherville Golf and Country Club), 3625 170th Street, (712) 362-4755, a semiprivate nine-hole course. Like many other golf courses, it has a clubhouse with a restaurant, but there the similarities with the other courses end, because Heartland Hills' *Deer Run Restaurant and Bistro* features superbly made Cajun and French dishes as well as selections of wild game.

Upon meeting Highway 9 at Estherville, turn left (west) and continue for 15 miles to U.S. Highway 71 and the Okoboji area where you began this tour.

Tour 2

Tour 2
A Place Called Siouxland

Sioux City—Hawarden—Orange City—Le Mars—Merrill—Hinton—Sioux City

Distance: approximately 110 miles

This tour includes a part of northwest Iowa that was the scene of some of Iowa's earliest historical events involving European-Americans, specifically the frontier expedition led by Lewis and Clark, who visited here in 1804 and again in 1806. Called Siouxland, a word coined by regional author Frederick Manfred, who wrote novels such as *Lord Grizzly*, this area is known for its hills and wide river valleys. It's also home to Iowa's largest prairie, what may be the world's largest ice cream freezer, the first national monument in the United States, and places where you can truly see the world through rose-colored glass.

Begin this tour in Sioux City, at the *Sergeant Floyd River Museum and Welcome Center,* just off Interstate 29 near Exit 149. The center, 1000 Larsen Park Road, (712) 279-0198, free, is in *Chris Larsen Park*, along the Missouri River. It is, appropriately enough, located in a former survey boat used on the Missouri by the U.S. Army Corps of Engineers. Although you may come just for information about the region, wander though the center, which is also a wonderful museum about all types of watercraft that have used the Missouri River, from dugouts and keelboats to palatial sternwheelers of the nineteenth century and tows that transport the nation's goods.

Near the welcome center is the *Sioux City Lewis and Clark Interpretive Center*, 900 Larsen Park Road, (712) 224-5242, free. Exhibits allow you to assume the role of one of the men of that famous expedition and learn what they packed, wrote, used, and did on their long journey. A pair of animatronic figures, dressed as Lewis and Clark, re-create the burial of Sergeant Charles Floyd atop a nearby bluff.

Continue east on the road that passes through *Chris Larsen Park*. On the way, you'll see Veterans Memorial Bridge that connects Iowa and Nebraska. The park contains a memorial to the victims, survivors, and rescuers of the crash of United Flight 232 in 1989; the elegant *Anderson Dance Pavilion*; and a playground. Near the far end of the park, *Argosy of Sioux*

City Casino, 100 Larsen Park Road, (712) 255-0080 or (800) 424-0800, has table games and more than 400 slot machines on three decks. If you're in the area over the Labor Day weekend check out *ARTSPLASH*, a large show of juried artists held in the park.

At the east side of *Chris Larsen Park*, circle the roundabout and take I-29 to the north for about 2.5 miles to Exit 151. As you pass along some bluffs on the right (north) side of the interstate, you might notice on one ridge the statue of *War Eagle*, an Isanti Dakota who aided the first whites in this area.

Lewis and Clark

Ordered to explore the Louisiana Purchase and seek a way to the Pacific Ocean, Captains Meriwether Lewis and William Clark led an expedition, consisting of 22 soldiers, 2 interpreters, and 17 other men (mostly French boatmen) through this area in 1804, while going up the Missouri River. Using a keelboat and two smaller boats, called pirogues, to haul their supplies, the men found traveling upriver to be hard, taking about five weeks to travel between Iowa's southern border and what is now Sioux City.

Just below Sioux City, Sergeant Charles Floyd died on August 20, 1804, possibly of appendicitis, and was buried on a bluff south of the city. The men then held the first election by Americans west of the Mississippi River and elected Patrick Gass to replace Floyd as sergeant.

At Exit 151, turn onto Riverside Boulevard, which runs north from the interchange and is also State Highway 12.

Quick Trip Option 1: As soon as you begin to go north on Riverside Boulevard, take War Eagle Drive and proceed up to the *War Eagle Monument* atop the bluffs, giving a great view across Siouxland.

Proceed north on Highway 12 for 2 miles to the fork in the road. Keep to the right to stay on 12, which is now named Sioux River Road and is part of the *Loess Hills National Scenic Byway.* By the way, the Big Sioux River—the border with South Dakota—is

The Loess Hills

The Loess Hills were born at the end of the last Ice Age, between 10,000 to 20,000 years ago, give or take a few centuries. As the glaciers that had covered much of North America melted more and more each summer, they unleashed heavy runoff that carried away the finely ground silt produced when the glaciers had crushed everything in their way. Each winter though, the runoff slackened and the silt was left high and dry.

Prevailing northwesterlies carried those fine, dry grains of silt, called *loess* (which rhymes with bus and comes from the German word meaning "loose"), to the edge of the waterway, where the winds broke and the grains tumbled, forming dunes. The dunes grew over the centuries and prairie plants took root, stabilizing the dunes. As the winds built the hills, rain and the waterways sculpted them further. Today, the tops of the hills rise up to 260 feet above the valley of the Missouri River.

When not covered by topsoil, loess withers when hit by rain. Slopes are particularly vulnerable but, oddly, loess forms a strong bond when the hills are cut vertically, which is the reason why cuts for roads often stand without reinforcement. These cuts show that most of the hills are pure loess, although some regions, such as those near Sioux City and Sidney (Tour 7), contain some rocks.

Many Iowans are proud of the Loess Hills, and from time to time a few say that the only other loess hills are in China along the Yellow River. Not true. Deposits of loess are found in other parts of the world, and those hills you see way over in Nebraska cross the Missouri? Yup, they're loess too, although not as tall as those in Iowa because of how the winds blew when they were formed. If one wants to be accurate, the thing to say is that nowhere else in the world are deposits of loess that high except in China. To be considered a loess formation, loess must be at least 60 feet deep.

When Lewis and Clark passed alongside Iowa, they wrote that the hills were covered with prairie. At that time, wildfires caused by lightning cleansed the hills of invading woody plants but wildfires are no longer possible because of roads, farm fields, and communities, so brush and trees now cover many of the hills. Still, of the 20,000 acres of prairie remaining in Iowa (considerably less than the 30 million acres here in the early nineteenth century), 15,000 acres are in the Loess Hills with the largest areas in the Broken Kettle Grasslands and north of Turin (Tour 4).

Because of their highly erosive nature, there is considerable discussion about how to use and preserve the Loess Hills. The best examination of the hills is the book *Fragile Giants* by Cornelia Mutel.

The *Loess Hills National Scenic Byway*, (888) 623-4232 and (712) 482-3029, traverses the hills for about 220 miles on its main route, all on paved highways, with 16 side trips that sometimes take gravel roads.

on your left and that's where it's going to be for a while on this tour. Not long after coming onto Sioux River Road, on the left (west) you will see *Milwaukee Shops*, 3400 Sioux River Road, (712) 276-3176, admission. Located at the site of a railroad roundhouse, this museum is open on Saturdays and covers the history of the railroads in this region.

Farther up the highway is *Dorothy Pecaut Nature Center*, 4500 Sioux River Road, (712) 258-0838, free, on the right side of the road. This facility is a great place to become acquainted with the nearby Loess Hills and their flora and fauna. (See Tour 4 for an extensive jaunt through the Loess Hills.) You'll also encounter some of the hills on

the present tour. One display in the center takes you through one of the hills so you can see what's underneath them.

Upon leaving the Pecaut Nature Center, go north for about 1 mile on Highway 12; turn into *Stone State Park*, 5001 Talbot Road, (712) 255-4698. At the entrance you have a choice. If you want to picnic at one of the 32 campsites, take the low road (directly ahead), but if you want overlooks of the region, turn right, ascend the hill, and drive across the ridges of the hills. You can also hike miles of trails in the park. The best way back to Highway 12 is the way you came.

From the park, continue on Highway 12 for about 15 miles to Westfield. The road here angles to the northwest and runs on a ledge between the Big Sioux River and the base of the bluffs. Notice how the hills diminish to the point that they disappear as you enter tiny Westfield.

Quick Trip Option 2: If traveling on gravel roads doesn't bother you, this route through the northern Loess Hills can be an entertaining interlude on your travels. About 5.5 miles after leaving Stone State Park, turn right (northeast) onto County Road K18, a paved road. (But beware: there are two K18s! *Do not take the first one*; that one cuts back sharply to your right rear and returns to Sioux City. Instead, take the second K18 turnoff, which goes to your front right and the northeast.)

More than 3 miles past the K18 junction with Highway 12, watch for the entry to *Five Ridge Prairie Preserve*, (712) 947-4270, free. A mile-long dirt road on your left (northwest), 260th Street, leads into the preserve, part of one of the larger roadless areas in Iowa. If the entry road is wet, do not take it. Of the preserve's 780 acres, nearly 300 acres remain as prairie, primarily on the ridges and south slopes, with little bluestem and sideoats gamma grasses as well as other prairie plants that attract butterflies. The ravines are thick with bur oak. Mountain biking is allowed on established trails.

Once you're back on K18, continue to the northeast. Shortly, at County Road C43—a gravel road—turn left (northwest); it runs along the open ridges of the Loess Hills. At the intersection with Butcher Road 2.8 miles later, turn left (southwest). Butcher leads along areas with great vistas of the *Broken Kettle Grasslands*, (712) 568-2596, free. At 3,000 acres, it's the largest expanse of prairie in Iowa and some of its wildlife and plants are not found for hundreds of miles to the west. The grasslands hold a small group of prairie rattlesnakes that are not only the easternmost of their kind in the nation but also the only ones in Iowa. Other residents include the black-billed magpie, upland sandpiper, coyote, badger, plains spadefoot, and Great

Plains toad, as well as many prairie butterflies. Among the plants are purple locoweed, purple coneflower, dotted blazing star, big bluestem, buffalo berry, and yucca.

In 3.5 miles, you'll reach Highway 12; turn right (northwest) and go about a half mile to the farm lane leading to the preserve's headquarters on the right (northeast). There's really nothing in the building to see but it's a good place to park and take to hiking in the hills.

To resume the main part of this tour, return to Highway 12, turn right (northwest), and go about 5 miles to Westfield.

At Westfield, continue north on Highway 12 for about 18 miles to Hawarden. Along the entire way, the road continues to parallel the Big Sioux River, which angles slightly to the northeast now. Before reaching Hawarden, you'll pass through Akron in 5 miles and Chatsworth 7 miles beyond that. In Hawarden is *Historical House*, 801 Avenue H, free, which has been furnished to resemble how it looked in 1900; and *Calliope Village*, 19th Street and Avenue E, (712) 551-2403/4433, free, a collection of 14 buildings that represent Sioux County's original county seat before the county records were seized and moved to Orange City in 1872. Among the buildings is the childhood home of Ruth Suchow, which is being refurbished to display items related to her. Born here in 1892, Suckow (pronounced "soo-koe") was highly regarded in her day for her novels and short stories that realistically depicted the lives of Midwestern families, independent women, and other people. After living some years in eastern Iowa, she died in 1960 in California.

At Hawarden, turn right (east) on State Highway 10 and drive for 25 miles to Orange City. Here is where those county records were taken in 1872; as a result, Orange City became the county seat of Sioux County. As you enter the south side of town, turn left (north) on South Central Avenue. That will take you downtown in eight or so blocks. Don't worry about missing it, the Dutch-style architecture of some buildings lets you know when you have arrived. Obviously, this town was established by Dutch settlers, and their heritage is displayed proudly, as evidenced by some of the buildings. There's no need to guess what's in the *Dutch Bakery* and the *Dutch Meat Market*—all good food.

At the intersection of First Street and Central Avenue is a windmill-shaped phone booth. Just south of downtown is the *Old Factory*, 110 Fourth Street SW, (712) 737-4242. In a former shoe factory—ahem, a wooden shoe factory— this gift shop carries delft, lace, tile, and foods imported from Holland. Of course, wooden shoes are still sold there, in 20 sizes.

On the third weekend of each May, Orange City celebrates *Tulip Festival*, (712) 737-4510,

The evening sun lights up the Broken Kettle Grasslands. North of Sioux City, they comprise the largest contiguous native prairie in Iowa.

when tulips are blooming and many residents dress in old-style Dutch clothing to wash the streets, hold a parade, and have a good time.

Return to Highway 10, continue east and then turn right (south) on Albany Avenue SW. As you leave town, watch on the right (west) side for the small windmill outside the headquarters of *Diamond Vogel Paint*, 1020 Albany Place SE, (712) 737-8880, free. If the mill's not open, ask at the nearby office for a key to let yourself in for a look.

Attired in Dutch dress, young girls dance in Orange City's annual Tulip Festival.

Continue south on Albany Avenue SW, which becomes County Road K64 outside of town. In 5 miles this meets State Highway 60. Turn right (southwest). Construction continues on Highway 60, widening it so it will be a four-lane highway connecting Sioux City with Minnesota's Twin Cities.

In about 10 miles you will approach Le Mars. When you meet U.S. Highway 75, veer left to go south and enter the city. There, count down the streets on the left: 6th, 4th (there is no 5th at the highway), 3rd, 2nd, 1st—and bingo! You're at the *Ice Cream Capital of the World Visitor Center*, at the junction of U.S. Highway 75 and State Highway 3, (712) 546-4090, admission. Set up by the Wells Dairy, which makes more ice cream in Le Mars than any other place in the world, the center tells how ice cream came to be and is made nowadays. There's also a very interactive room at the end of the self-guided tour that's a hit with kids. Beyond that (and accessible without paying to visit the museum) is a 1920s-style ice cream parlor that serves it all—sundaes, sodas, floats, phosphates, banana splits, and special concoctions. Have you been served golf-ball-sized scoops of ice cream anyplace lately? Well, get used to baseball-sized scoops here. A regular two-scoop sundae costs about $3.49 and you may need a friend to help eat it. Besides regular ice cream flavors and toppings, the soda fountain has yogurt and fat-free and sugar-free ice creams.

Le Mars Facts

—Settled in 1866, Le Mars was originally called St. Paul Junction. But in 1870, as a group of men plotted the town's new streets, their wives plotted the town's new name. Combining the initials of their first names, Lucy Underhill, Elizabeth Parson, Mary Weare, Anna Blair, Rebecca Smith, and Sarah Reynolds, ended up with what they thought was a pretty name, Le Mars. So if you thought it was French, it isn't. Besides, the town was settled mostly by British, Scotch, Irish, and Welsh immigrants, followed later by Germans and the Dutch. A number of the British were second sons of titled families; unable to inherit their fathers' titles, they were sent here to learn how to manage farms, and for a while polo, steeplechases, and fox hunts were popular in this town.

—Begun in 1913 with a horse-drawn milk wagon, Wells Dairy is now the largest family-owned dairy in the nation and distributes its chilly refreshments to every state and some foreign countries. On the south edge of town is the company's 11-story, 100 million-cubic-foot warehouse that holds up to 13 million gallons of ice cream at minus-20 degrees Fahrenheit. The third-largest ice cream manufacturer in the nation, Wells makes 100 million gallons of ice cream each year, including 14 types of vanilla alone.

—In 1890, Le Mars was the fourth-fastest growing community in the nation.

Once you waddle away from the soda fountain, go east on Highway 3, which is also Plymouth Street. At First Avenue SW, turn right (south) and go three blocks. In the former high school building is the *Plymouth County Historical Museum*, 335 First Avenue SW, (712) 546-7002, free. The museum has a Civil War era log cabin, schoolroom, as well as a collection of antique musical instruments, including a nineteenth-century music box that played 25-inch-in-diameter disks, the grandfather of today's much smaller CDs.

To return to Highway 75, take 4th Street SW to the west for a few blocks.

On Highway 75, drive southwest for 7 miles to Merrill. This small community is the home of *Bogenrief Studios*, 124 Main, (712) 938-2162, which is less than a block to the right (west) side of the highway at the flashing yellow light. In business since the 1970s, Mark and Jeanne Bogenrief have changed their small firm into one with a 20,000-square-foot studio that produces stained glass creations that have been used across the nation and in other countries. Visitors can look at the custom-designed stained-glass windows, domes, ceilings, lamps, and doors that use jeweled and beveled glass.

Leaving Merrill, continue southwest on Highway 75 for 7 miles to Hinton. Turn right (west) at Main Street. This will give you an opportunity to visit another glass studio owned by a Bogenreif; this time, it's *B&B Art Glass*, 103 West Main, (712) 947-4572, run by Mark's brother, Nick. Actually, this is where Mark started years ago. The brothers amicably went their separate ways, and Nick began working in this smaller, more intimate space but with no less intensity on custom-made stained and leaded glass windows for homes, churches, and businesses. Again, visitors are welcome.

Continue on Highway 75 for about 10 miles to Floyd Boulevard; turn right and proceed southwest into Sioux City. Along your way on Floyd, you will see the large complex of the American Popcorn Company, makers of Jolly Time popcorn, on the right (west). Started in 1914, it was the first company to process popcorn and the first to sell brand name popcorn; the family-owned company is now one of the nation's leading popcorn producers. It also has had the Good Housekeeping Seals of Approval longer than any other company—since 1925.

Drive a bit more than 2 miles on Floyd Boulevard to 33rd Street. There, you'll find *Trinity Heights*, (712) 239-8670, free. This Roman Catholic-oriented site has large gardens around epic-size stainless steel statues of the Virgin Mary and of Jesus, while more than 30 other pieces of art depict the history of Christianity. A life-size wood carving of the Last Supper is in the St. Joseph Center and a gift shop is on the grounds.

Continue into town on Floyd and turn right (west) at 27th Street. Go about one mile to Jackson Street; turn right (north). On the far left (northwest) corner of the intersection of Jackson and 29th Street is the *Sioux City Museum*, 2901 Jackson, (712) 279-6174, free. In an 1893 mansion built of pink-gray Sioux quartzite, the museum has a great collection of artifacts related to the Native Americans of

Siouxland and exhibits about the region's early settlers and local wildlife.

From the Sioux City Museum, drive west on 29th Street for six more blocks to Summit Avenue. Turn left (south). This takes you alongside *Grandview Park*, which has a band shell and a rose garden that's accessible from Summit. Grandview is where *Gateway's Saturday in the Park*, (712) 277-2575, is held on the Saturday closest to the Fourth of July. It features 10 hours of music; in the past, entertainers such as Santana, Blues Travelers, and the Brian Setzer Orchestra have performed here.

At 24th Street, turn left (east) and go two blocks to Grandview Boulevard. Turn right (south) onto Grandview and drive to 7th Street; turn left (east). In one block is the *Woodbury County Courthouse*, 620 Douglas Street, (712) 279-6525, the largest municipal building in the nation designed in the Prairie School Style. If you think the outside is something, go in and be awed by the magnificent architectural details and paintings in the atrium.

Go east one more block to Pierce Street, turn right (south), and go to the intersection of Pierce and 6th Street. To the southeast is the restored *Orpheum Theater*, (712) 258-9164, which hosts live theater, film, presentations, and concerts ranging from the Sioux City Symphony to Anne Murray.

Continue south on Pierce to 2nd Street (which may not be marked well), turn left (east) and at the middle of the block, turn right (south) into a parking lot for the *Sioux City Art Center*. Many art museums hold works of art . . . that's understood. This center, 225 Nebraska Street, (712) 279-6272, free, is a work of art in itself as well. From the outside it looks like tan blocks stacked around a steel and glass drum: the center's atrium. The wings hold works from the permanent collection, traveling exhibits, classrooms, and art studios for visiting artists.

From the art center, go east on 3rd Street for four blocks. At Virginia Street, turn left (north) and go for one block later to 4th Street; turn right (east). Now you're in the middle of the *Fourth Street Historic District*, a clutch of historic warehouses and commercial buildings built between 1889 to around 1915. Within a two-block area are boutiques, antique stores, pubs, and great restaurants.

When you're finished shopping and eating in the historic district, go east on 4th Street, which shortly becomes 3rd Street. At Lewis Boulevard, which is also Business Highway 75, turn right (south) and drive for about 2 miles. The *Sergeant Floyd Monument* will

appear on the right (east). This 100-foot-high, tan obelisk, the first national landmark in the nation, marks the bluff where Sgt. Charles Floyd was buried in 1804. He was the only person on the expedition led by Lewis and Clark to die during the entire trip. The bluff is also a good place to look out at Siouxland.

Many people consider the Sioux City Art Center itself to be a work of art.

Return to Lewis Boulevard and turn left (north). Backtrack to the first stoplight, which is at Glenn Avenue. Turn right (east) and go to South Lakeport Avenue, less than 2 miles away, and turn right (south). In a little more than a mile this leads to *Southern Hills Shopping Mall*, the only commercial site certified by the National Park Service on the entire Lewis and Clark Trail, which stretches from near St. Louis, Missouri, to the Pacific Ocean. Why's that? you wonder. Well, the mall has 38 murals that depict the journey of Lewis and Clark from the time when Lewis discussed the trip with President Thomas Jefferson to when the two explorers returned to Saint Louis in 1806.

From the shopping mall, continue south for less than a mile to U.S. Highway 20 and turn right (west). Proceed on Highway 20 for 1.5 miles to I-29. Follow it for about 4.5 miles to Exit 149, the beginning of this Siouxland tour.

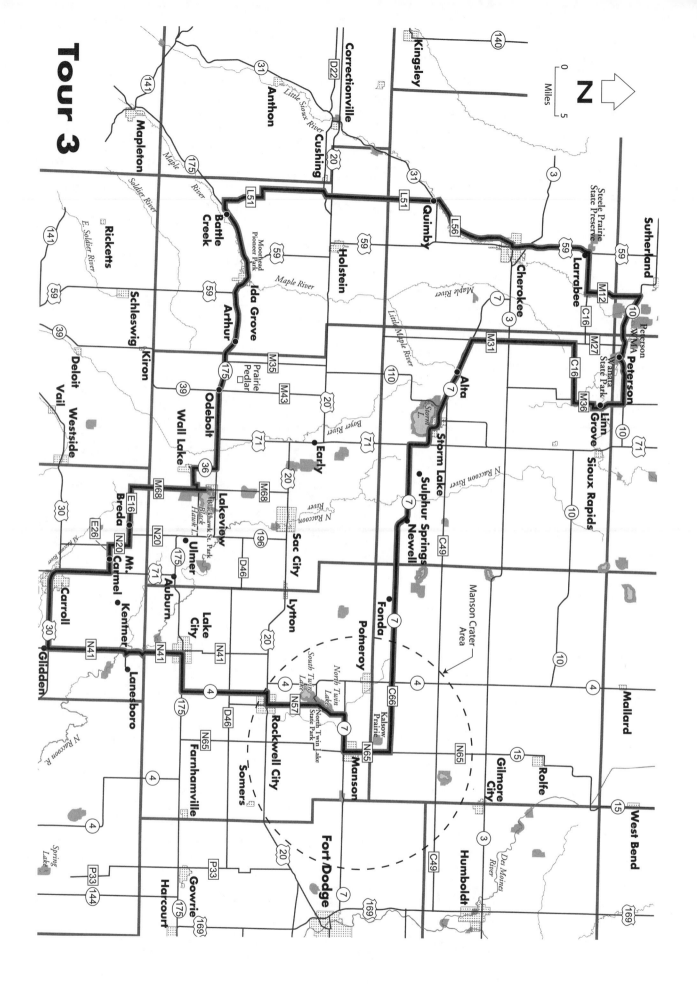

Tour 3
Glacial Lakes, Prairie, and the Biggest Crater No One Has Seen

Battle Creek—Ida Grove—Odebolt—Wall Lake—Lake View—Carroll—Lake City—Rockwell City—Storm Lake—Peterson—Cherokee—Battle Creek

Distance: approximately 238 miles

Ranging across the plains of northwest Iowa, this tour introduces you to the Spanish architecture of one community, the world's largest wind farm, a place to admire the flowers of the prairie, some pretty lakes with nice beaches, and one place that literally shook the world millions of years ago. Along the way, you can learn about Arabian cultures, listen to some antique radios, canoe quietly on the Little Sioux River, and perhaps see some square-dancing tractors—now that's a doe-see-doe not many can do!

Begin this tour at Battle Creek on State Highway 175. As you go east along the south side of this community of about 750 residents, you will see the *Battle Hill Museum of Natural History*, Highway 175 E, (712) 365-4414, free. Located in two one-room schools, this museum was started by one man's curiosity about natural history and what it holds is surprising—rocks, fossils, sea shells, more than 600 mounted animals from around the world, bones of creatures that roamed here thousands of years ago (including a sea lion bone found in the area . . . which no one can explain) and a replica of a limestone cave.

Continue east on Highway 175 for 7 miles to Ida Grove. As you approach the town and pass the turnoff to U.S. Highway 59, on your left (north) is *Moorehead Pioneer Park*, (712) 364-3257, which has campsites, picnic areas, a playground, boating, and fishing. Besides an 1884 schoolhouse, there's a stagecoach inn that began as a log cabin built in 1856 by John H. Moorehead (who named the county and city for his daughter); it also was the county's first post office, church, school, and hospital.

From the park, go east on Highway 175 to Oak Grove Drive and turn right (south). Right there is *Skate Palace*, 201 Oak Grove, (712) 364-3430, which has two unique qualities. The first is very evident—its medieval Spanish exterior, an architectural feature you will also notice elsewhere around this town. The second is inside—its modern but old-style inlaid wood floor, something most skating arenas just don't have anymore. Nearby is *Cobb Memorial Park*, a

nice green area that's home for geese, ducks, and swans. On some holidays it's full of flags.

Continue on Oak Grove Drive as it turns east and becomes Ash Drive. When it connects to Moorehead Avenue, turn right (south); the avenue jogs a bit and becomes Main Street. This leads to the town's business district, which is centered on 2nd Street. *Ida Grove Pharmacy*, 506 2nd Street, (712) 364-2734, serves up frosty treats from its old-time soda fountain.

A few more blocks south on Main is the Ida County Courthouse and across the street to the west is *Moorehead Museum*, 400 Main, (712) 364-3257. An 1883 Victorian house with a square tower, it now houses historical artifacts from around the county.

Byron Godberson

Ida Grove is the hometown of Byron Godberson, Iowa's most prolific inventor. Raised on a farm, Godberson first achieved fame for inventing a farm wagon that used a hoist powered by a tractor's hydraulic system to dump its loads. Later, he attached a winch to a boat trailer and people across the world have since been using that.

For a while, Godberson made one-fifth scale, radio-controlled aircraft that were considered the Cadillacs of that hobby. When he died in 2003 at the age of 78, Godberson had more patents than anyone else in Iowa—over 50. Named Inventor of the Year in 1996, he was also the Small Businessman of the Year in 1973.

Today, his GOMACO Trolleys makes reproductions of the trolleys of yesteryear and reconditions historic ones, his Midwest Industries makes boat trailers, and his GOMACO builds concrete paving machines used across the world.

Godberson liked medieval architecture, which is easily seen throughout the town in places he was involved with, including the local newspaper, golf course, Skate Palace, airport, and, near that, his half-scale *HMS Bounty*.

From the courthouse area, go east to Moorehead Street (not Moorehead Avenue) and turn left (north). Pass through the downtown again, following Moorehead Street as it becomes Washington Avenue north of the tracks. At Highway 175, turn right (east). You'll pass a group of industrial buildings on both sides of the highway. Not far beyond those on the right (south) is a lake with a three-masted sailing ship, but it's private property and nothing you can visit. The airport, with a Spanish-style hangar, is just beyond there.

Continue east on Highway 175 for about 12 miles to Odebolt, passing the turnoff for Highway 59, which branches off to the south, and the tiny town of Arthur. In Odebolt, you'll find historical items from the region, including farm tools and equipment, at the *Odebolt Historical Museum*, 512 West 2nd Street, (712) 668-4860/4377/4532, free.

Quick Trip Option 1: A little more than 2 miles past Arthur, turn left (north) on County Road M35 to visit one of Iowa's more popular garden spots, *Prairie Pedlar*. Go up M35 for 6 miles and, at the Prairie Pedlar sign at 210th Street, which is a gravel road, turn right (east). In 2 miles, Prairie Pedlar is on your left (north). Note that once you enter Sac County, 210th Street becomes 270th Street.

Created by Jane and Jack Hogue, Prairie Pedlar, 1609 270th Street, (712) 668-4840, free, has 60 theme gardens sprouting herbs and perennials, and everlasting flowers, dried in the loft of their barn, are sold on the floor below in the gift shop. The Hogues host various classes and festivals each growing season.

To return to the main tour, go east on 270th Street for 2 miles. At County Road M43, turn right (south) and drive into Odebolt, 6 miles away.

Popcorn Capital of the World

In the 1930s, the region near Odebolt was the world's popcorn capital although now all of Sac County claims that title. In 1995, residents of the county built the world's largest popcorn ball, which measured more than six feet across and weighed more than 2,000 pounds. At least 20 million pounds of popcorn raised in this area are used by Cracker Jack every year.

From Odebolt, continue on Highway 175 for 8 miles to County Road M64. Turn right (south) and drive 3 miles to Wall Lake. As you approach Wall Lake, you will undoubtedly see its new wind turbine, 230 feet high and generating 200 million kilowatts a year. It's one of many located across Iowa.

Where's Wall Lake?

At Wall Lake, you might wonder, where's the lake? Well, at one time just west of town was a wetland—the lake, if you will—that had an embankment—the wall, if you will—against one side of it, but that slough was drained and is now a farm field.

Enter Wall Lake on Center Street. Go to 1st Street on the south side of town and turn left (east). Right there is the *Andy Williams Birthplace*, 102 East 1st Street, (712) 664-2119,

admission. Built in 1890 by his grandparents, this is where singer Andy Williams was born in 1927, the youngest of four boys who began singing in the choir where their father, a railroad mail clerk, was the choir director of the local Presbyterian church and their mother played the piano. Realizing their vocal talents, the parents moved the family to Des Moines in 1935 as the Williams Brothers and Andy went on his own in 1952, often joining composer Henry Mancini. Among his many hits are "Moon River," "The Days of Wine and Roses," and the theme song from *The Godfather*. Williams also hosted a popular TV show in the 1980s.

Go west on 1st Street for a few blocks, crossing Center Street. You'll arrive at Wall Lake's other success story, *Cookies Barbecue Sauce*, 614 West 1st Street, (712) 664-2662. Started in the local volunteer fire department by D. L. "Cookie" Cook in 1976, Cookies made 200 gallons of barbecue sauce that year. Now, it makes about 20,000 gallons of barbecue and taco sauces and salsa each week and distributes them to at least 32 states. In 2002, Cookies Western Style Barbecue Sauce was chosen as the best sauce at the American Royal Barbecue in Kansas City. A gift shop at the plant sells sauces, some barbecue accessories, T-shirts, and cooking aprons.

Return to Center Street, turn left (north), and go to County Road D54 on the north edge of Wall Lake. Turn right (east) and go to County Road M68; turn left (north) and drive for about 2 miles to Lake View. Along the way, the road swerves to the north and then back to the east, soon leading to some small lakes and right into Lake View, which does have a lake—957-acre Black Hawk Lake, the southernmost glacial lake in Iowa. Also in town is *Golf Products, Inc.*, Lake Street and Highway 175/71, (800) 238-8679. Started in 1987 as a golf ball retrieval company, it is now one of the older and larger suppliers of used golf balls in the world. If you've lost a golf ball in the last few years, chances are that it passed through here on its way to a new owner. Visitors are welcome.

Go to Third Street in Lake View and turn right (east). At the intersection with McClure, on the right (south) is the northern trailhead of the *Sauk Rail Trail* (712) 662-4530, fee, a hike-bike trail that passes through farm fields, woods, and open stretches of land before reaching Carroll, 33 miles away. Also close by is a nice stone overlook of the area. Check it out by taking Third Street, which drifts to the north, then turns right (south) onto Lakeshore Drive.

Return to Third Street and turn right (northeast) on what is now Lake Street; drive a short distance. On the left is *Speaker Park*, a grassy area with picnic tables. On the right is

Crescent Park, which has a beach, concession stand, picnic areas, boat launch, and camping.

Just past Crescent Park, turn right (southeast) on Crescent Park Road, which turns into North State Road. This drive runs along the lake's north shore and to *Denison Beach State Park*, (712) 657-8712, which has a nice beach on Black Hawk Lake.

While rounding the north side of the lake, you will meet County Road M54. Turn right (east) onto M54, which is also called Rolf Avenue and goes around the east side of the lake to its south side. There, take South State Road back toward town. This takes you through *Black Hawk State Park*, (712) 657-8712, which lines the south shore and has another beach, picnic areas, 176 campsites (68 with electricity), trails, a Frisbee course, fishing, and boating. The lake is stocked with channel catfish, crappie, walleye, bluegill, sunfish, and bass.

Continuing west on South State Road, cross the neck of Arrowhead Lake, and then South State Road turns to the right (north). This drive leads to Ice House Point, a nice fishing spot.

By continuing straight instead of going on South State Road, however, you reenter town on South Blossom Drive. At Third Street, turn left (west) to meet County Road M68. Turn left (south). On M68, you are approximately on the divide where waters flow to either the Mississippi River or Missouri River.

Go about 9 miles to County Road E16, turn left (east) and proceed for 4 miles to Breda. This small community was named for a town in Holland. The restored train depot provides access to the Sauk Rail Trail. Note the old but nice baseball park.

Continue for 2 more miles past Breda, and at County Road N20, turn right (south). In another 2 miles, turn left (east) on County Road E26 and proceed into Mount Carmel. On the left is a beautiful small-town church called Our Lady of Mount Carmel, which has ornate stained-glass windows. For years it was the only Catholic church between Boone and Council Bluffs. Madison County may have its covered bridges but Carroll County has its pretty, historic churches, 14 to be exact, including two made of stone.

East of the church is *Mount Carmel Store*; in an 1879 building, it was a mainstay of this community for decades and is now a museum that's being restored. It can be toured by contacting the Carroll County Historical Museum (see below).

Continue east out of Mount Carmel until you reach U.S. Highway 71, less than 2 miles away. Turn right (south) and drive

Black Hawk Lake is one place to cool off on a hot summer day in northwest Iowa.

about 5 miles into Carroll. Turn left (east) onto U.S. Highway 30, which goes through the city. At West Street turn right (south) and, a block later, turn left (east). By now you should see the *Chicago and Northwestern Depot* near the tracks; its interior is being restored so keep your eye on it as time goes on. Just east of it is the *Carroll County Chamber of Commerce*, 223 West 5th Street, (712) 792-4383, which has information about regional attractions such as the historic churches of Carroll County and walking and driving tours of historic sites in the city. On Wednesday afternoons and Saturday mornings during the summer and fall, a *Farmers Market* is held at the intersection of Carroll Street and Highway 30; area farmers bring in fruits, vegetables, handmade crafts, honey, and baked goods.

From the chamber of commerce, go one block north to 6th Street (Highway 30); turn right and go to the old Carnegie library building at the intersection of Court Street. Now it houses the *Carroll County Historical Museum*, 123 East 6th, (712) 792-3933/1582, free, which displays historical items from each community within the county.

From the museum, go north on Court for three blocks. Turn right (east) onto 9th Street and enter Graham Park two blocks later. Tours of the park's red, one-room school-house and a log cabin can be arranged at the historical museum.

Leave Graham Park by taking Grant Road, on the park's east side, to the south. Cross Highway 30 and, 2 miles later, turn left (east). Now you're at *Swan Lake State Park*, (712) 792-4614, at the south end of the Sauk Rail Trail and home of the *Swan Lake Farmstead Museum*, (712) 792-4614, free, which occupies a large red barn and exhibits historical agricultural equipment. A new exhibit building was added to the park in 2003; during the Christmas season, the park has animated outdoor lighting exhibits.

Return to Highway 30, turn right (east) and drive about 7 miles to Glidden. About a half mile west of Glidden is a cemetery with a memorial to Merle Hay, a local farm boy who was among the first three Americans to die in World War I, on November 3, 1917.

In Glidden, turn left onto County Road N41 and go north for about 13 miles to State Highway 175 on the east side of Lake City. Like Wall Lake, this town has no lake. No wonder the sign outside town reads, "Everything but the lake." Lake City is the home of *Dobson Pipe Organ Builders*, 200 North Illinois, (712) 464-8065, one of the premier builders of pipe organs that have been installed from Los Angeles to Washington, D.C. Since its 1974 founding, Dobson's has made new organs and restored old ones more than a century old. If you make an appointment, you can visit Dobson's, which is on the city square.

What a Blast!

Be glad you were not here about 74 million years ago. Although this region was much like the shores along the Gulf of Mexico today, all that ended abruptly when an asteroid measuring about one and a half miles in diameter slammed into Earth right about here at 35,000 mph. In an instant, the fireball from that blast (estimated by a geologist with Iowa's Department of Natural Resources to be ten times that of all the world's nuclear weapons combined) incinerated everything within 130 miles. Shock waves killed animals up to 650 miles away and threw large ones off their feet 850 miles away. Humans, if there had been any then, would have been knocked unconscious as far away as present-day Buffalo, New York, and Houston, Texas.

The crater was about 24 miles wide, and some scientists have theorized that the impact threw 240 cubic miles of debris into the air, contributing to the demise of some species of animals, including some dinosaurs.

By comparison, Arizona's famous crater is only three quarters of a mile wide, and the only larger crater within the U.S. was formed 40 million years after this one when an asteroid gouged out a section of the Chesapeake Bay. Because that one hit water, the Manson Crater is considered to be the largest terrestrial crater in the United States.

By now, you're wondering, where's the crater? Well, over millions of years, sediment filled the crater, especially when the glaciers did their thing. A cross-section of the land shows the crater floor ranges from 300 feet below the surface to about 70 feet down at the impact crater's central peak, which is near Manson.

In Lake City, turn right (east) onto State Highway 175 and go 4 miles to State Highway 4. Turn left (north) and proceed for 9 miles to U.S. Highway 20. Turn right (east) and enter Rockwell City. Turn right (south) at 8th Street and drive four blocks to Court Street; turn left (east) and go just past 5th Street. There, you can drop in on *Cooper's Radio Service*, 425 Court Street, (712) 297-7232. In a former hardware store on the courthouse square, Larry Cooper repairs and restores antique radios, ranging from the earliest ones to those of the 1930s and 1940s, many of which were housed in elegant wooden cabinets.

Aside from radios he repairs for clients across the nation, Cooper has some for sale in his store, which also features other types of antiques.

Continue on Court Street to 4th Street; turn left (north) and return to Highway 20, where you turn right (east). A few blocks down the way is the *Calhoun County Museum and Machinery Exhibit*, 150 Highway 20 E, (712) 297-8139/8585, free. A former school contains 34 rooms with exhibits related to the county's history. Horse-drawn equipment is in nearby buildings.

At First Street, turn left (north) on what soon becomes County Road N57 and proceed for about 5 miles to County Road D26. Turn left (west) on the conjoined roads for a very short distance to where you turn right (north) on the east side of North Twin Lake. This route takes you along North Twin Lake to *Twin Lakes State Park*, (712) 297-7131, which has shelters, a playground, and modern toilets. At the north end of the lake, North Twin Lake Road goes left (west) to *Featherstone County Park*, (712) 297-7131, which has 61 camper pads with electricity and water, 50 tent sites, and two seasonal cabins that sleep six each.

In a little more than a mile past the north end of North Twin Lake is State Highway 7; turn right (east). Drive for 4 miles, turn left (north) on County Road N65, skirting the west side of Manson.

Go north on N65 from Manson for about 4 miles to County Road C66. Turn left (west) and proceed for 7 miles to State Highway 7.

Quick Trip Option 2: About 3 miles north of Manson on County Road N65, turn left (west) on 630th Street, a gravel road. After passing a north-south gravel road, go for another mile to *Kalsow Prairie*, (712) 325-4395, on the left (south). At 160 acres, it's a remnant of the tallgrass prairie that covered this section of Iowa and has wet prairie, potholes left by glaciers, rare butterflies, and mima mounds. From 6 to 72 feet across and at most 36 inches high, these mounds are created by pocket gophers, some scientists say. To return to the main tour, go north on the gravel road you crossed, and in a mile you'll see County Road C66. Turn left (west) and drive about 5 miles to State Highway 7.

Upon meeting Highway 7 again, go straight west on it for 8 miles through Fonda, then for another 9 miles to the south edge of Newell. If you leave Highway 7 at Fulton Street and go north, you will come upon *Keith's Arab Heritage House*, 302 South Fulton, (712) 272-3527, admission, a Victorian home with three

Grasses bow before the wind at Kalsow Prairie near Manson.

floors of handmade coffee pots, weavings, oriental rugs, works of art, and other items collected by Keith Carter, who taught for 30 years in Saudi Arabia and Libya; call ahead for a visit. Keith also makes Mideastern luncheons for 6 to 12 people; again, make an appointment.

Also in Newell is *Allee Mansion*, (712) 272-4277/4566/4356, admission, a Victorian mansion built in 1891 on a farm. Although restoration is in progress, it is open only by appointment. To reach the mansion, go south on Fulton Street, pass Highway 7 for a mile on a gravel road and then three-quarters of a mile west.

About 8 miles past Newell, Highway 7 joins U.S. Highway 71. Turn right (north) and go for 2 miles, following Highway 7 to the left (west) and entering the town of Storm Lake. The road becomes Lakeshore Drive but, when Highway 7 splits to the right, stay on Lakeshore and drive along the north side of the lake of the same name. Here, you see a string of parks. But first along the way you can rent paddleboats and canoes at *Lakeside Marina*, 96 Lake Shore Drive, (712) 732-7465, which has a boat ramp and facilities for power boats and sailboats. Farther up the shore, a drive goes off to the left (south) into *Chataugua Park*, (712) 732-8027, which juts into Storm Lake. Trees shade the park, which is part of a 5-mile trail system.

More trees are farther along the shore, specifically the *Living Heritage Tree Farm*, (712) 732-3780. One of the larger tree museums in the nation, this grove has 51 trees raised from cuttings of those found at historic places such as Mount Vernon and Bunker Hill and from the tree that dropped an apple on Sir Isaac Newton. Here you can find public docks and a band shell for evening concerts in the summer.

Also along the shore is *Circle Park*, which marks the end of Lakeshore Drive.

Square Dancing Tractors

Southwest of Newell is Nemaha, home of Farmall Promenade, a group of eight men, mostly area farmers, who square dance—while riding their red Farmall tractors! Organized to celebrate the town's centennial in 1999, the men found their big-wheeled version of square dances, including the Virginia Reel and Tea Cup Chain, to be in such demand that they received 240 requests one year (although they only do about 20 shows annually). The group has appeared in several publications and on CBS's *Sunday Morning* and NBC's *Today Show*.

At Grand Avenue, which is at the entrance to Circle Park, head north on Grand for a couple of blocks, passing through the campus of Buena Vista University, turn left (west) at West 4th Street, go one long block to Early Street, and turn left (south) again. At the end of the street is *Scout Park*, where you'll see a small lighthouse, a rarity in Iowa, on the shore of Storm Lake. (If you want to know where others in the state are, see Tour 23.)

From Scout Park, go north on Early Street to West 5th Street, passing the campus of Buena Vista University. Turn right (east). Just past the railroad tracks and between Geneseo and

A lighthouse overlooks a portion of Storm Lake.

Michigan Streets, an old Ford garage is home to the *Buena Vista County Historical Museum*, 214 West 5th Street, (712) 732-4955, admission.

Continue east on West 5th Street, cross Lake Street through the business district, and two blocks after Lake turn left (north) on Cayuga Street. There sits the *Witter Gallery*, 609 Cayuga Street, (712) 732-3400, free, a very nice public art gallery for a town this size.

From Cayuga, go to East 7th Street, turn left (west), return to Lake Street and turn right (north). At Highway 7, turn left (west) and drive for about 9 miles to County Road M27, passing through Alta on the way. Turn right (north) on M27. Along the way, you will see a number of sleek, modern windmills that make up the world's largest wind farm. Here, 268 wind turbines arrayed in an 11-by-17 mile area produce 193 megawatts of electricity, enough power for 71,000 homes. Each turbine is 208 feet tall with a diameter of 164 feet. Al-though the blades take about two to three seconds to complete a revolution, there's something gracefully hypnotic about watching dozens of these windmills turning at the same speed as you drive among them.

About 11 miles after leaving Highway 7, turn right (east) onto County Road C16, which is also part of the *Old O'Brien Glacial Trail*, one of Iowa's scenic byways. This tour will take you about three quarters of the way around this circular trail, which passes through rumpled land formed by the Little Sioux River and its tributaries.

Drive 6 miles to County Road M36, turn left (north), and stick with the highway as it turns east and then north again. You then descend a slope into Linn Grove, situated on the Little Sioux River. On the left side of the road in this small community is *Linn Grove Landing*, (712) 296-3635, where you can rent canoes and kayaks and get provisions, bait, tackle—and even espresso—for whatever you want to do on the Little Sioux. While in the store, check out the carvings and furniture made by owner Monte Scholten and ask about the other members of the Cedar Ridge Artisans Group who live in the area. They include a saddlemaker, potters, painters, and a cattleman who also makes furniture at his Rocking M Furniture and Cattle Company. A short distance from the store is an access for putting in or taking out a canoe on the Little Sioux, near the only dam on the river's entire length.

Continue north on M36 for 2 miles to State Highway 10; turn left (west) and drive for about 4 miles to Peterson. If you detour left (south) on Ash Street in town, you will reach *Wanata State Park*, which has picnic facilities alongside the Little Sioux. A block farther in town, on Park Street, is the original, two-story, hewn-log blockhouse built in the wake of the Spirit Lake Massacre. It was moved here from its original location outside of town. As the highway curves to the northwest as it leaves town, watch on the right (north) for a historic home and an 1868 schoolhouse in a park.

Head west on Highway 10 from Peterson. In the summer of 2005, the *Prairie Heritage Center* is to open about 3.5 miles northwest of Peterson. Built by the O'Brien County Conservation Board, (712) 448-2254, the center will be on a bluff overlooking the Little Sioux River. Inside will be a 2,000-square-foot space housing displays about regional fish, reptiles, and amphibians, local architectural sites concerning the Mill Creek Culture Indians, early settlers, the effect of glaciers upon the landscape, and changes in how the prairie has been used over the years.

Drive about 7 miles to County Road M12, and turn left (south), staying on the Old O'Brien Glacial Trail byway. After about 5 miles, turn right (west) onto County Road C16 and go 4 miles to U.S. Highway 59. Turn left (south) and drive for 8 miles to Cherokee.

Quick Trip Option 3: If you're up for another prairie encounter, go 1.25 miles west of Highway 59 on C16 and turn right (north) onto P Avenue, a gravel road. In another half mile is one part of *Steele Prairie State Preserve*. The other section, which is larger, is reached by turning left (west) at the next gravel road and traveling 1 mile.

Spread across 187 square miles northwest of Storm Lake, the world's largest wind farm has 268 wind-powered turbines.

In downtown Cherokee, turn left (east) at East Willow Street. Be sure to check out the *Sanford Museum and Planetarium*, 117 East Willow Street, (712) 225-3922, free, offering exhibits featuring everything from the region's prehistoric days to contemporary art exhibits to seeing the stars and planets in the state's first planetarium.

Proceed to East Main Street, one block south of Willow, then turn right (west), cross the railroad tracks, and reach South 5th Street, where you turn left (south). This road angles to the southwest; when it turns west to become West Beech Street, turn left on South River Road. This soon becomes County Road L56. Enjoy the drive as it snakes along the pretty valley of the Little Sioux River.

After leaving Cherokee, drive for about 11 miles on L56 to County Road L51. Turn left (south), cross the Little Sioux River and enter Quimby. This town of just under 368 residents is one of three Iowa communities that begin with the letter Q.

At Quimby, cross State Highway 31 and continue south on L51 for 10 miles to U.S. Highway 20. Right after crossing it, L51 joins County D22 and jogs to the right (west) for less than a mile. Stay on L51 when it turns to the left (south) and continue on for 13 miles back to Battle Creek. Enjoy the rollicking ride along this stretch, which includes two turns to the east and quite a few hills and which returns you to the start of this tour.

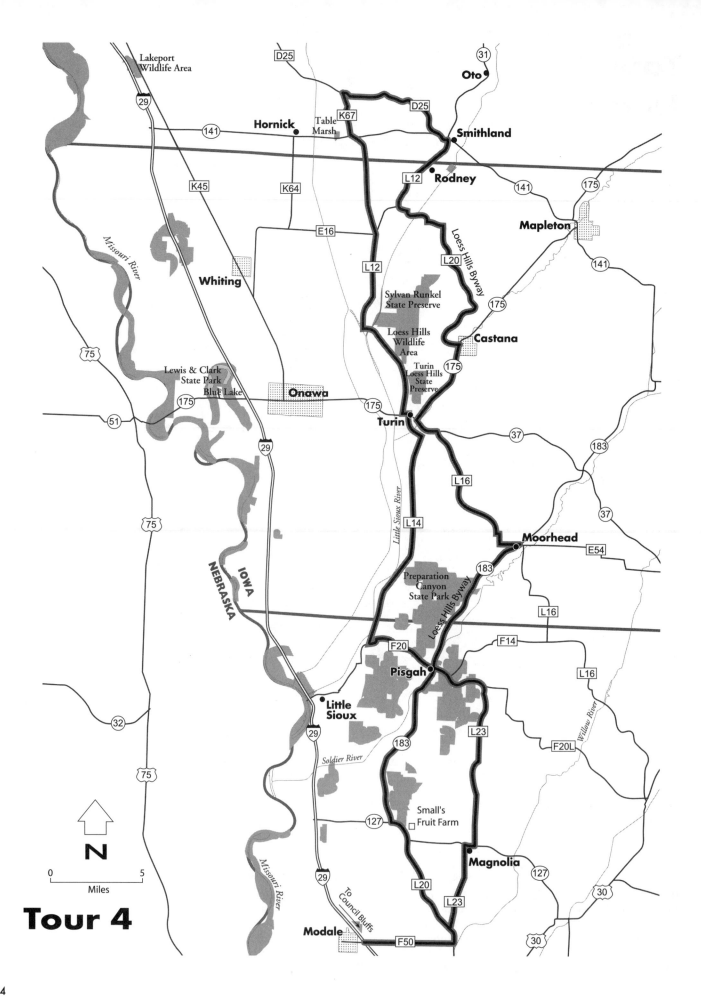

Tour 4

Tour 4
Heart of the Loess Hills

Modale—Magnolia—Pisgah—Moorhead—Castana—Smithland—Onawa—Murray Hill—Modale

Distance: approximately 110 miles

The Loess Hills may be Iowa's most unique geological feature. Shaped thousands of years ago by winds, they line much of Iowa's western border. This tour will concentrate on their midsection that stretches across Harrison, Monona and southern Woodbury Counties. During this drive you will visit some of the hills as they once were, topped with only prairie, and see many more crowned with woods. The roads here are unlike many others in Iowa, which seem to be lines running straight to infinity; here, they curve around hills and follow waterways of various sizes. Along the way, you'll come to the birthplace of one of America's favorite ice cream treats, touch a replica of the keelboat used by Lewis and Clark, munch on apples at an orchard, travel a former stagecoach route, and see where a swindler led his faithful followers astray.

The tour includes two stretches of gravel roads, approximately 6 and 10 miles in length; alternative paved routes are suggested, although they won't be as scenic as the gravel roads. Also, for a few miles, this tour overlaps a portion of Tour 5 and has more than an average number of Quick Trip Options. Lots of great choices here.

To begin this tour, leave I-29 at Exit 82 near Modale, roughly 25 miles north of Council Bluffs. At the bottom of the exit, turn right (east) onto County Road F50. Ahead of you, stretching from north to south, are the Loess Hills, which range from gently rolling slopes to steep bluffs and from open prairie and fields to thick woods. Depending on the time of year, you may see flocks of birds as they use the Missouri River flyway as a migratory route between places far to the north and south. While geese are identified by their V formations, occasionally you might see a flock of white birds in the distance that suddenly disappear—these are pelicans, which sometimes fly in circular patterns. When they cross your line of vision you can see them easily but as they turn to fly directly to or from you, they seem to vanish.

When you reach the base of the hills, a bit more than 4 miles from I-29, turn left (north) onto County Road L20. In less than a

The Loess Hills National Scenic Byway wanders for more than 200 miles through western Iowa's Loess Hills.

mile, the road curves to the left, but take County Road L23 as it angles off to the right. Take L23 for about 4 miles to Magnolia. Alongside the road is a blue sign stating that you're on *Sawmill Hollow Run* of the Loess Hills National Scenic Byway. Gently, the road lifts into the hills. Not all the curves on this road are marked with signs to let you know what's ahead, so use some caution, especially on the ones that are marked (perhaps only the proven killers have been given signs here). After some curves, L23 straightens out to go up and down the hills for a couple miles. Then the road curves to the right once more as you approach Magnolia.

When you reach State Highway 127 in Magnolia, turn right (east) and one block later turn left (north) onto L23 once more. Now you're on *Orchard Ridge Loop* of the Byway.

Although you won't encounter orchards on this part of the loop, you will later, so be patient. This road does not wind around much but it still has its curves and ups and downs.

Continue on L23 for less than 9 miles to County Road F20L; turn left (west) and drive for about 3 miles to Pisgah. As you head toward this town of about 300 residents, note a farm on your right where a wooden sign out front spells out, "Lone Pine Limousin." No, it's not some rural limousine service with the e missing; it's a particular breed of cattle that is pronounced like *limousine*.

In Pisgah, continue straight ahead, crossing both First and Front Streets. You're now at the *Loess Hills State Forest Visitor Center*, 206 Polk Street, (712) 456-2924, free, a great place to pick up information about what there is to see and do in the Loess Hills. Besides having free literature, the center has good displays about this region, including a large 3-D relief map that shows the surrounding terrain and a 3-D cutaway of Loess Hill. In one area, floor tiles show the footprints of the various animals inhabiting the hills, from the small plains mouse to coyote and bobcat, which have been seen more often in the last few years. Also, photos, paintings, and more works about the Loess Hills by various artists are featured.

From the visitor center, return to First Street, which is also State Highway 183 and turn left (north). Just as you turn, note the *Old Home Fill 'Er Up and Keep on Trucking Cafe*, (712) 456-9797, on the northwest corner of the intersection. For those of you old enough . . . who lived in the Upper Midwest . . . you might remember a set of Old Home Bread television ads in the 1970s about a bread trucker who had a crush on a hip-swiveling waitress who worked in a small town cafe. Well, the ads weren't filmed here, but in a case of life imitating art, this little cafe became famous and changed its name to the one featured in the commercials.

As you go north, you will eventually cross the Soldier River, one of the many tributaries of the Missouri River in western Iowa. Continuing up the valley of the Soldier River, you will see signs pointing the way to a scenic overlook and Preparation Canyon State Park.

Drive a little more than 5 miles to 314th Street, turn left (west) and go for about 2 miles to the main entrance to *Preparation Canyon State Park*. Just as the paved road ends, you'll see the entrance on the left. Heavily wooded, the 344-acre park, (712) 423-2829, has picnic shelters near this entrance and nine walk-in campsites near the park's other entrance. To get to the campsites, go back east on 314th to Peach Avenue, the only road going to the right (south; and it's gravel, by the way). Take that to a parking area that is the trailhead to the campsites. To return to the rest of this tour, go back to Highway 183 the way you came.

Preparation Canyon State Park is named after the town of Preparation, which was formed in 1853 by Charles B. Thompson, who diverted up to 60 Mormon families away from their migration to Utah. Soon Thompson claimed that a spirit had told him that all people in this region they called Monona—an Indian word meaning "peaceful valley"—should give him their material possessions. Eventually the residents asked Thompson to return their property but he refused. Shortly afterward, Thompson fled ahead of his disillusioned followers, never to return. Although many residents then went to Utah, some stayed. By 1900, nothing was left of the town.

Quick Trip Option 1: From where the pavement ends at the entrance to Preparation Canyon State Park, go right (west) on a good gravel road. In 1 mile the road forks. Keep right to stay on 314th Street. In another half mile a parking lot that can accommodate buses and RVs is near a handicapped-accessible overlook platform. The view to the south shows lots of forested land and some prairie-topped ridges near the overlook; a foot trail leads along those ridges. To the west, you can see the grain elevator in Blencoe, about 8 miles away on the Missouri River's floodplain. Beyond that on the horizon is Nebraska.

There are a few things to note while you're here. One of them are the badger holes near the boardwalk leading to the observation deck, but don't worry—badgers are not fond of showing themselves when humans are around. Another is the foot trail that is shallower than the surrounding ground, showing how easily loess can erode, something that has happened since the lookout was built in the early 1990s. The final thing is that the burnt areas of trees and grass here, or anywhere else in the hills, are more than likely the result of a prescribed burn.

To continue on Tour 4, return to Highway 183 the way you came. Turn left (north) and head into Moorhead, about 2.5 miles away. Follow the signs on 183 that point

the way to continue on the Loess Hills National Scenic Byway. But upon entering Moorhead, don't continue on the byway just yet. Go straight into the small downtown. At the intersection of 2nd and Oak is the *Loess Hills Hospitality Association*, (800) 886-5441 and (712) 886-5441, now in Cover School House, a former one-room school. In the vesti-bule is free information about western Iowa and the region covered by the Loess Hills. In the bright, airy main room is a gift shop offering items about the Loess Hills and featuring pottery made by Jerry and Deb Kessler, residents of the hills. The association offers step-on tour guide service for individual travelers as well as bus tours.

Across Oak Street is the *Moorhead Cultural Center* (same phone as the Loess Hills Hospitality Association), where works of art are displayed; it is open every afternoon from Thursday through Sunday. And next to Cover School House is *Bluebonnet II*, (712) 886-5465, a pleasant cafe with luncheon specials and homemade desserts.

At the bottom of Oak Street in Moorhead, turn right (west) on County Road L16. On the way out of town, note the big brick home on the left (south). Appropriately called "The Brick," it was built for J. B. Moorhead in 1871; it also was the local post office for a while.

Quick Trip Option 2: Around a bend from The Brick is a sign that reads "Danish Church" and points to the left and County Road E54, a gravel road. Stay on E54 as it travels through the hills. About 4 miles out of town is the *Ingemann Danish Lutheran Church* near a cemetery on the right (north) side of the road. Nestled picturesquely among the hills, the church was built in 1884 by Danish settlers. If you do not want to drive all the way back to Moorhead to meet L16 again, backtrack on E54 until you see another gravel road going off to the left (north). That's Peach Avenue; turn onto it and drive for a mile to L16.

Stay on L16 as it winds through the hills until the T intersection with State Highway 37. There, turn left (west). In less than 2 miles, turn right (north) onto State Highway 175 and drive for 5 miles to County Road L20 at Castana. Turn left (west). This county road cuts across the valley of the Maple River and then enters a spur of the hills again, rising, falling, and twisting and turning for about 8 miles, generally heading north.

Quick Trip Option 3: For those who are in the mood for a little hiking and don't mind taking gravel roads for approximately 3 miles, leave L20 as soon as it enters the hills, turning left (west) at the sign on Oak Avenue that points to Whiting Cemetery. At the first fork, stay to the right on

Oak. Eventually you will come to another fork, which has a parking area on the left (south). Park here and head out on trails that lead initially through woods but then go across the prairie-topped hills.

At this point, you're at the junction of the *Loess Hills Wildlife Area* and the *Sylvan Runkel State Preserve*, (712) 423-2426, one of the largest protected areas in the Loess Hills and one of the larger areas of native prairie in Iowa. This is also the site of the *Loess Hills Seminar*, (712) 274-6000, ext. 6080, fee for meals, an outdoor educational seminar for all ages that is held for a weekend early each summer. Return to L20 the same way you came.

Prescribed Burns

To maintain some natural areas of prairie in the hills, humans have taken to setting prescribed burns, doing what wildfires did years ago. These kill the invading woody plants, particularly sumac and cedars, and renew the prairie soil with ash. Although one might think a fire is a fire, that's not so.

Depending on the time of year, a fire can help some plants rejuvenate themselves while killing others. Also, if a fire is set to advance with the wind, the flames will remain high off the ground, killing trees yet leaving the low-lying plants relatively unscathed. But if the fire is set to head into the wind, it scours the grasses and brush while not harming the crowns of the trees.

Crews that set the fires monitor the weather conditions constantly, measuring wind direction and speed in particular, but also how dry the area is. Besides being trained to set the fires, the crews are trained to put them out. Between 5,000 to 7,000 acres are burned each year in the hills and another 1,500 to 2,000 acres are cleared by cutting down trees. Ideally, the Nature Conservancy reports, 20,000 acres should be cleared each year in the hills.

From Castana, take L20 for about 8 miles to its intersection with County Road E16. Turn left (west), cross the Little Sioux River, and go straight to County Road L12. At L12, turn right (north) and drive for about 4 miles to Smithland. Along the way, you'll pass through Rodney, which was named for Rodney Rice, the first passenger to step off the first train to stop at the town's depot in the 1880s.

Quick Trip Option 4: If want to take the *Smokey Hollow Loop* of the Loess Hills Scenic Byway, this trip is for you. Once you're at the stop sign at Highway 141 in Smithland, continue north toward Oto on what is now State Highway 31 and follow the Smokey Hollow Loop signs. As you go north on 31, note the historical marker that's on the left side of highway. This marks a campsite used by the Sioux warrior Inkpaduta before he and others fell upon settlers in what became known as the Spirit Lake Massacre (see Tour 1).

In Oto, turn left (west) onto 290th Street, a gravel road. Then turn left (south) onto Knox Avenue. After about 3.5 miles, at an intersection, veer to the left to go southeast on Kossuth

A car travels through part of the Loess Hills near Little Sioux.

Avenue. This gravel road leads to County Road D25 at Smithland.

At the intersection of L12 and State Highway 141 in Smithland, turn left (west) onto 141. Within a short distance, turn right (north) onto County Road D25. To visit a nice park with a playground that's a great place for children to unwind, continue past the D25 turnoff for a moment, and you will see on the left (south) Fowler Preserve, which also has picnic facilities; after that, return to D25, which was once a stagecoach route between Sioux City and Des Moines.

Proceed for about 7 miles to County Road K67, turn left (south), and drive a short distance back to Highway 141.

Note: at this point you have a decision to make: either travel on a stretch of gravel road for about 5.5 miles or a series of paved roads for 14 miles. Either way will get you to the same destination.

(1) If you opt for the gravel route, from the intersection of K67 and Highway 141, continue southeast on K67, which becomes a gravel road, for 5.5 miles to County Road E16 (paved). Turn left (east) and go a short distance to County Road L12. K67 is one of the few Iowa county roads with a gravel surface. Along the way, you'll soon see a solitary knob of the Loess Hills, a rarity, and will be rewarded with some of the more scenic views of the Loess Hills'

western front. Even though the road is fairly straight, 40–45 mph should be your top speed to stay out of trouble and to enjoy the scenery.

(2) If you want to avoid gravel, at the intersection of K67 and Highway 141, turn right (west). Go 3 miles to County Road K64 and turn left (south). In 5 miles, at County Road E16, turn left (east) and drive for less than 6 miles to County Road L12.

No matter which route you chose, turn right (south) on L12 and proceed for 5 miles to County Road L14. As you head down L12 the Little Sioux River is on your left. Just beyond that, some prairie-topped hills stand out as stark reminders of how all these hills looked when Lewis and Clark saw them in 1804.

Quick Trip Option 5: About 3.5 miles south of E16, Nutmeg Avenue, a gravel road, takes off to the left (east) from L12. Follow Nutmeg as it bridges the Little Sioux River and leads to the parking lot at the juncture of the Loess Hills Wildlife Area and the Sylvan Runkel State Preserve, which we saw in Quick Trip Option 3.

At County Road L14, you have another decision to make between two routes. The first alternate route continues along the Loess Hills, but it runs on gravel for about 10 miles before meeting the second route at Murray Hill, a lookout point. The second route is nearly twice as long, but it's on paved roads and runs through Onawa and Lewis and Clark State Park before rejoining the first route at Murray Hill.

Alternate Route 1 (approximately 15 miles):
If you don't mind a gravel road, turn left (southeast) onto L14 and drive for about 5 miles to Turin. Early in this stretch, you'll see a parking area on the left; this is for people who want to visit the *Turin Loess Hills Nature Preserve*, (712) 423-2426. Later, note that the speed limit drops suddenly to 20 mph upon entering tiny Turin (population under 100). Watch for the sign about the Turin Man. In 1955, a young girl found some bones here, which led researchers to uncover the remains of four humans who died here about 5,500 years ago; together they were called the *Turin Man* and for a while were the oldest human remains found in North America. Originally Turin was called Bluff Point but it was renamed for the Italian city on the advice of some Italian railroad workers.

Cross State Highway 175 and continue south on L14 (which for the next 10 miles is a gravel road) to County Road F20. L14 is also called Charles L. Larpenteur Road, after an early fur trader, trapper, and settler who lived in this region in the nineteenth century. As L14 goes south along the base of the hills, at 286th Street, you'll see a sign pointing to the left that reads, "Scenic Overlook, three miles." The overlook is the same one you might have visited earlier near Preparation Canyon.

If you turn onto 286th Street as it ascends the first hill and curves to the left, you will see a large, old oak with its branches spread in an unusually open pattern. Although there's no hard evidence to support this observation, the tree bears a strong resemblance to others in western Nebraska seen by the author that were deformed by funeral platforms made by Native Americans.

Also, along the way, you'll pass Little Sioux Scout Ranch, a regional campsite used by Boy Scouts. A few miles south of there, a windmill stands along the left side of the road. Also, look carefully to spot an old shelter built into the side of the hill just past the windmill and before you get to F20.

At County Road F20, turn left (east). As this road goes uphill, you will see some turnouts on the left side of the road. Although you can pull over and enjoy the views, there are more scenic ones to come. Turn on your right blinker and just as the road curves to the right, slow down and be prepared to turn into a parking area that appears suddenly on the right (south). Welcome to *Murray Hill*, where you can take in some of the most spectacular views of the Loess Hills.

Park your vehicle and make your way up the footpath. Murray Hill is deceiving. As you walk up from the parking lot, you think you are approaching the top. But after a short walk, you find out that what you thought was the top isn't . . . and you walk up some more and find out that

that's not the top either. To the west is the fertile floodplain of the Missouri River. To the north, south, and east, more Loess Hills. Yucca and cactus are in this stretch of prairie.

Alternate Route 2 (27 miles): **At the junction of County Roads L12 and L14, continue on L12 for about 6 miles to Onawa and State Highway 175.** By staying on L12, you will go farther into the flats of the Missouri River floodplain. At Onawa, the county seat of Monona County, immediately after you turn to the right (west) watch for the *Monona County Arboretum*, 318 East Iowa Avenue, (712) 423-2400, free, which has more than 300 types of trees and shrubs as well as various prairie grasses that once covered this region.

One thing you can't help but notice as you continue into town on Iowa Avenue is that it is a very wide main street, the widest in the world, the town claims. On the third Saturday night of each June, bring your best old car to town to celebrate Graffiti Night when the main drag turns into a popular place featuring 1950s-style music, clothing, food, and, of course, the dream machines of yesteryear that cruise up and down the street.

Another of Onawa's claims to fame is that it's where a high school teacher named Chris Nelson invented the Eskimo Pie around 1920. By 1922, about a million a day were being sold after Nelson joined forces with candy maker Russell Stover to make and distribute the ice cream treats. It was originally called the I-Scream-Bar, in case any trivia fiends want to know.

As you go through town, you will pass the *Monona County Courthouse* on the right and, in a park on the left, the city's Carnegie Library. Built in 1908, the library is one of the finer examples of a public building designed in the Prairie School style of architecture.

Continue west on Iowa Street and turn right (north) onto North 12th Street. Up this street is a complex of three free museums: *Kiwanis Museum Complex*, (712) 423-1801, has a schoolhouse, blacksmith shop, firehouse/jail, and a C & NW Depot containing more than 800 railroad items; *Monona County Historical Museum*, (712) 423-2776/2867, has farm equipment, a barbed wire collection, and a display about Eskimo Pies; and *Monona County Veterans Memorial Museum*, (712) 423-3780/2411, honors the county's veterans with uniforms, displays, and equipment such as a WWII Jeep, 105 mm howitzer, tank, Huey helicopter, and Corsair fighter.

From the museums, return to Iowa Avenue (Highway 175) and turn right (west). Cross I-29 and go 2 more miles to *Lewis and Clark State Park*. Blue Lake, which you pass as you approach the park, is a former channel of the

A replica of the keelboat used on the Lewis and Clark expedition is at Lewis and Clark State Park near Onawa.

Missouri River. In the park, (712) 423-2829, is a replica of the keelboat used by Lewis and Clark and near it, copies of smaller boats, called pirogues, which were also used by their men. The keelboat was used in Ken Burns's PBS series *Undaunted Courage*, and is manned by reenactors during special celebrations, including Lewis and Clark Days held each June. The park has a beach, boating, camping, and picnic facilities shaded by tall trees.

As you return to Onawa on Highway 175, first turn left (north) at the flashing yellow light between Blue Lake and I-29. Follow the paved road to *Casino Omaha*, 1 Blackbird Bend Boulevard, (712) 423-3700 and (800) 858-8238, which has 450 slots and blackjack, craps, roulette, and poker. A buffet and gift shop are also on the premises.

Return to Onawa. At 10th Street, turn right (south); take this road, which becomes County Road K45, for 17 miles to State Highway 301. Along the way you'll go through the town of Blencoe. A note: K45, which parallels

I-29, was the main road between Council Bluffs and Sioux City before the interstate was built.

Turn right (west) at Highway 301, cross I-29, and when you come to the RV/trailer park, turn to the right (north). This road circles the park and eventually stops at the confluence of the Little Sioux River and the Missouri.

Return to Highway 301, cross I-29 again, and enter the little town of Little Sioux. Go to Main Street, turn left (north), and follow this road, which becomes County Road F20, for a few miles to Murray Hill. See Alternate Route 1 for more information on this scenic overlook.

Whether you've taken Alternate Route 1 or 2, from Murray Hill go east on F20 a few miles back into Pisgah; this time you're coming from the west on Jackson Street. Turn right (south) onto Highway 183. Here you'll rejoin the Loess Hills National Scenic Byway and will pass some trailheads in the Loess Hills State Forest.

Ten miles south of Pisgah, Highway 183 joins State Highway 127. Turn left (east) on the combined highway. As this road quickly curves to the south, note the small parking lot on the left (north) side of the road. It's another trailhead for those willing to hike through the Loess Hills State Forest and actually it's a relatively easy hike compared to some others and passes through grassy spaces before ascending a ridge where prairie and woods meet.

On Highway 183/127, go a short distance to County Road F32. Turn left (east) and proceed to *Small's Fruit Farm.* Russ Small is the fourth generation to work this produce farm, (712) 646-2723, begun by his great-grandfather in the 1880s. Each year, the growing season starts with strawberries in the early summer and winds up with pumpkins, squash, and apples in the fall. If you're not into picking your own, stop at the store to find what you want. If no one's in the store, use the honor system to pay for what you're taking. Besides fruit and vegetables, the store has a kitchen where the helpers prepare fresh-baked goods and frozen pies you can bake later.

Return to Highway 183/127 and continue south along the bottom of the hills on what is the Byway's Sawmill Hollow Run. When you reach the point where 127 splits off to the left, keep going straight on 183 (but note that its designation changes to County Road L20). Drive for 6 miles to County Road F50 and turn right (west). Proceed for about 5 miles to Modale and Exit 82 on I-29 where you began this tour.

Loess Hills Apples

At one time, produce farms like Small's were common throughout the Loess Hills. In 1911, Iowa ranked among the top ten apple-producing states and was fifth in growing fruit overall. Ironically, the apple industry in Washington, which leap-frogged ahead of Iowa's, got its start when young apple trees were hauled there on a wagon train from Iowa in 1847. As other states got more and more into growing apples, Iowa fell further and further behind until it produced only 559,000 bushels of apples in 1940, nine million fewer than had been grown in 1911.

In 1940 the bottom of Iowa's apple barrel fell out. After a mild fall, a hard freeze hit on November 11. Temperatures dropped from 34 to 0 degrees in hours. Sap that was still high in the trees froze, splitting open the trees and killing them. In 45 western counties, 95 percent of the apple trees were wiped out. In one orchard of 25 acres, just 12 trees remained alive. In 1941, only 48,000 bushels of apples were produced in Iowa.

Because it takes up to seven years for an apple tree to bear good fruit, many orchard owners tore up what was left of their trees and planted crops that returned money relatively fast—corn and soybeans. A few, like Russ Small's father, held on although they did not see a good crop of apples until 1952.

Today, efforts are being led by government agencies, such as Golden Hills Resource Conservation and Development in Oakland, to reintroduce crops like grapes to the region. In a few years it's expected that wine production will begin again on a small scale in the Loess Hills.

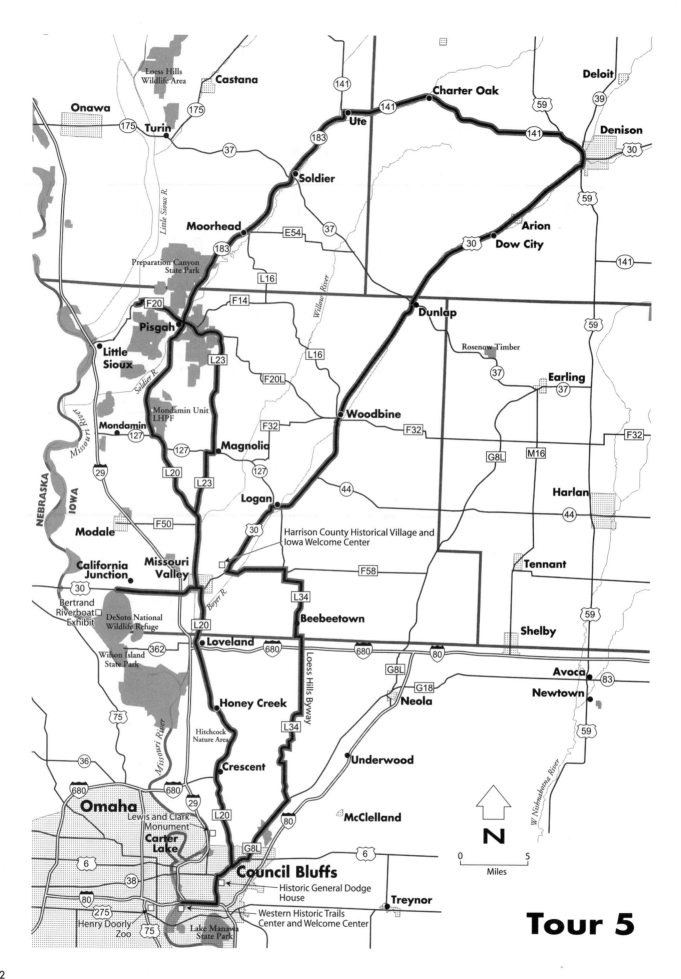

Tour 5

Tour 5
The Valleys of Western Iowa

Council Bluffs—Logan—Woodbine—Denison—Charter Oak—Soldier—Moorhead—Pisgah—Missouri Valley—Council Bluffs

Distance: approximately 155 miles

Before much of Iowa was settled in the nineteenth century, the western edge of the state, especially the region around Council Bluffs, was developing much faster than the interior. That was because of its proximity to the Missouri River, which was the region's key transportation link to the rest of the Midwest back then. So it's only fitting that you begin this tour in "CB," as the city is often called today.

Now, don't let the thought that it's a historic town that sprang up in the 1840s fool you. There's a lot that has gone on here recently and will be happening in the near future. So, CB and the other parts of Iowa that you'll encounter on this tour are definitely not standing still. Along the way, you'll have a chance to see a great acting seminar taught by professionals from Hollywood, parts of a national scenic byway, quaint country churches, a place where a half-million snow geese make a temporary home each year, one of the best places in the nation to watch raptors migrate, and the nation's first transcontinental highway. So hop into your car or van and let's go.

This tour begins in southwest Council Bluffs at the *Western Historic Trails Center and Welcome Center*, which is just south of Interstate 80/29 at Exit 1B. The center, 3434 Richard Downing Avenue, (712) 366-4900, free, is at the end of a long lane that passes stands of trees and open stretches of prairie. If you're wondering about that distant glass and steel dome, that's the Desert Dome at Henry Doorly Zoo in Omaha, Nebraska, across the Missouri River—more on that later.

Inside the center, a series of metal figures and interactive displays tells of those who traveled through this area, from the days of Lewis and Clark, wagon trains, and the first transcontinental railroad to the Lincoln Highway and the present-day interstates. The entry is paved with bricks engraved with names of individuals and Indian nations, and alongside that walkway is a polished granite wall cut to resemble a profile of the plains and mountains between the Mississippi River and the Pacific Oregon. A trail leads to the Missouri River and is linked to the city's hike-

bike trails. Each July, a reenactment of *White Catfish Encampment* recalls when Lewis and Clark stayed here for several days in 1804, and every Thursday afternoon, country music musicians and fans gather here for a free jam session.

New Attractions on Council Bluffs's West End

North of the Welcome Center

Mid-America Convention Center and Arena, 1 Arena Way, (712) 323-0536, is the new home of the River City Lancers hockey team and has been host to entertainers like Cher and John Cougar Mellencamp. The center is also near an outdoor shopping complex, restaurants, theaters, and a hotel.

Bluffs Run, 2701 23rd Avenue, (712) 323-2500, features a casino with slots, restaurants, an RV park, and a greyhound race track with daily races. Two more casinos, *Ameristar*, 2200 River Road, (712) 328-8888, and *Harrahs*, 1 Harvey's Boulevard, (712) 329-6000, each have large hotel-convention complexes and restaurants with live entertainment and motor their riverboat casinos along the Missouri River on summer mornings.

South of the Welcome Center

Council Bluffs Drive-In, 1130 West South Omaha Bridge Road, (712) 366-0422, is a perennial summertime favorite that opened in 1950 and is now one of the three remaining drive-ins in Iowa; once there were 68.

Lake Manawa is a 1,529-acre lake that's popular for boating, swimming, fishing, biking, and more, especially Dream Playground, a wonderful wooden labyrinth of child-size bridges, platforms, watch towers, ladders, and tunnels. On the south side of the lake is Lake Manawa State Park, 1100 South Shore Road, (712) 366-0220, with a beach, campsites, and picnic areas.

From the welcome center, hop on I-80/29 and turn right (east). Leave the interstate at the very next exit, at the South Expressway. Turn left (north) at the bottom of the ramp and proceed into downtown Council Bluffs. Leave the South Expressway at the 16th Avenue exit and turn right (east) onto 16th Avenue; a short distance later, turn left (north) onto Main Street. Now pull up to *Rails-West Railroad Museum*, 1512 South Main Street, (712) 323-5182, admission. Built in 1899 as the Rock Island Depot, this is the last of seven depots in what had been the nation's fifth busiest rail yard. The station's agent is maintained as it once was and artifacts fill the rest of the building, which also has a large HO-scale railroad.

From the depot, return to 16th Avenue and head east again. As you drive, you will see *Acorn Supply*, 329 16th Avenue, (712) 325-9282, free, on the right (south) side. At most any time of the week this is a feed supply store, but on Saturday afternoons many country music fans come to participate in or listen to an informal jam that usually starts about one o'clock. So, if you're here on a Saturday afternoon, you're in luck. *Acorn Supply* was one of 29 sites across America that received Rand McNally's 2004 *Best of the Road* award.

The RailsWest Railroad Museum in Council Bluffs is located in the former Rock Island depot.

Turn left (north) at 3rd Street, cross 9th Avenue, and continue straight up the hill for one block. Go just past Fairview Avenue. On the right (east) you'll see two large, well-kept Victorian houses. Park near the first and enter there to gain entry to the further one, the *Historic General Dodge House*, 605 3rd Street, (712) 322-2406, admission. The mansion was built in 1869 by Grenville Dodge, a Civil War general and a prominent official of the Union Pacific Railroad.

From the Dodge House, continue north on 3rd Street to 5th Avenue and turn left (west). Go two blocks to 4th Street. (No, that's not a typo . . . 3rd and 4th Streets are two blocks apart.) In the two-story, brown, brick building across the intersection is *Kanesville Kollectables*, 530 South 4th Street, (712) 328-8731, which has half a million 33, 45, and 78-rpm records, 8,000 CDs, countless cassettes, 20,000 comic books, and 20,000 books.

Continue west on 5th Avenue to the next intersection, which is Main, and turn right (north). Go one block on this one-way street, move to the left lane, and turn left (west) onto Willow Avenue; cross Pearl Street. It would be a good time to park your vehicle near *Bayliss Park* and take in a few nearby attractions. *Veteran's Plaza* is on the park's east side, and in its center, a fountain changes patterns of spray and is lit colorfully at night.

South of the park old Carnegie library now houses the *Union Pacific Railroad Museum*, 200 Pearl Street, (712) 329-8307, free. Its exhibits, many interactive, describe railroad history on the plains from the first transcontinental railroad, which proceeded west from Council Bluffs, to the present-day operations of the UP. Next door is the *Squirrel Cage Jail*, 226 Pearl Street, (712) 323-2509, admission. This nineteenth-century building, with a three-story, drum-shaped set of cells that revolved within a barrel, is now a museum.

From Willow Avenue and Pearl Street in Council Bluffs, go one block west on Willow and turn right (north) onto 6th Street. Drive for two blocks and turn right (east) onto Broadway. This will lead you through another part of Council Bluffs's L-shaped downtown. Some of the buildings here are the oldest in the city, dating back to the 1860s.

Go past two traffic lights (at North Broadway and North Avenue), and then on out to a fourth traffic light, about 2 miles past North Avenue and near a K-Mart. Turn left onto County Road G8L, which runs northeast. Proceed for about 4 miles to County Road L34. Turn left (north). In a short distance, L34 leads up a hill to run through what had been rolling prairie but is now rolling farmland. It's tempting to put down the gas pedal on this road because of its wide-open feeling but it can curve quickly, so keep your head. You'll be driving through a linear neighborhood of people who commute to their businesses in the Council Bluffs-Omaha metro area. By the way, you're on part of the *Loess Hills National Scenic Byway*.

Drive for about 20 miles on L34 to County Road F58, passing Interstate 680 and the small community of Beebeetown along the way. At F58, turn left (west) and drive for

Across the River in Omaha

Well, only someone who's really in the dark would not know this but just west of Council Bluffs is Omaha, Nebraska. With a population of over 386,000 people, it's the largest community in the metro area, which has about a half million residents.

To enter downtown Omaha, drive across the Interstate 480 bridge from Council Bluffs, and take in some of the city's attractions.

Downtown

Lewis and Clark Landing is a new 23-acre park with a plaza, trails, a 500-seat restaurant with outdoor seating, boardwalks, a marina, and a riverboat landing. Soon to come there are the National Park Service's regional headquarters and a pedestrian bridge to Council Bluffs.

—*Qwest Convention Center and Arena*, is a new facility near Lewis and Clark Landing.

—*Heartland of America Park* links Lewis and Clark Landing with *Gene Leahy Mall*, an urban park that stretches into downtown Omaha with an undulating waterway, waterfalls, grassy slopes, and shady trees. At the mall's west end, a $90 million performing arts center with a 2,000-seat concert hall, outdoor concert area, and chamber music hall will open in 2005.

South of Downtown

—*Old Market*, a former warehouse district at 11th and Howard, is now a trendy neighborhood of shops, apartments, upscale restaurants, art galleries, boutiques, street musicians, cobblestone streets, and carriage rides.

—*Durham Western Heritage Museum*, 801 South 10th Street, (402) 444-5071, admission. Located in the elegant, art-deco Union Pacific Depot, the museum shows how Omaha grew over the years.

—*Lauritzen Gardens*, 100 Bancroft Street, (402) 346-4002, admission, is a very nice assortment of gardens that expands and gets prettier each year.

—*Henry Doorly Zoo*, 3701 South 10th, (402) 733-8400, admission, is truly a national-class zoo with many superlatives. The Desert Dome is the world's largest indoor desert environment displaying arid areas of North America, Australia, and North Africa. Beneath that is Kingdoms of the Night, the world's largest nocturnal animal exhibit, which features their habitats—caves, underground waterways, a Louisiana swamp, an Amazon rain forest, and more. The Lied Jungle, the world's largest indoor jungle, has wildlife of the jungles of South America, Africa, and Asia in natural settings of thick undergrowth, waterfalls, and rocky cliffs laced with vines. The list can go on and on but start with those. Hint: Visit the zoo from about 4 p.m. on when the crowds are thinner. The grounds close at 7 p.m.

—*Rosenblatt Stadium* is the home of the *Omaha Royals*, (402) 734-2550, the Triple-A farm team of the Kansas City Royals, and the stadium is the annual host of the *College World Series* in late spring, (402) 554-4404.

West of Downtown

—*Joslyn Art Museum*, 2200 Dodge Street, (402) 342-3300, admission, has strong holdings of American frontier art, and has a gift shop and a fine restaurant. Admission is free on Saturdays, 10 a.m.–noon. North of Downtown.

—*Hot Shops Art Center*, 1301 Nicholas, (402) 342-6452, north of downtown, a unique arrangement of 80 artist studios, classrooms, a small café and coffee shop, and three galleries.

—*Freedom Park*, 2497 Freedom Park Road, (402) 345-1959, admission, is alongside the Missouri River and home to USS Hazard, a World War II minesweeper and the largest warship to travel the nation's inland waterways. A training submarine, World War II landing craft, naval armament, and aircraft are there, too.

about 4 miles to U.S. Highway 30, on the northeast edge of the town of Missouri Valley. At Highway 30, turn right (northeast) and go a quarter mile to the *Harrison County Historical Village and Iowa Welcome Center*. Even though you may have visited the Welcome Center in Council Bluffs, consider stopping at this one, (712) 642-2114, free, because it carries more informational literature than most. The center has a gift shop with Iowa-related items and free cherry juice, which has been made regionally for years. Inside the main building is a museum, admission, containing an impressive collection of barbed-wire strands and artifacts from the county's early days, including an 1880s peddler's wagon. Outside are historic buildings, including a one-room school and a church, and an original Lincoln Highway marker.

From the welcome center, continue northeast on Highway 30 through the valley of the Boyer River. As was done often in the early

days of railroads, the Union Pacific laid its tracks in this valley; no doubt you will see long trains heading to and fro on the nearby tracks. After the railroad came the *Lincoln Highway*, the nation's first transcontinental highway, which is now Highway 30.

About 3 miles past the welcome center, turn left (north) on Niagara Trail. There, a sign points to the *Museum of Religious Arts*, 2697 Niagara Trail, (712) 644-3888, admission. The museum has the Midwest's largest collection of religious artifacts, which have been collected from a wide variety of religions. Among its items are nun dolls showing habits from across the world and a replica of an early, southwestern Mission-style church interior.

Return to Highway 30 and resume traveling northeast, passing through Logan, the seat of Harrison County. In another 9 miles the highway turns sharply to the right to

The Squirrel Cage Jail in Council Bluffs has a three-story drum-shaped set of jail cells that revolved so that only one cell could be opened on each floor at any one time.

bypass Woodbine, but you should go straight (paying attention to the traffic on Highway 30 from the right) to enter town. After crossing the train tracks, you will be on Lincoln Street, a cobblestone street that was part of the famed Lincoln Highway. The historic road is recalled by the red, white, and blue signs and the concrete marker near *Merry Brook School*, a one-room schoolhouse from the 1890s that's now a historic site. The cobblestone street is considered to be the finest example of an original Lincoln Highway brick street in Iowa.

They Went Thataway

The story goes that in December 1910, burglars broke into Dow City's bank, blew open its safe, and made off with about $5,000. Authorities believed the men were Shorty Gray, Texas Whitey, and Big Mitch, and they may have been aided by Indiana Frank, Dynamite Bill, and Illinois Slim.

At Merry Brook School in Woodbine, turn right (east) and then turn left (north) at the next intersection, Walker Street, which runs through the small downtown. Watch for *Eby Drug*, 423 Walker, (712) 647-2840, which has a nice old-time soda fountain that serves up refreshments sure to please everyone.

Return to Lincoln Way, turn to the right (north), and follow it for a mile to Highway 30.

Quick Trip Option 1: From downtown Woodbine, start going back to Highway 30 the way you came but, at First Street, turn to the right (west). This will become County Road F32, which shortly curves to the right (northwest) to become County Road F20L. About 6 miles out of town is *Willow Lake Recreation Area*, a nice park with a beach, fishing, campsites, picnic facilities, and year-round cabins.

At Highway 30, turn to the left (northeast) and proceed for 9 miles to Dunlop. At Iowa Avenue, turn right (east). For an authentic glimpse into the past, visit *McLean Museum and Dougal House*, 1211 Iowa Avenue, (712) 643-5908, free, where a square grand piano and pump organ are in the house and farm items are outside. The folks here can help you find the *Z. T. Dunham Barn*, a brick structure that was built in 1870 about a mile west of town near the junction of State Highway 37 and County Road L51. Built to shelter horses and mules on the lower level and store hay on the main floor, the barn features hand-hewn beams fastened with wooden pegs.

From Dunlap, keep going northeast on Highway 30 for 8 miles to Dow City. Proceed to Prince Street, turn right (south), and follow it as it ascends a hill and you can't go any farther (be careful of the dips encountered at the cross streets). Now you're at *Dow House*, (712) 263-2693, admission. Built in the 1870s by the town's founder, Simeon Dow, who introduced shorthorn cattle to the area and was the postmaster, this pretty, two-story home with 12-inch-thick brick walls overlooks the valley and is nicely restored to the way it looked when Dow lived there.

Return to Highway 30 and continue going northeast for 9 miles to Denison. As the road approaches Denison, it becomes four lanes. When it joins U.S. Highway 59 on the south side of town, turn left (north), then go right (east) at the next intersection, all the while remaining on Highway 30. Just past the last intersection is *Cronk's Restaurant*, (712) 263-4191, on the left. Started in 1929, it's a good place not only to eat but also to collect informational pamphlets on regional attractions from the racks in the foyer.

Continue on Highway 30 for a few blocks until you reach Main Street; turn left (north). Drive for a few blocks to Broadway, turn right (east) and park. You will no doubt notice the large theater. Built in 1914 as the Opera House, it's now called the *Donna Reed Theater for the Performing Arts*, named in honor of the hometown girl who attained fame in Hollywood.

On the right side of the theater is *Reiney's Soda Fountain*, 1301 Broadway, (712) 263-4752. Stills and posters from Reed's movies hang on the walls near customers sitting in booths, at tables, or at the marble-topped counter, eating sandwiches, soups, and ice cream treats. Note the door near the left end of the soda fountain: in the 1930s, a young woman wanted to be sure her engagement diamond was real, so, knowing diamonds cut glass, she engraved her name into the door's glass face-Irene Topping's name is still there.

On the left side of the theater is the *Donna Reed Foundation for the Performing Arts*, 1305 Broadway, (712) 263-3334, which preserves the memory of the actress, who died in 1986, primarily through the Donna Reed Festival.

Back on Broadway in Denison, proceed east, turn left (north) at 15th Street, and at the next block, 1st Avenue North, turn left (west). You're now at the *W.A. McHenry House*, admission. Built in 1885 at a cost of $25,000, it had many modern features for its time, including pipes for hot and cold running water and speaking tubes. Home of the Crawford County Historical Society, the house displays many items, including the Oscar won by Donna Reed.

While there, get a copy of the walking tour brochure and stroll around town to enjoy the architectural beauty of 38 houses on the tour. Of particular interest is 1424 2nd Avenue N., former home of Clarence Chamberlain who, two weeks after Charles Lindbergh flew from New York to Paris, flew further than Lindbergh—to Berlin. In August 1927, Chamberlain made the first transatlantic mail flight.

Continue west on 1st Avenue North for three blocks to where Avenue C goes off to the right (northwest). Take that road out of town to the intersection with State Highway 39; turn left (south). The county fairgrounds and NASCAR racetrack will be on the right.

At the intersection with U.S. Highway 59, turn right (northwest). In about 2 miles, as 59 splits to the right (north), proceed west on what is now State Highway 141 for 11 miles to Charter Oak. There, you can make a quick stop at the town's arboretum, which is on the left side of the highway and has marked fruit trees, evergreens, flowers, and shrubs.

Continue on Highway 141 for 6 miles to State Highway 183 at Ute. Turn left (southwest). If you wonder why an Iowa town is named after Utah's Utes, it's because they befriended Isaac Cummins, the postmaster who named this town, when he lived near them.

Drive on 183 for 6 miles to Soldier. You'll pass through the valley of the Soldier River. The town was named after the river, which in turn was supposedly named because the body of a man wearing an army coat was found along the riverbank (however, when Lewis and Clark arrived here in 1804, it was already named Soldier River).

Donna Reed

Born in Denison in 1921 as Donnabelle Mullenger, Donna Reed left in 1937 to live with an aunt in California and work as a secretary. In her off-hours, she attended acting classes with friend Alexis Smith, and both caught the eye of agents who signed them to work in movies. Later she starred in the perennial Christmas favorite *It's a Wonderful Life* with Jimmy Stewart. (By the way, in that movie she gave Stewart a kiss that so impressed director Frank Capra that he did not care that Stewart and Reed had dumped a page of dialogue; however, censors cut the torrid smooch from the movie.) Then, she won an Oscar in 1953 for portraying a prostitute in *From Here to Eternity*. Reed shifted to television, starring in her own show that aired from 1958 to 1966; she was also the show's producer and director, rare roles for women in those years.

During the third full week of each June, the Donna Reed Foundation puts on the week-long Donna Reed Festival, which has more than 60 workshops that cover producing, directing, acting, choreography, commercials, radio, script writing, music, and makeup; some classes are designed for children. Among the instructors have been people who worked with Reed in Hollywood, including her television son and daughter, Paul Peterson and Shelly Fabares (who is now one of the festival's organizers). Other instructors have been actor Alan Young, director/producer Gene Reynolds, choreographer Andrea Muller, writer Lloyd Schwarz, and dozens of other Hollywood talents who have enriched those attending the festival. With classes costing $35 to $150, the festival attracts many people from the Midwest and beyond.

Quick Trip Option 2: Just past Soldier, look for the first left, a gravel road named Redwood Avenue, and turn onto it. Go 1.5 miles south to 280th Street and turn left (east). In about a half mile you will find *Soldier Norwegian Country Church*, on the left (north) side of the road. Built in 1904, it's known for its unique interior and beautiful stained glass windows. To return to the main tour, go west on 280th, pass Redwood and in 1 mile you will come upon Highway 183. Turn to the left (south).

By the way, don't expect any redwoods along Redwood Avenue, nor sequoias along Sequoia Avenue, which is not far away. When the 911 emergency telephone system was set up to cover rural areas around the 1990s, roads that once had no names had to be given names so the computers could identify what was where in the countryside.

Continue southwest on Highway 183 for 6 miles to Moorhead. Parts of the rest of this trip are also covered in Tour 4.

As you come to Moorhead, turn right (west) on County Road E54, which leads across the south end of town. At Oak Street, turn right (north). At the far end of the block on the right (east), the *Loess Hills Hospitality Association*,

(800) 886-5441 and (712) 886-5441, is quartered in Cover School House, a former one-room school. Inside is a gift shop that has books and artwork about the Loess Hills (see Tour 2), and in the vestibule is information about places to see in the hills that you just entered. The association offers guide service if you call ahead.

Next to the school is the *Bluebonnet II*, (712) 886-5465, a small café with a pleasant atmosphere and good food, especially the desserts. Across the street is the *Moorhead Cultural Center* (same phone as the association), where works of art can be viewed afternoons from Thursday through Sunday.

Quick Trip Option 3: To view another picturesque church, go west on E54, which is also County Road L16, and on the west side of Moorhead, follow the sign that points the way to the Danish Church. In a few miles down this gravel road (which is still E54), the *Ingemann Danish Lutheran Church* sits at the far end of a cemetery on the right. Built in 1884 by Danish immigrants, this church is a favorite of photographers and artists. To rejoin the main tour, return to Moorhead and Highway 183.

Up to a half-million snow geese can be seen each fall at DeSoto National Wildlife Refuge west of Missouri Valley.

From Moorhead, continue southwest for about 2.5 miles on Highway 183, watching for signs to *Preparation Canyon State Park*. Turn right (west) at 314th Street and drive about 2 miles until the pavement ends. Immediately on your left, you'll spot the entrance

to the park, (712) 423-2829, which includes a scenic overlook. (See Tour 4 for more information on Preparation Canyon.) After visiting the park, return to Highway 183 the way you came.

Quick Trip Option 4: To explore another facet of Preparation Canyon, see Quick Trip Option 1 in Tour 4.

From the park, return to Highway 183 and continue south for 7 miles to Pisgah. This small community is famous as the home of the *Old Home Fill 'Er Up and Keep on Trucking Cafe*, at the northeast corner of First and Main Streets, (712) 456-9797 (see Tour 4). Pisgah is also the home of the *Loess Hills State Forest Visitor Center*, 206 Polk Street, (712) 456-2924, free. The center has literature about regional attractions, and in its main room visitors get a comprehensive understanding of the Loess Hills. A three-dimensional map orients you to this section of the state and exhibits show the wildlife, plants, and the composition of the hills. Works of art about the hills are also on display.

Quick Trip Option 5: For a nice overlook of the front of the Loess Hills, go one block south of the center and turn right (west) onto County Road F20. This takes you through some of the Loess Hills; about 4 miles after leaving Pisgah you will reach the turnout to the Murray Hill parking lot on your left (south). Park here and enjoy a nice hike on a prairie-topped hill. To resume the main tour, return to Pisgah and Highway 183.

At Pisgah, continue south on Highway 183 for 10 miles until it is briefly joined by State Highway 127. A short distance south of the junction is County Highway F32. Turn left (east) there. *Small's Fruit Farm*, (712) 646-2723, is just up the hill. Stop here anytime from the early summer (strawberry time) through the fall (apples, pumpkin, squash, and more) and you will find some pretty fine locally grown produce. The small café at the store serves freshly baked goodies, but you can buy some frozen pies to take home to bake in your own oven if you want.

Continue south on Highway 183 and note that at the intersection with County Road F27, Highway 183 changes to County Road L20. Continue on L20 along the base of the hills all the way into Missouri Valley once again, although this time you zigzag into the west part of town on North 1st Street. At the intersection with Erie Street, which is also U.S. Highway 30, turn left (east). At 6th Street, which is a continuation of L20, turn right (south). Take this for about 9 miles to Honey Creek. The road crosses a large set of Union Pacific Railroad tracks and runs across a

The Jacob Krumm Preserve, located just north of I-80 at Exit 179, provides a glorious Iowa vista.

Built in 1846 the Wagaman Mill in Lynnville had been in continuous operation for over a hundred years.

A couple sit near the entrance to Dancehall Cave in Maquoketa Caves State Park.

A fisherman enjoys the Winnebago River in Mason City.

Hanging on a line, puppets made by famed puppeteer Bil Baird are found in Mason City's Charles MacNider Museum.

Catfish Bend Casino is based on a riverboat at both Fort Madison (here) and Burlington.

A part of the Loess Hills National Scenic Byway appears through the trees near Little Sioux.

The Iowa Capitol sits atop a hill west of downtown Des Moines.

Hot air balloons fill the sky in Indianola during the annual competition there.

A set of winding stairs leads between the floors of the Old Iowa Capitol in Iowa City.

Children play in the fountains at Memorial Auditorium in Burlington.

Farm buildings and a windmill create a scenic view near Rock Rapids.

Originally hidden by a wall, an opening in the basement of the Hitchcock House near Lewis reveals where runaway slaves would hide as they went north on the Underground Railroad.

Built in 1899, the RailsWest Railroad Museum station in Council Bluffs has been kept in its original condition.

A row of conical mounds represents just some of the many found in Effigy Mounds National Monument north of Marquette.

flat portion of the Missouri River floodplain. Less than 2 miles south of town, L20 suddenly makes an S-curve and goes through a narrow underpass beneath a set of train tracks. You then pass through the tiny hamlet of Loveland, cross under I-680, and cruise alongside the base of more hills.

Quick Trip Option 6: At Erie Street in Missouri Valley, turn right (west) and go about 8 miles to the *DeSoto National Wildlife Refuge*, on the left side of Highway 30. There are at least two super reasons to make a special visit to the refuge, (515) 642-2772, admission. First, in the late fall, up to half a million snow geese rest at DeSoto on their southbound migration. Although some spotting scopes are available to use in the visitor center's glass-walled galleries, bringing your own scopes and binoculars is a good idea.

The second is that the visitor center houses artifacts recovered from the steamboat *Bertrand*, which sunk in the Missouri River in April, 1865 on her way to the gold fields of Montana. When the Bertrand was discovered a century later, mud was found to have preserved her cargo, and as a result, items recovered from her cargo are among the best preserved of existing mid-nineteenth-century artifacts. These recovered items range from toys, cloth goods, high-button shoes, and dinner plates to shovels, fancy kerosene lanterns, and bottled foodstuffs.

After passing through Honey Creek, L20 ascends into the hills. About a half mile after cresting a ridge south of the community, watch on the right (west) for a sign for the *Hitchcock Nature Area*. Turn right (west) at Page Lane and go to the T intersection with Ski Hill Road. Turn right (north) and follow the signs. Hitchcock Nature Area, 27792 Ski Hill Road, (712) 545-3282, entry fee, is an 800-acre preserve with 10 miles of trails, mostly through wooded portions of the Loess Hills. The preserve has campsites just north of its entrance as well as an overlook and a lodge that serves as another overlook. On the deck of the lodge, a pair of 51-pound binoculars made for the Russian Navy are permanently mounted on a 90-pound pedestal and provide close-up views of the hills and valleys. Trails near the lodge lead to three hike-in campsites.

Returning to L20, continue south for about 4 miles to Crescent. Along the way, watch for a large red barn on the left side of the road; it's a llama farm. Just past that, on the right side, is the turnoff to the *Mount Crescent Ski Area*, 17026 Ski Hill Road, (712) 545-3850. Yes, there is downhill skiing in Iowa—and manmade snow if needed.

From Crescent, continue south on L20 for 6 miles back into Council Bluffs, where this tour began.

Ski Iowa? You bet—at several places, including Mount Crescent north of Crescent.

Hawk Watch

Hitchcock Nature Area is one of more than 70 North American viewing stations for Hawk Watch, a program that monitors the fall migration of raptors. In the fall of 2001, 591 bald eagles were spotted here; only four other stations recorded more than 500 bald eagles that fall. In the fall of 2002, nearly 8,000 raptors were seen from here, putting Hitchcock among the top 30 viewing sites in terms of overall numbers. Regarding species though, because about 20 types have been seen here each year, Hitchcock ranks third in that category. The five most commonly seen raptors here are red-tail hawks, Swainson's hawks, broad-winged hawks, sharp-shinned hawks, and kestrels. At the other end of the scale are the ferruginous hawk, which is rare in Iowa, and the black vulture, which had not been seen in Iowa since 1959 until one was spotted here in 2002.

On an average day, about 250 raptors pass through the region but in October, 2002 more than 900 Swainson's hawks were counted on just one day. Because the species of raptors migrate at different times, the site is manned by volunteers from mid-August to mid-December.

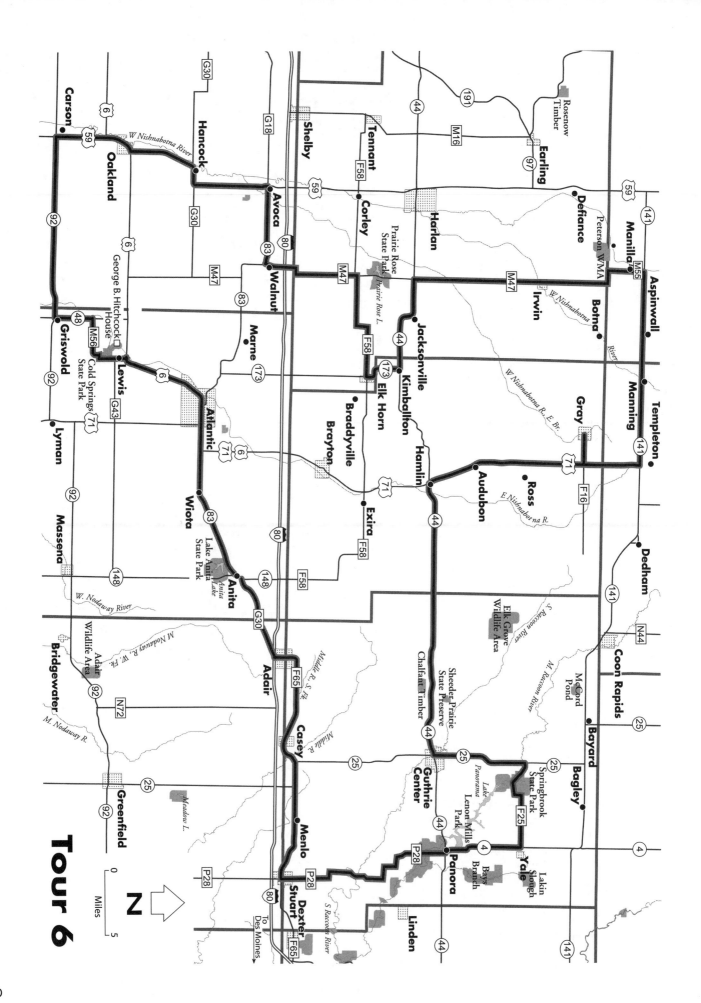

Tour 6

N

0 Miles 5

Tour 6
The Cultures of West Central Iowa

Walnut—Avoca—Griswold—Lewis—Atlantic—Adair—Stuart—Panora—Guthrie Center—Audubon—Gray—Manning—Manilla—Elk Horn—Walnut

Distance: approximately 225 miles

You may not visit any of Iowa's oldest places on this tour, but you're certainly going to see some of its oldest *things* when you visit Walnut, regarded as the state's "Antique Capital." After this start, it's on to additional superlative attractions: the largest bull in the nation, the largest rural settlement of Danes in the U.S., a couple of unique trees—one growing in the middle of a road and another that has grown around a full-sized plow—a way station on the Underground Railroad, the last bank ever robbed by Bonnie and Clyde, and the first train ever robbed by Jesse James. Along the tour, you can walk through a house-barn built in 1660 and a windmill built in 1848. Are you wondering how they got here? Then read on.

To begin this tour, go to Walnut, just south of Interstate 80 at Exit 46. The signs that claim Walnut is Iowa's Antique Capital aren't kidding, a conclusion you'll quickly come to as you drive into the downtown and begin to notice its 18 antique stores and malls. Also, around town are a dozen replicas of antique signs that were painted as a city beautification project. Orient yourself at the *Antique City Welcome Center*, 607 Highland Street, (712) 784-2100, free, which has information about area stores; public rest rooms are here too. Across the street from the center is *Monroe #8 One-Room Country Schoolhouse*, 610 Highland Street, (712) 784-3663 or (712) 784-2100, admission, which has been restored to the way it looked in the 1920s. The *Walnut Creek Historical Museum*, 301 Antique City Drive, (712) 784-3663 or (712) 784-2100, admission, in a former Masonic Lodge, tells of the region's German past.

Go to the south end of Antique City Drive, turn right (west) onto State Highway 83, and drive 6 miles to downtown Avoca and Elm Street; turn right (north). Between Wool and Crocker Streets on the right (east) is the *Eastern Pottawattamie County Courthouse*. Because Pottawattamie County is Iowa's second largest county, with 954 square miles, it has two courthouses: one in the county seat of Council Bluffs, 34 miles to the west, and another here.

Several of the county offices were moved back to Council Bluffs in the 1990s, but court is still held here once a week and the county sheriff maintains an office here too. Farther up the street is the *Sweet Vale of Avoca Heritage Museum*, 504 North Elm, (712) 343-2477, free, which has a large collection of stuffed animals from around the world, historical displays, and a collection of Danish plates.

Return to Highway 83 and head a couple blocks east until you reach U.S. Highway 59; turn right (south) and drive for about 6 miles to tiny Hancock. Right before it enters town, the road curves west, then turns south again as it enters town. At this point, go straight (west) on what is now Kimball Avenue and County Road G30. Across the railroad tracks is *Botna Bend Park*, (712) 741-5465. Run by the Pottawattamie Conservation Board, the park has 60 campsites with electricity, picnic areas, and small herds of buffalo and elk. Canoeists can access the West Nishnabotna River here.

Return to Highway 59 to continue south to Oakland, 6 miles away; in town, turn right (west) on Linden Street. You'll soon be in Oakland's small but pretty downtown, which has retained many of its original Victorian storefronts. Occupying five of those is the *Nishna Heritage Museum*, 118–123 North Main, (712) 482-6802 and (712) 482-3075, free, which has exhibits about prehistoric animals and rocks of southwest Iowa, settlers' equipment, an ice wagon, a traveling coach, and collections of dolls and tools.

From Oakland, continue south on Highway 59, cross U.S. Highway 6, and drive 4 miles to State Highway 92 near Carson. Cross the bridge and turn to the left, a route that will circle you around to Highway 92. Turn right (east) at the stop sign and proceed for 14 miles to Griswold. Along the way is a crossing of the Mormon Trail. Actually, it was also the Pioneer Trail, but its heavy use by the Mormons who moved to Utah in the nineteenth century has led many to call it the Mormon Trail.

On Main Street in Griswold, you will soon come upon the *Cass County Historical Society Museum*, 412 Main, (712) 778-2700 or (712) 778-4182, free, which is located in a nineteenth-century bank on the right. Just across the street from there is the *Rush Farm Antique Display*, 500 Main, (712) 778-2213, free. In a building that housed a car dealership and a John Deere dealer in the past, this collection consists mostly of International Harvester equipment collected and nicely restored to their original red-and-white schemes by Dale Rush, a retired area farmer. Along with the IH equipment are McCormick-Deering Farmall implements and downstairs a number of horse-drawn implements from the nineteenth century. Other restored antiques include kitchen stoves and cupboards. The collection is not open regular hours, so although you can call once you're in town, think about calling ahead.

Proceed east on Main Street until you reach State Highway 48. Turn left (north) and proceed for about 1 mile. There, you'll see *Conklin Fish Farm County Park*, (712) 778-2408 or (712) 243-6665, a pleasant place that has a meandering lake, about 50 campsites with electricity, picnic areas, and fishing. North of the park is a collection of three old windmills.

Hitchcock House near Lewis was once a stop on the Underground Railroad.

Continue north for little more than a mile to County Road M56. Turn right (east) and drive for about 3 miles to *Cold Springs State Park*. After the road winds through pastures and turns north, you'll see the park entrance, (712) 769-2372 or (712) 243-6665. At least 110 campsites are at the top of a hill amid oak and shagbark hickory. The 16-acre lake is stocked with bass, crappie, and bluegill, and it's where the Cass County Conservation Board raises catfish.

From Cold Springs Park, continue north a short distance on M56 until you reach a T intersection with County Road G43. Turn left (northwest) onto G43, which curves into the small community of Lewis. Here, you have a decision to make: whether to take a shorter route (less than 1 mile) on a paved road or a 23-mile trip that includes some gravel.

Alternate Route 1 (less than 1 mile): **If you do not want to travel on gravel roads, go straight north through Lewis on G43, which very soon runs into U.S. Highway 6; turn right (east).**

Alternate Route 2 (27 miles): **At Smith Street in Lewis, turn left (west) and continue until the paved road turns to gravel.** As you go a few blocks in town, you might see signs indicating that you are on Minnesota Street and wonder how you got there, because you just turned onto Smith. Well, that's the way some things are in this world—don't worry; you're on track. Soon after you're on gravel, you'll spy the *1849 Old Ferry House* on the right (north). A portion of the Mormon-Pioneer Trail ran this way and when the East Nishnabotna River was almost at the house, a ferry shuttled people, livestock, and wagons across it. Renovations are proceeding on the building, one of the oldest in western Iowa.

Continuing west on the gravel road, pass 567th Street and, just past the crest of the next hill, turn left at the sign for *Hitchcock House*; drive to the end of the lane. Built in 1856 by Reverend George Hitchcock, this two-story, unassuming brownstone (literally made with brown stones), (712) 769-2323, admission, overlooks the valley of the East Nish. It was a stop on the Underground Railroad for blacks seeking freedom from slavery in the North. In the basement is a secret room where the runaway slaves hid.

Return to the gravel road, turn right (east) and, at 567th Street, turn left (north). In a half mile you will meet U.S. Highway 6; turn right (east).

Whichever route you took, go east, then northeast on Highway 6 for about 7 miles to Atlantic; just west of town the road is joined by State Highway 83. Before reaching Atlantic on Highway 6, you may notice a sign or two calling this the White Pole Road. This name came about years ago, before highways had numbers, when white poles outlined the route. Watch the gravel roads intersecting the highway from the right side—one has a huge tree growing in the middle of the road just to the right of the highway.

Atlantic is known as Iowa's Coca Cola capitol because of the large bottling plant in town.

Highway 6 passes the *Cass County Courthouse* on the right (south), a downtown park, and the downtown itself, which is to the left on Chestnut Street. For fudge lovers, visit *Main Street Grill & Whitney Inn*, 222 Chestnut, (712) 243-1818, which makes about a dozen types of homemade fudge. Located in a former hotel, the restaurant also serves very good food and has murals and paintings created by a local artist. At the far north end of Chestnut, the massive brick *Rock Island Depot* is slowly being restored.

From Atlantic, continue east on Highway 6/83. About 4 miles out of Atlantic, 6 curves off to the left (north), but you should continue straight ahead on 83. In another 3 miles, at Wiota, 83 angles toward the northeast and arrives in Anita in 7 more miles. As you approach Anita, you may wonder why there are yellow cones set off to the right of the road. The reason is that they're outlining a small grass runway that lies between the highway and the railroad tracks, which have paralleled the highway since Wiota. Barely a mile south of Anita on State Highway 148 is *Lake Anita State Park*, (712) 762-3751. The 1,082-acre park has trails (including an equestrian path), a beach, boating, fishing, and 144 campsites (75 with electricity).

Highway 83 ends in Anita but keep going northeast on the road, which becomes County Road G30, for 5 miles. Slow down and look for a lone steam locomotive wheel on the right near some large trees. It was near here on July 21, 1873, that Jesse James and associates loosened a rail on the nearby tracks. They had heard that a train carrying $75,000 was to pass here and, when a train came along, they jerked the loose rail away. The locomotive toppled, killing the engineer outright and mortally wounding the fireman. However, it wasn't the train the robbers wanted. They emptied the express car's safe of $2,000 and took another $1,000 from the passengers, a robbery that is said to be the first of a moving train.

Continue for 2 more miles on Highway G30, crossing I-80 and entering Adair. Head to *Melvin Park*, which is marked with tall cement pedestals and colonnades. Turn left (north) onto County Road N54. This town of less than 1,000 has two well-known landmarks seen by thousands of travelers on I-80 every day: a yellow water tower bearing a Happy Face and a tall, wind-powered turbine. This route will pass by the town's business district, which is to the right (east) on Audubon Street.

Just north of Adair, at County Road F65, turn right (east) and continue for 7 miles to Casey. Along the way is a large red barn on the left with an American flag painted on a wood panel. If you're here some evening, you get to see the flag lit up along with a pig and a star outlined by lights.

F65 skirts the south side of Casey as it goes east. At the only stop sign on F65 in town, turn left (north) on McPherson to see another patriotic display. A short way up the street on the left (west) are the remains of a former storefront set between two buildings; part of the facade frames a lot that has become *Veterans Memorial Park*. A wall on a neighboring building has been turned into a gigantic red, white, and blue mural honoring servicemen and servicewomen from the Revolutionary War to the present.

From Casey continue east on F65 for about 9 miles to Stuart. About halfway there you'll pass the south side of Menlo where, on the left, you'll see a sign from yesteryear—a gas station attendant wearing a blue coat and bow tie—who still greets travelers.

When Stuart comes into view, watch along the road for a sign pointing the way to *O'Brien's Chocolates*, Victory Lane, (712) 523-1927. You can go north on that gravel road for a quarter mile and find fine homemade chocolates, toffee, fudge, caramels, and more that are usually made between the months of October through February each year.

In Stuart, turn left (north) onto County Road P28, which is also Division Street. Some buildings here really catch the eye: the 1907 *Carnegie Library*; the red, white, and blue *Morrison Chevrolet dealership*, and, on North 2nd Street, the *Masonic Lodge* that was built in 1894 and is crowned with the town clock. The *Rock Island Depot*, built in 1879 and visible from the F65/P28 intersection, is being restored.

On April 16, 1934 famed robbers Bonnie Parker and Clyde Barrow left town hastily after making an unauthorized withdrawal of about $1,500 from the First Union Bank. The bank robbery was the last by the couple who were killed a month later in Texas. Ironically, the bank they robbed is now the *Stuart Police Station*, 100 Northwest 2nd Street.

If you want to buy O'Brien's Chocolates in town, stop at *Stuart's Flowers*, 108 Northeast 2nd Street, (515) 523-2264. Also, as you pass through town, take note of a burned stone church a block east of the highway. Although one might think that the fire that gutted this edifice was recent, it occurred in 1995 when an arsonist set *All Saints Church* afire; funds are still being raised to restore it to its former glory. Built in 1908, it was once voted the most beautiful church in Iowa.

Quick Trip Option 1: This trip involves a visit to a nearby town that was the scene of another Bonnie and Clyde encounter. The year before they visited Stuart, they and their gang had been in Dexter, 5 miles east of Stuart on F65. On July 20,

Stuart is the location of the last bank robbed by Bonnie and Clyde; ironically, it is now the town's police headquarters.

Another place to visit is *Drew's Chocolates*, 426 State Street, (515) 789-4540 or (800) 243-7397, where one-of-a-kind, fork-dipped chocolates have been made since 1927. Every day, this chocolate shop makes a couple thousand pieces of candy, including chocolate-covered nuts (such as black walnut, cherry nut, and English walnut), creams, chocolate-covered fudges, toffee, and their favorite item, Drew Drops, which are chocolate-covered pecan caramels.

From Stuart, take County Road P28, which is part of the Western Skies Scenic Byway, north for about 14 miles to Panora. Turn left (west) at South Street and go three blocks to the *Guthrie County Historical Village*. The road from Stuart twists and turns through the rolling terrain, giving travelers a jauntier ride than on the area's usual straight-as-an-arrow stretches. Located at 206 West South Street, (641) 755-2989, free, the artifact-filled historical village educates the traveler about the history of Guthrie County very well; attractions include a depot, a church, a log cabin, a caboose, a general store, and a blacksmith shop, and a museum building. Two blocks beyond the village is *Lenon Mill Park*, (641) 755-3061, where the Middle Raccoon River drops over a small dam. Camping, picnic areas, and a comfort station are in the park.

From Lenon Mill Park, turn around on South Street and go east to West 3rd Street. Turn left (north) and go to State Highway 44; turn right (east). At the intersection with State Highway 4, turn left (north). As you leave town, you can see *Lake Panorama* on the left side of the highway. Surrounded by private developments, the lake has no public areas. While driving north, notice that the land ahead and to the right (east) is much flatter than where you were just a short time ago; this is where the leading edge of a glacier flattened everything about 13,500 years ago in what experts call the Des Moines lobe of the Wisconsin glaciation.

A bit more than 6 miles north of Panora, turn left (west) onto County Road F25 and drive for about 5 miles to *Springbrook State Park*, (641) 747-3591. Heavy with woods, this 920-acre park has 121 campsites (81 with electricity) and six rustic seasonal cabins. Its 17-acre spring-fed lake has a sandy beach and contains crappie, largemouth bass, bluegill, sunfish, bullhead, and catfish. Besides the 12 miles of trails that wander through it, Springbrook is on part of the 160-mile-long Central Iowa State Park Bike Route that connects the park with Ledges and Big Creek State Parks, as well as 14 towns. Boat ramps are located on the lake and on the Middle Raccoon River that flows through the park's southwest portion.

1933, the Barrow gang, which included Clyde's brother, Marvin "Buck" Barrow, and Buck's wife, Blanche, came to Dexter following a gunfight a few days earlier with law officials in Platte City, Missouri in which Buck had suffered a head wound. The gang stayed in Dexfield Park, now a cornfield, while members tended to Buck's wounds. Alerted to their presence (perhaps the gang's bullet-punctured cars were clues), about 50 law officials and armed citizens attacked the outlaws on July 24. After a two-minute gun battle, Bonnie, Clyde, and gang member W. D. Jones escaped on foot—all were wounded—but Buck was wounded again and captured with Blanche. On July 29, he died in a Perry hospital. At the site of the shootout, officials found two revolvers, 32 automatic pistols, and two automatic rifles. The *Dexter Museum*, 719 Marshall, has some items related to the shootout.

Leave Springbrook State Park's west entrance and go to State Highway 25. Turn left (south) and drive 7 miles to State Highway 44 at Guthrie Center; turn right (west). Highway 44 is another part of the Western Skies Scenic Byway at this point.

Quick Trip Option 2: About 5 miles after leaving Guthrie Center, watch for signs pointing the way to *Sheeder Prairie State Preserve.* Turn right (north) onto the gravel road and go to the T intersection a mile away; turn right (east). Watch for the small pullout to Sheeder Prairie immediately on the left. You can also park along the road but use care because vehicles could come over the hill immediately to the east. Some trees have invaded this 25-acre patch of prairie but big and little bluestem grasses continue to occupy most of the site, which comes alive with a brilliant show of prairie flowers in late June and August. The best way to return to Highway 44 is the way you came.

Quick Trip Option 3: This trip shows two of Iowa's more unusual trees and involves driving on some gravel roads.

About 12 miles after passing the turnoff to Sheeder Prairie on State Highway 44 is County Road N36; turn left (south). This highway joins County Road F58 more than 5 miles later. Turn left (east) and stay on F58 as it curves to the south. Where it begins to curve away to the east once more 2 miles later, watch for the signs to *Tree in the Middle of the Road* and go straight.

Follow the signs from then on. Eventually you will see a 100-foot-tall cottonwood dead ahead of you and yes, it is in the middle of the intersection of Nighthawk Avenue and 350th Street. In 1850 a surveyor working in this region had cut a young cottonwood sprout to use as a walking stick and when he realized he had nothing to mark a section corner, he hammered the stick into the ground with a rock—and it grew!

Return to the intersection of N36 and F58 and keep going west on F58 for 3 miles to Exira. From 1874 to 1879, this town was the Audubon County seat and the original wood frame courthouse is now the *Courthouse Museum,* 200 East Washington Street, (712) 268-2831, free, housing collections of county history, Native American displays, and a genealogy library. The building has also been an opera house, dance hall, roller rink, café, bakery, library, and the local lodge of *Knights of Pythias.*

Continue west of town a short distance to U.S. Highway 71. Turn left (south). In about 1 mile, turn right (west) into *Plow in the Oak Park,* (712) 268-2762. At the far (southeast) corner of the small preserve is the park's namesake—uh-huh, a large oak that has grown around a plow left by someone who, as legend has it, went off to the Civil War. The park has bathrooms and picnic areas.

To return to the main tour, return to Highway 71 and turn left (north); go for about 6 miles to Hamlin.

From Guthrie Center, drive west for 21 miles on Highway 44 to Hamlin and the junction with Highway 71. If you go straight ahead into town, cross the railroad tracks, and take the first left, you'll come to *Darrell's Place,* (712) 563-3922. People who have been to this restaurant say there's nothing fancy about it, but they swear that it has the state's best pork tenderloin sandwiches.

At Highway 71, turn north and drive 4 miles to Audubon. In this town of nearly 2,500 residents, you will notice *Nathaniel Hamlin Park,* (712) 563-2516, free, on the left. It's pretty hard to miss because of the 18 antique windmills outside the main house. Also in the park are a schoolhouse, farm implements, a stand of native timber, a few elk, and the world's largest collection of nails. Closer to town is *Albert the Bull.* Made of 45 tons of concrete and steel and measuring 30 feet high, Albert, built to honor the regional beef industry, is claimed to be the world's largest bull.

In Audubon, a life-size bronze statue of naturalist and illustrator John James Audubon is in the city park, which is right up Broadway to the right (east) of Highway 71. The town has memorialized Audubon in other ways, including a beautiful tile mural in the local library that sits on the northwest corner of the park; the entry through the original Carnegie portion is now closed, so use the library's new entrance on North Park Place. Another mural, made as a WPA effort to depict Audubon, is in the post office that sits on the northeast corner of Chicago and Tracy Streets, a block south of the park.

Downtown is *Hansen's Gallery,* 225 Broadway, (712) 563-3335, where original oil paintings by local artist Clint Hansen are shown and sold. Hansen has worked mostly as a freelance commercial artist for corporations like IBM and Coca-Cola and is known for his scratchboard works, but the gallery holds a range of his more personal items with subjects ranging from farms and lighthouses to wildlife.

Leave Audubon on Highway 71 and go north about 8 miles to County Road F16. Turn left (west) and drive 2 miles along a rolling landscape to the tiny town of Gray. Considering that Gray has only eight or so blocks (and fewer than 100 residents), it's easy to find the *Gray Heritage Rose Garden,* a stretch of formerly empty lots that some local women have beautified with at least 250 roses, other perennials, annuals, statues, benches, trees, Victorian-style lights, arches, and a pergola topped by a steeple from a town church. Even the town's water tower has roses painted on it.

Next to the garden is the *Long Branch*, 107 Second Street, (712) 563-2377, a place people talk about because of its good sandwiches, shrimp, steaks, home-seasoned Iowa chops, and chicken, along with homemade fries, onion rings, and pies.

Although there are two other ways out of Gray, just return the way you came, on F16 (that's because it's the only paved route). Upon reaching Highway 71, turn left (north) and drive for about 5 miles to State Highway 141. Turn left (west) and go for about 7 miles to Manning. Watch for the sign directing you to the *Hausbarn and Heritage Park*, 12196 311th Street, (712) 655-3131 or (800) 292-0252, admission, which are on your left near a thick grove of pines. The Hausbarn—pronounce that slowly and you'll understand what it is: a combination of a house and a barn—was built in Offenseth, Germany in 1660, dismantled, and rebuilt here in 1999 with the help of German thatchers. Heritage Park has a farmstead with a restored 1915 bungalow-style home and seven other buildings, including the *Hausbarn Restaurant*, (712) 655-3095, which serves German and American food.

Just south on the gravel road is *Forgotten Corner Museum*, 1305 East Street, (712) 653-3029, donation, a private collection of just about anything from household goods to farm equipment and a 30-inch-wide crystal ball.

Back on Highway 141, continue 8 miles west to County Road M55. Turn left (south) and go a short distance to Manilla. As the road sways into town, you will see the *Klondike Hotel*, 332 3rd Street, which opened on a limited basis in 2003. Built in 1897, the original Italianate structure was once the hotel for railroad passengers and crews who changed trains at this town, which was the main junction between two divisions of the Chicago, Milwaukee, and Saint Paul Railroad. Artifacts include the rope

fire escapes in the second-floor rooms, original furniture, and a metal coin box where railroad employees deposited money for their overnight stays. As restoration continues, parts of the hotel are planned to become a tearoom, a gift shop, and a bed and breakfast.

From the Klondike, go south to Main Street and turn left (east) into the downtown area. Go to 8th Street and turn right (south). This becomes County Road M47, which eventually jogs to the east for a mile, cuts south again, then goes straight for 5 miles, passing through Irwin. From there, continue south on it for about 10 more miles to State Highway 44.

Turn left (east) onto Highway 44, which is also another leg of the *Western Skies Scenic Byway*. In about 8 miles, turn right (south) onto State Highway 173 at Kimballton. This village of about 300 residents was one of two villages (the other is nearby Elk Horn) settled by Danish immigrants in the late nineteenth and early twentieth centuries. On Main Street, a statue of Hans Christian Andersen's *Little Mermaid* sits in a fountain amid water spraying on her from all directions. The *General Store Museum*, 112 North Main, (712) 773-2430, free, has displays featuring early Kimballton and serves as the national corn husking museum.

Continue south on Highway 173, which curves to the east before entering Elk Horn 3 miles away. As you enter the largest Danish rural settlement in the United States, you can see the 60-foot-tall *Danish Windmill*, 4038 Main Street, (712) 764-7472 or (800) 451-7960, at the south end of town. Although there are other places you could visit, go to the windmill first because it has an *Iowa Welcome Center* (free) with lots of information about the region's attractions and guides who give tours inside the windmill (admission). There's also a gift shop featuring Danish items ranging from Legos, silver jewelry, and ornaments by Georg Jensen to Holmgaard glassware, candies, books, and figurines by B&G and Royal Copenhagen. The windmill was built in 1848 in Norre Snede, Denmark, but was dismantled in the 1970s and brought to Elk Horn as a national bicentennial project to honor the Danish who first settled here.

Near the windmill is the *Danish Inn*, 4116 Main Street, (712) 764-4251, which has American meals as well as Danish dishes such as *frikaddler* (meatballs), *rodkall* (red cabbage), *smorrebrod* (open-faced sandwiches), and *moredard* (pork stuffed with apples and prunes). Among the other attractions in Elk Horn, which is bright with the red and white flags of Denmark fluttering next to the Stars and Stripes and benches painted like the Danish flag, is the *Danish Bakery*, 4324 Main Street, (712) 764-2151, with a host of sweet baked goods. Around the corner is *Bedstemor's Hus*, College and Union Streets, (712) 764-6082 or (800) 759-9192, admission, which means "Grandmother's House" in Danish (there's an irony here because the house was built by a lifelong bachelor).

Just west of town is the *Danish Immigrant Museum*, 2212 Washington Street, (712) 764-7001 or (800) 759-9192, admission, which is the only museum in the United States about the Danish immigrants and is designed in the style of a large Danish farm building. Exhibits include items brought by the immigrants from their homeland, records from a Danish-American *folkschule* and a piano used by Danish-American comedian and pianist Victor Borge. A genealogical library provides reference materials for those wanting to research their Danish backgrounds.

Alternate Route: Back at the intersection of State Highway 44 and County Road M47 about 8 miles west of Kimballton, go south on M47 for about 3 miles to *Prairie Rose State Park*. The park, (712) 773-2701, has a 214-acre lake, camping, picnic facilities, a beach, and trails.

To reach Elk Horn from the park, continue south on M47 for about 2 miles to County Road F58 and turn left (east). Drive for about 9 miles to Elk Horn. You'll pass the Danish Immigrant Museum (see above) on your left before reaching town.

From Elk Horn, continue south on Highway 173 for about 12 miles, crossing over I-80 to State Highway 83. Turn right (west) and proceed for about 10 miles back to Walnut, completing this tour.

Yes, the Danes have windmills too! This one, in Elk Horn, was brought to the town as part of its celebration of the U.S. bicentennial in 1976.

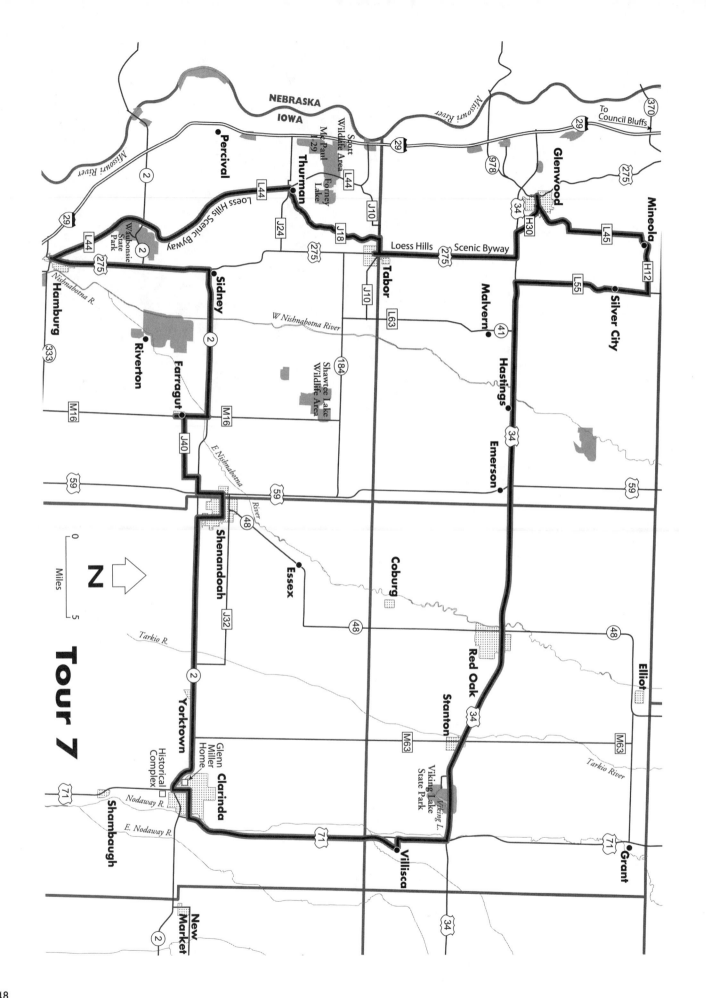

Tour 7

NEBRASKA
IOWA

Missouri River

To Council Bluffs

Percival

Scott Wildlife Area
McPaul L29

Thurman
Forney Lake

Glenwood

Mineola

Loess Hills Scenic Byway

Waubonsie State Park

Loess Hills Scenic Byway

Tabor

Silver City

Hamburg

Sidney

Malvern

Nishnabotna R.

W Nishnabotna River

Hastings

Riverton

Farragut

Shawtee Lake Wildlife Area

Emerson

E Nishnabotna River

Shenandoah

Essex

Coburg

Red Oak

Elliot

Tarkio R.

Stanton

Yorktown

Clarinda

Glenn Miller Home

Viking Lake State Park

Tarkio River

Historical Complex

Nodaway R.

Shambaugh

E. Nodaway R.

Villisca

Grant

New Market

N
Miles
0
5

Tour 7
Great Tastes, Music, and History—
Iowa's Southwest Corner

Glenwood—Tabor—Hamburg—Sidney—Shenandoah—Clarinda—Villisca—Red Oak—Glenwood

Distance: approximately 155 miles

Southwestern Iowa seems so sleepy, so out of the way, so "Nothing happens here." That's part of its charm but in some ways that sentiment is oh so wrong. As you travel this tour, you get to belly up to the marble counter of the nation's oldest family-owned soda fountain, plus visit a couple of others, walk though the hometowns of some of our nation's most famous musicians, enter a small school that is the birthplace of 4H, and see a house that was the scene of one of the nation's most infamous murders . . . all in Iowa's quiet southwest corner.

This tour begins in Glenwood, about 18 miles south of Council Bluffs. At the intersection of Locust and Sharp Streets, go east on Sharp one block to the town square. Like most small town squares, this one is basically an outdoor shopping mall. Glenwood's has a jewelry store, bank, hardware store, floral shop, chiropractor, county sheriff's office, optometrist, senior center, movie theater, card shop, insurance company, beauty shop, barber shop, and more. Stroll around the square; it's the perfect opportunity to take in a quintessential Iowa scene.

A nice place to stop is *Two Sisters & Me*, 418 1st Street, (712) 527-1111, on the north side of the square near the theater. It offers espresso and homemade foods, which include egg salad on croissant, bacon and cheese soup, cookies, and other sweets. Art from local artists hang on wall racks, along with regular tables, a couch, and overstuffed chairs are in the rear.

Head east on Sharp Street and cross Keg Creek. To the right is the entrance to *Glenwood Lake Park* and the *Mills County Museum*, Highway 34 E, (712) 527-5038, admission. The park's lakeside paths are frequented by strollers and joggers while geese and ducks prefer the water. On the far side of the lake is *Davies Amphitheater*, (712) 527-3334, where dramas, comedies, and live musical presentations occur throughout the warm months, many at extremely reasonable prices if not free.

One might suppose that the *Mills County Museum* is like so many other county museums with collections of settlers' equipment, artifacts

from various wars, old newspapers, and so on. Well, it has those, but the thing that sets it apart from the others is its fine collection of artifacts from late prehistoric times. Museum personnel can arrange tours of the igloo-shaped earth lodge just across the road. Also at the museum are a caboose, a restored 1895 barn, jail, and a building containing agricultural implements and vehicles.

Early Residents

Native Americans who lived in the Mills County area between 1000 and 1600 A.D. were part of the Central Plains tradition, which had elements also in Kansas, Nebraska, and Missouri. Most Indians who lived in western Mills County during that era, called the Glenwood Culture, lived on individual farms, especially in and near the Loess Hills, although it was not uncommon for a few families to cluster together. These Indians hunted wild animals, collected wild plants, fished, and raised crops. It is believed that the climate became warmer around 1300, which adversely affected flora and fauna. Because of dwindling resources and perhaps, as some researchers think, because of raids by northern Indians, members of the Glenwood Culture moved elsewhere in the sixteenth century.

It is not known exactly where these Indians went, although it is thought they went west where they may have joined the Pawnee, who had a similar culture. In their wake, they left countless arrowheads, spear points, cutting tools, grinding bowls, and pieces of pottery. More than 80 earth lodge sites have been identified in Mills County, mostly near Glenwood.

Later, Ioway, Oto, Omaha, and perhaps some Missouria and Dakota lived here. For a few years, Pottawattamie were here too. They called themselves Neshnabek, or "The True People." Pressured by westward-moving Americans, about 3,000 Pottawattamie were moved to a region south of Glenwood in 1836 from their Great Lakes homeland. Three hundred of them lived in a village that had a post office, stagecoach stop, and a U.S. Army blockhouse. In 1845, the Pottawattamie were forced to move to northeast Kansas, which they did in 1846. However, Waubonsie, a leader of the Pottawattamie, remained here until his death in 1848.

Return to Sharp Street and turn right (east). Take the road, which is also County Road H30, for a couple of miles to U.S. Highway 34/275. Turn left and go east for less than 2 miles to where Highway 275 splits from 34. Turn right (south) on 275 and drive for 9 miles to Tabor. Note how many of the fields that have been terraced to reduce erosion.

Upon entering Tabor, turn right (west) onto Elm Street. Go for two blocks, alongside the city park, and turn left (south) at Park Street. About the middle of the block is the *Todd House*, 705 Park, (712) 692-2675, a one-and-a-half-story, white, frame structure. This was the residence of John Todd, a Tabor minister but, more important to some, also an abolitionist. His house, built in 1853, served as an arsenal for fellow abolitionists and a way station on the Underground Railroad, a series of routes used by blacks escaping enslavement in southern states.

Continue to the next intersection and turn left (east) on Orange Street to return to Highway 275 two blocks away. You might want to check out *The Diner*, a small restaurant, and *2nd Time Around*, an antiques store, both near this intersection.

In Tabor, the Todd House was a place where runaway slaves would hide on their journey north on the Underground Railroad.

Continue south on Highway 275 for about 2 miles to County Road J18. Turn right (west) and proceed for about 5 miles to Thurman. This two-lane road rolls through the Loess Hills with some broad curves. Watch for an open-front farm shed on the right side of the road; in it is a pair of wicker horses made out of tree branches.

Just outside of Thurman, J18 meets County Road J24. Turn right (west) to enter tiny Thurman, then turn left (south) at County Road L44. This leads along the base of the bluffs of the Loess Hills that rise high up on the left. To the right lie fertile farm fields and the Missouri River, which is more than 5 miles away.

Watch on the left for a white barn with round, colorful hex signs painted on it. In other parts of the nation, these are associated with the Amish, who believe they ward off evil spirits, and the presence of the signs here is a rarity since no Amish live in the area.

Drive south on L44 for about 16 miles to Hamburg. Along the way, you'll pass State Highway 2 and continue to skirt the base of the bluffs. You will eventually see *Mincer Orchard*, (712) 382-1484, on the right, but their main outlet is at the entrance to Waubonsie State Park.

In Hamburg, where L44 becomes E Street, go to the intersection of E and Main Streets, which is marked by a flagpole. Hamburg has the distinction of being Iowa's southwestern-most community. On the left side of Main Street, near the intersection, is *Stoner Drug*, 1105 Main, (712) 382-2551, which has an old-time soda fountain that's still pouring great cold treats. The house specialty is the Fried Egg Sundae, which is not really what it sounds like; it's actually a delicious sundae of vanilla ice cream covered by a marshmallow topping in such a way that it only looks like an egg done over easy.

To the right (east) of the intersection is *Swedish Touch*, 610 Main, (712) 382-1809, a flower and gift shop that's connected to one of the largest peony nurseries in Iowa (considering all the peonies grown here, it's no wonder that Hamburg claims to be the Peony Capital of the World).

At the intersection of E and Main, continue east on E Street for two blocks to U.S. Highway 275. Turn left (north) onto 275 and go for 7 miles to State Highway 2. Along the way, you'll see the hills of Missouri to the right, barely a mile away.

At Highway 2, turn left (west) and go for 1 mile to *Waubonsie State Park*. The 1,247-acre park, (712) 382-2786, sits atop heavily wooded hills although some patches of the prairie remain here and there. One of the prettier trails is Sunset Ridge Trail, which rambles out to some prairie-topped bluffs overlooking the broad Missouri River valley. The park has other trails totaling 15 miles, 40 campsites (24 with electricity, picnic areas, and 34 more campsites for horseback riders and their steeds.

Return east to Highway 275, then turn left (north) and proceed for 4 miles into Sidney. Once in this quaint county seat, head downtown and keep to the right at the courthouse square. The *Fremont County Historical Museum Complex*, (712) 374-3248, free, is on the right side of the square. For a well-deserved icy treat, continue around the square until you're going south on Illinois Street. With an ice cream soda painted on its front window is *Penn Drug*, 714 Illinois Street, (712) 374-2513. Bought by Dr. John Newton Penn during the Civil War, it's now run by the fifth generation of his family, making this the oldest family-owned drugstore in the nation. The specialties of the soda fountain are banana splits and homemade lemonade. Some hot lunches are available.

Go around the square to Filmore Street, which is also Highway 2, and turn right. Drive for about 9 miles to County Road M16 and turn right (south) toward Farragut 2 miles away. Just before reaching Farragut, turn left (east) on County Road J40 and go for about 4 miles to *Manti Memorial Park*. As the road curves north, look for the entrance on the right. The park, (712) 542-3864, has its origin in the nineteenth century. Around 1851, about 40 families, mostly dissident Mormons, lived in Manti, which had two stagecoach stops among its businesses. In the 1870s, the railroad went to nearby Shenandoah and Manti folded. Although none of Manti's buildings remain, a half-mile trail leads through 32 acres of woods to the old cemetery in the preserve's far southeastern corner.

Continue on J40, which now goes north, for a short distance to Highway 2; turn right and proceed to U.S. Highway 59, about 1 mile to the east. At 59, turn left (north) and go about 2 miles to the west side of Shenandoah. At the third stoplight, turn right (east) onto Sheridan Avenue, Shenandoah's main thoroughfare. At the turn is an octagonal, Victorian-style visitor center with stained glass windows and lots of regional information. The center also serves as a gift shop for the *Bricker Butterfly House*, Sheridan Avenue and Fremont Street, (712) 246-5455, free. Housing countless native butterflies along with tropical and native plants, the Bricker is, in a way, paying homage to the large nurseries that have played a role in Shenandoah's economy throughout the last century.

Shenandoah is the hometown of Don and Phil Everly who created a string of musical hits in the 1960s and 70s. Although no place in town is directly connected to them, the *Depot Deli*, 101 Railroad Avenue, (712) 246-4444, which is near railroad tracks on the left (north) side of Sheridan Avenue, is something of their unofficial headquarters; a monument to them is outside the restaurant. Across Sheridan Avenue from there, the *Greater Shenandoah Historical Society Museum*, 800 West Sheridan, (712) 246-1669, free, covers the history of the city as well as some of the smaller, outlying communities.

For something cool and scrumptious, stop at *George Jay Drug*, 612 West Sheridan, (712)

Hikers take to the trail in Waubonsie State Park in the Loess Hills near Sidney.

246-2635, which has, as you might guess by now, a soda fountain from years gone by. The prices for those cold treats are just right: pop and phosphates (flavored pop) are 35 and 75 cents; malts and milkshakes, $2.50; sodas, $1.85; and sundaes, 85 cents and $1.20. A list of home-made concoctions is posted near the cash register, and in-cludes apple pie ice cream (vanilla with chunks of spiced apples, pie crust, and caramel apple revel) and candy bar whirl (chocolate-and-peanut-butter-candy-bar-flavored ice cream with roasted peanuts and caramel and fudge swirl).

Picturesque touches highlight the downtown, including gooseneck lights, American flags, and some neat murals, but the icing on the cake is the short, brick pedestals adorned with colorful tiles made by local children. On the sidewalks is *Iowa's Walk of Fame*, which consists of plaques honoring famous people with Iowa ties, including comedian Johnny Carson, twin columnists Ann Landers and Abigail Van Buren, writer Hugh Sidey, Olympic wrestler Dan Gable, Meredith "Music Man" Willson, artist Grant Wood, and Presidents Herbert Hoover and Ronald Reagan. Also honored are two local men: Henry Field created one of the nation's largest mail-order seed companies here in 1892, and one of his competitors, Earl May, also started a mail-order seed and retail garden business here some years later.

At the next intersection, turn left (north) onto North Sycamore Street and go to West Ferguson Avenue. Turn right (east). If you're carrying bicycles or skates—or if you like to hike—stop at the old *Shenandoah railroad depot* (not to be confused with Depot Deli) just off Ferguson; the depot is part of a complex containing a performing arts theater and a swimming pool. This pretty gray-and-white depot is an access point on the *Wabash Trace Nature Trail*, user fee, a 69-mile-long hiking and biking trail that stretches between Council Bluffs and Iowa's southern border. Topped with finely crushed limestone, the Wabash is the longest

Glenn Miller

Glenn Miller began playing musical instruments while a youngster. In 1931 he formed his own band and ten years later had earned the first gold record ever for selling more than a million copies of "Chattanooga Choo Choo." He was also known for composing "Moonlight Serenade" and "In the Mood."

In World War II, Miller joined the U.S. Army Air Force and led a 50-member band to play for the troops as a morale builder. On December 15, 1944, Miller boarded a small airplane in England to fly to Paris with the pilot and another officer and disappeared in the fog of war.

Although the story has never been proven, a British Royal Air Force airman later recalled that his bomber jettisoned its bombs over the English channel that day and as he watched them exploding in the water, he also saw a low-flying plane of the same type as that carrying Miller being tossed by the explosions.

Every June, Clarinda hosts the *Glenn Miller Festival*. One of Miller's four trombones, kept safely throughout the years, is displayed with other memorabilia. Big band fans and musicians come from as far as Canada, Holland, Finland, Japan, and Britain to participate in the fun. Events cost between $5–20 per person but the Friday evening concert on the courthouse square is free and defines Clarinda perfectly. People set their lawn chairs on the blocked-off streets as the musicians warm up and then, as the last light of a summer day leaves the tip of the courthouse tower, the hot music of a cool night sweeps over everyone and Clarinda cooks.

recreational trail in the state.

The best way out of town is to drive east on Ferguson Avenue to North Center Street and turn right (south). Drive for about 2 miles back to Highway 2 south of town, then turn left (east) toward Clarinda.

Alternate Route: Some drivers may think that a better way to head east out of town is on East Ferguson, which becomes County Road J32. Well, that's true but, once out of town, the road becomes narrower, bumpier, and hillier than Highway 2 that it parallels. If you're up for thrills, follow J32 for about 12 miles as it runs east, then swings south to meet Highway 2, and resume traveling the main route.

From Shenandoah, follow Highway 2 for about 18 miles to the west edge of Clarinda.

Changing Names

Originally, the town of Shenandoah was called Fair Oaks. However, when a veteran returned to the town from the Civil War, he commented on the way the area reminded him of Virginia's Shenandoah Valley—and Fair Oaks soon had a new name.

Here Highway 2 splits into Business Highway 2 (straight ahead) and the bypass (to the right). Take the bypass. This brings you to the south end of town where you turn right (south) on South 16th Street. Within sight of the intersection is *Goldenrod School*, the birthplace of 4-H, which was begun by a young teacher named Jessie Field Shambaugh in 1901 to strengthen her students in head, heart, hands, and health as a way to prepare them to help themselves and others. Near the school is the *Nodaway Valley Historical Museum*, 1600 South 16th Street, (712) 542-3073, admission, which has more information about 4-H among its many items. The grounds have other historic buildings that can be visited, including a general store and barbershop.

After leaving the museum, take 16th Street north into Clarinda. Along the way are signs stating that the street is also Glenn Miller Avenue. Along the way is the *Glenn Miller Birthplace Home*, 601 South 16th Street, (712) 542-2461, free, on the left (west). This unpretentious green frame house is where the famed bandleader spent the first years of his life, from 1904 to 1908, before following his family elsewhere. The house contains memorabilia from Miller's career, and there are plans to erect a museum behind the house to honor the big band music that Miller helped create.

Upon reaching the courthouse square, turn right (east) onto East Main and park your vehicle. To complete your exposure to Clarinda's favorite son, visit the *Glenn Miller Birthplace Society*, 107 East Main, (712) 542-2461, free. Besides books and literature about Miller, it has lots of information about the big band sound and manages the Glenn Miller Festival. The square also gives you a chance to catch your breath and take in the town's serene atmosphere.

From East Main, go east to North 15th Street and turn left (north). At East Washington one block away, turn right (east) and head out of town on what becomes County Road J35. If you're hungry, Hua Yung Buffet, 822 East Washington, (712) 542-5156, and J Bruners, 1100 East Washington, (712) 542-3364, are along the way.

Take J35 for a couple of miles east to U.S. Highway 71. There, turn left (north) and go about 13 miles north to Villisca. All along the way, you'll be running parallel with the West Nodaway River on the left.

Just south of Villisca, look for Old Highway 71 and turn right on it after crossing the Middle Nodaway River. Proceed to West 4th Street, turn right (east), and enter the small downtown area. At the far side of the square is the *Olson/Linn Museum*, 343 East 4th, (712) 826-2756 or (641) 322-4202, admission. Besides having a number of artifacts and an extensive collection of antique automobiles, it's also the starting point for tours related to one of the most infamous crimes of the early twentieth century, the Villisca ax murders.

To view the exterior of the *Villisca Ax Murder House*, go north on South 4th Avenue to East 2nd Street. Turn right (east) and go two blocks until East 2nd Street ends at a T intersection with South 6th Avenue. The house is the one on the northwest corner of the intersection. When last seen, it was being renovated. Tours of the house can be arranged at the Olson/Linn Museum.

Turn north onto South 6th Avenue for one block, turn left (west) onto East 1st Street, then right (north) at South 5th Avenue. Go to High Street and turn left (west), which leads back to Highway 71. Turn right (north) and proceed for 3 miles to U.S. Highway 34. Turn left (west) and drive about 3 miles to *Viking Lake State Park*. The entrance to this 1,000-acre park, (712) 829-2235, is on the left. It has fishing, 126 recently renovated campsites (95 with electricity, 22 with full hookups), six miles of trails, picnic facilities, no-wake boating, and swimming at an unsupervised beach, which has a food-and-boat concession stand and a tackle and bait shop. A lakeside restaurant opened in 2002 and serves lunches and dinners April through December. Beaver, turkey, muskrat, duck, shorebirds, and white-tailed deer are common in the park.

Four miles past the park on Highway 34, turn left (south) onto County Road M63 to enter Stanton. Where that road splits a moment later, take the left fork, Halland Avenue. At Center Avenue, turn right (west) and go a short distance, following the street as it jogs a bit, to the intersection with Hilltop Avenue. There, an old, large, brick schoolhouse now houses the *Swedish Heritage and Cultural Center*, 410 Hilltop, (712) 829-2840 or (877) 329-2840, admission, where in six rooms of exhibits, artifacts, papers, photos, and more tell the story of the region's Swedish immigrants.

From the center, return to Halland Avenue and turn right (south) again. As you travel down the street, look to the left to see Stanton's prize attraction—the *world's largest Swedish coffee pot*, which is really a water tower shaped and painted like a coffee pot. The coffee pot honors a hometown gal who made good. Virginia Christine acted in movies, including *High Noon* and *Judgment at Nuremberg*, but she's most remembered as Mrs. Olson of the Folger's Coffee television commercials that aired for 21 years in

the 1970s and 1980s. Within the past few years, another, larger water tower was erected south of town and, appropriately enough, it's painted like a coffee cup. That can be seen by taking Halland Avenue south of town. By the way, the coffee pot can hold about 240,000 cups of coffee, and although the coffee cup is shorter, it can hold 2.4 million cups of coffee.

From the world's largest Swedish coffee cup, return north on Halland; at the fork in the road, keep left on what will become Broad Avenue and head into Stanton's business district. While there, think about lunch at *Susie's Kok* or, in English, *Susie's Kitchen*, 404 Broad Avenue, (712) 829-2947. By the way, if you did not notice, all the houses in town are painted white, which is why Stanton is sometimes called "The Little White City."

To leave town, head north on Broad Avenue to Highway 34. Turn left (west) and drive for about 8 miles to Red Oak. At North 4th Street, turn right and go for about two blocks to the *Montgomery County Historical Center*. The complex, 2700 North 4th, (712) 623-2289, free, has an 1853 log cabin, schoolhouse, and restored barn outside and plenty of exhibits inside. Of particular interest are the artworks used by the Murphy Calendar Company, which produced calendars here and was the first firm to feature photos in its calendars.

While at the museum, pick up a booklet for the self-guided "Heritage Hill Tour" of significant buildings in Red Oak. Head south on 4th Street to the town square. Unlike many other county seats, the square is not occupied by a courthouse. That's located a couple blocks to the east and faces Coolbaugh Street, an eastbound one-way street. Take a look-see at this magnificent red brick building with a tall limestone base, and then begin your walking tour of Red Oak.

Near downtown, the *World War II Memor-*

An old Fordson tractor is one of several on display at the Indian Creek Historical Museum west of Red Oak.

ial Museum occupies the beautifully restored Burlington Northern Depot, 305 2nd Street, (712) 623-6340, free. A multimedia show, photos, uniforms, and copies of news broadcasts and music from that era present an overall view of the war overseas and on the home front. With more casualties per capita than any other city in the nation, Red Oak was honored by the U.S. Navy when it named one of its cargo ships *Red Oak Victory*.

From downtown Red Oak, head west on Reed Street to North Broadway Street, which is also State Highway 48. Turn right (north) and go a short distance back to Highway 34; turn left (west) and go about 12 miles. Between mileposts 35 and 34, at Nishna Valley School, turn left (south) and

go a quarter mile to the *Indian Creek Historical Museum*. Opened in 2001, this facility, (712) 824-7730, free, was created when a million dollars worth of farm equipment was donated by a family that homesteaded in the area in the nineteenth century. Among the equipment are 60 tractors that date back to 1917 and are all in operating condition, including a Waterloo Boy, one of the first gas-powered tractors ever made. Demonstrations include shelling and grinding corn, spinning and weaving wool, and many other "touch and do" projects. On a 27-acre county preserve, the museum includes a one-room schoolhouse, prairie, and a lake that was the local swimming hole years ago. A few campsites with electricity are on the property.

Return to Highway 34, turn left and con-

tinue west for 10 miles to County Road L55. Turn right (north) and proceed for about 6 miles to Silver City. Along the way, you'll travel through a narrow underpass beneath the tracks of the Burlington Northern Santa Fe Railroad, which is also AMTRAK's main route across Iowa. Watch the farmsteads on the left side of the road . . . one has a rather unique outhouse (more than likely not in use) just north of the main house.

In Silver City, you'll encounter, once more, the Wabash Trace Nature Trail. In a building quaintly reminiscent of a railroad depot, the *Studio Grill,* 410 South Main, (712) 525-9080, serves noon specials, announcements for which are posted outside its front door.

Continue north on Road L55 for 2 miles to County Road H12; turn left (west) and head for about 3 miles to Mineola. As you approach this small town, you encounter the Wabash Trace yet again. The highway rounds the west edge of town, but if you're hungry now, go one block east on Main Street to the *Mineola Steak House,* 408 Main, (712) 526-2078. It's a popular hangout for bicyclists on the Wabash Trace.

Continue past Mineola on H12 and about a mile from town, cut south (left) on County Road L45, and continue for 8 miles to Glenwood. For most of its length, L45 goes south, but when it turns to the west, it ascends a hill that gives a nice view to the north. Many of the houses in this part of the countryside have been built in the last few years by people who want to live in the country but who work in the nearby metro area of Council Bluffs and Omaha, Nebraska. In short, this part of Iowa is becoming a rural bedroom community, evidence of continuing urban sprawl and the gentrification of Iowa's countryside.

Back in Glenwood, at the T intersection with State Highway 949 (Sharp Street), turn right (west). Before you know it, you'll be back at the courthouse square, the beginning of this tour.

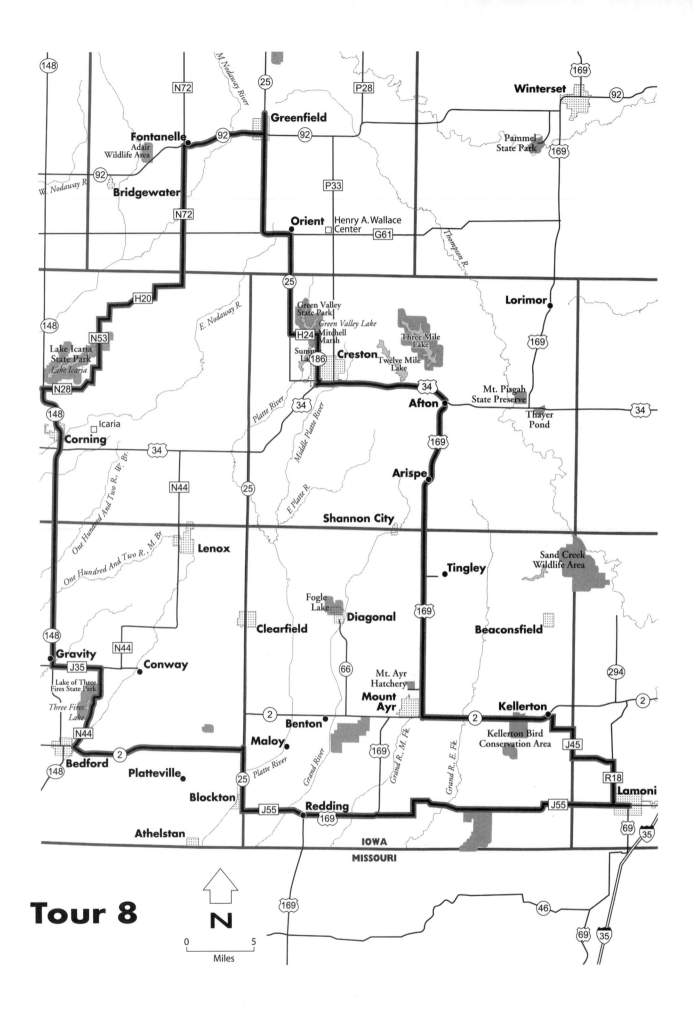

Tour 8

N

0   5
Miles

Tour 8
The Wide Skies in the Center of Southwest Iowa

Greenfield—Orient—Creston—Mount Ayr—Lamoni—Bedford—Corning—Greenfield

Distance: approximately 175 miles

This tour definitely takes you through the highs and lows of Iowa—all the way from the sky-high adventures of some of Iowa's most famous aviators to the soils used by farmers to raise organic foods. Along the way, you'll come across the homes of a former governor, a former U.S. vice president who changed the way people look at the world of agriculture, and the leader of one of the nation's churches. You'll also visit a small gas station that honors a barber who started one of the nation's largest petroleum companies. And if you're into sweets, you're in for some treats at one town that's lucky enough to have two old-time soda fountains!

This tour starts on the north edge of Greenfield at the airport, about 12 miles south of Exit 86 on I-80 in Adair County. There you'll find, on the east side of the small airport, the *Iowa Aviation Museum*, 2251 Airport Road, (641) 343-7184, admission. Outside is an A-7, an attack jet used by the Iowa Air National Guard, but inside is the real story. The museum has memorabilia from aviators and aircraft that date back to early in Iowa's aviation history. The Iowa Aviator's Hall of Fame honors famed aviators, such as 1930s air racers and brothers John and A. B. "Bite" Livingston; Major Gen. Charles Horner, who directed Desert Storm's air campaign; Eugene Ely, who developed the arresting gear used on aircraft carriers; Walter Cunningham, *Apollo* 7 astronaut; and Ann Pellegreno, pilot and author.

In the hangar are numerous light aircraft that include some Tiger Moth biplanes; a Piper J-3 that used skis, floats, and wheels; a 1928 Curtiss Robin powered by an OX-5 engine (it's the oldest Robin known to exist); and a 1941 Aetna-Timm Aerocraft 2SA, built as a military trainer and now the last of its kind found anywhere.

From the airport, drive south on State Highway 25 into Greenfield. At East Iowa Street, turn right (west) and proceed a few blocks to the town square. The square is like none other in Iowa: all traffic enters the square at the middle of each side and all traffic that departs does so at the corners of the square. As you come to the square, you should see *Schild-*

berg Antique Car Museum, (641) 337-5469 and (641) 743-8444, on the east side. Inside is a collection of 15 antique and classic autos, including a 1963 Stingray and other Corvettes, and a 1902 Oldsmobile. Also on the square are the *Adair County Courthouse*, the *E. E. Warren Opera House* and *Inspiration Point*, 362 Public Square, (641) 743-8248, a coffeehouse that serves organically raised fruits and vegetables along with soups and sandwiches.

From the square, make your way south a few blocks to State Highway 92. Turn right (west) and proceed about a mile to the *Adair County Historical Museum*. This multi-building complex, (641) 743-2232, admission, includes a 1896 wedding chapel, a railroad depot, and the home of former Governor George Wilson. Nearby is *Lake Greenfield*, a 236-acre park with a 44-acre lake, picnic facilities, a two-mile walking trail, Frisbee golf, fishing, and boating.

Famous Greenfielders

Greenfield is the home of Time magazine columnist Hugh Sidey, who has written about the presidency since the days of Dwight Eisenhower. The *Greenfield Free Press* newspaper is still owned by Edwin Sidey who has won several awards for his editing and columns.

Return east on Highway 92 and go to Highway 25. Turn right (south) and drive 2 miles. There, you'll see the *Neely-Kinyon Research Farm*, (641) 743-8412, free, a part of the Iowa State University Extension Service. As the nation's largest agronomic organic research project, the farm deals primarily with raising organic crops such as grapes and alternative crops such as *edamame* (a vegetable soybean). Call ahead for a tour.

Quick Trip Option 1: Before turning south on Highway 25, drive about 7 miles east of Greenfield on Highway 92 to *Miller's Country Zoo*, (641) 743-6345, admission. Along with 150 mammals and birds from across the world, the zoo has a section representing an 1860s-era homestead.

About 5 miles south of the research farm, the highway turns left (east) and passes through Orient before turning south again in town. In town is the *Bank of Memories*, 107 First Street, (641) 345-2283, donation. This small museum, located in a former bank, has displays about the Mormon Trail, Henry A. Wallace, and Baseball Hall of Fame pitcher "Dazzy" Vance, who had a 28-6 record in 1924 (in one game that year, he struck out three batters in a row with nine pitches).

Now the Union County Tourism Office in Creston, this was one of Iowa's first Phillips 66 gas stations, a company started by Frank Phillips, who was once a barber in town.

Quick Trip Option 2: If, instead of turning south to follow Highway 25 out of Orient, you keep going straight east on that street, it becomes County Road G61. When you're 3 miles east of Orient, turn left (north) onto County Road P33. Go north one mile to 290th Street and then turn left (west) and go a quarter mile to the *Henry A. Wallace Country Life Center*, 2773 290th Street, (641) 337-5019, donation. This is the birthplace of Henry A. Wallace, founder of Pioneer Hi-Bred International, editor of *Wallace's Farmer* magazine, U.S. Secretary of Agriculture and vice president under Franklin Roosevelt from 1941 to 1945. Now the farm is a center for studying the production of organic crops and foods, and visitors can tour either with guides (call for appointment first) or on their own. Return to Orient the way you came.

On the Crest

Creston derives its name from being on the ridge, or crest, that divides the watersheds of the Missouri and Mississippi Rivers.

About 7 miles south of Orient on Highway 25, turn left (east) onto County Road H24 and go for about 2 miles to State Highway 186. Turn left (north) to *Green Valley State Park*. Along H24, you'll cross a dam, behind which, to the north, is Green Valley Lake. The 900-acre park, (641) 782-5131, has 145 campsites (45 with electricity), picnic facilities, a beach, two year-round cabins, and trails.

Back on Highway 186, turn right (south) and proceed for about 2 miles to the intersection with Highway 25 on the northwest edge of Creston. Turn left (east) onto Highway 25, which immediately turns south into Creston and becomes Sumner Avenue. Proceed south on Sumner, cross the railroad tracks, which are the main east-west line across Iowa for the Burlington Northern Santa Fe Railroad, and continue to U.S. Highway 34. There, turn right (west) and drive a very short distance to the *Phillips 66 station*. Built in 1931 as one of the first Phillips 66 gas stations in Iowa, this little brick building with the high-peaked roof is now the *Union County Tourism and Information Center*, 636 New York Avenue, (641) 782-4405. However, the structure has a strong historical connection with Phillips. Frank Phillips was a young barber in Creston who married the daughter of a local banker. In 1905, he and his brother, L. E., struck out for Oklahoma at the height of its oil boom and (by now you may have guessed it) formed Phillips Petroleum Company or, as many people know it, Phillips 66.

From the visitor center, go north on adjacent South Park Street and pass under the railroad tracks. In a moment you will be in McKinley Park, the site of the *Union County Historical Village and Museum*, (641) 782-4247/4405, free, featuring a complex of 14 buildings from the late nineteenth century, including a school, church, barn, blacksmith shop, and a railroad caboose. A modern building houses the museum and its artifacts. A swimming pool is in the nearby park, which also has campsites.

Go east from the park on West Adams Street to downtown Creston. The center of town is on the north side of the busy Burlington Northern Santa Fe Railroad tracks. In keeping with the town's railroading history, be sure to visit the three-story, tan brick *CB&Q Railroad Depot*, 116 West Adams, (641) 782-7021, free. It has been renovated to hold various offices, but the waiting room on the first floor is much as it was when passenger trains ran through town. Also, the room contains some railroad memorabilia and down the hall is a working scale-model railroad.

From the depot, backtrack west to South Elm Street, turn left (south) and drive south to Highway 34 again. **Turn left (east) and drive about 5 miles to County Road P43; turn left.** You'll soon come to *Twelve Mile Lake*, (641) 782-1755, which has 650 surface acres and is surrounded by 1,500 acres of public land.

Return to Highway 34 and continue east for a few more miles to County Road P53; turn left (north) and proceed a short distance. There you'll be met by a similarly named body of water, *Three Mile Lake*, (641) 782-1755, which has 900 surface acres and is embraced by 2,100 acres of public land that includes 48 modern campsites, 37 primitive campsites, trails, and eight year-round cabins.

Return to Highway 34 and continue into Afton, where you will turn right (south) onto U.S. Highway 169.

Quick Trip Option 3: Continue east on Highway 34 past Afton. After 6 miles, turn left (north) onto U.S. Highway 169. After less than 3 miles, watch for the sign pointing the way to *Mount Pisgah Cemetery State Preserve*, (641) 782-4405, and turn left (west) onto County Road H29. In about 1.5 miles, the gravel road turns to the south, passes a T intersection on the right, and enters the grounds of Mount Pisgah, which was a stop on the Mormon Trail. About 300 people who died here are buried in the area. A reconstruction of a small cabin, reminiscent of those used in the winter by the travelers on the trail, is in the park. To return to the tour, go back to Afton and turn south there onto Highway 169.

Drive 23 miles south of Afton until Highway 169 meets State Highway 2 on the east side of Mount Ayr. Turn left (east) onto Highway 2 and go 10 miles to Kellerton. As Highway 2 curves to the left (north), turn right onto 1st Street and take that for a half mile to the T intersection with County Road J45. Turn right (south) and follow J45 east and south for about 7.5 miles until it meets County Road R18.

At R18, turn right (south) and proceed for 2 miles to County Road J55. Turn left (east) and drive toward Lamoni. Before reaching town, you will see a large yellow house with a sign out front announcing it as *Freedom Hall*. When the Mormons left Nauvoo, Illinois, in the 1840s, most went to Utah, but some followed the family of Joseph Smith, Jr., who had founded the group, also known as the Church of Jesus Christ of Latter-day Saints. After he was killed in Illinois, Smith's family created a separate group, the Reorganized Church of Jesus Christ of Latter-day Saints (now called the Community of Christ), and set up their home and headquarters in Freedom Hall for many years, with Joseph Smith III as their leader, before moving to Mis-

Lots of Hot Air

Creston hosts the Southwest Iowa Hot Air Balloonfest on the third weekend of each September.

souri in 1906. *Freedom Hall*, 1300 West Main Street, (641) 446-4841, free, is furnished as it was about a century ago.

To get literature about the region and state, head over to the *Southern Iowa Gateway Welcome Center*, (641) 784-3688. Located about 2 miles east of Lamoni at the entrance to I-35, it's housed in a former farm implement dealership.

A portion of the Creston Depot remains as it was for years.

From Lamoni, head west on J55 for about 16 miles until the road joins County Road P46 and turns south for a mile. It then turns west once more, joining U.S. Highway 169 less than 3 miles later. Follow this road for about 6 miles into Redding. There, follow Highway 169 as it curves to the south, but at 1st Street, turn right (west). One block later, turn right on what will be J55 again, which ultimately runs to the west. Follow J55 for about 5 miles to the T intersection with County Road P14. Turn right (north). In approximately 4.5 miles, turn left (west) onto State Highway 2. Proceed for 13 miles until you approach Bedford.

Just east of Bedford, turn right (north) onto Lake Road (which is also County Road N44) and go for 3 miles to *Lake of Three Fires State Park.* This 691-acre facility, (712) 523-2700, features an 85-acre lake, a beach, year-round cabins, 8 miles of trails, 140 campsites, and another 22 campsites at an equestrian campground. The park's name is based on a Pottawatomi legend concerning a council of three nations that was marked by a set of three fires.

Return to Highway 49 and continue for 5 miles to County Road J35; turn left (west) toward Gravity. By now you should realize a strange force is pulling you and your vehicle to the west. Well, that's how Gravity acts on you . . . sorry, couldn't resist the pun.

At State Highway 148 on the east side of Gravity, turn right (north) and proceed for 15 miles to U.S. Highway 34 and Corning. This town of about 1,700 is where late-night television host Johnny Carson was born on Octo-ber 23, 1925, although he spent most of his youth in Nebraska. His father, Homer "Kit" Carson, worked for the Iowa Nebraska Light & Power Co.

Liberty Hall in Lamoni was the home of Joseph Smith III and the headquarters of the Reorganized Church of Jesus Christ of Latter-Day Saints, now called the Community of Christ.

Quick Trip Option 4: At Highway 34 south of Corning, turn right (east) and, about 3 miles from that intersection, at the junction with County Road N52, look for a historical marker near the former location of *Icaria.* This is where a Frenchman named Etienne Cabet established a utopian society in 1853. It lasted for 45 years, and some efforts are under way to relocate the community's dining hall and school to the property again, which is just more than a mile north of the marker on N52.

To rejoin the main tour, take Highway 34 back to Highway 148.

At the intersection of Highways 34 and 148, turn right (north) on 148 and drive to 6th Street in Corning. Turn left (west) and go for two blocks to Davis Avenue; turn right (north) and proceed into downtown. Here you'll be rewarded with something that's unusual in a town this size anymore—two soda fountains! And they're within a block of each other! *Getter Pharmacy,* 709 Davis, (641) 322-3722, serves up refreshments with Pepsi while *McMahon's Drug,* 625 Davis, (641) 322-3454, serves Coca-Cola products. The choice is *yours.* On the north end of downtown are the *Adams County Courthouse* and the *Corning Opera House,* which is being restored.

Return to Highway 148 and turn left (north). Just outside of town the road weaves to the left (west) before continuing north. About 4 miles north of town, turn right (east) onto County Road N28. This leads into *Lake Icaria State Park,* (641) 322-4793, a 1900-acre park with fishing, boating, a beach with concession stand, campgrounds, and eight year-round cabins. The lake has 700 acres of surface area and has a one-and-a-quarter-mile-long skiing area.

From the state park, return to N28 and go east for about 2 miles to County Road N53; turn left (north) and proceed for about 5 miles to County Road H20. N53 meanders east and north and soon crosses the northeast end of Lake Icaria.

At H20, turn right (east), then follow it for about 6.5 miles north and east to County Road N72. Turn left (north) and proceed for 10 miles to Highway 92 in Fontanelle, where you turn right (east). On the side of the American Legion building on the town square, which Highway 92 skirts, the *Fontanelle Veterans Mural,* painted mostly by high school students, depicts a variety of scenes from America's military history.

To return to the beginning of this tour in Greenfield, continue east on Highway 92 for 6 miles.

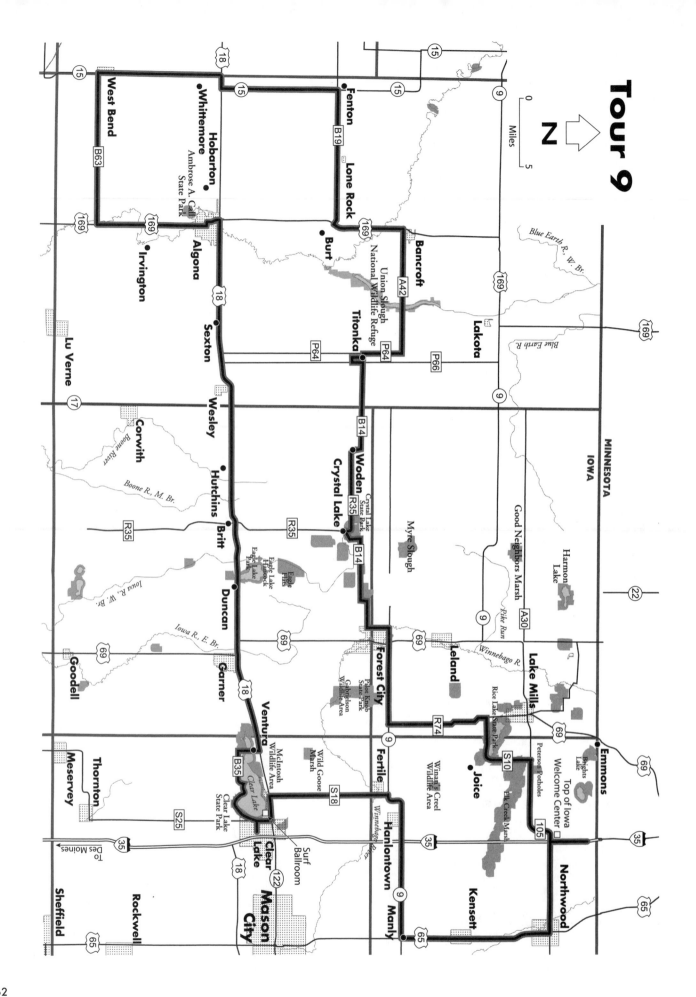

Tour 9
The Top of Iowa

Top of Iowa Welcome Center—Forest City—Crystal Lake—Titonka—Union Slough National Wildlife Refuge—West Bend—Algona—Britt—Clear Lake—Fertile—Manly—Northwood—Top of Iowa Welcome Center

Distance: approximately 215 miles

North central Iowa is deceptive in that it looks like few things are there to be seen. Yet out in the open on this tabletop land are a number of pretty lakes, large and small, common and unique, and one that's higher than the land around it. Along the way are a number of other surprises—a farm silo that's a home, the world's largest grotto, the newest in windmills, a place that honors hobos, semitrailers that tilt up into the air, a picturesque mill, and a ballroom where the music was last played before it died in a farm field just a few miles away.

Begin this tour at the *Top of Iowa Welcome Center*, about 3.5 miles south of the Iowa-Minnesota border on Interstate 35. The first official item that people see as they come into Iowa from the north on I-35 is the "Welcome to Iowa" sign at the border. The next thing, a few miles down the road, is the *Top of Iowa*, Exit 214 on I-35, (641) 324-3184, free.

Designed as a large red barn with a white-topped silo, it's an attractive stop, with two floors of information about the entire state and especially about north central Iowa. So if you're looking to learn about attractions, restaurants, places to stay, and more, this is certainly the place to find out. A gift shop, the Barn Boutique, has various items made in Iowa. On the third Sunday of each July, the center hosts its Annual Norwegian Celebration, which features music and other aspects of Norwegian culture.

From the welcome center, go west on County Road 105 for 8 miles and turn left (south) onto County Road S10. Drive for about 5 miles, as S10 goes past the east side of Rice Lake. At 425th Street, turn right (west) and follow that for a little less than 1 mile to County Road A34. Follow A34 for a little more than 1 mile to the entrance to *Rice Lake State Park*, (641) 581-4835. Even though it's one of Iowa's smallest state parks at 15 acres, it's set alongside a 900-acre natural lake and offers swimming, boating, fishing, and picnic facilities.

Quick Trip Option 1: For years the only windmills seen on the plains were those spindly

Shaped like a huge barn, the Top of Iowa Welcome Center, located just south of the Minnesota border on I-35, is one of the state's more unusual rest stops and information centers.

things that pumped water for livestock. Now, a new type that creates electricity has been popping up in many places, particularly north central Iowa, where the wind blows at a brisk and steady clip. One of the newest groups is the *Top of Iowa Wind Farm*, (641) 588-3800, which is easily seen from Rice Lake. It consists of 89 wind generators, as these windmills are called, which are each 237 feet tall at the hub and have a 171-foot-in-diameter rotor. In a 38-mph wind, each generates 1,184 horsepower, and the entire farm supplies enough electricity for up to 30,000 homes, about twice the number of homes in nearby Mason City.

For a close view of the farm, continue south on County Road S10 for about 2 miles to County Road A38 at the south edge of Joice. Turn left (east) and about 3 miles later, turn at the Top of Iowa Wind Farm sign, which is Evergreen Avenue. A couple hundred yards up this gravel road is the farm's operations center, in a barnlike structure, where you can pick up some literature about this farm and using the wind to create

A stone observation tower crowns the state's second highest point in Pilot Knob State Park east of Forest City.

was a landmark for those traveling on the prairie. Now the knob, which is the second highest point in Iowa, is topped with a 35-foot-tall stone observation tower built in the 1930s by the Civilian Conservation Corps and offers a good view of the countryside.

The park has two lakes—concentrate on the smaller one. Called Deadman's Lake, about half of this 8-acre, glacially made lake (called a kettle) is a sphagnum bog, which is basically a spongy bed of vegetation and the water so acidic that no fish live here. This little lake is the only one of its kind in Iowa and is more representative of those found in Minnesota. Besides three types of water lilies found nowhere else in Iowa, it has other plants not commonly found in the state. In contrast, the bigger lake supports bass and bluegill for fishing enthusiasts.

Overall, the park has 528 acres, 60 campsites, 48 with electricity, hiking trails, bridle trails, and picnic facilities. A trail leads to Forest City, your next destination, so those in your party who are so inclined can hike or bike to that community while someone else drives there.

Return to Highway 9, turn left (west), and proceed to U.S. Highway 69 in Forest City. Turn left (south) and go a short distance to the south end of town. This town earned its name in the pioneer days because of the abundant number of trees that grew near the Winnebago River. It is also home to an industry most appropriate for this book.

Located on Highway 69, Winnebago Industries is the world's largest manufacturer of recreational vehicles: those that are made under the Winnebago name as well as others. Freshly made RVs can be seen at the *Winnebago Industries Visitor Center*, 1316 South 4th Street, (641) 385-6936 and (800) 643-4892, free. The company offers free, 90-minute tours of the production facilities, beginning at 9 a.m. and 1 p.m. Monday through Friday. A gift shop is in the visitor center.

By the way, if you want to buy a RV here, that won't happen. You must go through a dealer but, luckily, Lichtsinn Motors, on the north side of town, sells RVs.

electricity. One of the wind generators is nearby so you can walk up to that too.

For trivia fans, although Iowa is the nation's tenth windiest state, it is third in wind production of electricity.

Leaving Rice Lake State Park, continue west on A34 for 1.5 miles until you reach County Road R74. Turn left (south) and cruise for 8.5 miles to State Highway 9, Iowa's northernmost east-west highway. Turn right (west) and drive for about 3 miles to State Highway 332. Turn left (south) and go 1 mile to *Pilot Knob State Park*. The park, (641) 581-4835, gets its name from a knob, or a deposit of rock and other materials left by the last glacier about 12,000 years ago. For countless years before trees grew on the mound, the knob

Highway 9

Back in the early days of auto travel, before highways had numbers, State Highway 9 was part of an intercontinental route called the Atlantic–Yellowstone–Pacific Trail.

Go south a short distance until 4th Street joins Highway 69. Near the intersection, follow County Road B14 as it goes west out of Forest City. In about 8.5 miles, turn left (south) onto James Avenue. Drive for about 1 mile to the T intersection with State Street, turn right (west), and proceed to the entrance to *Crystal Lake State Park*, (641) 923-2720. About 25 acres in size on the southeast shore of Crystal Lake, this oak-shaded park has 95 campsites, 65 with electricity, a playground, and a beach.

Past the park, the road curves to the south into the town of Crystal Lake. On the way into town, you'll encounter a rarity—the world's largest statue of a bullhead, resting atop a stone base and overlooking the lake.

In town, turn right (west) at 1st Street, go one block, then turn right (north) onto County Road R35. Drive for about 6.5 miles to Woden, and turn right (north) onto County Road R20. Drive for 1 mile to County Road B14 and turn left (west). Proceed for a little more than 7 miles to County Road P66, on the east edge of Titonka. Turn left (south). As you drive toward a solitary farm silo about a mile away, you will soon notice something different about this one—it has an octagonal penthouse. That's right, this one's a home from top to bottom. Built by Arthur "Hap" Peterson in 1983, he used a standard silo with special frames for the windows. Inside are four levels, and the penthouse, which is the living room, forms the fifth, all connected by a curved staircase. Tours of "Silo Home," (515) 928-2734, admission, must be arranged in advance.

From the silo home, go north to Elevator Avenue, about a half mile away, turn left (west) and drive a short distance to Titonka. At Main Street North, you'll find a sculpture made of several metals of an old-fashioned plow breaking open the tight soil of the prairie.

From Main Street in Titonka, go north a couple of blocks to County Road B14. Turn left (west) and go a short distance to County Road P64. Turn right (north) and take that for 3 miles to County Road A42; turn left (west) and go about 3.5 miles to the headquarters of *Union Slough National Wildlife Refuge.* At 3,334 acres, Union Slough, (515) 928-2523, straddles two watersheds, forming a union between the basins of the Blue Earth River to the north and the southward-flowing East Fork of the Des Moines River. If you wonder which way the water in the slough flows some days, just note which way the wind is blowing. On some days in the late summer and early fall, some of the gravel roads may be open for visitors to use, depending on weather conditions.

Approximately 100 species of birds are commonly seen here at various times of the year, including grebes, pelicans, cormorants, herons, egrets, ibises, swans, geese, hawks, kestrels, shorebirds, gulls, owls, vireos, and about 20 types of ducks. Birds occasionally seen here include osprey, bald eagle, loon, and the red-bellied woodpecker. The refuge is working to reintroduce trumpeter swans to the region and is known for successfully raising wood duck.

Continue west on A42 for 6.5 miles to U.S. Highway 169, south of Bancroft. Turn left (south) and drive about 5.5 miles to County Road B19 just north of Burt. Turn right (west) and go 9 miles to State Highway 15 at

Fenton. Turn left (south) and cruise for 9 miles to U.S. Highway 18, where Highway 15 (and you) will jog one mile west before going south again for about 2 miles. You'll come to a set of six Harvestore silos, which you may have already seen in other places around Iowa. Made of glass-coated steel, these blue silos—all of which sport the U.S. flag—were a new breed of high-tech storage system when they first appeared in 1946. Now, more than 70,000 are scattered around North America, made by A. O. Smith, a Milwaukee firm that started in 1874 as a manufacturer of parts for baby carriages.

Busting the Prairie Sod

More than 95 percent of Iowa's land is dedicated to agriculture, more than any other state. Also, although Iowa is the 23rd largest state, it has a fourth of all the grade A agricultural land in the nation. Farming is a tough business and it was even tougher in the nineteenth century when the sod covering Iowa's rich soil had to be busted by strong men and their oxen. Here's an account from years ago.

Three yokes of good-sized oxen drawing a 24-inch plow with two men to manage the work, would ordinarily break about two acres a day; five yokes with a 36-inch plow, requiring no more men to "run the machine," would break three acres a day. When the plow was kept running continuously, the "shear" had to be taken to the blacksmith often as once a week to be drawn out thin, so that a keen knife-edge could be easily put on it with a file, by the men who managed the plow. If the team was going around 80-acre tract of prairie, the "lay" or "shear" had to be filed after each round to do the best work. The skillful "breaker" tried to run his plow one and one-half inches deep and deeper. This was for the purpose of splitting the sod across the mass of tough fibrous roots, which had lain undisturbed for uncounted years and had formed a network of interlaced sinews as difficult to cut as india rubber, where the prairie was inclined to be wet; and it was not easy to find an entire 80-acre tract that was not intersected with numerous "sloughs," across which the breaking-plow had to run. In many places the sod in these "sloughs" was so tough that it was with the greatest difficulty that the plow could be put in the ground (*Annals of Iowa*, July 1902).

Continue south on Highway 15 to West Bend, 7 miles away. As you enter this town on Highway 15, there's no way you can miss seeing the *Grotto of the Redemption*, 300 North Broadway, (515) 887-2371 and (800) 868-3641, free, which is a block west of the highway.

The grotto has its beginnings when a young German, Paul Dobberstein, promised to build a shrine to the Virgin Mary should he recover from an illness. In 1912, after he had become a priest and was living in West Bend, Dobberstein began

Made of stones from around the world, the Grotto of the Redemption at West Bend claims to be the world's largest grotto.

to fulfill his promise by building the first of nine grottos with stones gathered from around the world. Sometimes when he returned from a trip, a train car would soon follow, filled with rocks, stones, and shells of all sorts that he had collected for building the grotto. Dobberstein worked on the grotto—the size of a city block and said to be the largest manmade one in the world—until his death in 1954. Near the grotto are a museum, a park with a pond, and a gift shop.

About five blocks south of the grotto is *The Villager*, 105 South Broadway, (515) 887-2801, a pharmacy and gift shop that contains an old-fashioned soda fountain that introduces youths to the rich icy treats of yesteryear and lets their parents and grandparents relive their youth with

cherry, lemon, and lime cokes as well as shakes, malts, and sundaes.

A block west of the Villager is the *Historical Museum*, 101 1st Avenue SW, (515) 887-2371, a former Presbyterian church that houses a collection of items about the history of West Bend. This is also where to arrange tours of Palo Alto County's first school and first post office, both at 101 3rd Street SE, and of a replica of a sod house used by settlers at 201 1st Street SE.

Continue south on Highway 15 until you're barely out of town. At County Road B63, turn left and head east for 9 miles to U.S. Highway 169. Turn left (north) and proceed for 9 miles to Algona. Before you enter the town, you'll see the county fairgrounds. There are two times to visit here—during the county fair each summer, of course, and from the first Sunday in December until the last day of that month. That's when a half-size nativity scene, built of wire and concrete by German prisoners of war during World War II, is displayed each year in its own building.

Iowa's Biggest

With 973 square miles, Kossuth County is Iowa's largest county. Originally it was two but one was dissolved and its land absorbed into Kossuth.

At the moment, the nativity is the only public reminder of a POW camp that was here. However, it should be noted that a movement is under way to create a museum to display the countless artifacts related to the POW camp. It's also hoped that the museum will contain items collected by Pharmacy Mutual Insurance Company, a local firm, such as a soda fountain and other articles associated with early drugstores, as well as artifacts belonging to the county's historical society. A conservative estimate for the year this museum is to open is 2005. More information about this project is available at the *Algona Chamber of Commerce*, (515) 295-7201, which is located in the Adams Building, a former financial institution designed by famed architect Louis Sullivan in 1913; it's located on the northwest corner of East State and Moor Streets in downtown Algona.

Follow Highway 169 through Algona a short distance to U.S. Highway 18 on the north edge of town. Turn right (east). If you are here during harvest, look toward the northwest corner of this intersection, at the Pioneer Hi-Bred Processing Plant. There, you can see something very unusual—entire semi-truck trailers, weighing up to 80,000 pounds each, being tilted 40 feet up on platforms, emptying ears of seed corn onto conveyor belts that transfer the corn to storage units.

Continue on Highway 18 for 23 miles to Britt. About every year since 1900, Britt has been the home of the Hobo Convention, an event that has brought national and even international attention to this town of about 2,000. Among those who have been anointed as hobo kings and queens have been many colorfully named individuals, including Scoop Shovel Scotty, Box Car Myrtle, Minneapolis Jewel, Blue Moon, Songbird McCue, Fishbones, Fry Pan Jack, and Ramblin' Rudy. The festivities are held on the second weekend of each August. In a former theater, the *Hobo Museum and Hobo Gift Shop*, 51 Main Avenue S., (641) 843-9104, admission, is thought to be the only museum dedicated to these kings of the road. So if you want to learn how some others lived life on the road, here's the place to see photos of them along with walking sticks, hobo nickels, and other items, including some distinctive jackets and hats.

For something a bit more sedate, a short distance away is *Hancock House*, 266 2nd Street SE, (641) 843-3037/3701, admission, an 1896 mansion with antiques and replicas of artifacts to show how life was a century ago.

Leave Britt and start going east on Highway 18. Soon after leaving town, you'll notice another wind farm. Called *Hancock County Wind Energy Center*, it has 148 wind generators, creating 98 megawatts of power that serve

about 30,000 homes. Built in 185 days, this wind farm was dedicated in May 2003.

About 16 miles from Britt, you'll arrive at Ventura, passing through Garner on the way. In Ventura, turn right (south) at Main Street, which is also County Road S14. In about 1.5 miles, turn left (east) onto County Road B35, which is also 235th Street. After leaving Ventura and passing the west end of Clear Lake, to the south you'll see some of the 55 wind generators that belong to the *Cerro Gordo Wind Farm*, which produces about 42 megawatts of electricity.

Drive 2 miles on B35 to Dogwood Avenue; turn left (north). This leads up to the south side of Clear Lake and South Shore Drive. Turn right (east). Measuring 2.5 by 7 miles and covering 3,648 acres, Clear Lake is Iowa's third largest natural lake. As you drive along the shore, you'll come upon *Clear Lake Boats and Powersports*, 15296 Ramsey Drive in PM Park, (641) 357-5293. If you don't have a boat and want to go on the water, this is the place to visit because it rents personal watercraft, pontoon boats, ski boats, fishing boats, and paddle boats, as well as water skis, tubes, and wakeboards.

Continue east on South Shore Drive for about 2 miles. Watch for *Clear Lake State Park*, South Shore Drive, (641) 357-4212. On the lake's southeast corner, the park has 200 campsites, 105

POWs in the Heartland

Algona was the headquarters of a network of 34 prisoner-of-war camps during World War II that stretched from southern and eastern Iowa to North Dakota; the camps held about 10,000 enemy soldiers, mostly Germans.

At Algona, about 3,000 POWs lived among eight guard towers, 60 barracks, 12 mess halls, guardhouses, storehouses, three recreation halls, a 150-bed hospital and 10 barracks for the American guards. The prisoners, who had created a 15-piece orchestra and a drama society during their stay, were gone by February 1946; and all the buildings were disassembled.

Some Hobo Trivia

No one is sure where the word hobo comes from. Some think it's a contraction of *homus bonus*, Latin for "good man." Others believe it came about after the Civil War when soldiers were asked where they were going and answered, "homeward bound," or "hobo" for short. Also, some wonder if *hobo* evolved out of *hoe boy*, a nickname for a migratory farm hand.

Hobos left signs for each other as they wandered the countryside. A pair of connected w's meant barking dogs were ahead. A circle with a line coming out of it meant to turn left or right or go straight ahead, depending on which way the line pointed. A rectangle with a small square drawn in the middle stood for danger.

When killing time, some hobos carved the heads side of a buffalo nickel, turning the Indian profile into profiles of various characters, often hobos. These coins are known as hobo nickels.

with electricity, picnic facilities, playground, a 900-foot sandy beach, fishing, and a boat ramp.

Clear Lake

Created by glaciers thousands of years ago, Clear Lake is an oddity in that it's about 100 feet higher than much of the land surrounding it in north central Iowa. In fact, at 1,247 feet above sea level, its surface is higher than Mason City's tallest building, about 10 miles to the east. The lake holds walleye, panfish, muskie, northern, perch, crappie, catfish, bullhead, and carp.

Round the southeast corner of the lake on South Shore Drive and go north to 12th Avenue S. Turn right and go east 1.5 miles until you reach South 24th Street, just before I-35; turn left (north) onto 24th Street. Shortly you will see the turnoff on the

The Lady of the Lake excursion boat docks near the city park at Clear Lake.

right to the *Guardian Angel Roadside Chapel*, no phone, free. Open during the day, this is the second small church here; the original, built in 1991 and destroyed by vandals, was replaced by this one in 1993. Its pews, altar rail, and windows are from area churches although the large stained glass window and baptismal fountain were built specifically for this chapel. If the gate is closed, there's a small parking area where you can leave your vehicle and walk about a hundred yards to the chapel.

Return to South 24th Street, go north for less than 1 mile to Main Avenue, and turn right (east). There you will find *Fort Custer Maze*, 2501 Main Avenue, (641) 357-6102, admission, one of the area's newer attractions. Aided by Adrienne Fisher, the world's foremost maze designer from England, locals Jack and Scott Kennedy designed this complex, which changes patterns weekly. Although occupying only a couple acres, it has nearly two miles of paths.

On Main Avenue, head west into the town of Clear Lake. Follow Main as it angles to the left after passing 8th Street (which is also County Road S25) and ends at the city beach. Between North 5th Street and the lake are some antiques stores, mostly on Main.

A short walk up the shore from the beach is the *Lady of the Lake*, Lakeview Drive and First Avenue N., (641) 357-2243, admission. A double-deck excursion boat, the *Lady* cruises around the lake on weekday evenings and weekend afternoons. The walk along the shore here is also a nice place to catch a lake breeze and watch the sun set.

From Main Avenue, go northwest one block to 1st Avenue N.; turn right (northeast) and go to North 6th Street. Turn left (northwest). You should be almost in front of the *Clear Lake Fire Museum*, 112 North 6th Street, (641) 357-2613, donations. Open weekends, this museum honors Clear Lake firefighters in a modern representation of a firehouse that holds old firefighting equipment, including an 1883 hand-pulled hose cart and a 1923 pumper.

A stroll southeast of the museum along 6th Street leads to a small, triangular park that has something one might not expect to see in Iowa—a sundial made of a model sailboat, with the shadow of its mast pointing to the correct time.

Taking any one of several streets from the area near the fire museum, return to the lake, turn right on North Shore Drive, and go a few blocks. You'll come to the *Surf Ballroom*, 460 North Shore Drive, (641) 357-6151. This is where Buddy Holly, J. P. "The Big Bopper" Richardson, and Ritchie Valens gave their last performances on February 5, 1959 before dying in a plane crash that night. Although greatly associated with those performers and rock and roll, the Surf dishes up everything else you can imagine—blues, country, jazz, bluegrass, polka, and swing. Even if you're not there for a concert, walk inside to see the mementos from the past, including autographs of some of the biggest names in music. Tours can be arranged for a nominal fee. A tribute is paid to Holly, Richardson, and Valens at the Surf the first weekend in February.

Backtrack just a half block from the Surf to Buddy Holly Place. Go north on that street, cross the tracks a few blocks later, and turn left (west) onto U.S. Highway 18. Drive 1 mile to Eagle Avenue, turn right (north) and go 9 miles to Fertile (on the way, the road becomes County Road S18).

Quick Trip Option 2: To see the place where "the music died" in 1959, take this tour. Upon coming up Buddy Holly Drive to Highway 18, turn right (east). Then turn left (north) at 8th Street. This becomes County Road S28 outside of town. In 5 miles this paved road curves to the left (west) but you should go *right* (east) onto 310th Street, a gravel road. In the blink of an eye, turn left onto Gull Avenue. Go north for a half mile and park just past the grain bins, near the first fence row on your left (west). You can walk along the fence to the west where, about a half-mile later, four trees mark where Buddy Holly, "The Big Bopper" Richardson, Ritchie Valens, and their pilot, Roger Peterson, died in a plane crash. There's also a small memorial made of a stainless steel guitar and three stainless steel records bearing the song titles "Peggy Sue," "Chantilly Lace," and "Donna." This is private property so be respectful.

To return to the tour, go back to the intersection of 310th Street and S28 and continue ahead to the west on what is now County Road B20. This leads to County Road S18 in 2.4 miles where you will turn right (north) toward Fertile.

As you enter Fertile, turn left (west) into William Rhodes Park. This is a pleasant, shady area on the south bank of the Winnebago River. Across the river is the red-painted *Fertile Mill*, built in 1858 to saw wood by the man whom the park was named after. Ten years later it began milling grain, which it did until the 1930s. Now privately owned, the mill is not open to the public, but it's still a pretty backdrop to the park.

From the park, head a few blocks north to State Highway 9 and turn right (east). Cruise for 12 miles to U.S. Highway 65 at Manly, passing through Hanlontown along the way. Founded in 1877, Manly is where countless trains passed each day in its early years, when a number of railroad companies ran their passenger and freight lines through here; now only a handful of trains rumble through daily. In recog-

nition of what used to be, a Rock Island caboose full of railroad artifacts sits a few blocks past U.S. Highway 65 at the intersection of Broadway and State Highway 9.

From Manly, drive north on Highway 65 for 11 miles to Northwood, passing through Kensett on the way. On Central Avenue in the center of Northwood are a town clock, erected here in 1907 by watchmaker L. T. Dillon in front of the store where he worked, and a water fountain that was once a horse trough in the late nineteenth century. Also in town is the *Worth County Historical Society Museum*, Highway 65 and County Road CO 105, (641) 324-6991, free, which has local artifacts and an 1892 creamery, an 1874 country school, a log cabin, and an 1880 Italianate building.

Go west on Central Avenue, which is also County Road CO 105, for a little more than 7 miles to I-35, where you began this tour at the Top of Iowa Welcome Center.

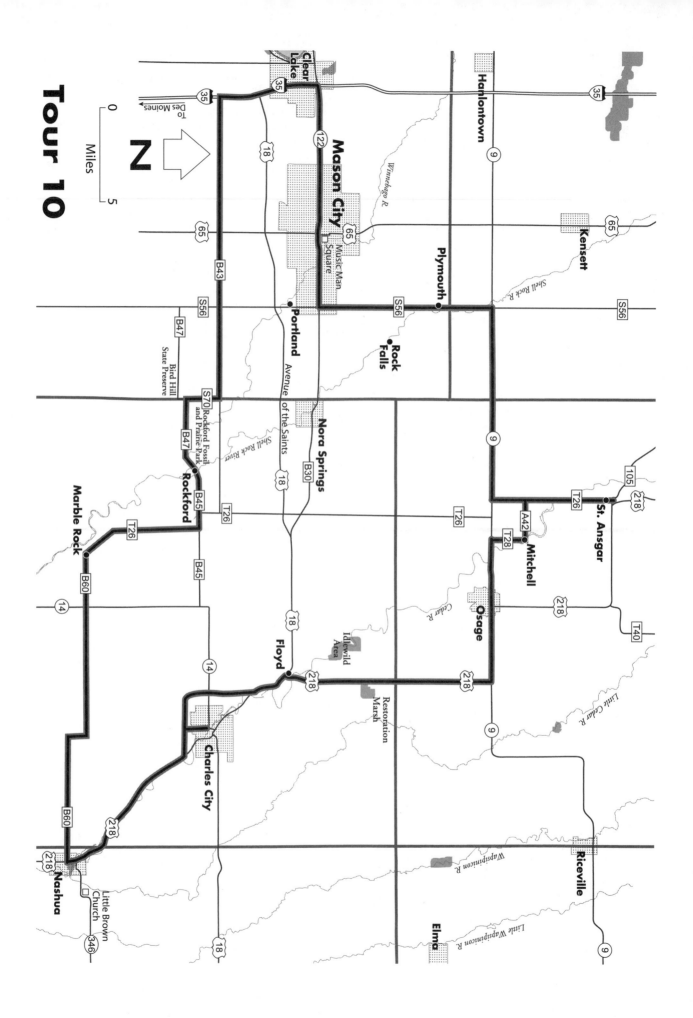

Tour 10
The Rivers of North Central Iowa

Mason City—Plymouth—Saint Ansgar—Rock Falls—Osage—Charles City—Nashua—Rockford—Mason City

Distance: approximately 120 miles

When some folks talk about the rivers in Iowa, they're usually describing those other than the ones in the north central part of the state. That shows what little they know about this region, where some of Iowa's prettiest waterways can be found. Over the years these rivers, primarily the Winnebago, Shell Rock, and Cedar, have brought pleasure to countless people who like to collect fossils millions of years old, camp, boat, fish, ski, and canoe. One area river even inspired a Broadway and Hollywood musical. Among the prominent personalities who have influenced and been influenced by this region are a fighter for women's rights, a writer who remembered his hometown in song, and one of the world's foremost architects.

This tour begins at the intersection of I-35 and State Highway 122 (Exit 194), about 9 miles west of the center of Mason City. Head east on 122. On the way to the largest city in north central Iowa, you will see the entrance to the Mason City Airport on the left (north); it's also the entrance to the *Kinney Pioneer Museum*, Highway 122 W., (641) 423-1258, admission. Besides rooms outfitted like they were years ago, such as a doctor's office, a dentist's office, a sweet shop, and rooms of a private residence, this privately owned museum has collections of fossils and dolls along with some antique autos, including a special yellow one, the world's only surviving Colby Car—more than 900 were made between 1911 and 1914 in Mason City. The museum also has an early studio of local radio station KGLO, and outside are a wooden jailhouse, a one-room school, a 1912 blacksmith shop, and a log cabin.

As you continue into the city, Highway 122 becomes 6th Street, a one-way, eastbound thoroughfare. At South Federal Avenue, which is also U.S. Highway 65, turn left (north). After crossing Willow Creek, follow the route you're on as it curves to the right to become South Delaware Avenue. Upon approaching Southbridge Mall, the main shopping center in downtown Mason City, you should see a large, cream-colored building on your right. That's *Music Man Square*, 308 South Pennsylvania (641) 424-2852 and (866) 228-6262, free, but note that the part of this facility you're seeing right now is its back side. To enter the square, turn right (east) onto 2nd Street SE and one block later turn right (south) onto South Pennsylvania Avenue, where you will find the entrance to the *Music Man Square*.

Inside the 30,000-square-foot *Music Man Square* are a number of items, including a 1912 street with period storefronts, a gift shop, and, hanging from the ceiling, 76 trombones. Also in Music Man Square is the *Meredith Willson Museum*, admission, which tells the story of this town's most famous son, who wrote the well-known musical *The Music Man*. Among the items in the museum are his piano and a recreation of his California studio.

Next to Music Man Square is the *Meredith Willson Boyhood Home*, 314 South Pennsylvania Avenue, (641) 423-3534 and (866) 228-6262, admission. Built in 1895, this Queen Anne Victorian home is where Willson lived until he was 17 and went to New York City to study music. Although Willson's long gone, the home is maintained as it looked when he and his family lived there in the early part of the twentieth century.

Meridith Willson

All right, some of the younger readers are wondering, "who is the guy with Meredith for a first name and an extra l in his last name?" Born in 1902, Meredith Willson grew up with a love of music in his family, a love that pulled him away from Mason City. He eventually played flute for Arturo Toscanini and in John Phillip Sousa's band. Willson went on to write hundreds of songs, including the fight songs for the University of Iowa and the Mason City High School, but in the 1950s he spent five years writing a musical that has its roots in his hometown. *The Music Man* opened on Broadway in 1957 and was a smash hit. Later it became a movie, as did another musical that he wrote, *The Unsinkable Molly Brown*. Willson, who died in 1984 in California, is buried in Elmwood Cemetery in his hometown.

His sister, Dixie, wrote children's books but also did the screenplay for the movie *God Gave Me 20 Cents*, which won one of the first Academy Awards—years before Meredith had his hits.

Proceed north on South Pennsylvania Avenue to East State Street, a distance of a couple

The boyhood home of composer Meredith Willson is just east of downtown Mason City, which he used as the model for River City in his musical *The Music Man*.

of blocks. Turn left (west), go a few more blocks, and park alongside *Central Park*. At the northeast corner of State and Federal Avenue, just east of the park, is the *City Center*, which holds offices and apartments now. Originally, though, it was the First National Bank, which on March 13, 1934, was visited by John Dillinger and friends, including John Hamilton and "Baby Face" Nelson (real name Lester Gillis), who made off with $52,000, Dillinger's second-largest haul. In a gunfight, Dillinger and Hamil-

Mason City Architecture

For having a population of about 30,000 people, Mason City has a better architectural reputation than that of some cities many times its size. Actually, its buildings and homes designed around the end of the nineteenth century are like many other communities' but things kicked into high gear when Frank Lloyd Wright arrived to design the Park Inn and City National Bank. During Wright's stay, Dr. George Stockman hired the architect to design a home for him. Built in 1908, it was the first building designed by Wright to be completed in Iowa. The inn and bank were completed within the next two years.

Beginning in 1911, others associated with Wright's style of architecture, notably Walter Burley Griffen (who later designed Canberra, Australia's capital city), William Drummond, Barry Byrne, and Einar Broaten, designed other structures, including the houses in the Rock Glen-Rock Crest Development, which is perched on the rocky walls overlooking Willow Creek.

With all these buildings, especially those of the Prairie School style, it's no wonder that some people come to Mason City just to marvel at its architecture.

ton were wounded, as was bystander R. H. James, but taking hostages as human shields, the gangsters were able to escape. However, they left behind $300,000 they did not know about.

On the south side of West State Street, across from the park, are two buff-colored buildings designed by Frank Lloyd Wright early in his architectural career. One, with a retail store on its first floor, was the *City National Bank*, which now has offices upstairs. Just west of there is *Park Inn*, 15 West State Street, a former hotel that's slowly being restored to how Wright designed it.

And next door to the inn is the *Mason City Convention and Tourism Bureau*, 25 West State Street, (641) 422-1663 and (800) 423-5724. Besides having the usual assortment of brochures and pamphlets about attractions, lodgings, and places to eat around town, the bureau has something you should really have, a booklet entitled *Mason City Walking Tour Guide*. It costs four dollars but it's money very well spent. That's because the booklet is a wonderful guide to 67 fantastic buildings around town, which is an architectural mecca. If you want to know what's what about one of the structures, who designed it, and what's significant about it, this is the book to use. Now, get on your walking shoes, load up the camera, and have a great time.

From the bureau's offices, go south on South Washington to 2nd Street SW. Turn left and go east for four blocks to the *Charles H. MacNider Museum*, 303 2nd Street SE, (641) 421-3666, free. Set in an English Tudor mansion that has been expanded to the rear without compromising its facade, the MacNider is an art museum that many larger communities would be proud to have. In it is the largest collection of puppets made legendary puppeteer Bil Baird, which range from small, string-controlled dancing horses to larger-than-life outfits that Baird wore. The museum also shows the works of regionally, nationally, and internationally known artists by displaying works from its permanent collection and traveling exhibits.

Just down the sidewalk from MacNider is the *Meredith Willson/Music Man Footbridge*, a white, pedestrian bridge that leads across the rocky gorge holding Willow Creek.

From there, walk up to 1st Street SE, turn right and follow the street as it bends to the north. Now you're in the Rock Glen-Rock Crest neighborhood where you can admire the houses as you walk by them. When you reach East State Street, cross it and go to the right where you will see *Stockman House*, 530 1st Street NE, (641) 421-3666, admission, which was designed by Frank Lloyd Wright. Moved here to save it from being demolished to create a parking lot elsewhere in the city, the two-story, four-bedroom, stucco house is furnished with Arts and Crafts furniture.

About a half mile east of the Stockman House is *East Park*, a nice greenspace where willows dip into the waters of both the Winnebago River and Willow Creek, making picturesque scenes. You can also try out the city's trail system, which measures more than 11 miles.

From East Park, head east on East State Street, which angles to the south and meets 4th Street SE, which, in turn, becomes County Road B30 as it leaves town. Follow it east for about 3 miles to California Avenue (which is also County Road S56). Turn left (north) and drive for about 7 miles to Plymouth. If you're into paddling, this is a great place to begin a trip down the Shell Rock River. Most people like to take it in three 10-mile segments. The first segment starts at Strand Park on the north side of Plymouth, passes through Rock Falls and a small rocky, limestone canyon, and ends at Nora Springs. This is where the next segment begins, winding up in Rockford. In the third segment, which begins at Rockford, the Shell Rock is joined by the Winnebago just south of town and finishes at Marble Rock. Some people, however, like to paddle the Shell Rock the rest of its length, another 46 miles, until it converges with the bigger Cedar River southwest of Janesville. Along the Shell Rock's length in this area, paddlers have seen a variety of birds, including geese, duck, great blue heron, kingfishers, hawks, turkey vultures, and wild turkey.

Plymouth, by the way, earned its name from a rock that reminded early settlers of Plymouth Rock in Massachusetts. The rock is on private land about a quarter mile south of town but it can be seen from the river.

From Plymouth, continue north on S56 to Iowa Highway 9, less than 3 miles away. Turn right (east) and go for about 11 miles to County Road T26. Turn left (north) and proceed for about 5 miles to the entrance to *Halvorson Park* on the right. Besides being a nice place to kick back, the 10-acre park, (641) 732-5204, provides access to another river, the Cedar, so if you did not have enough canoeing on the Shell Rock, here's another place to slip a canoe into the water. If you haven't brought your own, you're in luck because *Cedar Run Canoe Livery*, (641) 736-2221, is right at the park. In 2003, canoes were renting for $15 a day, including a shuttle that takes you to an access point at Otranto, about eight miles upriver, and to the take-out at Acorn Park, a couple miles northwest of Halvorson (some people prefer the stretch of the river between Otranto and Acorn Park because when they leave the river they can eat at the restaurant at the Acorn Park Golf Course).

At *Halvorson Park*, which has 32 campsites with electricity, the Cedar River is like a lake because of the water backed up by a dam five miles away at Mitchell. Of course, this makes for

a great place for swimming, boating, water skiing, and trying to hook some of the largemouth bass, crappies, and northern pike known to lurk here. Below Mitchell, the river has no rapids and is better suited to paddling canoes than anything else, but be aware of the lowhead dams along the way. If you're really up for a good workout, it's about 30 miles downriver to take-out point above the dam at Charles City.

On T26 again, go north another 1.5 miles and enter Saint Ansgar on what is Main Street. A pretty community, Saint Ansgar calls itself the Garden Spot of Iowa because of the showy gardens around town. Each June, the town hosts its Parade of Ponds, a tour of the privately owned gardens (some of which have ponds, hence the name of the tour). Saint Ansgar's *First Lutheran Church*, 212 North Main, (641) 713-4873, is the oldest continuously used Lutheran Church west of the Mississippi. Made of hand-cut stones with a white steeple, it was built in 1866 by Scandinavian settlers.

The town is also known as the home of the *White Deer*. An albino, this doe was born in 1980 and roamed the region north of town, protected by laws specially enacted to guard her. She gave birth to several normally colored offspring, and when she died in 1988 her remains were mounted and are now displayed in a glass case in, what else, White Deer Park, a small green space at 4th and Mitchell Streets.

Check around downtown for various specialty shops and a tearoom—as a testament to their popularity, it's not unusual to see bus tours from Minnesota in this town.

If you want to stay overnight, check with the *Blue Belle Inn*, 513 West 4th Street, (641) 713-3113 and (877) 713-3113, a bed and breakfast that the locals are proud to talk about. Built in 1898, the Victorian-style inn has six guestrooms and outside, as one would expect in this community, gardens and a small pond.

Leave Saint Ansgar by returning south on T26. After about 4.5 miles, turn left (east) onto County Road A42. Drive for less than 3 miles to County Road T28. Turn left (north), and almost immediately after crossing the Cedar River turn left into *Interstate Park* on the west edge of Mitchell. Here, in a nice setting, a dam straddles the Cedar where an old powerhouse sits off to one side. The park, (641) 732-5204, has 28 campsites with electricity, picnic facilities, and a beach. Here, also, is the north end of the *Cedar River Greenbelt Trail*,

(641) 732-5204, a hiking, biking, and horse trail that runs next to the river, crosses limestone bluffs, and rambles through woods until it reaches Osage, 4 miles to the southeast. A small shelter sits halfway between Mitchell and Osage.

From the park, head south on T28 to State Highway 9, about 2 miles away. Turn left (east) and drive about 1.5 miles. You'll come to the *Mitchell County Conservation Board Nature Center*, 18793 Highway 9, (641) 732-5204, free, which provides canoe access to the Cedar River and has wildlife displays. Right next to that is *Cedar Valley Memories*, 18791 Highway 9, (641) 732-1269, admission. Operated by the Mitchell County Historical Society, this museum has at least five working antique steam engines as well as the first gasoline-powered auto made in Iowa. Built by George Frazee in 1901 in Osage with an engine of his own design, this blue two-seater that's trimmed in red is paraded under its own power during the museum's Power Show, held the second weekend in August. By the way, Frazee built the car, which was the tenth auto licensed in the state, on the second floor of his house—ask at the museum for further details about that episode. The museum also has the world's largest steam-powered tractor, a 4140 Reeves; built in 1912, this two-story behemoth requires a driver (who's upstairs) and a fireman (who's downstairs) to operate it. Another one-and-only may be the world's first steam-powered traction engine, an 1878 Blumetrit.

Avenue of the Saints

When you are on the highway from Floyd to Charles City, you're not only on a road with three highway designations (U.S. Highway 218, U.S. Highway 18, and State Highway 27) but also on the Avenue of the Saints, a 536-mile-long series of four-lane roads between Saint Paul, Minnesota and Saint Louis, Missouri. Although no towns named "Saint" in Iowa are directly on the route, Saint Paul, due west of Burlington in the southeast corner, is less than 3 miles from the route.

On Highway 9 immediately east of the nature center and the museum, turn right (south) at Spring Park Road and go a short distance to *Spring Park*. Bordering the Cedar River, the park, 3540 Spring Park Road, (641) 732-3709, has 20 campsites, picnic facilities, and waters from a nice cool spring that flow from a metal pipe now. A trail connects the park with Osage, 1.5 miles away.

Return to Highway 9, turn right (east) and proceed for about 2 miles into Osage. As you drive down State Street, you will pass the large, Greek-Revival-style county courthouse built in 1858. Because of the great number of maple trees here, the city advertises itself as "The City of Maples" and it truly does turn extremely brilliant

with the changing colors each fall. Speaking of names—although one might think that Osage was named after the Native Americans of the same name, that's not the case. Originally called Cora, the town was renamed after Massachusetts benefactor Orrin Sage, who gave money for the town to start a library and acquire a fire engine and a church bell.

From 1870 to 1881, author Hamlin Garland lived near Osage as a youth. After moving to Boston, he became a teacher and lecturer and began writing articles and books. His most famous novels portray the hardships of Midwest pioneer life. In 1922 he was awarded the Pulitzer Prize for his writings.

From Osage, take Highway 9 east for 4 miles, then turn right onto U.S. Highway 218. Take that 11 miles south to Floyd (where the highway is also called Monroe Street) and to the junction with U.S. Highway 18/State Highway 27 on the south side of town. Continue south on this combined highway for 8 miles, rounding the west edge of Charles City and continuing to Exit 218 on the city's south side. There, turn left (north) and go into town on Business Highway 218, which is also called Grand Avenue. In Charles City, just as you pass a fire station and Grand Avenue curves to the left (northwest), you'll find the *Charles City Chamber of Commerce*, 610 South Grand Avenue, (641) 228-4234, which has information about places to see in the city. Be sure to pick up a walking tour booklet about the city's interesting buildings, including some of the Prairie School design, among them a private residence designed by Frank Lloyd Wright.

From the chamber, follow South Grand as it jogs northwest and soon becomes Gilbert Street. Just three blocks beyond the chamber is a large tan and white building housing the *Floyd County Historical Society Museum*, 500 Gilbert, (641) 228-1099, admission. With 50,000 artifacts, this is one of Iowa's larger county historical museums. Its main attraction is its collection of antique tractors, including a 1913 Hart-Parr, one of the earliest gasoline-powered tractors, which were first made in Charles City and were a main part of the economy here for decades. The museum also sells original and reproductions of tractor shop, parts, and equipment manuals from the earliest days of tractors.

Continue up Gilbert for three blocks to Main Street, turn right (northeast), and cross the Cedar River into downtown Charles City; go four blocks beyond the river. On the left (northwest) is the flashy facade of the *Charles Theater*, 409 North Main, an art deco movie theater from the 1930s that is also used for a community theater group's stage productions.

On Main, go to the next intersection, with Ferguson Street, turn left (northwest) and then a block later turn left again (southwest) onto North Jackson Street. Just beyond the next block, the vine-covered *Charles City Arts Center*, 301 North Jackson, (641) 228-6284, is located in the former Carnegie Library. The center is where works from the permanent collection and traveling exhibits are shown.

From the art center, go to Clarke Street, turn right (northwest), and go to the end of the street to a pedestrian bridge. This 270-foot-long footbridge was built in 1906 to connect the main part of the city with Sherman Park on the other side of the Cedar River. A pretty time to see this suspension bridge is in the evening when it's lit up.

From the pedestrian bridge, take Illinois Street to the southwest, where you have no choice but to turn left a block later onto Riverside Drive, which parallels the Cedar River. Continue on Riverside for four blocks and turn left (northeast) at Jackson Street. Go one block, turn right (southeast) at Clark Street and take that one block to Main. From there, make your way back to Highway 218/18/27 south of town.

Take that road southeast for 10 miles to Nashua and State Highway 346. Turn to the left (east) and drive about 2 miles. Where the road turns north, you will see *Old Bradford Pioneer Village*, Highway 346, (641) 435-2567, admission. Located near where the now-vanished village of Bradford was built around the middle of the nineteenth century, this museum is a collection of more than a dozen buildings gathered from around the county. Among the buildings is the office of William Pitts—more about him in a moment.

Next to the museum is the world-famous *Little Brown Church*, Highway 346, (641) 435-2027, free. Built over four years beginning in 1860, this simple church was made famous by William Pitts, who wrote the classic Christian hymn "The Church in the Wildwood." Ironically, he was inspired to write the song not by the church but by a visit to its site before it was built. Years later he returned here and was surprised to see that a church had actually been built here.

Expect a lot of activity here on weekends—this is a very popular place for weddings, more than 70,000 so far. Because the parking lot is across the highway, be careful when visiting here.

Quick Trip Option 1: Less than 20 miles east of Nashua is *Hawkeye Buffalo Ranch*, 3034 Pembroke Avenue, (563) 237-5318/6175, admission. On this 500-acre preserve that began when the owner's great-grandfather settled here in 1854, you can pet buffalo on guided tours and learn of their relationships with the Native

Carrie Chapman Catt

One of the leaders of women's rights, Carrie Chapman Catt, moved to Charles City in 1866 when her family arrived here from Ripon, Wisconsin, where she was born in 1859. Graduating from high school here in 1877, Catt became San Francisco's first female reporter, and then returned to Charles City in 1887 where she became involved with the Iowa Woman Suffrage Association. Later she became president of the national and international associations, leading the way for women's rights, including the right to vote in the United States, which was finally guaranteed when the 20th Amendment became law in August 1920. Afterward she helped form the League of Women Voters, worked on establishing child labor laws, helped with the relief of Jewish refugees during and after World War II, and supported the establishment of the United Nations. Catt's childhood home, a red brick, two-story house with a partial-octagonal porch over its front door, is located 3 miles southeast of Charles City. Built by Catt's father, this is where 13-year-old Carrie asked why her mother was not voting in the 1872 election as were the men and was told, with laughter, that voting was too important for women to do—that conversation determined her future. The house, at 2379 Timber Avenue, can be toured by contacting the *Carrie Lane Chapman Catt Childhood Home Restoration Project*, (641) 228-3336.

Americans who revered them and the European-Americans who practically wiped them out.

The ranch also has burros, llamas, and a gift shop featuring buffalo-related items, including meats such as sausage, bacon, jerky, roast, and sirloin cuts. Campgrounds and a bed and breakfast are on the premises.

Go back to Nashua and turn south on Highway 218. Almost immediately, turn right (west) onto Lexington Avenue, which is also County Road B60, and drive about 18 miles to Marble Rock. This is another community on the Shell Rock River. On the west edge of town is a riverside park that's dominated by a former powerhouse that was in use until 1950; picnic facilities are available here.

In Marble Rock, turn north on River Street N. and proceed to a T intersection with North Street, which is also County Road T26. Turn left (west) and follow it northwest, then north, for about 6 miles to County Road B45.

Turn left (west) on B45 and drive 2 miles into Rockford. Pass though town, cross the Shell Rock River, and on the west side, turn left (south) on 8th Street SW. Go a short distance, then turn right (west) onto County Road B47. Just past that intersection, pull into *Fossil and Prairie Park*, 1227 215th Street, (641) 756-3490, donations. Located where clay was once dug from along the Winnebago River and then fired into bricks, this 400-acre preserve is one of the best spots in the Upper Midwest to find marine fossils dating back 350 to 400 million years ago in the Devonian Age. Finding fossils at this site, which looks like a small section of the banded hills in South

Because of its history, the Little Brown Church at Nashua is a popular spot for weddings.

Dakota's Badlands, is pretty easy. Just start kicking around or flip a few rocks and you're sure to see something. However, collecting is permitted for noncommercial purposes only.

A word of advice is to use the old gold miner's trick of looking where the water has washed through gullies; it's a good chance you'll be able to find something in those washes. Watch your footing though, the surface of the slopes is rather crumbly. Besides a nice visitor center that explains the history here, a marine aquarium, a children's discovery area, and a sod house, the

park has a 50-acre prairie that supports more than 100 types of prairie plants.

From the preserve, head west on B47 about 2 miles to County Road S70, also called Zinnia Avenue, and turn right (north).

Quick Trip Option 2: If you haven't been fossilized yet, another area rich with fossils is nearby. When you reach S70 from the Rockford Fossil and Prairie Park, turn left (south) and then turn right (west) at 190th Street a short distance away. Not even a quarter mile up the hill from there is an area on the right (north) that looks like nothing more than a small pullout of cream-colored gravel—that's the parking area for *Bird Hill State Preserve*, (641) 423-5309, which is on a small shoulder of the hill overlooking the farm fields to the north (by the way, there is no sign here). Once called Fossil Hill, this gently sloping preserve is where natural erosion continues to unearth more fossils from the Devonian Age. Again, you can pick what you want for personal reasons, and you should use the same technique you used earlier at Fossil Park; that is, look where the rains have created small washes.

Proceed north for about 2 miles to County Road B43. Turn left (west) and drive to I-35, 16 miles to the west. Turn right and drive north for about 3.5 miles back to the junction with Highway 122, where this tour began.

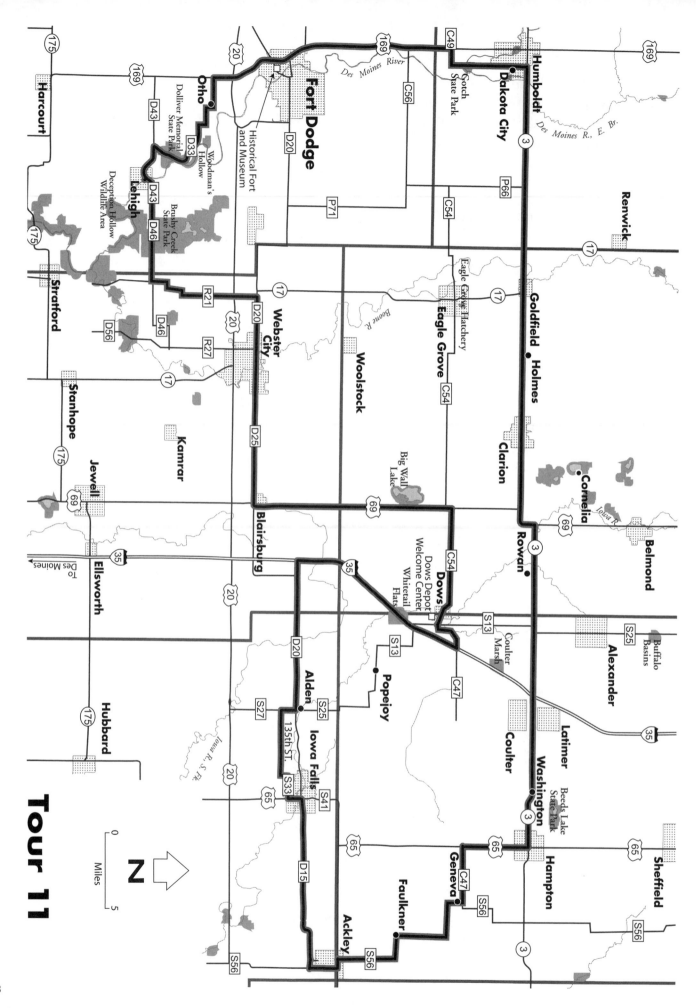

Tour 11

Tour 11
The Northern Plains

Dows—Webster City—Fort Dodge—Humboldt—Dakota City—Clarion—Hampton—Geneva—Ackley—Iowa Falls—Dows

Distance: approximately 163 miles

If there's one area that makes people think that Iowa's flat, this is it. But don't let flat land fool you. At first glance, you think you can observe everything that there is to see, and sometimes it looks like there's not very much. Wrong. From the dusty gypsum mines of Fort Dodge came one of the nation's biggest hoaxes. In Ackley, an abandoned gravel pit has become a beautiful city park filled with ponds and bridges. Once every five years, teddy bears magically transform Clarion from a sleepy little town into an international hot spot. And even the landscape is deceptive. A few moments after you leave what had been flat prairie, you're near 100-foot-tall cliffs towering over a gentle stream. A pedestrian bridge in Iowa Falls leads from limestone bluffs to a riverside park; and south of Iowa's smallest county seat, the forks of the Des Moines River, which begin as several streams in Minnesota, finally converge to form one of Iowa's more famous rivers.

So look around. There's plenty to see out here in the flat lands. *Also note that this tour involves driving about 3 miles on a well-maintained gravel road.*

This tour starts at the intersection of I-35 and County Road C47 at Exit 159. There, about 75 miles north of Des Moines, you'll find one of Iowa's new, second-generation rest stops on the southwest corner of the intersection. Accommodating both northbound and southbound travelers, the rest stop is like the other new ones in that each has a theme; here, the theme is the role that Iowans played in the Civil War.

From the rest stop, head west on County Road C47 for 2.8 miles to County Road S13. Turn left (south) and go for less than 1 mile to Dows. At Ellsworth Street, turn right (west). Just past the railroad tracks, turn right (north) onto Railroad Street; park your vehicle and take to your feet for a while. Right at that corner is *Vernon Township Center School #5*, a one-room schoolhouse where first-through eighth-grade students learned their lessons beginning way back in 1887.

Just north of the schoolhouse and sometimes in the shadow of the nearby big grain elevators is the *Dows Depot Welcome Center*, Train and Depot Streets, (515) 852-3595. Built in 1896, the tidy, little railroad depot is half railroad museum, half visitor information center about this part of Iowa, so take in the building and pick up some literature about the region's attractions. The gift shop features hand-made items.

Immediately across the street and facing East Train Street is the *Quasdorf Blacksmith Wagon Museum*, Train and Depot Streets, (515) 852-3595, free. Operated as a blacksmith shop from 1899 to 1990, this structure with the two big white garage doors is pretty much as it was when the Quasdorfs operated their business here. Except for the addition of wagons and some museum displays, it's as if the owners just stepped out for a cup of coffee down the way.

Walk to the next street to the west and then go a block south to Ellsworth. There you will find the *Dows Mercantile Store*, a two-story brick building with an arched entryway. After having housed various businesses, it's now the home of the Dows Historical Society and features a store with Iowa-made items, an antique mall, and a place to get sandwiches and desserts.

By the way, if you visit Dows on the first weekend in August, take in *Sweet Corn Days* (but remember to bring dental floss).

Get back in your vehicle and head west on Ellsworth for about six blocks to Burrows

A Lot of Chicks

On the south side of Webster City, southeast of the intersection of State Highway 17 and U.S. Highway 20, is the 26,000-square-foot building housing *Murray McMurray Hatchery*, 191 Closz Drive, (800) 456-3280. Despite the jokes about the availability of chicks here, this is one serious operation. Murray McMurray, which began in a home in 1917, is the world's largest rare bird hatchery. Besides offering the eggs of more than 100 types of chickens, it also supplies buyers around the world with eggs from pheasant, quail, peafowl, duck, swan, geese, and guinea fowl. Although the vast majority of its orders are completed by mail, if you're here between January and June, you can stop in to collect your order at the front counter or just pick up a catalog if you want. No tours are given, however.

Street; turn right (north). Just outside of town, the road becomes County Road C54 and curves to run straight west for 7 miles to U.S. Highway 69. Turn left (south) there and travel 13.5 miles across some very flat country. At County Road D25, turn right (west) and go for 9 miles to State Highway 17 on the north side of Webster City. Originally the town was called Bone's Mill and then Newcastle before being given its current name in 1857, although no one is sure just who Webster was. Author MacKinlay Kantor, who wrote 40 books, including the highly acclaimed and popular *Andersonville*, was born here in 1904.

In Webster City, D25 miraculously becomes D20 as you continue straight west for 4 more miles to State Highway 17. Turn left and head south for 9.5 miles (note that right after crossing U.S. Highway 20, the road you're on becomes County Road R21). At County Road D46, turn right and go west for about 3 miles. Here is the main entrance to *Brushy Creek State Recreation Area*, (515) 543-8298. Actually, the state land is on both sides of the highway with the main part being to the north. That's where the campgrounds, picnic facilities, and beach are. At 6,000 acres, Brushy Creek is Iowa's largest park, and it's a favorite

with equestrians, having two campgrounds equipped with horse wash areas, hitching rails, lots of shade, and a 1000-by-2000-foot arena. All told, the campgrounds have 230 sites, 120 with electricity. The parkland that's south of D46 has trails that lead along the Des Moines River.

Continue west on D46, which becomes County Road P73 just past the park, and in another 2 miles it becomes County Road D43—all without you making a turn. Right after the road becomes D43, it suddenly turns and drops into the Des Moines River valley, where it passes through Lehigh.

Go about 2 miles west of Lehigh to Quail Avenue, or County Road D33. Turn right (north) and drive a short distance to *Dolliver Memorial State Park*. Note that just after you enter the south end of the park, the road you're on fords Prairie Creek—that's right, you don't cross over the water, you go *through* it. And if rains make the ford impassable, signs are erected to inform motorists. In that case, go past D33 for 3 miles to County Road P59. Turn right (north). Go for about 4 more miles until you're approaching Otho from the south and turn right (east) where you see D33 again. This leads back into Dolliver, this time from the northwest.

Limestone bluffs overlook a creek at Dolliver Memorial State Park south of Fort Dodge.

Dolliver State Park, (515) 359-2539, is where Prairie Creek flows into the Des Moines River. Here, sandstone cliffs rise about 100 feet above the creek and people love to wade through its shallows. Some Indian mounds are south of the ford and are accessible by trails. At the north end of the park is Boneyard Hollow where countless buffalo bones have been found, leading to speculation that Indians drove buffalo over the nearby cliffs or cornered them in the ravine. Dolliver has 31 campsites, 19 with electricity, picnic facilities, hiking trails, boat ramps, and a seasonal cabin that sleeps four.

From the north end of the park, take County Road D33 west for about 4 miles to U.S. Highway 169, passing through tiny Otho on the way. Turn right (north), drive for 5 miles to Business Highway 169/20 on the southwestern edge of Fort Dodge.

At Business Highway 169/20, also called Kenyon Road, turn right (northeast) toward the center of town. Look immediately to your left for the entrance to the *Fort Dodge Museum and Frontier Village*, Highway 169/20 and Museum Road, (515) 573-4231, admission. Although the original fort that was built here in 1850—and used for only 30 months—was erected where downtown is now, this replica shows what life was like for soldiers posted on the frontier about 150 years ago. Originally called Fort Clarke, the post was renamed after Henry Dodge, a governor of the Wisconsin Territory that included Iowa. Among the officers here was Lewis Armistead, who died while leading Confederate soldiers in Pickett's charge at the battle of Gettysburg.

The replica of the log-walled fort has barracks, headquarters, and blockhouses and outside the walls are some original buildings moved from other areas, including an 1855 log home, an 1857 school, and the cabinet shop owned by the grandfather of Conrad Hilton, the hotel magnate. The trading post serves as a gift shop. On the fourth weekend of each August, the fort hosts a Civil War reenactment and the gray and blue clash all over again.

Continue toward the center of Fort Dodge on Kenyon Road. Cross the Des Moines River and, just after a set of railroad tracks, veer left (north) onto 7th Street. Go two blocks and turn right (east) onto 3rd Avenue South. In less than two blocks is *Blanden Art Gallery*, 920 3rd Avenue South, (515) 573-2316, free. Built in 1932 as the state's first permanent art gallery, Blanden has a facade in which a trio of arches forms the entryway. In the galleries are displays from its permanent collection as well as

Hoaxes Far and Near

Far from Fort Dodge, in October 1869, two hired hands were digging at the farm of Stub Newell south of Syracuse, New York, when they hit something solid a few feet down . . . the body of an ancient giant. Immediately the news spread and Newell began charging 50 cents a person to see this 10-foot-long, 3,000-pound petrified body of a man. Thousands lined up to see it and a railroad even added a stop on its line to accommodate the visitors.

Soon, though, it was revealed that what everyone was looking at was not a petrified body at all. It was actually a block of gypsum that had been quarried at Fort Dodge and carved and aged with sulfuric acid in Chicago before being buried late the previous year at Newell's farm by his brother-in-law, jokester George Hull, who was also from New York.

The carving was named the Cardiff Giant, after the town close to the spot where it had been discovered. P. T. Barnum tried to buy it but, after being turned down, made his own to display to paying customers. The original is now at the Farmer's Museum in Cooperstown, New York (a full-size replica, also made of a block of gypsum from Fort Dodge, is housed in the Fort Dodge Museum).

A little more than 40 years later, in 1912, some picnickers found a lead tablet in a popular place about 10 miles southeast of Fort Dodge. With words inscribed in Latin, some claimed it had been made in 1701 by Father Louis Hennepin, who is credited with exploring the Des Moines River. Soon, this too was proved to be a hoax, but such attention was brought to the area where it was allegedly found that the land there later became Dolliver Memorial State Park.

traveling exhibits and showings by regional artists. Among its more recent exhibits have been art works from Haiti, photos of Iowa in the early twentieth century, the art of animated films, and fanciful quilts. The museum also has a handicapped-accessible garden and gift shop.

From 3rd Avenue South, go a short block up to 2nd Avenue South and turn left (west). Go about 1 mile to Highway 169, crossing the Des Moines River again. Turn right (north) and proceed for about 11 miles to County Road C49; turn right and go for 2.5 miles east, then north to *Gotch State Park*. This is where the east and west forks of the Des Moines River converge after wandering down from their sources in Minnesota. Honoring area resident Frank A. Gotch, who won the 1911 World Wrestling Championship and has been called the greatest wrestler ever, the park, (515) 332-4087, has 30 camping spaces with electricity, ramps to drop in canoes and other boats, and picnic facilities. The park anchors one end of Three River Trail, a 32-mile-long trail system that goes to nearby Humboldt and on to Eagle Grove and Rolfe. As the name implies, the trail crosses three rivers—the east and west forks of the Des Moines and the Boone River—and passes through woods, prairie, marshy areas, and grasslands.

Return to C49 and go north about 3 miles into the twin communities of Humboldt

The Fort Dodge Museum is a faithful re-creation of the fort that was built in Fort Dodge in 1850.

seat. At the east end of town, Main Street jogs one block north and leads to the *Humboldt County Historical Museum*, 905 1st Avenue North, (515) 332-5280/5447, which is housed in an 1879 Victorian home that overlooks the East Fork of the Des Moines River. On the grounds are a church, a log cabin, a barn, and a jail.

From the museum, continue east, cross the East Fork of the Des Moines River, and when you reach County Road P56 after a short distance, turn left (north). After about a half mile, turn right (east) onto State Highway 3 and drive 31 miles to Clarion. As you come into town, on your right (south) is the *Heartland Museum*, 119 9th Street SW, (515) 602-6000, admission, which opened in 2001. With the facades of four nineteenth-century buildings gracing its 100-foot-long front, the museum has various collections, including at least 6,000 farm implements, more than 9,000 farm toys, and, in *Alvina's Hat Parlor*, many of the hats collected by Iowa's Hat Lady, Alvina Sellers. Born in 1915, Sellers collected hats and began lecturing about them in 1968. By the time she died in mid-2003, she had given 5,636 presentations across the nation and had appeared on *The Late Show with David Letterman* to talk about her more than 6,000 hats, hundreds of which are at the museum.

A few blocks closer to town on the left (north) is the *4-H Schoolhouse Museum*, Gazebo Park on Central Avenue, (515) 532-2256, free. For those interested in the history of 4-H, this 1907 country school has a wealth of items related to 4-H and O. H. Benson, who designed the four-leaf clover logo of 4-H in the early twentieth century.

Gazebo Park is also the home of *Festival in the Park*, a celebration that takes place on the second Saturday of June. The festival features a parade as well as arts, crafts, and food, and is held in conjunction with the *Annual Celebration of Boyds*, a tribute to teddy bears and those who make and collect them. Originated by Steve Schutt, a local artist who designs and makes teddy bears, the festival is noted for having a different teddy bear designed for it each year by Boyds Bears, a teddy bear manufacturer in Pennsylvania that also has a hand in the event.

For those who can't get enough of teddy bears, think about visiting Clarion on the years ending with zero or five. Since 1990, the town has hosted *The Teddy Bear Reunion in the Heartland* every five years. Compared to the annual event, which locals call The Little One, this is The Big One; and big it is, with 40–50 workshops, charity auctions, special sales, shows, appraisals, and more. Let's just say the fur flies—in a fun way—when this international event brings more than 15,000 people to this town of about 3,000 residents for a four-day weekend. By around 2005, the Heartland Museum will have another area set aside as its

and Dakota City. As you enter the towns, jog to the right (east) onto what becomes 2nd Street South in Dakota City (if you had gone straight and followed the curve to the left, you would have been in Humboldt). Go a few blocks north to Main Street and turn right (east) just past the Humboldt County Courthouse, 203 Main, to enter the downtown. With a population of a little more than 900, Dakota City is Iowa's smallest county

Gypsum

Sitting atop a rich deposit of gypsum, Fort Dodge was the nation's largest supplier of the mineral in the 1870s with 13 mills mining and processing it. Although that superlative distinction now belongs elsewhere, the gypsum quarried and mined at Fort Dodge has helped place Iowa as the nation's second-leading state in production of gypsum. Gypsum is most often associated with its use in wallboards found in almost every residential and commercial building erected in the last century or so. It's also the source for plaster of Paris, chalk, and the molds used to make platterware and silverware; it's used in toothpaste as well.

A farm sits pretty amid the croplands of Franklin County.

Teddy Bear Museum.

About a block east and another block south of the park is the *Clarion Depot*, 302 South Main, (515) 532-2256, a restored Rock Island train station on the north side of the tracks. Inside are railroad artifacts and the town's chamber of commerce, which has information about the community and the surrounding area.

From Clarion, go east on Highway 3 for 28 miles to Hampton, crossing I-35 along the way. As you enter Hampton, note the fairgrounds on your right. Located on their east side is the *Franklin County Historical Museum*, (641) 456-5777, free, which is open every afternoon. The museum building holds many items and artifacts related to the history of Franklin County. Outside is a village consisting of numerous buildings that include a depot, blacksmith shop, saloon, general store, and an ice cream parlor, which features homemade ice cream when the whole village is open during the county fair in July. At all other times of the

year, the buildings may be visited by making prior arrangements with the museum.

Continuing into central Hampton, you will see the *Franklin County Courthouse*, Federal Street and Central Avenue. Built in 1889, this is a nice example of the Richardsonian style of architecture and features a domed tower that rises 133 feet above the ground.

Just east of the courthouse is *Soldier's Memorial Hall*. The only one in Iowa that's dedicated to the memory of those who served in the Civil War, the building feels like a small chapel. It can be seen if you call the historical museum, (641) 456-5777, ahead of time.

Quick Trip Option: On the way to Hampton and nearly 9 miles after passing I-35, take County Road S42 to the left (north). In about 1.5 miles is *Beeds Lake State Park*, (641) 456-2047. Centered around a lake that was formed by William Beeds when he built a dam and gristmill here in 1857, the 319-acre park is a nice oasis with 114 campsites (74 with electricity), picnic facilities, concessions, hiking trails, fishing, boating, and swimming. You can go to Hampton either the way you arrived or by leaving the park's southeast corner on a road that leads to County Road S43, which drops straight south into Hampton's west side.

From the courthouse in Hampton, continue east for a few blocks until you reach 4th Street, which is also U.S. Highway 65. Turn right (south) and drive about 3 miles. You'll arrive at another element of the Franklin County Historical Museum, the *Rural Electric Association Museum*, which was a power plant built in the early part of the twentieth century as part of a nationwide effort to bring electricity to rural areas. In particular, this was the first farmer-owned power plant west of the Mississippi to go online and was used until the 1950s. Inside are some of the original equipment and other items showing life before and after electricity came to the countryside. Tours are arranged in advance by contacting the museum, (641) 456-5777.

Continue south on Highway 65 for about 1 mile to County Road C47. Turn left (east) and proceed for 2 miles. You'll come upon the large, two-story *Stone House* that is another property of the county museum. Built in 1854 by Leander Reeve, a settler who had come from Ohio a year earlier, it was made of limestone quarried at nearby Maynes Creek and lumber made from the walnut trees that grew there. Reeve lived here with his wife for only three years when, homesick for Ohio, she demanded to move back east. Although a total of 16 owners or residents lived here before the museum acquired the house in 1979, it was never wired for electricity until that year. Tours of the house, furnished as it might have been in the nineteenth century, are arranged by contacting the museum, (641) 456-5777.

Continue east for another 2 miles into the small community of Geneva; from its east side, take County Road S56 south and east to the north edge of Ackley, about 12 miles away. After following the highway through a series of left- and right-hand turns, when you're about a half mile from Ackley, watch on the right (west) for *Prairie Bridges*, 310 North Franklin, (641) 847-3332. Years ago if you came here, you were going to the pits, literally—a series of abandoned gravel quarries. Awarded some grants in the 1990s, a few locals slowly transformed the pits into a nice 72-acre city park with six interconnected ponds crossed by eight bridges of various designs. North of Beaver Creek, only grasses, bushes, and trees that are native to the plains are allowed, while to the south, hostas and other ornamentals have been planted in the park.

Also in the north end are campgrounds that have 44 sites with electricity.

Continue south on S56, cross Old U.S. Highway 20 and then a set of railroad tracks, and proceed into central Ackley. Turn left (east) onto Main Street and go about three blocks. There, you'll find *Victory Park*, a small triangular park where flocks of chickens were tended by drovers before being loaded onto nearby railroad cars headed for eastern markets along with iced ducks. Similarly, rail cars loaded with grain went east from here too. The park is near the *Ackley Heritage Center*, State and Main Streets, (641) 847-2201, free. Located upstairs in the Municipal Building, the center has displays and genealogical information about the settlers who came here years ago from Ostfriesland in Germany.

Walk across Victory Park to the *Heritage Museum and Soda Shop*, 701 Park Avenue, (641) 847-6975, where you can look at displays while having your favorite ice cream treat from an old-time soda fountain that's open every afternoon.

From Victory Park, go east on Main for three blocks and turn left (north) on Butler Street; drive about four blocks to Old Highway 20. You'll end up at *Settlement on the Prairie*, (641) 847-6975, another element of the local heritage center. Surrounded by a low white fence is an 1870s-era I-house. What's an I-house? you wonder. That's a type, rather than a style, of house that was commonly associated with rural areas in Indiana, Illinois, and Iowa. It usually was a two-story frame house like this one, with a simple floor plan consisting of common rooms on the main floor and the bedrooms upstairs, with a central hallway on each floor. Besides the house, the grounds contain a one-room school, an old-fashioned barn, garden sheds, a garden with cash crops, and a restored prairie with a windmill. To visit the buildings, make arrangements at the heritage center on Main Street.

Return to Butler Street and continue south for about 1 mile out of town to County Road D15. Turn right (west) and drive for 12.5 miles into Iowa Falls. Sure, sure, you could have taken Old Highway 20, which is joined by U.S. Highway 65 about midway to Iowa Falls, but D15 is more pleasant and has less traffic.

Once you're in Iowa Falls, D15 becomes Rocksylvania Street. Continue west on that through town and go two blocks past the junction with Highway 65 to the *Iowa Falls Chamber of Commerce*. Housed in the former Carnegie Library, the chamber, 520 Rocksylvania, (641) 648-3432, can provide useful information on area attractions and other places of interest. The building also is the home of the *Pat Clark Art Gallery*, which consists of more than 200 paintings, sculptures, etchings, lithographs, photographs, and more gathered from around the world by Iowa Falls native Pat Clark when she worked as a diplomat for the U.S. State Department.

Across the street to the south is *Estes Park*, a pleasant shady place where the real treat is at the park's southeast corner: an old-fashioned popcorn stand with a neon sign serves popcorn in paper bags.

At Main Street, which is on the west side of the park and the chamber's offices, go north three blocks to Union Street. Turn left (west) and proceed a few blocks to the Iowa River. There, you'll see the *Scenic City Empress Boat Club*, 1113 Union Street, (641) 648-9517 and (800) 873-1936, which is where the two-level excursion boat *Scenic City Empress* docks. On Sunday afternoons, she takes visitors on a 90-minute cruise of the Iowa River.

A short walk from the dock down Cedar Street, which is atop the bluffs that overlook the Iowa River from the east, is the *Swinging Bridge*. It not only lets pedestrians cross the Iowa River but takes you from the bluffs down to *Assembly Park* at the water's edge. The bridge was erected years ago to provide access between a church and the downtown area.

Drive a few blocks south on Cedar Street to Washington Avenue and turn left (east); go for about four blocks. Between Stevens and Oak Streets is the beautiful three-story *Metropolitan Theater*, 515 Washington, which looks like a yellow and white wedding cake. Opened in 1899, it was renovated in the 1990s.

Go east to Oak Street, which is also Highway 65, turn right (south) and, after crossing the river, turn right onto Park Avenue. Follow Park along the south side of the river to River Street South and turn left (southwest). Follow this for about a quarter mile to Georgetown Road, which is also County Road S33, and turn right (west).

When the road turns markedly to the south, watch for signs about the *Calkins Nature Area* and follow them to the right (west) to 135th Street, a total of about 4 miles from Iowa Falls. Go a very short distance on this gravel road. Soon, you will reach the entrance to this 78-acre preserve, 18335 135th Street, (641) 648-9878, free. Located on the south side of the Iowa River, Calkins Nature Area has woods, wetlands, and prairie as well as an arboretum and, at the visitor center, wildlife exhibits and a gift shop.

From Calkins Nature Area, head west again on 135th Street for about 3 miles to County Road S27. Turn right (north) and head to Alden, 1 mile away.

A couple pauses on the pedestrian bridge over the Iowa River at Iowa Falls.

At County Road D20 in Alden, turn left (west) and go for 10 miles to I-35 at Exit 147. Turn north onto the interstate and cruise to Exit 159 and the rest stop where you began the tour

Alden's Library

In 1914, after receiving a $9,000 grant from Andrew Carnegie, the city library in Alden (which is just north of 135th Street on County Road S27) opened its doors, making it the smallest community in the nation to have a Carnegie library. In 2000, an addition doubled the library's size.

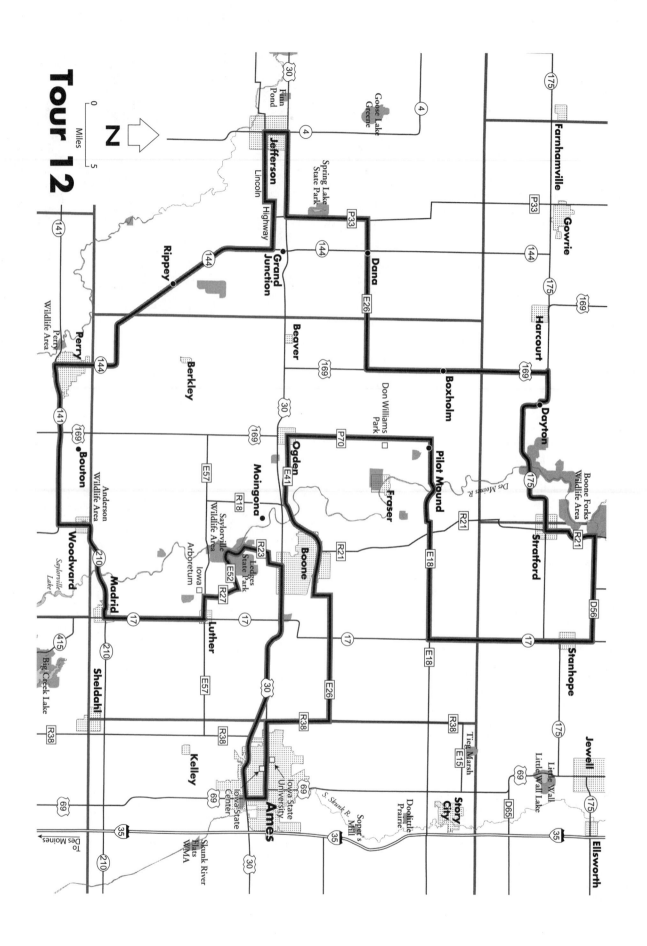

Tour 12
The Central Valley of the Des Moines River and the Lincoln Highway

Ames—Boone—Stanhope—Stratford—Dayton—Jefferson—Perry—Madrid—Ames

Distance: approximately 203 miles

Surprises abound in the center of Iowa where the plains give way suddenly to tall bluffs, deep forests, and the wide, deep valley of the Des Moines River as it courses through this region. Lush, colorful gardens are encountered along this tour, as is the childhood home of one of our nation's First Ladies. And if you get tired of driving, let someone else give you a ride on the rails that take you across one of the nation's highest bridges—that's right, here in the middle of Iowa!

To begin this tour, leave U.S. Highway 30 at Elwood Drive on the south side of Ames and go north on Elwood for a short distance to the second stoplight at South 16th Street; turn left (west) into the football stadium parking lot. No, we haven't come here to try to catch a glimpse of the Iowa State University football team. The lot is also close to *Reiman Gardens*, 1407 Elwood Drive, (515) 294-2710, admission, where a stylized version of ISU's famous campanile rises above the flowerbeds and trees. Reiman contains formal gardens, a bog garden, aquatic plants, a children's garden, trial gardens, and a rose garden with more than 2,000 bushes of at least 300 varieties. A butterfly garden has butterflies from six continents. Besides greenhouses, in the main building is *Hazel's Kitchen*, which serves sandwiches, desserts, and beverages for brunch and lunch. Note that you're only allowed to photograph the gardens for non-commercial purposes. If you intend to sell your pictures, you must register and pay a $25-per-hour fee; and tripods and monopods are not allowed under any conditions.

From Reiman Gardens, return to Elwood Drive, turn left (north), and go about 1 mile to Lincolnway. On the way, at South 4th Street, you may want to stop briefly at the Iowa State University information booth on the right. Even if you are not visiting the school, this stand has brochures and literature about attractions, restaurants, lodging and more in the area and the guides can help direct you around town.

Before reaching Lincolnway, you'll also see on the left the *Iowa State Center*, a complex consisting of *Jack Trice Stadium*, home of the

Reiman Gardens, on the campus of Iowa State University in Ames, has outside plantings, a large indoor botanical center, and a butterfly garden.

Cyclones football team; *Hilton Coliseum*, site of many intercollegiate sports events; *C.Y. Stephens*, the university's main performing arts theater, and *Fisher Theater*, a more intimate theater for small productions. For information about events here, contact (515) 294-3347 or (877) 843-2368.

At Lincolnway, turn left (west). If you want to walk around the campus, just after Knoll Road, take the next right (north), which leads to a parking ramp near the *Memorial Union*, (515) 292-1111. Like many other student unions, this has lecture halls, arts and crafts studios, recreation areas, food services, and something most others don't—the *Maintenance Shop*, (515) 294-2772; concert information,

(515) 294-2969. A former maintenance area, the *Maintenance Shop* hosts live entertainment, including locally and nationally known musicians as well as small stage productions in a very intimate atmosphere—there are only 200 seats. Among the well-known names who have performed here are Leo Kottke, Arlo Guthrie, Smashing Pumpkins, Suzanne Vega, Taj Mahal, and Muddy Waters.

North of the union is the tall, tan brick campanile that has long been a symbol of this campus, chiming every hour and often accompanied by songs on its carillon. A short walk to the northwest of the campanile, past Curtiss and Ross Halls, is the *Farm House Museum*, (515) 294-7426, free. The first building on the campus, the Farm House is maintained as it was during its early years.

A Calculating Mind

In the late 1930s, mathematics and physics professor John Atanasoff and graduate student Clifford Berry developed what is acknowledged as the world's first electronic digital computer, which was disassembled during World War II because space was needed for other projects. It was about half the size of a billiards table, weighed over 700 pounds, had 300 vacuum tubes, and solved a problem every 10 seconds (whereas modern computers can handle billions of operations each second). A working replica was built in the 1990s at a cost of $35,000 and is in the Durham Center.

Continue west on Lincolnway for about 3 miles to County Road R38. Turn right (north) and drive for about 4 miles to County Road E26 on the left (west). Be careful: E26 appears earlier on the right (east) but *don't* take that. At E26, turn left (west) and proceed for about 10 miles to the north side of Boone, where the road becomes 22nd Street.

At Story Street in Boone, turn left (south) and proceed to 11th Street. Turn right (west) and go to Harrison Street, where you will see a number of passenger train cars and some locomotives to your front left. Turn left (south) onto Harrison. After crossing the tracks, you'll arrive at one of Iowa's more popular attractions, the *Boone and Scenic Valley Railroad*, 225 10th Street, (515) 432-4249, admission. Begun as a preservation effort by railroad enthusiasts in this town that has had a long relationship with the railroads, the B&SVRR now entertains thousands of visitors each year. You can ride a train for a 15-mile round trip or take the dining or dessert trains, both of which have 22-mile round trip runs. On weekdays the trains are pulled by diesel engines and on most weekends a Chinese steam locomotive does the honors. Going west of town, the trains cross two bridges: the first one is the

tallest interurban bridge in America, looming 156 feet above Bass Point Creek (yes, just a few moments ago you were traveling across flat, flat Iowa, so this comes as a big surprise to some). A little later you cross the Des Moines River.

You can also ride the railroad's 1915 electric trolley to downtown Boone from 11 a.m. to 4:30 p.m., Saturdays and Sundays in the summer. Children under 13 ride the trolley free. The B&SVRR's depot contains a museum and gift shop. On the weekend after Labor Day, Boone celebrates *Pufferbilly Days*, which celebrate the town's railroad history.

Quick Trip Option 1: For those who want a close look at the nation's longest and highest double-track bridge—yes, another superlative in the middle of flat ol' Iowa—turn south from the B&SVRR's parking lot onto Harrison, and at 10th Street, turn right (west). Go to Marion Street, about three quarters of a mile away, and again turn right (north). Proceed to 12th Street, which is also County Road E26, and take a left (west) there. Stay on the road when E26 runs to the right. About 3.5 miles out of town, you'll come to the *Kate Shelley Bridge* standing 185 feet above the valley floor. It is named after a local girl who became a national hero more than a century ago (more about her later in the tour). Completed in 1901, it is 2,685 feet long, and serves the main line of the Union Pacific Railroad.

From the B&SVRR's parking, turn right onto Harrison, go to 10th Street, and turn left (east). Three blocks later, at Carroll Street, turn right (south). Between 8th and 7th Streets is the *Mamie Doud Eisenhower Birthplace*, 709 Carroll Street, (515) 432-1896, admission. In this unassuming but pleasant home was raised a young woman who, in 1916, married an army lieutenant named Dwight D. Eisenhower, who went on to become one of the nation's most famous generals and best-loved presidents. Kept much as it was when Mamie lived here, the house has furnishings from her family and two cars that she and Ike owned. The home also contains a small museum, a gift shop, and a library.

Turn left (east) on 7th Street and drive a short distance to Story Street in downtown Boone. Turn to the right (south) and proceed to the *Boone County Historical Center* on the left side of the street. The center, 602 Story Street, (515) 432-1907, admission, a former Masonic Temple, tells the history of those who have lived in this region from prehistoric times to the present. A diorama tells the story of 15-year-old Kate Shelley, a local girl who, in 1881, saved a passenger train from plunging into a nearby creek west of town when a railroad bridge washed out during a storm.

From the historical center, go south two

blocks to 4th Street, also called Mamie Eisenhower Avenue, and turn right (west). In fewer than ten blocks, the thoroughfare shifts slightly to the south and becomes West 3rd Street. Follow this out of town to where it soon becomes County Road E41. As you go, you may notice something a bit different about Boone—the county courthouse, which is along this street, is not near the main business district as in most other county seats. The road begins a long descent to the valley floor of the Des Moines River. As you cross the valley, note the Kate Shelley Bridge about a mile and a half to the right.

Quick Trip Option 2: After you cross the Des Moines River on County Road E41, you soon will come to County Road R18. Turn left (south) and cross U.S. Highway 30. An outdoor recreation area called *Seven Oaks*, 1086 222nd Drive, (515) 432-9457, admission, is on the right side of R18. During the winter it's a nice place to downhill ski or go snowboarding and snow tubing. When it's warmer, practice your golf swing on the ranges there, go mountain biking, or canoe the Des Moines River.

At the crest of the hill farther south on R18 from Seven Oaks, turn left (east) where the sign points to Moingona. Take that road as it descends the hill to curve north and enter the small town, where you should turn left (east) on 232nd Street. At the far end is the *Kate Shelley Museum*, 1198 232nd Street, (515) 432-1907, free. Among the honors Kate Shelley received for her bravery was a gold medal fashioned by the Tiffany studio in New York City. Along with the depot at the site is a Rock Island Rocket passenger car. A trail leads to the location of the long railway bridge that Shelley crossed during a storm to alert railroad agents about a bridge that had been washed out a short distance away

Continue west on E41 from Boone for approximately 6 miles to Ogden, where the road becomes East Walnut Street. At the intersection with North 1st Street, turn right (north) and proceed through town, where the road becomes County Road P70. The red-white-and-blue signs on the poles serve notice that you're on the original Lincoln Highway, which later became U.S. Highway 30 until it was replaced by the four-lane highway just south of town.

After leaving Ogden, drive for less than 6 miles on P70 to *Don Williams Recreational* Area on the right. Some county parks are so-so and some are really nice. This one is definitely in the latter category, (515) 353-4337, free. Around a pretty 160-acre lake are arrayed beaches, campgrounds, picnic areas, a small restaurant (with a sign prohibiting bait buckets), a nine-hole golf course, boat ramps, a rental cabin, and more, all nestled among gently rolling

hills. Of particular note are the sculptures cut out of trees with a chain saw—eagles, a Viking, an Indian, bears (and bears and bears), and a *Sesame Street* favorite, Elmo. Near the park entrance is *Hickory Grove Country School Museum*, (515) 432-1907, free, which was built in 1889 and used until 1956. Inside are double-seat desks, a pot-bellied stove, a pump organ, and textbooks.

Return to P70 and continue north for about 2 miles to County Road E18. Turn right (east) and go for about 16 miles to State Highway 17. Turn left (north). Along the way, note that the folks around Pilot Mound have a sense of humor. They've put up a highway sign announcing the upcoming exits to their community, which numbers about 200 people. A few miles beyond Pilot Mound you again drop into the valley of the Des Moines River and ascend on the far side. Just as you turn north on Highway 17, look back to the west (left) to see *Saint Paul's Lutheran Church*. It was once selected by the readers of the *Des Moines Register* as the state's prettiest countryside church.

On Highway 17, drive north for 8 miles to Stanhope. Upon entering town, you will see a large mural on the left (west) side of the highway and the *Stanhope Meat Locker*, 465 Parker, (515) 826-3280, a very good place to buy meats. The town also boasts some neat antique stores.

Continue north on 17 for about 1.5 miles to the intersection with County Road D56. On the northeast side (far right) of the intersection is *Country Relics Village*, (515) 826-4386, admission. Although this attraction features the original, full-size Stanhope railroad depot built in 1882, the village's other buildings are one-third to one-half the scale of the real things. These other buildings include schools, homes, service stations, and more, all populated by more than 100 scale figures and set among various gardens. There are also collections of mechanical toys, music boxes, figurines, Raggedy Ann and Andy dolls, Christmas decorations, tops, pedal tractors, and more. On the fourth Sunday of each June, the village hosts its Big Little Engine Show, a display of working scale-model engines and scale-model machines.

Go west on D56 for 6 miles to the T intersection with County Road R21. Turn left (south) and proceed for about 3 miles to Stratford. Along R21, you'll experience a few turns, bends, and twists as the road goes south for a few miles, turns to the west for a short distance, and then resumes going south into Stratford. On the second weekend of each July, the town hosts its annual *Bluegrass Festival*, (515) 838-2311, admission, in the city park.

At State Highway 175 in Stratford, turn right (west) and drive for 9 miles to Dayton. Once again, you'll dip through the Des Moines River Valley along the way. As you enter Dayton, note the natural amphitheater that forms a great setting for the *Dayton Rodeo*, (515) 547-6336, admission, which has been held each Labor Day weekend since the late 1930s and draws thousands of spectators.

A Little Shakespeare Please

Okay, what's with the name Stratford here in Iowa? Well, some huff and puff and bluff. In the nineteenth century, Hewitt Ross created Rosstown with high hopes that the town would prove attractive as a stop on a major railroad line, giving it instant economic viability. But Ross and the chief railroad engineer laying out the line could not come to an understanding, so the Toledo and Northwestern Railroad put its tracks on the north edge of Rosstown.

Just to make sure Ross got the message he wasn't liked, the railroad located its depot on the north side of the tracks, effectively using them to block residents and businesses to the south. Next, the railroad laid out the streets in its new town so they would not line up with Rosstown's.

One railroad worker in the area suggested Stratford as a name for the railroad's new town, after Stratford, Pennsylvania, which was named after England's Stratford-upon-Avon, home of renowned playwright William Shakespeare. Streets in Stratford were named after Shakespeare and other famous English writers—Burns, Milton, Moore, Byron, Goldsmith, and Tennyson—and the river Avon.

Not long afterwards, Rosstown was no more, although one of the last vestiges of the founder's legacy, Ross Avenue, still exists—on the south edge of town, of course.

Continue west on Highway 175 for 2 miles past Dayton, then turn left (south) onto U.S. Highway 169. Drive for 6 miles to Boxholm. As you enter, you'll spot a farm implement toy store on the north side of town.

Keep going south on Highway 169 for 5 more miles to County Road E26. Turn right (west) and proceed for 9 miles to County Road P33, where you turn left (south). Go for about 2 miles to *Spring Lake Park*. Along E26, you go through tiny Dana (population 84) and cross State Highway 144 (you can do both pretty much at the same time). *Spring Lake Park*, (515) 738-5069 and (515) 386-5674, on the right-hand side of the road, has 240 acres, 124 campsites with electricity, and an open area for campers who don't need power. It also fea-

tures trails, swimming, boating and its 50-acre lake is stocked with largemouth bass, bluegill, bullhead, channel catfish, and northern pike.

Continue south on P33 for 3 miles to U.S. Highway 30; turn right (west). Proceed for about 5 miles to State Highway 4 and turn left (south) into Jefferson. When you reach Lincolnway, turn left (east), go two blocks, and park on or near Wilson Street; then take to your feet. By now you probably have noticed something for quite awhile, the 168-foot-tall *Mahanay Bell Tower*, Lincolnway and Wilson, (515) 386-2155, $1 admission. On the courthouse square, this carillon with 14 bronze bells has a 120-foot-tall observation deck that allows you to see for miles around—simply because it's the tallest thing for miles around. If the weather is right, you might be able to see the water tower in Scranton about 9 miles to the west. Built in 1897, that 148-foot-tall, 48,000-gallon, all-steel tank is the oldest water tower still in use in Iowa and the ninth oldest in the United States.

Each June, the *Mahanay Bell Tower* is the focal point of Jefferson's Bell Tower Festival, a celebration of the arts. Particular attention should be given to the *Alpha Studio*, 704 North Elm, (515) 386-3598. Open primarily during this festival, the studio shows the works of photographers, painters, sculptors, potters, and other artists during the festival as well as the bronze sculptures of the studio's owner, Alice Nipps.

After you've come down from the Mahanay Tower, walk across Wilson Street to the west and just beyond Drug Town is the new *Lincoln Highway Museum*, 110 West Lincolnway, open Monday, Wednesday, and Saturday, 1–4 p.m., or by phoning (515) 386-3419. Although small, this museum tells the history of the first paved highway to cross the United States . . . and Iowa.

Continue your walking tour of Jefferson by going one block south of the bell tower on Wilson, then turning right (west) on Harrison Street. At 105 West Harrison is the *Jefferson Telephone Company Museum*, (515) 386-4141, free. In the offices of the Jefferson Telephone Company, this museum recounts the history of the telephone, including displays of operator consoles and switching gear.

About a block east of the Mahanay Tower on East Lincolnway is the *Greene County Historical Society Museum*, 219 East Lincolnway, (515) 386-8544, free, which describes the region's history.

Near the intersection of Lincolnway and Cedar Street, about four blocks east of the carillon, is the restored, yellow and white Milwaukee Depot on the right. It's also the northern trailhead for the *Raccoon Valley Recreational Bike Trail*, (515) 386-4629, a hard-surface trail that leads to the western suburbs of Des Moines 57 miles away; the trail features a 600-foot-long bridge across the North Raccoon River.

Rules of the Road, 1916 Style
Here's what *The Complete Official Road Guide of the Lincoln Highway*, published in 1916, has to say about speeding: "The laws of Iowa hold that a motor vehicle must be so driven in a careful and prudent manner as not to endanger the property of another or the life and limb of any person. A speed in excess of 25 miles an hour is presumptive evidence that an automobile is not being so driven."

Now it's time to jump back into your car and head east out of Jefferson on Lincolnway. If you paid attention in the Lincoln Highway Museum, you should know this road is the original Lincoln Highway.

About 7 miles after leaving Jefferson, the Lincoln Highway comes to a T intersection with State Highway 144 just south of Grand Junction; turn right (south). At the turn is a former one-stop called Cozy Camp. Behind the main building are cabins that served as accommodations for travelers of the Lincoln Highway.

Take Highway 144 to the southeast for 16 miles to Perry, passing through Rippey along the way. In downtown Perry, turn left (east) onto Willis Avenue. Immediately on your left is the *Hotel Pattee*, 1112 Willis Avenue, (515) 465-3511 or (888) 424-4268. Restored beautifully in the 1990s, this hotel recalls a time when just going to hotels like this elegant one was enough of a vacation for many people. Even if you don't plan to stay there, the management welcomes you to see some of the 40 rooms and suites, which are individually decorated and set up for families as well as couples. There's even a bowling alley in the basement, but one thing not to miss is *David's Milwaukee Diner*, which is known for its superb meals, many made from locally grown organic foods and chicken (not to mention cheese made from milk produced by Tillie, the hotel's goat). By the way, a doorman greets everyone at the front of the hotel, something not often seen in a town the size of Perry.

Fitting in with the decor of the Hotel Pattee is, immediately next door on the right, *Ray B. Smith Museum Store*, 1118 Willis Avenue, (515) 465-4848. Located in a former pharmacy, this jewel of a store is not really connected with a museum but you feel like you are in one nonetheless. Books about Iowa and the region are here as are locally made works of art and pieces from far away, such as Swedish plates, Irish glassware, and works inspired by Frank Lloyd Wright. Regional artists also produce the jewelry sold here and the chocolates come from a Dubuque monastery.

Step out the back door of the store and you can meet the mayor . . . well, sort of. A statue of the former mayor, George Soumas, sits at a table

The Mahanay Bell Tower stands 168 feet tall near the courthouse in Jefferson.

in an outdoor eating area, as though he's welcoming you to join him for coffee, tea, or lunch.

Across Willis Avenue from the Hotel Pattee is the old Carnegie library, which is destined to become a historical museum.

At the corner just beyond the Hotel Pattee on Willis Avenue, turn left (north) on 2nd Street. In the past few years, the population of Perry has diversified with a number of Hispanics who have come to work in the area. As a result, places like *Tienda Latina*, 1104 2nd Street, a Mexican store and restaurant, and *Coco Loco*, 1110 2nd Street, a Mexican/Central American store, have sprung up, bringing in a rich variety of foods and household items that you don't often find in Iowa.

About three blocks further north on 2nd Street is an interesting store—*Mars Daisy Bar*,

The Lincoln Highway

Greene County has had a long-standing connection with the Lincoln Highway, the first auto route across America, stretching 3,389 miles between New York City and San Francisco.

In 1924, the county became the first in Iowa to have its section of the highway paved. Today, Greene County has more miles of the Lincoln Highway still in existence than any other county in the state. West of Jefferson, the county seat, is the old Eureka Bridge; built in 1912, it was one reason engineers brought the Lincoln Highway through this town. And immediately near that is Danger Hill, although it's not really that dangerous as it had been when it was a mud road. An old roadside motel, now closed, is just east of the bridge.

The demise of the Lincoln Highway came in the late 1920s when government agencies decided to replace named highways with a numbered system that remains in effect today. Still, Boy Scouts across America put in concrete posts, one per mile, on September 1, 1928, to mark the route of the nation's first transcontinental highway.

For more information about the Lincoln Highway in Iowa, see Drake Hokansen's book, *The Lincoln Highway: Main Street Across America*, or visit http://www.lincolnhighwayassoc.org/iowa

1421 2nd Street, which is a cellular phone store and a soda fountain! That's right, pick up a phone and a chocolate shake to go if you want.

Return to Willis Avenue and turn left (east). Head to K Avenue, turn right (south), and go a short distance to the *Forest Park Museum and Arboretum*, just south of State Highway 141. This 17-acre park, 1477 K Avenue, (515) 465-3577, free, was started more than 50 years ago by a local farmer who had such an interest in history that his friends donated artifacts to his collection. The park has more than 100 species of native trees and shrubs as well as many wildflowers. Also there is a one-room schoolhouse that was used for 96 years after it was built in 1867. The museum houses a rare dynamo that some believe was being developed as a perpetual-motion machine by its inventor.

Return to Highway 141, turn right (east), and go for about 9 miles to Exit 138. Turn left (north) onto State Highway 210 and go 1 mile to Woodward, where 210 turns to the east. On the north end of town are the grounds of the Woodward State Resource Center, in case you're wondering what that campus is all about. A few miles past Woodward, you cross the Des Moines River again (last time, honest).

Continue for 6 miles on Highway 210 to Madrid, turn right (south) on Water Street and, one block after that, turn left (east) on 2nd Street. Located in an old bank is the *Madrid Historical Society Museum*, 109 West 2nd Street, (515) 795-2287/2640, free. Inside are more than 1,000 dolls, antique toys, and, in an adjacent building, "Mine #7," a reproduction of one of the coal mines that was in operation in the area between 1910 and 1945.

From the museum, go one block south on State Street to 3rd Street, turn left (east) and go for three blocks to Kennedy Avenue (also State Highway 17). There, you'll find a display showing the locations of the mines and a wooden statue of a coal miner, honoring the immigrants from Sweden, Norway, Italy, Wales, Croatia, and England.

Turn left (north) on State Highway 17 and leave Madrid; go for 6 miles to County Road E57 just south of Luther. Turn left (west) and proceed for 3 miles to Peach Avenue, which is gravel. Turn left (south) and, following the signs, go 1 mile to the *Iowa Arboretum*. Created in the 1990s, the 378-acre arboretum, 1875 Peach Avenue, (515) 795-3216, admission, has 19 plant collections, ranging from herbs, hostas, and perennials to nut trees, shade plants, and a butterfly garden. Classes cover all sorts of subjects, including the basics of bonsai, grafting, pruning, growing roses, and making your own stepping stones. Self-guided trails lead across the grounds and the Hughes Educational Center has a gift shop. If you find the front gate shut; you can still let yourself in and out; just remember to secure the gate when you leave.

Although located in a medium-size community, Perry's Hotel Pattee exudes the excellence of first-class hotels found in much larger cities.

From the arboretum, return to E57, turn right (east), and go a short distance to County Road R27. Turn left (north), drive about 2 miles to County Road E52, then turn left (west). This leads to the east entrance of *Ledges State Park*, (515) 432-1852, one of central Iowa's favorite parks. At the entrance, either go straight into the park or follow E52 as it curves to the south and then turns west again. Either way leads through the park and down to an area alongside the Des Moines River, although the former route, which goes along Pea's Creek and is a beautiful drive, may be closed at times.

Archeologists have found evidence that the region has been used by humans as long as 4,000 years and more recently by the Sauk and Fox when the first European-Americans arrived in Iowa. Now the park has 94 campsites (40 with electricity), picnic tables and shelters, fishing, and trails that go below and on top of the 100-foot-tall sandstone ledges that give the park its name.

At the bottom of Ledges State Park, take the park road north to the park's north entrance, where it becomes County Road R23. This quickly rises to the upper plain and twists and turns its way toward Boone from the south.

Go north a short distance to U.S. Highway 30, turn right (east), and cruise for about 12 miles back to the south side of Ames, where this tour began.

A butterfly visits a purple coneflower at the Iowa Arboretum south of Boone.

Gallup Home

The octagonal house in Jefferson where George Gallup, founder of the Gallup Poll and the father of modern public opinion polls, lived until he finished high school in 1919 is at 703 South Chestnut. Because it is a private residence, be respectful of the property, which is not open for tours.

Swedish Madrid

Despite the Spanish overtones of its name, the town of Madrid was originally called Swede Point—and with good reason. Settled in 1846, it's the oldest, continuously inhabited Swedish settlement west of the Mississippi. And the name is pronounced *Mad-rid*, unlike the Spanish capital.

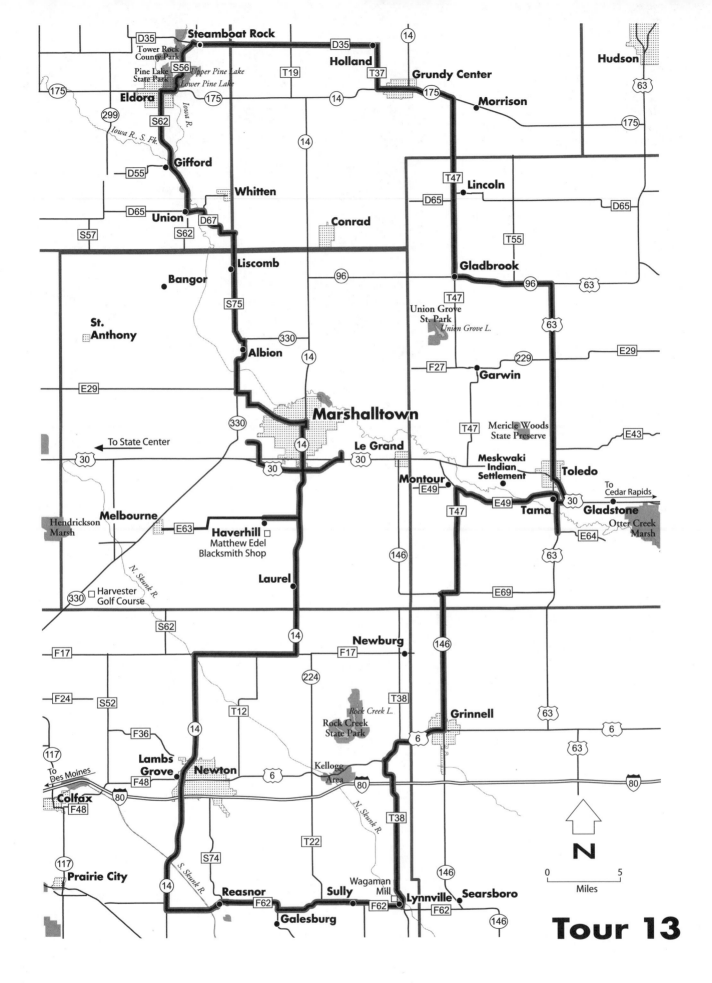

Tour 13

94

Tour 13
The Towns and Countrysides of Central Iowa

Marshalltown—Union—Eldora—Steamboat Rock—Grundy Center—Gladbrook—Toledo—Tama—Grinnell—Lynnville—Newton—Haverhill—Marshalltown

Distance: approximately 195 miles

This tour covers a region that is one of the more deceptive areas of Iowa. Like some other parts in the center of the state, it looks like an endless plain, but the Iowa River courses through this territory, creating some remarkable scenery that appears suddenly in vivid contrast to the surrounding farmlands. Rocky cliffs, dense woodlands, and wetlands form wonderful state and county parks, and rolling hills help create one of the greatest golf courses in the nation, yes, right here in Iowa. This land is also rich with the history of the Meskwaki and Sauk who have inhabited this part of North America for hundreds of years as well as the history of those who came later building schools, mills, and small businesses that have become international corporations. Others from this region include a writer who detailed the days of the early pioneers and one artist whose works remain unmatched by other artists. So take to the road around Marshalltown and see how much more there is here than first meets the eye.

This tour begins at the intersection of State Highway 14 and U.S. Highway 30, on the south edge of Marshalltown. Go north on Highway 14, which is also Center Street for about 2 miles. The road passes through a corridor loaded with businesses, shops, and various restaurants. Closer to the center of town, you'll see *Fisher Community Center*, 709 South Center Street, (641) 753-9013, on the west side of the street, sitting back from the road a bit. The Fisher represents many things to local residents and visitors. For you, the main thing to note is that the *Marshalltown Convention and Visitor Bureau*, (641) 753-6645 and (800) 697-3155, is here, so stop in awhile to learn what's old, what's new, and what's to do in this city and the surrounding area.

While in the Fisher, check out its art gallery that displays pieces from its permanent collection, including 17 paintings by French impressionists such as Degas, Cassat, and Matisse. It also hosts traveling exhibits throughout the year. In the Ceramic Study Collection, works from America and other countries such as New Guinea, Spain, and Holland have brought praise upon this collection by ceramics scholars and artists. Outside are sculptures, including *Dedication to the Future*, the last sculpture done by Christian Petersen, who was renowned for his works at Iowa State University.

From the Fisher, head north on Center, crossing Anson Creek, and passing over a large rail yard to come to the *Marshall County Courthouse*, bounded by Main, Church, and Center Streets, and 1st Avenue. Park awhile and walk around this impressive Beaux Arts building that was built in the 1880s with a 175-foot-high tower that's easily seen for quite a distance and is the pride of the community. At different times from the 1950s to the 1970s, residents turned down suggestions to build a new courthouse and have at least twice authorized projects to restore and improve it.

Walk to the *Marshall County Historical Museum*, 202 East Church, (641) 752-6664, donation, which is just southeast of the courthouse. Exhibits include a new geological collection with fossil crinoids recovered from a quarry east of town and displays about prominent local residents, including the late actress Jean Seberg; Adrian C. "Cap" Anson, the first major league baseball player to have 3,000 hits, a feat he accomplished in the late nineteenth century; and Dale Paul, a boyish actor who older folks might remember as the page who called for Phillip Morris in cigarette commercials years ago. The museum also has Native American artifacts, rooms representing different elements of life in the past, and a display about local businesses, including one started by David Lennox, of air conditioning fame (unlike his counterpart in the television ads, the real one wore a coat and tie at work).

Walking north on 2nd Avenue leads you to *Taylor #4 Country School*, 60 North 2nd Avenue, which was in use from 1911 to 1955 and handled students in grades one through eight. Next to that is the *Glick-Sower House*, 201 East State Street, which was built in 1859 and is decorated with furnishings from the mid-1950s. Tours of the home and school are arranged by contacting the Marshall County Historical Museum.

Return to your car and drive west on State Street, which is one block north of Main. At North 9th Street, turn right (north) and go two blocks to Summit Avenue. Turn left (west). On the right, you'll pass the well-kept grounds of the *Iowa Veterans Home*, (641) 752-1502, which has cared for and memorialized Iowa's veterans of conflicts from the Civil War to those of the present day.

Continue west on Summit as it leaves the city limits, then angles to the northwest and west; follow it to State Highway 330, about 4 miles beyond the edge of town. Turn right (north) onto 330 and go about 1.5 miles. Here, you can make a stop at *Turners Grove County Park*, (641) 754-6303, which straddles the Iowa River, which you will encounter several other times on this tour.

Iowa's Tarheels

So many of Union's earliest residents were Quakers who came from North Carolina that the town's annual celebration is called Tarheel Days in their honor.

Continue north on Highway 330 through Albion until the road turns to the east just north of town. Turn left (west) on County Road S75, which then swings north after a short distance. Drive for about 4 miles to Liscomb, then continue for 2 more miles to County Road D67. Turn left (west) and follow the road as it stair-steps to the north and west for about 5 miles to Union, following and crossing the Iowa River.

Quick Trip Option 1: As you travel on D67, you will come to where the road turns west toward Union, but if you keep going straight north, you will meet County Road D65. Just a quarter mile up this road is *Daisy Long Memorial County Park*, (641) 648-4361. Astride the Iowa River, this small but pretty park has primi-

tive camping as well as 40 campsites with electricity, fishing, and picnic facilities. Also on the grounds are the remains of the area's first water-powered gristmill, built in 1856.

At Union, turn right (north) onto County Road S62.

Drive 9 miles north from Union on County Road S62 to Eldora, where the road becomes Washington Street. A picturesque community with a pretty town square, Eldora is a good spot to begin exploring the *Iowa River Greenbelt*, a series of wetlands, woods, and cliffs that line the Iowa River, creating a stark but pleasant departure from the farmlands that occupy most of this part of the state.

On the south side of town is the *Hardin County Historical House*, 1603 Washington, (641) 858-5173/939-5173, donation. A very fancy and ornate Victorian home built in 1892 for a rich widow, the house is the jewel in the crown of the *Hardin County Historical Society*, and items from across the county are displayed here. Nearby is a two-story carriage house.

Continue north on Washington through the center of Eldora and almost a mile outside of town to the *Hardin County Farm Museum*. The facility, 207 Washington Street, (641) 858-3946, donation, was created around some restored existing buildings, including a round-roofed dairy barn; the museum has since added the one-room Goose Creek Schoolhouse. The museum also has a variety of farm equipment that was used before electricity, gas, and diesel fuels powered everything, such as hand-carried corn pickers, potato planters, a self-propelled combine, cream separators, a threshing machine, and a horse-drawn sleigh and mower. Two machine sheds house the large items while the smaller artifacts and household goods are in the other buildings.

Return to town and turn left (east) at Edgington Avenue near the 1892 *Hardin County Courthouse*. In a departure from how Justice is often depicted—standing while holding her scales—here a statue of her sits in an alcove midway up the tall clock tower. Blindfolded as usual, she still holds her scale while statues of Mercy and Liberty attend to her. Also at the intersection is the *Ahoy Fountain*, 1266 Edgington Ave-nue, (641) 858-5881, which, as you might guess, has a soda fountain and some old-time Coca-Cola memorabilia.

As you pass through the town's east end, watch for the *Eldora Welcome Center and Railroad Museum* on the left (north) side of the road in Deer Park, (641) 939-2393/5137. Located in the depot that once stood in Osawa, the center has a collection of railroad artifacts and memorabilia and is open Saturday and Sunday afternoons, Memorial Day through September. Near the center are a caboose, a wildflower garden, a petting zoo with llamas and goats, and the trailhead of a paved hike-bike trail that runs to Pine Lake State Park just outside of town.

By the way, if you wonder why you are being directed to a welcome center upon leaving town, remember that Eldora is not so big that you can't go back and easily visit a place that you missed.

Continue east on Edgington, which is also State Highway 175, for a short distance to County Road S56; turn left and head toward the town of Steamboat Rock, about 4 miles to the north. Along the way, you'll quickly come to *Pine Lake State Park*, a pleasant and pretty 585-acre park that is a stunning departure from the plains of central Iowa. Here, in two beautiful tree-lined lakes, anglers find bass, crappie, northern, and catfish while others enjoy 10 miles of trails, a beach, boat rentals, 128 campsites (75 with electricity), picnic facilities, and the Iowa River, which runs near it all. Along with these amenities is a nine-hole golf course that many say is the most beautiful in the state. Also in the park and overlooking the Iowa River are four sandstone-and-timber cabins built in the 1930s; recently remodeled, they can be used year-round. To reserve the cabins, contact *Twin Lakes Bait Shop*, 23204 County Road S56, (641) 858-2084. Also, Pine Lake is linked with George Wyth Memorial Park, 50 miles away in Cedar Falls and Waterloo, by the *Lake-to-Lake State Park Bike Route* that follows the valley of the Iowa River.

Go a short distance farther north on S56. You'll soon arrive at *Rock 'n' Row Adventures*, an outfitter, (641) 858-5516, that can arrange float trips down the Iowa River in 36- and 48-inch-diameter tubes. Covering either four or eight miles (the latter takes about three to four hours), the journeys usually begin below the dam at Steamboat Rock, a couple miles north of the park on S56. *Rock 'n' Row* has recently added kayaks to its equipment and has a miniature golf course for its guests to use where they leave the river.

As you approach Steamboat Rock, watch for the arrow sign directing you to *Tower Rock Park*, (641) 648-4361, on the left (west), and enter there. A pleasant winding road rolls along the edge of a field; unfortunately the drive is spoiled by the presence of large discarded appliances in the nearby woods. Hold on though because the payoff is at the end of the drive, which goes down a slope to parking areas next to a beautiful curve in the Iowa River. Downstream, the namesake of the park, Tower Rock, looms large above the river, quite a sight in this part of Iowa. Other rocky formations, all heavily

Tower Rock looms above the Iowa River at Tower Rock Park south of the town of Steamboat Rock.

laden with trees, are nearby, and it's no wonder that nearby Steamboat Rock was once named Lithopolis, Greek for rock city. However, a few years after living in the area, some early residents began looking at the rocks and decided one in particular resembled the pilothouse of a steamboat, and the town's name was changed to Steamboat Rock in 1870. Sadly, lightning hit a tree growing in that rock and blew the rock to pieces in 1885, leaving us only to imagine what it must have looked like.

A footpath leading from the west parking area leads into adjacent *Fallen Rock State Preserve*, (641) 648-4361, which has more bluffs, woods, and rocky outcroppings.

Return to S56 and drive into Steamboat Rock. Go one block past Main Street and turn left (west) on Market Street. Three blocks down is the large city school—well, it was a school. Now it's *Steamboat Emporium*, 306 Market Street, (641) 920-7060. On the first floor are the Schoolhouse Café, a western wear store, and a consignment shop. On the main level are a tearoom and several antiques shops, while on the uppermost floor are more stores, including a Christmas shop, another store featuring original jewelry, and a bookstore. The *Iowa River Greenbelt Art Gallery* is there too, featuring the works of regional artists; two in particular, Colleen Carson and Shirley Shirley (that's not a misprint, that's her real name), are doing exceptional work.

If you wish to camp or visit another riverside park, continue west on Market Street until its end, where you must turn left (south); at Main Street, turn right (west), cross the Iowa River and immediately turn into *Pine Ridge County Park*, (641) 648-4361. The park has some primitive campsites along with 40 equipped with electricity and picnic facilities.

Local Author

Born in Grundy County in 1861, Herbert Quick was a well-known early-twentieth-century author. Crippled as a youngster by polio, he took to reading lots of books and became an educator soon after finishing school. In 1889 he became a lawyer and moved to Sioux City to practice there and also served a two-year term as that city's mayor. In 1916 Quick moved to Washington, D.C., for three years and then served with the Red Cross in Russia for a while. During all this time he had been interested in writing and in 1901 had published his first book, a collection of fairy tales. He was also writing various articles in magazines and in 1905 abandoned his law practice after publication of his first successful novel. Among his 18 books was a trilogy that made him famous: *Vandemark's Folly, The Hawkeye,* and *The Invisible Woman*. He was working on another novel and his autobiography when he died in 1925. Some literary critics regarded Quick as a mediocre writer, but his eye for detail, developed as a journalist, won praise from historians. He was lauded for his keen portrayal of the early days of Iowa's settlers, especially in *Vandemark's Folly*.

Return to Main Street and head east out of town, where the road becomes County Road D35. Follow that for 13 miles to Holland. Just past Holland, turn right (south) on County Road T37. Go 2 miles to State Highway 14/175 on the west side of Grundy Center and turn left (east) to enter the town on G Avenue. In Orion Park, which is between 14th and 13th Streets, is the small, white-frame *Herbert Quick Schoolhouse*, (319) 824-3838, free. Named for the author of books about the early days among Iowa's settlers, this one-room school is furnished with chairs, desks, maps, and books from years ago, and has mementos related to Quick.

Continue east on G Avenue as it passes through Grundy Center. Along the way, you will pass the Grundy County Courthouse with its tall clock tower. If you turn left on 7th Street on the east side of the courthouse square and proceed one block to the north, you will come to the *Center Theater*, 602 7th Street, (319) 824-6571. Run by members of the community, the Center shows first-run movies for 99 cents.

About 3 miles past Grundy Center on State Highway 175, turn right at County Road T47, also called J Avenue, and take that 12 miles south to Gladbrook. On the town's east side, turn right onto Front Street, which runs sharply to the northwest. Go three blocks and turn left (west) at 2nd Street. In a very nice building that houses the local tourist center is a restored theater and *Matchstick Marvels*, 319 2nd Street, (641) 473-2410, admission. Without resorting to puns, it's safe to say that few places have creations like those found here, made of millions of matchsticks. In the 1970s, when he was in his twenties, Pat Acton began using sandpaper, glue, and a razor blade to create models out of matches. At first he made a simple country church and then advanced to more intricate structures. He began using so many matchsticks that he ordered them in bulk from a manufacturer but without their sulfur coatings so he would not have to spend time cutting them off. Acton has created matchstick versions of cathedrals, aircraft, aircraft carriers, side-wheel riverboats, sailing ships, steam locomotives, and more. If, before you visit here, you think these are small models, think again. A World War II U.S. Navy fighter is almost as big as Acton, and a 12-foot-long model of the U.S. Capitol required 500,000 matchsticks. Acton's creations are also displayed in Ripley's Believe It or Not museums in several countries.

From 2nd Street, turn south on Gould Street and go six blocks south to State Highway 96; turn left (east). Drive 7 miles to U.S. Highway 63, turn right (south) and proceed to Toledo, 13 miles away. Upon entering town, turn left (east) onto West High Street and drive a couple of blocks. You'll come upon the *Tama County Courthouse* on your left (north), which has a five-story-high tower with four clock faces. You might not believe this, but the courthouse, built in the Richardsonian style in 1892, was built around an earlier, two-story one designed as brick Italianate building.

Enjoy the downtown with its old-fashioned stoplights just beyond the courthouse. A block north of West High Street, on North Broadway Street, is the *Tama County Historical Museum*, 200 North Broadway, (641) 484-4767, free, where Native American and pioneer artifacts are shown in the former jail along with a nineteenth-century Bohemian cabin. South on South Broadway is

Hotel Toledo, 114 South Broadway, (641) 484-2808, a fine old structure that dates back to the days of early cross-country travel.

Drive south on Broadway until you meet U.S. Highway 30 in about 1 mile and turn left (southeast). Less than 2 miles away, in neighboring Tama, you will see a small, tri-angular park on your right (south) as the highway turns to go east. Turn into the park and, after a very short distance, make another right turn (west) onto 5th Street. Drive *very slowly* for a good look at something. You're about to cross one of the few remaining original bridges of the Lincoln Highway. Built in 1915 like many other concrete bridges on the first transcontinental highway, this one is unique because its three-foot-high concrete railings spell out the words "Lincoln Highway."

Quick Trip Option 2: From the Toledo-Tama area, head west on U.S. 30 for 4 miles to the *Meskwaki Bingo Casino Hotel*, 1504 305th Street, (641) 484-2108 and (800) 728-GAME. With traditional and video slot machines, the casino has table games, bingo, a 24-hour buffet, and live entertainment.

Drive about a half mile west of the bridge on East 5th Street and turn right (north) at State Street, which is also U.S. Highway 63. Follow Highway 63 as it turns left (west) onto West 13th Street. When Highway 63 turns north again three blocks later, keep going straight west on West 13th Street, which then becomes County Road E49, for 7 miles to Montour. The road is part of the *Iowa River Valley Scenic Byway.* Crossing the Iowa River west of town, E66 stays in the river valley and skirts past the south side of the *Meskwaki Settlement.*

Just before entering Montour, turn left (south) onto County Road T47 and proceed for 7 miles to County Road E69. Turn right and go west 1 mile to State Highway 146; turn left (south) and drive to Grinnell, 12 miles away. Named by several publications as being among the hundred best places to live in the United States, Grinnell has also gathered attention because of its many well-kept homes built in a variety of architectural styles, including Victorian, Greek Revival, Gothic Revival, Georgian, and Prairie School. It's also the home of *Grinnell College*, a liberal arts college rated as the best all-around college in the country by Kaplan/Newsweek's annual "How to Get into College" guide.

On the campus, which is just northeast of downtown, is the *Faulconer Gallery*, in the Bucksbaum Center for the Arts, (641) 269-4660, free, which gets high marks for its permanent collection and traveling exhibits; one show

The Meskwaki

Originally from the region around the Saint Lawrence River, the Meskwaki were called Renards, or Fox, by the French who first came upon them, soon became their enemies, and forced the Meskwaki to move into Michigan and then Wisconsin. During his army's conflict with the Meskwaki, one French king issued a proclamation for his troops to completely eliminate them. In 1733, to avoid reprisals by French authorities for the killing of an officer who was foolhardy enough to ride into one of their villages, the Meskwaki and their Sauk friends headed east, crossing the Mississippi into what is now Iowa. Behind them came a punitive force of 84 French soldiers and about 200 of their Indian allies. In March, 1735, the avengers finally found the Meskwaki and Sauk near present-day Des Moines and attacked. However, the French force was outnumbered and nearly surrounded—and a farce ensued. The French asked the Meskwaki and Sauk if they had been punished enough. The Meskwaki and Sauk, no doubt surprised since they held the upper hand, said yes and the battle was over. The French-led force left Iowa but the Meskwaki and Sauk stayed, settling over much of the state.

In 1845, the American government removed most of the Meskwaki and Sauk to Kansas, but about 250, yearning for their Iowa lands, returned in the 1850s to buy 80 acres of land between the Tama-Toledo area and Le Grand. Although the land was sold to them at twice the going rate, the Meskwaki and Sauk paid the price so they could once more be in Iowa. Over the years, the Meskwaki (which means "red earth people") and Sauk have been thought of as one people, but they've retained their separate identities. Now more than 700 live on the 3,300-acre Meskwaki Settlement, which is not a reservation. Each August, residents of the Meskwaki Settlement hold a colorful powwow that is open to all.

arranged by the gallery earned Iowa's Tourism and the Arts Award in 2000. Among the works are historical and contemporary paintings, sculptures, photographs, multi-media shows, and more. The gallery is open daily most of the year except for school breaks and major holidays.

At 4th Avenue in Grinnell, turn left (east) and go two blocks. On the left is *Cunningham's Drug*, 827 4th Avenue, (641) 236-3151, a pharmacy that's well known for its soda fountain, which attracts lots of high school and Grinnell students, townsfolk, and visitors from out of town. If you want a good Green River, here's where it is. Ditto with the cherry cokes, malts, and other treats.

At the end of the block is the *Merchants National Bank*, 833 4th Avenue. Now housing the *Grinnell Chamber of Commerce*, (641) 236-6555, a foundation, and another business, this building is one of the jewel box banks designed by famed architect Louis Sullivan in the early twentieth century and it's definitely worth a look inside and out. A small city park is kitty-corner southeast of the bank.

Go north two blocks to 6th Street (also U.S. Highway 6) and turn left (west). Drive about 4 miles out of town, turn left (south) onto County Road T38, and follow it across I-80 to Lynnville, 9 miles away. As you

Evening light falls softly on the Wagaman Mill, which is now a museum in Lynnville.

approach town and cross the North Skunk River, look to your right and get a view of the mill that we'll be visiting shortly.

On the south side of the North Skunk, turn right on East Street and proceed to *Wagaman Mill*, (641) 792-9780, admission. Built in 1848 as a gristmill by John Sparks, the mill was used by different owners for various purposes. In 1925, it began generating electricity at the rate of 15,000 kilowatt-hours per month. A water turbine that was used for 80 years is displayed, along with gears, wheels, grain-cracking equipment, and other items used here over the years.

From the mill, head south a few blocks to 1st Street and turn right (west) onto what is also County Road F62. Take that for 10 miles to the intersection with County Road T14. Remain on F62 for 4 miles as it turns north, then west again as it rolls through Reasnor. Continue on F62 for about 4 more miles to State Highway 14. Turn right (north) and head to Newton, about 8 miles away.

In Newton, turn left (west) at South 12 Avenue West—that's the first stoplight north of I-80—and wind your way down to the *International Wrestling Institute and Museum*, I-80 at Exit 164, (641) 791-1517, admission. Created mainly by journalist and former wrestler Mike Chapman, the museum covers the history of wrestling from its mention in the Bible to today's amateur collegiate and Olympian athletes, without overlooking those who wrestled as professionals prior to today's showy productions. Here you'll find photographs, wrestling gear, Iowan Dan Gable's Olympic gold medal, and a scaled-down wrestling ring that anyone can enter, as well as the Glen Brand Wrestling Hall of Fame. A special display discusses the wrestling history of Iowan Frank Gotch, and others such as Verne Gagne, Lou Thesz, and Cael Sanderson are honored too.

Return to the stoplight at Highway 14, cross that highway, and go east on South 12th Avenue West. Watch for the sign at West 8th Street South that comes up fast pointing the way to the *Jasper County Historical Museum*, 1700 South 15th Avenue West, (641) 792-9118, admission, a short distance away. The museum's rooms are individually designed to show facets of Newton's history, including a 1930s home and a country store. Other areas have tools used by settlers, displays about quilts and sewing, and information about the region's coal mining. And then there is an exhibit about the companies that have made washing machines here . . . of which one has clearly emerged as among the largest appliance manufacturers in the world, Maytag Corporation. In the exhibit are washers made from about 1900 to the present, including Maytag's first round porcelain tub washer and its last wringer washer, made in 1983.

Quick Trip Option 3: If you're around Newton on a nice summer evening, you're in luck because *Valle Drive-In Theater*, (641) 792-3558, admission, is just west of town on County Road F48, which starts out as First Avenue West. It's one of three drive-ins left in Iowa—the others are at Maquoketa and Council Bluffs.

Return west to Highway 14, turn right (north), drive less than 1 mile along the west edge of Newton to 1st Avenue West. Turn right there and go about 1 mile to the east. At West 4th Street North, turn to the left (north). A few blocks up the street is the headquarters of the *Maytag Corporation*, 403 West 4th Street North, (641) 792-7000, where you can visit the Maytag Store. No, you can't buy washers, dryers, and other appliances here, but you can see models of those made over the years by the company. However, you can purchase promotional items, so if you have wanted shirts, hats, jackets, and such with the Maytag name on them, here you go.

The company began in 1893 when Frederick Maytag partnered with three others to form a farm implement company. Within nine years, it was the nation's largest feeder manufacturer and was making other machinery, including, for a while, tractors and two types of cars. In an effort to utilize workers when they weren't making farm equipment, Maytag began making clothes washers in 1907. Four years later electric motors were added to the washers, and by 1922 they were selling so well that Maytag quit making farm equipment.

Maytag also made Maytag Toy Racers, small cars powered by the same motors that powered some washers. Between 1934 and 1941, 498 of these one- and two-cylinder engine vehicles were made; about 35 are known to exist now, making them some of the rarest collectibles around today.

In World War II, the company made parts for military aircraft, including the B-17, B-29, and P-51. After the war, Maytag resumed making washing machines although it helped make Army tanks during the Korean War. In 1953, Maytag began manufacturing clothes dryers too.

With more than 29,000 people employed in plants across the world, Maytag now manufactures numerous useful items, including clothes washers and dryers, dish washers, vacuum cleaners, stoves, ovens, refrigerators, coin changers, and soft drink vending machines.

The company has the distinction of having the nation's first corporate airplane, the *Smilin' Thru,* which was based at the Newton airport. Plans are under way to develop a small aviation museum there.

Return to 1st Avenue West and turn left (east). In a couple of blocks is the *Newton Convention and Visitor Bureau*, 113 1st Avenue West, (641) 792-0299 and (800) 798-0299, which is just south of the Jasper County Courthouse. Visit the bureau and see what else you can learn about Newton and the area.

A couple of blocks to the east is a type of restaurant not usually found in Iowa, the *Gaucho Café*, 207 1st Avenue East, (641) 792-1411, which serves Argentinean food as well as American favorites. A bit further down the road is another dining experience, *La Corsett Maison Inn*, 629 1st Avenue East, (641) 792-6833, a mission-style, four-and-a-half-star restaurant that serves six-course meals and also operates as a bed and breakfast.

Continue east on 1st Avenue East to East 31st Street North and turn to the left (north). Here, you'll want to take in the *Newton Arboretum and Botanical Center*, 3000 North 4th Avenue East, (641) 791-3021, free. Trees, bushes, grasses, and flowers that are native to Iowa or have been brought from elsewhere are found throughout the grounds. A paved half-mile trail leads through the gardens and connects to the trail system that is expanding within and around the city.

Continue north on East 31st Street North and follow it around the curve to the left (west) at North 19th Avenue East, which is also Beltline Road. Take that west to East 8th Street North, turn right (north), and go less than 2 miles. You'll arrive at *Maytag Dairy Farms*, 2282 East 8th Street North, (641) 792-1133, free, where you can see the famous Maytag Blue Cheese being made. Fritz Maytag, son of Frederick Maytag, heard that researchers at Iowa State University were exploring new ways to make blue cheese in the 1930s, and in 1941 he began operations here with Holsteins owned by the Maytag family; the rest, as is said, is history. Visits include a short video and cheese tasting.

Return south to North 19th Avenue East, go west about three quarters of a mile to West 4th Street North, turn right (north) and proceed about a half mile to the junction with State Highway 14. Follow Highway 14 north, east, then north again for about 17 miles to Laurel. Continue for another 4 miles to County Road E63; turn left (west) and cruise to Oaks Avenue just north of Haverhill. Turn left (south). At the south end of this tiny town is the *Matthew Edel Blacksmith Shop*, 214 First Street, (641) 752-6664 and 475-3299, free. Now a state historic site, this shop was started by German immigrant Matthew Edel in 1883 and looks pretty much as it did when he worked there up to his death in 1940. That's because his son, Louis, closed the doors then and left everything pretty much intact. Besides housing the forge, the building also was the home of the Edel family until a house was built nearby in the 1890s. Along with doing the usual chores of a blacksmith, Edel invented tools to use around the farm and garden and made decorative iron cemetery markers, which can be seen in the shop and the graveyard just east of Immaculate Conception Church in town.

Quick Trip Option 4: This one is for golfers. As you drive north of Newton on State Highway 14, at the point about 5 miles north of town where the road turns right (east), turn left (west) instead onto County Road F17. Take that for about 13 miles to State Highway 330, the main four-lane thoroughfare between Des Moines and Marshalltown, about 12 miles away. At Highway 330, turn right (northeast). You may notice that you enter Story County and then, about 100 yards later, Marshall County. The simple explanation is that 330 cuts diagonally across the counties, and you just nicked the very southeast corner of Story County.

About 5.7 miles after leaving F17, you'll come to the turnoff to *The Harvester Golf Club*, 1102 330th Street, (877) 963-GOLF, on the right (east) side of the highway. Called one of the nation's top ten new golf courses in 2001, this public 18-hole layout was rated as the number-one public golf course in the state by Golf Digest in 2003. The course measures 7,340 yards from the back tees and, surprisingly for the middle of Iowa, varies in elevation by 110 feet. Designed by Keith Foster, the course has a clubhouse, the *View Restaurant* (reservations required), and a pro shop.

To return to the rest of the tour, continue up Highway 330 for 6.5 miles to 285th Street, where you turn right (east) and enter Melbourne a moment later on 2nd Street. Upon meeting Main Street, turn right and go 2 blocks south to 4th Street, where you will turn left (east). Go four blocks to Hart Avenue, also called County Road S62, and go a few hundred yards south to County Road E63. Turn left (east) and proceed about 7 miles to the Matthew Edel Blacksmith Shop just north of Haverhill.

From Haverhill, return to County Road 63, turn right, and proceed back to Highway 14. Turn left (north) and drive about 4 miles toward Marshalltown. However, don't think you're finished with this tour yet. There are still places to see.

At U.S. Highway 30 on the south edge of Marshalltown, turn right (east) and drive less than 3 miles to Shady Oaks Road. Turn left (north). In a few seconds you'll see something that will put any tree house you have ever seen previously to shame (perhaps a few regular homes too)—*The Big Treehouse*, at the *Shady Oaks Campground*, 2370 Shady Oaks Road, (641) 752-2946, free tours. Now with 12 levels, this 55-foot-tall, 5,000-square-foot tree house that began as a hobby in 1983 has spiral stairs, viewing platforms with picnic tables, 14 porch swings, a sound system, a refrigerator, a microwave oven, and running water, all in a towering, shady silver maple topped by a bell. Visiting the tree house is by appointment.

The site of Shady Oaks Campground has long been used by travelers. In 1848, its grove of bur oaks alongside Brush Creek was a stop on a stagecoach line between Marengo and Fort Dodge. Later, it was a cabin camp on the Lincoln Highway that ran up Shady Oaks Road; some of the buildings from that era, including an original cabin, have been restored. Presently the campground has 13 full-service sites, 2 more with only electricity, and some primitive tent sites.

Go back to Highway 30 and drive west about 5.5 miles to Exit 182, Highland Acres Road, passing Highway 14 on the way; turn right (north) onto Highland Acres Road. After less than 1 mile, turn left onto 223rd Street. Just as 223rd Street finishes arching to the west and begins to turn south, you'll find *Grimes Farm Nature Center*, 2359 223rd Street, (641) 753-6303, free. Bordering a creek, this 160-acre preserve encompasses woods, wetlands, prairie, and prairie potholes. Trails and boardwalks wander through the grounds, and an interpretative center built in 2003 educates the visitor about the biological forces at play in this part of Iowa.

Quick Trip Option 5: About 13 miles west of Marshalltown on Highway 30 is State Center, a town that calls itself the Rose Capital of Iowa. When you get there, turn right (north) at 6th

Avenue SE and then turn left (east) onto 3rd Street SE. In moments you will find *State Center Rose Garden*, (641) 483-2559, free, which is also lit from 8 to 11 in the evening.

From the gardens, go to 1st Avenue South and turn north. In a couple blocks is *Watson's Grocery Store*, 106 West Main Street, (641) 483-2110. Built in 1895, the store looks pretty much as it did years ago with all sorts of dry goods and groceries on its shelves and in its oak cabinets.

From 223rd Street, return to Highland Acres Road, turn right (south), and go back to Highway 30. Turn left (east) and return to Highway 14, where you began this tour.

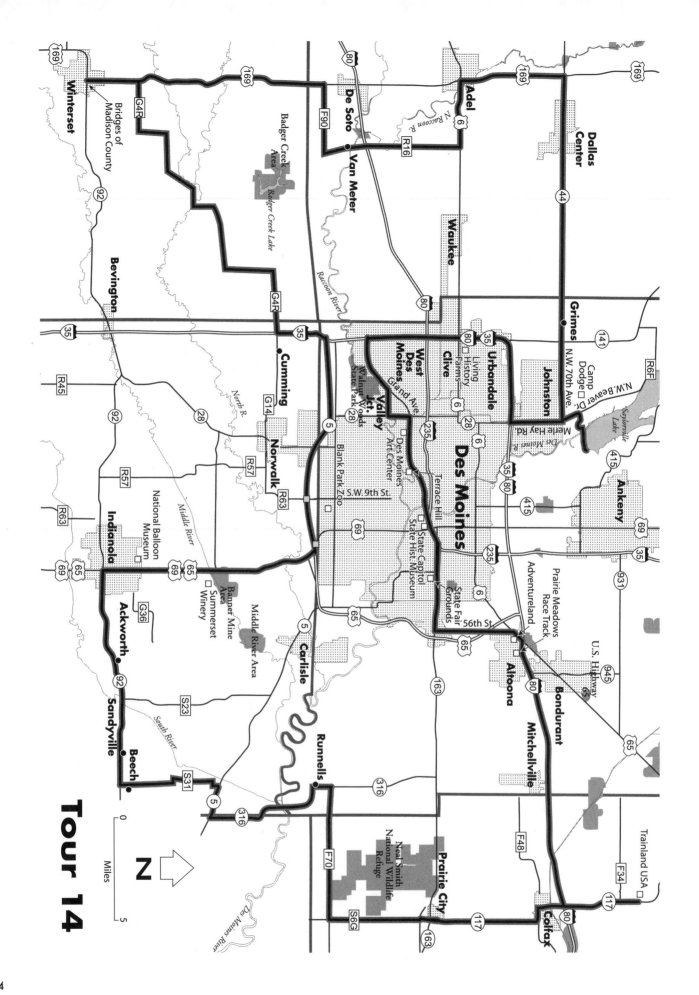

Tour 14

N

Miles
0
5

Tour 14
A Capital Time: In, Through, and Around Des Moines

Altoona—Des Moines—West Des Moines—Saylorville Lake—Adel—Van Meter—Winterset—Indianola—Colfax—Altoona

Distance: approximately 182 miles

Here's a tour that takes you through the state's capital city as well as around it. Along the way, you can ride roller coasters, walk inside the dome of the Iowa Capitol, see flowers blossoming in a botanical center anytime of the year, boat on one of Iowa's largest lakes, walk through the covered bridges made famous by a movie and a book, learn about hot air balloons that lumber across the sky like colorful giants, and meet the brown, shaggy giants of the great plains, the American bison, at a national wildlife refuge.

You'll start this adventure at the junction of U.S. Highways 6 and 65 and I-80 (Exit 142) on the far east side of the Des Moines metro area in Altoona. You will immediately run into Iowa's largest theme park, *Adventureland*, (515) 266-2121 and (800) 532-1286, admission. This is where visitors are ejected into the sky on the Space Shot, have a choice of four roller coasters, each with a different thrill factor, stroll the midway, and enjoy about 100 rides in all. There's also live entertainment and it's very easy to spend a day here—many do!

Near to Adventureland is *Prairie Meadows Race Track and Casino*, (515) 967-1000 and (800) 325-9015, where visitors can bet on the quarter horse and thoroughbred races and take their chances with 1,500 slot machines. Concessions, a restaurant, and a cocktail lounge are on the premises.

Head southwest down Highway 6 a short distance to NE 56th Street; turn left (south). Go a little more than 3 miles to University Avenue. Turn right (west) and proceed for about two blocks. This is the location of *White Water University*, 5401 East University, (515) 265-4904, admission, a swell place to cool off on warm days. The aquatic park has four water slides, a wave pool, tube runs, a children's play area, and a three-foot-deep lazy river. On land the park has a miniature golf course and the state's only twin-engine-powered go-carts.

Go west on University Avenue for about 3 miles. If you're around here in mid-August, there will be no question about when you are

Downtown Des Moines is situated on the west bank of the river bearing its name.

near the grounds of the *Iowa State Fair*, East 30th Street and East University Avenue, (515) 262-3111 and (800) 545-FAIR, admission. Considered the epitome of state fairs everywhere, the Iowa State Fair has been immortalized in books, films, and on stage. As the state's largest event—it has an 11-day run—the fair draws almost a million visitors every year to its livestock shows, grandstand shows where big-name entertainers perform, dances, colorful 10-acre midway, rides, and more.

Continue west on East University for about 1.5 miles to Interstate 235, turn onto it going south, and go to the second exit, at East 6th Street. Drive south a very short distance to Grand Avenue and turn left (east). This is the best way to approach the *State Capitol*, East 9th Street and Grand Avenue, (515) 281-5591, free, which is perched atop a hill. The main dome is 275 feet high and was regilded in the late 1990s with 100 ounces of gold leaf at a cost of $400,000. The four lesser domes are made of copper and trimmed with gold. Built in 1886, the building is open to the public. On the main floor are the offices of the governor and lieutenant governor, the chambers of the State Supreme Court, and historical displays. The House of Representatives and Senate are on the second floor, along with a beautiful law library that can be visited by anyone. At the center of the second floor, a staircase leads up to a balcony where you can get a good look around the inside of the massive dome. Visitors can tour on their own or take a free, hour-long guided tour (call for tour times).

Within walking distance is the *Iowa Historical Building*, 600 East Locust, (515) 281-5111, free, a modern complex where historic aircraft hang from the ceiling as you enter the galleries to see Native American artifacts, feel the tight confines of a coal mine, understand how horses helped Iowa's agriculture, and learn why so many insurance companies are in Iowa, as well as seeing a host of other displays. A gift shop and cafeteria are at the museum.

Court Avenue

One of metro Des Moines' special areas is *Court Avenue*, a collection of trendy restaurants, coffee shops, a brewpub, galleries, and specialty shops, all gathered around Court Avenue from about 2nd to 4th streets just east of the ornate Polk County Courthouse.

From the historical center, go west to East 6th Street, turn right (north) to get to the other side of I-235, and follow the signs that lead to the *Des Moines Botanical Center*, 909 East River Drive, (515) 323-8900, admission. On the east bank of the Des Moines River, the center's glass-and-steel, geodesic dome covers around 15,000 plants from tropical, semi-tropical, and desert climes. Displays change seasonally. A gift shop and café are on the premises. Outside are displays, including an herb garden and a portion of *Two Rivers Walk*. The walk connects with downtown, the Capitol, and Simon Estes Plaza, the scene of many outdoor concerts and performances overlooking downtown and the river. Along the east bank of the river, an Asian garden and the Chinese Cultural Center of America are scheduled to be built by about 2008. The garden, which will have a pond and a waterfall, will honor former Governor Robert Ray who led the state in welcoming thousands of Vietnamese to Iowa after the fall of South Vietnam.

Iowa Cubs

On the south side of downtown is *Sec Taylor Stadium*, 350 SW First Street, (515) 243-6111 and (800) GO-ICUBS. This is the home of the *Iowa Cubs*, a Triple-A farm team of the Chicago Cubs. The prices are reasonable, the seats have great views, and it's a good way to get close to professional baseball.

Return to Grand Avenue from the botanical center, turn right (west), and go through downtown Des Moines. After passing 19th Street and going a half mile, keep an eye out on the left (south) side for Forest Drive; turn onto it. Atop a hill lush with trees is *Terrace Hill*, 2300 Grand Avenue, (515) 281-3604, admission, the governor's residence. Built by a local banker in 1869 at a cost of $250,000, this high-Victorian home has ground floor rooms with 14-foot-high ceilings. Tours of the public rooms begin in the carriage house near Forest Drive.

Continuing west on Grand, turn left (south) at 42nd Street; then after a short distance turn left again (east) at the sign for *Salisbury House*, 4025 Tonawanda Drive, (515) 274-1777, admission. Although built in the 1920s, the house was designed to resemble King's House in Salisbury, England, which mixes a variety of English styles of architecture. Formerly the home of pharmaceutical and cosmetics king Carl Weeks, the 42-room mansion covers 22,500 square feet and contains rafters, paneling floors, and other interior elements that he collected from various sixteenth-century British structures. Because Weeks wanted his house to look a century old on the day construction was finished, his mason chose the sorriest-looking limestone he could find for the exterior.

Return to Grand Avenue and once more go west, this time for just a few blocks to the *Des Moines Art Center*. In addition to the works of art in its permanent collection and traveling exhibits, the center, 4700 Grand Avenue, (515) 277-4405, free, displays the architecture of three very distinguished architects, Eliel Saarinen, I. M. Pei, and Richard Meier, each of whom did a specific part of the complex. The center is also known for something else besides its art and architecture: the meals in its restaurant that have earned top ratings in local reviews; it's open for lunch daily and reservation-only dinners on Thursday evenings.

To the south of the center in Greenwood-Ashworth Park is the Science Center of Iowa, 4500 Grand Avenue, (515) 274-4138, admission. (At the time of this writing the center is still there although there are efforts to move it elsewhere.) The center is filled with all sorts of stations where all members of the family can participate in activities that reveal the world of science, including seeing your voice and watching the energy you create while riding a special bike. Once you tour the center, you'll understand that Bernoulli has nothing to do with Italian food.

Continue to go west on Grand for about 1 mile, where you leave Des Moines and enter West Des Moines. Here the numbered streets start all over again. Thus 63rd Street

in Des Moines is 1st Street in West Des Moines (some people just can't work together on numbering their streets . . . sigh). By the way, just to add to the confusion, it's also State Highway 28.

Whatever its name, turn left (south) onto 63rd or 1st Street or Highway 28 and go a little less than 1 mile to Elm Street; turn right (west). In four blocks, Elm brings you right into the center of *Valley Junction*. Once a mining town and then a railroad community, this area turned into a trendy shopping mecca a few decades ago featuring—are you ready for this?— clothing stores, a place that has every type of helium-filled balloon you can imagine, floral shops, an architect, interior designers, quilting supplies, stores selling homemade items ranging from crafts, lace, and candies to furniture, sculptures, and stained glass, purveyors of skateboarders' apparel, a stationery, a blacksmith, dressmakers, a jeweler, a gallery selling paintings and photographs by local and nationally-known artists, a place to get face peels, a dentist, salons, and a spa. Now, if you need to rest, catch up with friends, rebuild your energy, or just enjoy something tasty, refresh yourself with espresso, tea, Chinese food, scratch-made American dishes, icy treats at a soda fountain, or cheesecake from a place that makes 30 kinds. All of these businesses are within an easy walk of each other and lo-cated in a host of buildings that can be described as historic, quaint, charming, and fanciful.

After you're shopped out, go south for less than 1 mile on 5th Street to Railroad Avenue and turn right (west). Just past 14th Street, follow the curve that goes onto Fuller Road, to your left (south). This slants to the southwest and in a moment you will come upon *Jordan House*, 2001 Fuller Road, (515) 225-1286, admission. This pretty house, which is shaded by big trees, is the oldest structure in West Des Moines; it contains historical information not only about the region but also about the Underground Railroad, on which it served as a hideaway for runaway slaves.

Continue going southwest on Fuller Road for less than 1 mile until you meet Grand Avenue again. Turn left (south) and in about 3 miles you'll come to Interstate 35, where you will turn north. Drive for about 5 miles, past the big interchange with I-80 and I-235, to the exit at Hickman Road, which is also Highway 6. Turn right (east) and immediately turn left (north) to enter *Living History Farms*. Simply put, this facility, 2600 NW 111th Street, (515) 278-5286, admission, is one of the best places to visit in Iowa. After you park, you enter an *Iowa Welcome Center*, (515) 334-9625, free, and its gift shop. Within that same building is the entrance to the complex of

With historic buildings from across the state, Living History Farms in Urbandale has created the fictional late-nineteenth-century town of Walnut Hill.

farms, which starts off in the fictional town of *Walnut Hill*, a collection of authentic homes and businesses from across Iowa that resemble a small community. After that, you can walk or ride a tractor-drawn cart to the farms of the Ioway, early settlers, and early twentieth-century farmers. The farms show what life was like in rural Iowa many years ago (in other words, kids shouldn't expect anything electric at these places). A relatively new feature of the farms is its *100-Year Crop Walk*, which leads visitors through plots of land showing the evolution of farm land from stands of prairie to early corn varieties to today's hybrid crops, including biotech types, and various grasses used to feed livestock.

The *Wallace Center*, another exhibit building, contains displays that include a 1950s kitchen with foods made from scratch, a modern farm kitchen with ready-made foods, and today's computers that link farmers to all types of information used in farming. Another exhibit shows changes in farming practices and food preservation, along with the shift from growing food for individual consumption years ago to producing food for today's global markets.

Also, the farms' *Get a Grip* program allows visitors to don gloves and voluntarily work on dozens of chores such as churning butter, moving hay, grinding wheat, and, if you're up to this, building an outhouse.

If you're in Des Moines between mid-November and the end of March, for a meal to remember, reserve a seat at the farm's *1900 Farm Traditional Dinner*, which includes horse-drawn transportation from a parking area to a farmhouse where everything is cooked on a wood-burning stove and watching calories and cholesterol levels is banned. The menus cover roast beef, chicken, real mashed potatoes, homemade jellies, jams, and breads as well as fruit pies

Camp Dodge

Created in 1910, Camp Dodge served as a training base during World War I and at one time as many as 28,000 soldiers were stationed here. In World War II, the camp served as an induction center for the military. Nowadays, national guard soldiers train at the post, which has more than 2,000 acres set aside for maneuvers. The post also has the Maintenance and Equipment Maintenance Center where soldiers from guard, reserve, and active units across the nation are trained in state-of-the-art maintenance facilities. Law enforcement officers from across Iowa also train at the post's Law Enforcement Academy.

and cake. Most visitors leave with a slight waddle to their walk.

Return to I-35/80 and head north, then east, for about 8 miles to Exit 131 at Merle Hay Road. Turn left and go north about 3 miles. Take the overpass over NW 70th Avenue and continue to NW Beaver Drive, where you turn left (northwest). Very shortly, you'll pass a large building on your right. That's the *State Area Command*, which houses

Iowa's Biggest Dip

The biggest swimming pool in Iowa is located just north of the museum in Camp Dodge. Built in 1927 and larger than a football field, the pool was where Ronald Reagan served as a lifeguard while living in Des Moines. A historical landmark, the pool is presently closed until matters can be decided about its upkeep and operation.

the headquarters of Iowa's National Guard and seven guard units and serves as an emergency command post for the state.

Proceed for less than 1 mile on NW Beaver to NW 78th Avenue. Turn right (east). This brings you to *Saylorville Lake*, where the grounds on its south end are administered by the U.S. Army Corps of Engineers, which created this 6,000-acre lake on the Des Moines River years ago. A visitor center, 5600 NW 78th Avenue, (515) 964-0672, free, on the east end of the dam can orient you about what's going on at the lake; nearby are campgrounds, a beach, and other facilities managed by the corps.

More camping and recreational areas are further north on both sides of the lake. Lewis A. Jester County Park, 11407 NW 118th Avenue, (515) 323-5300, camping fee, is on the lake's west side; and *Big Creek Recreation Area*, State Highway 415, (515) 964-6473, camping fee, is on the east. Near the latter is *Big Creek Marina and Boat Rental*, Highway 415, (515) 984-6083, which rents houseboats, sailboats, kayaks, canoes, water bikes, and paddleboats. The marina also provides sailing lessons.

Return to NW Beaver and proceed south-

east back to Merle Hay Road. Along the way you will see military tanks, artillery pieces, and an A-7 attack aircraft in a small park atop a rise that overlooks Camp Dodge, the main training area of the Iowa National Guard. A nearby entrance is closed to the general public now but see the directions below for another way into the post to see the museum there.

Go south on Merle Hay a very short distance, then keep to the right at the first exit, which leads to NW 70th Avenue. Turn right (west) and go a little more than a half mile to the main entrance to *Camp Dodge*. At the security gate, be prepared to show a photo ID and tell the guards you would like to visit the *Iowa Gold Star Museum*, (515) 252-4531. If things are normal, which they are most of the time, you will be permitted to enter. Although the guards can also provide directions, the museum is fairly easy to identify as you get close to it—not many other buildings here have a number of artillery pieces, tanks, and aircraft arrayed around them. Inside the building, displays describe the exploits of Iowans who have served in the military as well as in the Iowa State Patrol.

Return to NW 70th Avenue, head west for about 3 miles, and cross State Highway 141. Continue west on what is now State Highway 44 and go about 9 miles to U.S. Highway 169. Turn left (south) and drive to Adel, 5 miles away. Once you're in town, turn right (west) at Court Avenue, one leg of the courthouse square, which has streets paved with bricks. Don't start oohing and aahing at the courthouse yet . . . you're only on the backside! Wait until you're on the south side of the square and get the full view of the front facade of this magnificent, three-story, white, French chateau-style building. Built in 1902, it's topped with red turrets and red, peaked roofs and is one of the prettier courthouses not only in Iowa but also in the nation.

The Raccoon River Valley Trail, a hike-bike path that runs between the west edges of the Des Moines metro area and Jefferson, passes through Adel just south of the courthouse square.

Return to Highway 169, called 8th Street here, and go south a few blocks to U.S. Highway 6. Turn left, go east for about 3 miles to County Road R16, and turn right (south). Drive for about 5 miles to Van Meter, crossing I-80 along the way. Upon entering this small community, you'll come quickly to the *Bob Feller Hometown Exhibit*, 310 Mill Street, (515) 996-2806, admission. Dedicated to Baseball Hall of Fame member Bob Feller, who grew up and started his pitching career here, the museum recounts the story of his long career with the Cleveland Indians through displays of his trophies, photos, uniforms, and more. Occasionally Feller comes from his Ohio home to greet visitors here.

Continue south on R16 from Van Meter for 1 mile to County Road F90. Turn right (west) and in a little more than 3 miles you will come upon Highway 169 again. Turn left (south).

Quick Trip Option 1: At Highway 169, turn right (north). Less than 2 miles away and just north of I-80 is the *Aircraft Super-Market*, 10 Ellefson Drive, (515) 834-2225. Here's where you can have a 15-minute-long mini-lesson in flying ultralight aircraft; the price in 2003 was $45 and the flight instructor can take you over the valleys of the North and South Raccoon rivers.

Take Highway 169 south for 13 miles to Winterset. For years the main thing that people knew about Winterset is that it was the childhood home of Marion Morrison—at least that's what he was called as a youngster. When his pharmacist father moved the family to California a few years after Marion was born in 1907, the boy played football, and caught the eye of a filmmaker. From then on he was known as John Wayne, who went on to create a legendary figure in western films and earn an Oscar as a crusty old sheriff in the movie *True Grit.* Now, the *John Wayne Birthplace*, 216 South 2nd Street, (515) 462-1044, admission, is set up the way it looked when the Morrisons lived there. There's also plenty of memorabilia from John Wayne's adulthood around, including the eye patch he wore in *True Grit,* his hat from *Rio Lobo,* and rare photos of his friends, including Jimmy Stewart, Kirk Douglas, and Ronald Reagan.

Along with the Wayne home, Winterset has long been the focal point for anyone interested in visiting a collection of covered bridges in and around the community. In the early 1990s though, those bridges were catapulted into superstardom when Iowa author Robert James Waller wrote a short novel about a photographer who was assigned to shoot those bridges and had a relationship with a farm wife during his short stay there. *The Bridges of Madison County* became a bestseller and not long afterwards a movie of the same name hit the screens, starring Clint Eastwood, Meryl Streep and, of course, the covered bridges.

In 2002, arson destroyed the 119-year-old Cedar Bridge and its replacement is due to be completed in 2004; it may be open to light traffic. In the meantime the other five bridges are open to the public, although not to vehicles. The best way to see the bridges is to first visit the *Madison County Chamber of Commerce*, 73 Jefferson, (515) 462-1185 and (800) 298-6119. On the courthouse square, the chamber has maps leading to the bridges and the other sites related to *The Bridges of Madison County.* Allow a few hours to take in everything con-

nected with the book and movie. As for the Northside Cafe, 61 Jefferson, (515) 462-1523, which was also featured in the tale, it's just a few doors from the Chamber of Commerce.

On the south end of town is the *Madison County Historical Complex*, 815 South Second Avenue, (515) 462-2134, admission, a collection of buildings from across the county, including the wonderful 1856 Bevington-Kaser House.

Those Bridges of Madison County

At one time Madison County had 19 covered bridges. They were built that way in the late nineteenth century to protect the heavy lumber used for the floorboards. Although Madison County has the greatest number of covered bridges in Iowa, a few are in other parts of the state.

Back in Winterset, return to Highway 169 and go north about 2 miles to County Road G4R. Turn right (east) and follow it as it stair-steps east and north for about 15 miles; watch for 130th Street on the right (east). Turn and drive about a half mile. You'll come to *Francesca's House*, 3271 130th Street, (515) 981-5268, admission. Although it's

The Roseman Bridge and other covered bridges in and near Winterset were made famous by the book and fillm *The Bridges of Madison County.*

far from the Madison County bridges, it's the house that was used in the movie and was named after the character played by Meryl Streep. If you want, you can sit in the bathtub she and Clint shared in the movie.

Continue going north on G4R, which soon turns right and becomes County Road G14.

Proceed east on that for about 3 miles to I-35. Take the interstate north for 3 miles to the very next exit, where you turn east on State Highway 5, a four-lane highway that skirts the south side of the Des Moines metro area.

A Surveyor's Trick

While approaching I-35 on G14, you might notice that you're driving slightly northeast. And if you look at a map, you will notice that just west of I-35 in the counties south of Des Moines, a number of roads and even the county lines and sections lines that usually run east and west suddenly are slanted northeast to southwest. That was done by surveyors in the nineteenth century to align some of the counties in this part of the state.

Also, in looking at an Iowa map you may have noticed that several counties have jogs in their north-south boundaries. That was also done to adjust the north-south lines that are affected by the curvature of the earth.

Drive east on Highway 5 for about 8 miles to Exit 96 at SW 9th Street. Turn left (north) and go about 1 mile. Just inside the southern city limits is *Blank Park Zoo*, 7401 SW 9th Street, (515) 285-4722, admission. More than 800 animals from five continents are gathered in various exhibits, including a prairie dog town, which the kids (and very nimble adults) can pop up in the middle of to get a close but safe look at the little critters. There's also a walk-through Australian exhibit. The newest addition, the *Myron and Jackie Blank Discovery Center*, is a great indoor exhibit that leads visitors through cool alpine environments, into a tropical cave, along waterfalls, and finally to a coral reef.

Hot-air balloons color the sky at Indianola, one of North America's premier ballooning sites.

From the zoo, return to Highway 5, go east about 3 miles to Exit 70 and then turn right (south) onto U.S. Highway 65/69. Just after you cross the Middle River in about 6 miles, turn onto the first road on the left side of the highway—Summerset Road. Go 2 miles east and at a T intersection, turn left (north). A quarter mile away is the big, red-roofed barn of *Summerset Inn and Winery*, 1507 Fairfax, (515) 961-3545, a B&B combined with Iowa's largest vineyard. Opened in 1997, Summerset makes up to 15 varieties of wine and by 2004 should be producing about 100,000 bottles a year. During harvest, which is between mid-August and October, volunteers help gather and stomp the grapes, taste the wines, and listen to live music on Sunday afternoons. The B&B has four rooms with private baths.

Return to Highway 65/69 and continue south for about 4 miles to Indianola. Although politicians are said to produce more hot air than anyone else, in August, Indianola outdoes them all when it hosts the National Balloon Classic, the state's largest hot-air balloon event. At times it also hosts the National Hot Air Balloon Championship.

Just inside the north edge of this community and on the right side of the highway is the *National Balloon Museum*, 1601 North Jefferson Way, (515) 961-3714, donation. At this location since 1988, the museum expanded in 2003 with an addition housing more display areas and a library with an extensive collection of books and papers about the 200-plus year history of gas and hot-air balloons. These items join the other exhibits related to balloon flights: gondolas, pilot histories, military units, accounts of record-setting adventures, and more. As one might expect, almost every balloon-shaped item that's been made and can be sold is in the museum's gift shop.

Quick Trip Option 2: For a pleasant respite from all the road tripping and a chance to kick back at a pleasant lake, go 5 miles south of Indianola on Highway 65/69 to County Road G58 and turn right (east). You're now at *Lake Ahquabi State Park*, (515) 961-7101, a great place to relax near a pretty lake with a beach, picnic facilities, and campgrounds.

Continue south on Highway 65/69 (Jefferson Way in Indianola) until you reach 2nd Avenue, which is also State Highway 92. Turn left and go east for 11.5 miles to County Road S31. Along the way you will pass through the very small communities of Ackworth and Sandyville.

At S31, turn left (north) and drive for less than 5 miles to State Highway 5. Turn right (east). When you reach State Highway 316

in about 1.5 miles, turn left (north). Proceed for 7 miles to County Road F70, crossing the Des Moines River and passing through Runnells on the way. Turn right (east) and cruise for a little more than 6 miles to County Road S6G. Turn left (north) and go for 3 miles to the entrance to the *Neal Smith National Wildlife Refuge* on the left. As Iowa's newest federal preserve, the 5,000-acre refuge, 9981 Pacific Street, (515) 994-3400, free, is home to buffalo, elk, badger, white-tailed deer, pheasant, and other animals. These can be viewed while on an auto tour through the grounds, which also have hiking

Buffalo

It's estimated that at one time up to 75 million buffalo lived in North America. After years of slaughter in the nineteenth century, only about 300 remained. Nowadays, about 200,000 are on private lands and public refuges like Neal Smith where about 40 buffalo live. Even though some buffalo grow to six feet high and 2,000 pounds, they are remarkably agile and can run up to 30 miles an hour. A cow has usually just one calf a year, most often in the late spring.

trails and more than 200 types of wildflowers and grasses. The *Prairie Learning Center* has exhibits about the flora and fauna of the tallgrass prairie that once covered most of Iowa as well as many other states in the central United States. The *Prairie Point Bookstore* carries gifts, clothing, books, and photographs.

Return to S6G and go north again. After you reach Prairie City in about 2 miles, the road becomes State Highway 117. Continue north on this for 7 miles to Colfax and I-80, then for another 3 miles to *Trainland U.S.A.* Originally one man's collection of Lionel O-gauge trains, *Trainland U.S.A.*, 3135 Highway 117 North, (515) 674-3813, admission, is a live-action museum of scale-model train cars and engines dating from 1916 to 1976. With about 4,000 feet of track that required 35,000 hand-made ties, the displays cover the history of railroads on the frontier, in the days of steam, and then in the diesel era. About 20 to 25 trains are operating at one time on sets that feature scale models of landmarks such as Mount Rushmore, Devils Tower, San Francisco trolley cars, a Kentucky coal mine, western scenes, and more.

Return to I-80 via Highway 117. Turn west and 13 miles later leave the interstate at Exit 142, finishing this tour through and around Iowa's capital city.

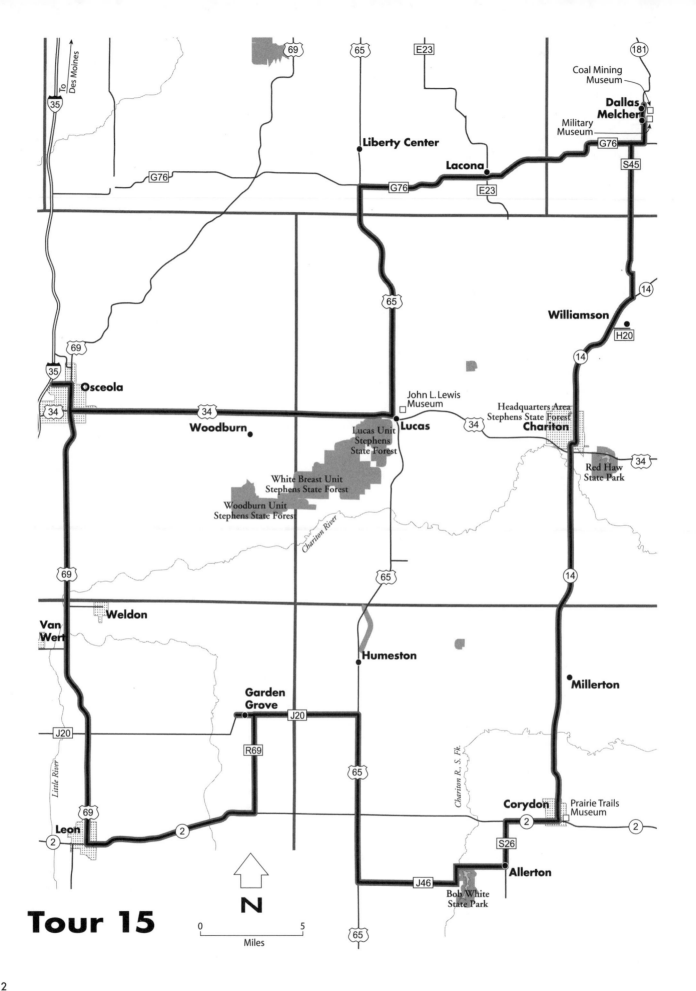

Tour 15

0   5

Miles

N

Tour 15
South Central Iowa—the Land of Amish, Mormons, and Coal Miners

Osceola—Leon—Allerton—Corydon—Chariton—Williamson—Melcher—Dallas—Lucas—Osceola

Distance: approximately 150 miles

Welcome to the rolling hills of south-central Iowa, where the land has not only supported the farming economy but also for many years supplied coal to the nation, a little-known fact about the state you can learn about in local museums. The area is also where you will encounter the Mormon Pioneer Trail and have a chance to meet some Amish. And you'll learn how some famous outlaws had a hard time convincing the residents of one town that they had really robbed a bank there, while in another town some bungling burglars failed to crack open a safe, yet blew up one side of a courthouse in the attempt.

Tour 13 begins at Exit 34 on I-35 on the north edge of Osceola, the seat of Clarke County. At the exit, go west a short distance on Clay Street, which is also County Road H33, to the *Lakeside Casino Resort.* Iowa's only floating casino situated on a lake, the facility, 777 Casino Drive, (877) 477-5253 and (641) 342-9511, has 900 slots along with 40 table games, three restaurants, live entertainment by celebrities, and 107 hotel rooms.

Upon leaving Lakeside, go back east on Clay Street into Osceola and turn right (south) onto Main Street, which is also U.S. Highway 69 to the business district. To the south is the *Clarke County Museum,* 1030 South Main, (641) 342-4200/6363, admission. Displays include artifacts from the early days of settlement in the region, a historical log cabin, a country school, and information about the Mormon Pioneer Trail.

From Osceola, go south for 21 miles on Highway 69 to Leon. The seat of Decatur County has several crafts shops and antique stores. One block east of 69 is Main Street and the *Decatur County Museum,* 111 North Main, (641) 446-4841, free. In a three-story building, the museum has rooms depicting various settings from the past, including a general store, a blacksmith shop, a parlor, a dining room, and more.

In Leon, turn onto State Highway 2 and head east through rolling terrain for about

8 miles to County Road R69. Turn left (north) and cruise for 5 miles to the east edge of Garden Grove; at Main Street, turn left (west) and keep going straight as the road, also County Road J20, turns to the south. A short distance out of Garden Grove on a road that turns to gravel is the *Mormon Pioneer Historical Trailside Park.* The outlines of small huts used by the Mormons that once stood in the grassy fields may still be seen. Trails lead through prairie and woods.

Courthouse Robbery

In 1877, someone broke into the treasurer's office in the Decatur County courthouse in Leon and, wanting to crack open the safe, set off dynamite under it. Although the explosion blasted away the west side of the courthouse, the safe remained locked, and it and its contents were removed from the debris by county officials.

Go back into Garden Grove on Main, cross R69, and continue east on J20. When that meets U.S. Highway 65 in 5 miles, turn right (south) and drive for about 9 miles to County Road J46, crossing Highway 2 along the way. Turn left (east) onto J46 and proceed for about 7 miles to Allerton. Along the way, you'll see the entrance to *Bobwhite State Park,* (641) 873-4670, which has trails, boating, fishing, and 32 campsites (19 with electricity). Upon arriving in Allerton, visit its small downtown that includes *Anathoth Artist Studio,* 106 North Central Avenue, (641) 873-6686, featuring locally made candles, pottery, herbal products, and hand-loomed rugs; and *Log Chain Apiary,* 204 North Central Avenue, (641) 873-4119, which sells honeys, including 15 flavored creamed honeys, beeswax items, gourmet coffee, and locally made gifts.

From Allerton, head north on County Road S26 to State Highway 2, about 4 miles away. Turn right (east) and go about 3 miles to Corydon. On the way into town, you'll see *Corydon Lake Park* on your right, which has camping, Frisbee golf, boating, and picnic facilities. In

Corydon, past the town square, is the *Prairie Trails Museum of Wayne County*, 515 East Jefferson, (641) 872-2211, admission, on the north side of the highway. The facility was named as one of the top ten small museums in the nation.

Round Barn

About a mile east of Allerton on East Maple Street (which connects with Central Avenue) is the *International Center for Rural Culture and Art*, (641) 873-4259, admission. The 93-acre site has a restored round, white barn that features a loft without support beams. A country school and church are on the property as well.

Grass outlines reveal the locations of small huts erected years ago by travelers on the Mormon Pioneer Trail just west of Garden Grove.

Its exhibits encompass the Mormon Pioneer Trail, early farm machinery, and a bank safe emptied by Jesse James when he visited the town in the 1870s.

From the museum, backtrack to the west on Jefferson Street (also Highway 2) and turn right (north) on Lafayette Street to start going around the town square. At Jackson Street, turn left (west) and a block later, turn right (north) onto North Washington. At the northwest corner of Jackson and Washington is Peoples Bank, which sits where the Ocobock Brothers' Bank was when it was robbed by Jesse James.

Go north on Washington Street, which becomes State Highway 14, for 17 miles to Chariton, the seat of Lucas County. As you go north on 14, you may see some horses and buggies of the Amish who live in this area. Drive safely when near them and be respectful of their religious beliefs, which include an admonition against having photographs taken of them.

About a mile south of Chariton is *Pin Oak Marsh*, (641) 774-2438, a 160-acre wetland, operated by the Lucas County Conservation Board, that is headquartered in a new lodge featuring exhibits from fossils to do-touch displays and aquariums. Birds of all sorts visit here at different times of the year. A 1,300-foot concrete path leads to the wetland, which features a lookout.

Quick Trip Option 1: The Amish residents living near Chariton are Old Order Amish, which means they live without the use of modern technologies. However, they welcome visitors to their businesses and a collection of these is just south of Chariton.

As you drive up Highway 14 from Corydon, just above the Lucas County line, the highway sways to the northeast and then north again. At that point, watch along the left (west) for *Gingerich Bakery and E&M Cabinet Shop*, which are located at the same place.

A few miles after that, at County Road H50,

Jesse James Visits Corydon

On June 3, 1871, no one in Corydon appeared too interested in the arrival of four cattle buyers. The townsfolk were more interested in going to the Methodist Church to hear a speaker talk about the possibility of a railroad coming through town. As the people listened, the four cattle buyers, all wearing long linen dusters, walked into the Wayne County Treasurer's office on the northeast side of the town square. One asked to change a $100 bill.

The clerk said he was unable to help—the safe was locked and the treasurer was at the big meeting. However, the clerk suggested the men could visit the Ocobock Brothers' Bank one block to the west. And there the men went.

Once inside the wood-frame structure, Jesse James, Frank James, Cole Younger, and Clell Miller asked for more than just change for a $100 bill, a request backed by cocked pistols. Literally under the gun, the lone cashier took all the money from the safe and stuffed it into a wheat sack. Then the robbers tied and gagged him, walked out of the bank, mounted their horses, and rode away.

But, according to legend, they did not flee. Instead, on their way past the Methodist Church, the robbers called out that the bank had been robbed. Some people thought it was a joke but, upon checking, found out the truth. A posse was formed but the James Gang made a clean getaway with between $6,000 and $10,000, pretty fair change for a $100 bill.

turn left (west). Go 1 mile and then turn left (south) onto a gravel road; go another mile to *The Basket Shop*. On H50 heading west again, about 4 miles from Highway 14, go to the right (north) for about a third of a mile to A&L Woodworking.

On H50, about 6 miles west of Highway 14 is *B&B Log Furniture*, on the left (south). Finally, 9 miles west of Highway 14 on H50 and then 2 miles south on a gravel road is *Pine Craft Shop*, which also carries crafts and rugs.

The Amish-owned businesses, in keeping with Amish religious practices, have no phones and are closed on Sunday.

After entering Chariton, Highway 14 curves to the right (east); right after it does, you should turn left (north) onto South Grand Street and drive three blocks. Near the courthouse square, park your vehicle and stretch your legs. This town of about 4,500 residents provides some great walking-around opportunities. The *Lucas County Chamber of Commerce*, 104 North Grand, (641) 774-4059, has plenty of information about local and regional places. One thing you should check out here is *Amish Meals*. This program is organized by the chamber to bring people into an Amish house for a noonday meal, usually on Wednesday and possibly on Tuesday and Thursday. The Amish woman who cooks the meal prefers to serve between 10 and 60 people at a time, but if you do not have that many check with the chamber anyway and they can try to join you with others to reach the minimum of 10 visitors. Expect a hearty meal with items such as real mashed potatoes covered by homemade noodles; this is one of those meals at which you will just have to drop your concerns about calories and cholesterol. In 2003, the meals were $11.95 each, without gratuity. No cameras are permitted.

Across the street to the south from the chamber's office is *The Sampler*, 102 South Grand, (641) 774-2116, a quilt shop, and across Grand to the west is the Lucas County Courthouse. Built in 1893, this Romanesque, two-story, sandstone building has a tower supporting a clock that came from the 1893 Chicago World's Fair. On the northeast corner of the square is *Piper's Old Fashioned Grocery and Candy Store*, 901 Braden, (641) 774-2131, a great, century-old place with wooden floors and a tin ceiling where kids of all ages can find homemade candy that's shipped all over the world . . . and sold here too, thank goodness. Among Piper's sweet concoctions are fudges, peanut clusters, chocolate creams, fruit slices, and Valentine's packages for your own sweetie; in short, if you can imagine something sweet, they have probably made it here.

Seven blocks west of the square (you may want to drive for this visit), near the intersection of Court Avenue and 17th Street, is the *Lucas County Museum*, 117 North 17th Street, (641)

A new bank sits on the site where a former bank was robbed by Jesse James when he and fellow outlaws visited Corydon in 1871.

What's in a Name

Corydon was originally called Springfield, but Judge Seth Anderson gambled on a chance to rename the town in a poker game. When he won, he named it after Corydon, Indiana.

774-4464, free. The complex of historical buildings, including a one-room school, a barn, a log cabin and a church, is dominated by the A. J. Stephens House, a large, two-story home fronted by a two-story white portico.

A few blocks past the museum on Court Avenue's south side is the trailhead of the state's first rail-to-trail, multi-use trail, the *Cinder Path Trail*, (641) 774-2438, which follows the former Burlington Northern Railroad route to the small community of Humeston 13 miles away. For part of the journey, the trail follows the Chariton River and also rolls through a covered bridge.

North of the trailhead, up 22nd Street, is the *Hy-Vee Distribution Center*, 1801 Osceola, (641) 774-2121, free, which brings in most of the food for the 200-store Hy-Vee Grocery chain and then distributes it to stores located in Iowa, Nebraska, Minnesota, South Dakota, Missouri, Kansas, and Illinois. The complex has one-hour tours by appointment, which take visitors through the center's offices, graphics department, 680,000-square-foot grocery warehouse, and perishable warehouse, which holds ice, fresh produce, and frozen goods.

Return to Highway 14, also called 7th Street here, and turn left (north). At Mitchell Street, turn left (west), and in one block, at 8th Street, you'll find the headquarters of the *Stephens State Forest*. If you plan to visit the various units of this 13,092-acre forest later

Iowa Coal Mining

For most of the first half of the twentieth century, coal mining was an important part of southern Iowa's economy. The range of underground and pit mines covered a region that included Melcher-Dallas, Lucas, Albia, and Centerville. Because the region's coal was soft and created pollution when burned, it fell from favor, and in the late 1940s coal mining came to an end in Iowa.

in the tour, stop here, (641) 774-4559, to get information about the forest and trails. For information about campsites in the forest, contact Red Haw State Park, (641) 774-5632.

Quick Trip Option 2: Just east of Chariton, on U.S. Highway 34, is *Red Haw State Park*, (641) 774-5632. Red Haw has a 72-acre lake that is considered one of the best panfish lakes in Iowa; it's stocked with bluegill, crappies, bass, and catfish. The park also has trails, picnic facilities, swimming, and boating. Sixty of its 80 campsites are electrified. Near Red Haw on the north side of Highway 34 are Lakes Ellis and Morris, which also offer good fishing.

From Chariton, continue north on Highway 14 for about 7 miles to County Road H20; turn right (east) and take it for about 1 mile into tiny Williamson. One block north of H20 on Williamson Avenue is the *Williamson School Museum*, (641) 862-3628, donation. A three-story brick structure, the former school recaps the region's history of coal mining, agriculture, and millinery work, and pays tribute to residents who served in the military; tours are

John L. Lewis

Born to Welsh immigrants on February 12, 1880 in a coal-mining camp about a mile east of Lucas, John J. Lewis began working in the local mines as a teenager. In 1900 he joined the United Mine Workers of America, and in 1908 went to work in the Illinois coal mines. He moved upward in the hierarchy of the UMWA and ultimately became the union's president, a position he held for 40 years. In the 1940s, his tough negotiating policies led to several long and bitter nationwide strikes, but they resulted in better working conditions for miners. Generally considered one of the twentieth century's most effective labor leaders, Lewis died in 1969.

by appointment. Nearby is the *Williamson Tavern*, (641) 862-3615, where the Pappa Burgers are so large—with one pound of beef each—you might want someone to help you eat it. By the way, there are Mamma and Baby Burgers for those who don't want the Pappa.

Return to Highway 14 and continue north for 2 miles to County Road S45, which cuts to the left (north) at a curve. Take it for about 5 miles. On the left is the *Gathering Barn*, 2368 50th Place, (641) 947-4005, which sells crafts made by locals, including some items made out of parts of old barns. During the fall, fresh produce is sold here.

Quick Trip Option 3: About 5 miles past the Williamson turnoff on Highway 14 is *Pierce's Pumpkin Patch*, (641) 862-3398, which has pumpkins, 25 types of squash, and Indian corn in the fall; it also hosts a festival featuring antique tractors on the second weekend of October. Another couple miles up the road is the *Belinda Toy and Antique Museum*, (641) 862-4439, admission. Located in a former church built in 1846, the museum features collections of toy trains, planes, tractors, cars, dolls, and cast-iron toys.

A few miles later, S45 meets County Road G76 at a T intersection. Turn right (east) on G76 and drive for less than a mile to State Highway 181; turn left (north) and proceed into Melcher-Dallas. The town, with a population of about 1,200, boasts two small but interesting museums. The *Melcher-Dallas Museum of Military History*, 123 Main, (641) 947-4506, free, has collections of uniforms, equipment, flags, firearms, photos, posters, and more, memorializing the men and women who have served this nation from 1800 to the present. Also in the museum's five rooms are English, Belgium, French, German, Dutch, Italian, Russian, and Iraqi items.

A bit farther up the street is the *Melcher-Dallas Coal Mining and Heritage Museum*, North Main, (641) 947-5651, donation, which recalls an era when this region of Iowa produced coal from below the ground as well as crops above. Located in the former Miners Union Hall, the museum has a reconstructed coal mine, blacksmith shop, and tools from the community's early days.

Return to Highway G76 and head west for about 8 miles to Lacona. Continue going west on what is now State Highway 206 for 6 miles to U.S. Highway 65. Turn left (south) and proceed for 12 miles to Lucas, where you meet Highway 34 on the south edge of town. Turn left (east) and drive a short distance to Division Street. Turn left (north) to enter Lucas. A couple blocks up the street is the *John L. Lewis Mining and Lake*

Museum, 102 Division Street, (641) 766-6831, admission. Along with tools from the days of mining coal in Iowa, the museum has displays about labor leader John L. Lewis, who was born near here, and a life-size, bronze statue of him. A half block east of the museum is the *Farmer's Market and Craft Shop*, (641) 766-6443/6831, featuring baked items, fresh produce in season, and locally-made crafts, open five days a week from mid-April through mid-October.

Quick Trip Option 4: Near Lucas are three units of the *Stephens State Forest*. Immediately southwest of town is the Lucas Unit with 1,192 acres. A bit farther south and west is the White-breast Unit, which has 2,868 acres, and south of the town of Woodburn, the Woodburn Unit has 1,590 acres. More than 30 miles of multi-use trails and 80 primitive campsites are scattered throughout these heavily wooded units, which include 36 equestrian campsites, three with water hydrants. Information about the trails is available in Chariton at the Stephens State Forest headquarters, (641) 774-5449, but information about the campsites may be found at *Red Haw State Park*, (641) 774-5632, east of Chariton.

From Lucas, return to Osceola, the beginning of this tour, by going west on Highway 34 for 16 miles.

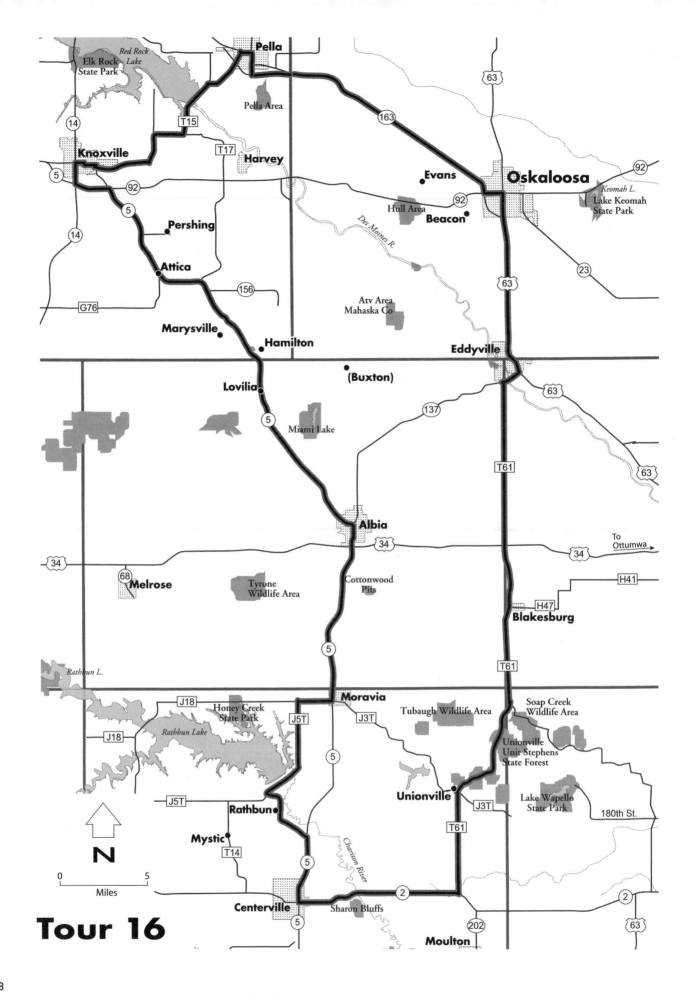

Red Rock Lake

Elk Rock State Park

Pella

Pella Area

14

T15

T17

Knoxville

Harvey

92

5

5

163

Evans

Oskaloosa

92

92

Beacon

Hull Area

Keomah L.

Lake Keomah State Park

63

92

14

Pershing

Attica

156

23

Des Moines R.

63

G76

Marysville

Hamilton

Atv Area Mahaska Co

Lovilia

(Buxton)

Eddyville

63

5

Miami Lake

137

T61

63

Albia

34

To Ottumwa

34

34

68

Melrose

Tyrone Wildlife Area

Cottonwood Pits

34

H41

H47

Blakesburg

5

T61

Rathbun L.

J18

Honey Creek State Park

Moravia

J5T

Tubaugh Wildlife Area

Soap Creek Wildlife Area

Rathbun Lake

J18

J3T

Unionville Unit Stephens State Forest

5

J5T

Rathbun

Unionville

J3T

Lake Wapello State Park

180th St.

Mystic

T14

T61

Chariton River

5

N

0   5

Miles

5

Centerville

2

2

5

Sharon Bluffs

202

63

Tour 16

Moulton

118

Tour 16
A Touch of Dutch, Race Cars, Lakes, and the Land of the Ioway

Pella—Lake Red Rock—Knoxville—Albia—Lake Rathbun—Centerville—Oskaloosa—Pella

Distance: approximately 135 miles

Welcome to the land of the Ioway, the Native Americans who lived here for many years and served as the inspiration for those who named this state after them (but with a different spelling and pronunciation). After the Ioway left, immigrants from the Netherlands arrived, forming their own community that remains very special in Iowa. Not far from there is a town that existed for only about two decades during the early twentieth century and that was perhaps the most successful racially integrated community in the nation. Just a short drive away, on summer evenings, you can hear the thunder of sprint cars zooming around one of the nation's top racetracks. Finally, nearby are the state's two largest lakes, where it's possible to lose yourself in nothing more than the sounds of the leaves rustling in the breeze, far above your tent. So let's see what's in this part of south central Iowa.

This tour begins in downtown Pella, at the intersection of Washington and Broadway Streets, where you should park on the northwest corner at Central Park. This is Pella's town square, which is unlike almost any other town square in Iowa because of all the Dutch-style architecture to be seen in the business district. The only exception is Orange City, which claims to be as Dutch as Pella is. (Take a hint: let them argue that point—you just sit back and enjoy what both have to offer.)

Cross Washington to the north to visit *Scholte House*, 728 Washington, (641) 628-3684, admission. After arriving in America, the town's founder, Dominie H. P. Scholte, built this 23-room house in 1847 as a promise to his wife that they would have as nice a home in America as they did in the Netherlands. Out back are pretty gardens along with statues of the town's early people in everyday poses.

You can leave your car where it is for now and just take off on foot. Nothing's all that far away if you don't mind walking a few blocks. Return to Central Park and take in its dominant feature, the 65-foot-high *Tulip Toren*, a pair of pylons rising above a platform. This is the center of activities during *Tulip Time Festival*, one of the state's largest and most brilliant events, held each May when tulips flood this

town with color. Walk across the park to its southeast corner, where you will find a small Dutch windmill that houses an information center about this city and the region. The park is also where family activities are held each Thursday evening in the summer.

Built of components made in the Netherlands, a windmill stands tall in Pella, which was settled by Dutch immigrants.

From the small windmill, you can visit a real one; that is, a *really* big one that you may have noticed by now. But hold your paarden (that's Dutch for horses) and note some other places while you're near the park. Sure, some are regular business prettied up in Dutch architecture (and there's nothing wrong with that), but some really tie into the Dutch heritage, such as *Jaarsma Bakery*, 727 Franklin, *De Pelikaan-Dutch Imports*, 627 Franklin, and *Boat Home Furnishings*, 620 Franklin.

As you walk along Franklin Street east of the park, be sure to notice the three-story *Klokkenspel* where, at 11 a.m., and 1, 3, 5, and 9 p.m., a number of mechanical figures put on a show at the second floor window to the tunes created by a 147-bell carillon. And while some figures, like the shoemaker and street scrubbers, are generic, some others are unique, such as Dominie Scholte and lawman Wyatt Earp, who lived in Pella during his early years. Be sure to walk through the opening beneath the Klokkenspel and see the figures that appear on the other side too.

Just past the Klokkenspel is the *Pella Opera House*, 611 Franklin, (641) 628-8628, admission for shows. Built in 1900, it was remodeled 90 years later and hosts a number of productions.

Now it's time to continue east on Franklin, cross East 1st Street, and size up the *Vermeer Mill*, 507 Franklin, (641) 628-4311, admission, the nation's tallest working windmill. The mill is 90 feet tall, and the tips of its blades reach as high as 124 feet above the ground. Using materials fashioned in the Netherlands, the windmill was built by local and Dutch workers and flour made there is sold in local restaurants and at the interpretative center housed in the windmill. The windmill also houses a 1/24-scale model Dutch town with townspeople and 80 buildings.

The windmill and interpretative center serve as the entrance to the *Pella Historical Village*, which contains 21 buildings, many with the typical steep roofs favored by the Dutch, and various gardens. One building is the childhood home of Wyatt Earp, the legendary marshal whose father was a marshal in Pella.

After walking back west and recrossing East 1st Street, you enter the *Molengracht*, a clutch of buildings that, although new, definitely make you feel like you're in Holland. In the Molengracht, which means "mill city," various businesses, including a jewelry store, an outlet for Stam chocolates, the Grand café, and the Royal Amsterdam Hotel line a canal that has a pedestrian drawbridge.

At the west end of the Molengracht, turn left (south) on Main Street and you'll find yourself right at the *Fire Station Museum*, 612 Main, (641) 628-2626 and (888) 746-3882, free but reservations are required. No longer an active firehouse, the 1882 station holds an antique fire truck and other fire-fighting equipment along with the city's old jail.

If you have children and want them to let off some steam, three blocks west of the old firehouse is West Market Park. Suffice it to say, the kids will know what to do here while you rest or enjoy the nearby butterfly garden—they'll bounce on the bridges, run through child-size structures, swing at the sky, plunge into the soft sand, climb, slide and just wear themselves out.

Okay, now it's time to return to your vehicle that was parked at Central Park. Go east to Main Street, turn left, and go two blocks north. Here, you'll arrive at the *Sunken Gardens*, a city park with a pond shaped like a wooden shoe and with a small windmill, formal gardens, and old-style lamps and benches.

Just north of the gardens is the *de Zee Meeuw House*, 1357 Main, (641) 628-3592, admission. Though it was built in the mid-twentieth century, its owners made it to remember their original homes in Holland and are willing to share their memories with visitors.

Return south on Main and drive five blocks south of Central Park to University Avenue; turn right and go west. Along the way, you'll pass the campus of *Central College*; then, just past West 5th Street and on the left (south) side of the road, you'll come upon the trailhead of Volksweg Trail, a paved trail that leads to *Fifield Recreation Area*, 14 miles away on the north side of Lake Red Rock.

Outside of town, University becomes Idaho Drive, which curves to the south and west to meet County Road T15, 2.5 miles after the Volksweg Trail trailhead. Turn left (south) onto T15 and after barely a half mile, you'll find yourself on the dam that creates *Lake Red Rock* out of the Des Moines River. Covering 19,000 acres, Red Rock is Iowa's largest lake and is surrounded by several campgrounds, nature trails, overlooks, beaches, and boat ramps. A marina is on the north shore along County Road G28, and near the dam is the *Red Rock Visitor Center*, 1105 Highway T15, (641) 828-7522 and 628-8690, which has a butterfly garden, observation deck overlooking the lake, and 45-minute tours of the dam.

Quick Trip Option 1: When you first meet T15, turn right (north) and link up with G28 to then head west 8 miles to *Cordova County Park*, 1378 Highway G28, (641) 627-5935, on the northwest corner of the lake near the State Highway 14 bridge. The park has four two-bedroom cabins with lofts, three three-bedroom cabins (all the cabins are year-round units), and trails. Also featured is a 106-foot-tall observation platform that was made out of a former water tower (a small fee is charged to visit the tower) and is the tallest observation tower in the Midwest.

Just west of Cordova, Highway 14 crosses

the lake's west end on a mile-long bridge and leads to *Elk Rock State Park*, 811 146th Avenue, Knoxville, (641) 842-6008, on the lake's south side. This lakeside, 850-acre park has trails for hiking, mountain biking, and riding horses, 90 campsites, 36 with electricity, picnic facilities, boat ramps, and fishing.

From the Red Rock dam, continue south 1.5 miles to County Road T17 and turn right (west). About 1.5 miles beyond that, T15 turns to the left (south). After another 1.5-mile stretch, you come to Old State Highway 92, where you turn right and go west for 3 miles to Knoxville. If you have no idea what Knoxville is, then you aren't into sprint car races. So, to learn about this sport—and you're at its international focal point here—you need to make your way to the main part of Knoxville.

After entering town on East Main Street, go to North Roche Street, which is just a block beyond 1st Street (in case you're counting down the streets as you drive through town); turn right (north). After two blocks, turn left (west) onto West Pleasant Street. A half mile later, turn right (north) at North Lincoln Street, which is also State Highway 14. Cross the railroad tracks and keep going north. If you are here on a race night, you're bound to hear that you're drawing near the

Iowa's Flag

After 75 years of not having an official state flag, Iowa finally got one in 1917 when Dixie Cornell Gebhardt of Knoxville designed the one that's still in use. It features broad bands of red, white, and blue and is centered with an eagle bearing streamers emblazoned with the state motto: Our Liberties We Prize and Our Rights We Will Maintain.

Knoxville Raceway, Highway 14, (641) 842-5431, admission. And the closer you get, the more you may wish you were wearing a pair of ear protectors because this place howls with screaming alcohol-fired engines. Every August, the national championship sprint car races attract about 80,000 fans who come from as far away as Australia to watch more than 150 sprint cars from the United States, Canada, and Australia race around the half-mile oval track that's covered with mud from the nearby Des Moines River—the best racing surface for sprint cars, the officials say. During this event, the *Knoxville Chamber of Commerce*, (641) 828-7555, administers its *Guest/Host Housing Program* that arranges for visitors to stay with area families during the four-day event. Beside the nationals, the track is busy every weekend from around mid-April to September, and an average of 6,000 fans watch each event.

A changing display of sprint cars can be seen at the National Sprint Car Hall of Fame and Museum in Knoxville.

Now, if you're in town when the air isn't being split apart by the sounds of sprint car engines, visit the *National Sprint Car Hall of Fame and Museum*, One Sprint Capital Place, (641) 842-6176 and (800) 874-4488, admission, which is a considerably quieter way to enjoy this high-speed sport. Located next to the raceway, it's the place you get an up-close look at sprint cars; on average, about two dozen are displayed and they are changed often. Two displays are particularly noteworthy: replicas of garages used by Hall of Fame members John Gerber and Bob Trostle. The gift shop has everything from small pins and bracelet charms to books and videos to prints, posters, and calendars. Of course, all are tied to sprint car racing.

Where All Things Were Equal

About 5 miles east of the spot where Highway 5 crosses into Monroe County, in a rather inaccessible area, the town of Buxton once stood. During the heyday of mining coal in this part of Iowa, Buxton had up to 5,000 residents. In several respects it was like many other coal towns—with one big exception: it was perhaps the most racially integrated community that one could find anywhere. Never incorporated as a city because it was a company town formed around 1900 by Consolidated Coal Co., Buxton was a place where blacks and whites were equals. Not only did they work together in the mines on an equal footing but also they played together at the town's parks and the YMCA, prayed together in the churches, and learned together in the schools. Among the professionals in town were many blacks, including a physician, a lawyer, two druggists, two constables, the postmistress, and a justice of the peace. Two of the town's five restaurants were owned or operated by blacks, as were Buxton's two milliners, a meat market, laundry, hotel, bakery, and a real estate firm. However, as other coal veins proved more lucrative, the controlling company focused its efforts elsewhere and by the early 1920s, Buxton was a shell of its former self. Blacks who lived in Buxton said they did not encounter prejudice until after they had left that town. Now hardly a trace of the town remains.

Return south to the intersection of North Lincoln and West Pleasant in Knoxville; turn right (west). A half mile later, turn left (south) onto Willets Drive and visit the *Marion County Historical Village.* On the grounds of Marion County Park, the complex, (641) 842-7274, free, has a museum with historical artifacts and a number of buildings, including

Honey Creek Resort

Iowa's Department of Natural Resources has plans to turn the hilly and heavily wooded Honey Creek State Park into Iowa's first destination park, basically a 1,600-acre resort that would encompass the present park at Rathbun Lake. Among the planned amenities are hotel suites, a restaurant, family cabins, convention facilities, an 18-hole golf course, expanded hike-bike trails, a beach, equestrian areas with horse trails, and a 60-foot-tall lighthouse that's also an observation tower. So, when you're in this area, keep an eye on what may be developing here in the next few years.

an 1850 stagecoach inn, 1835 log cabin, general store, and a depot built in 1912.

Return once more to the intersection of North Lincoln and West Pleasant and turn right, to the south this time. After about 1 mile, turn left (east) onto State Highways 92 and 5 and then, after another 2 miles, follow Highway 5 to the southeast for 28 pleasant miles to Albia.

As you enter Albia, turn left (east) onto A Avenue East and immediately find the Monroe *County Historical Museum*, 114 A Avenue East, (641) 932-7046/3319, free. It's located in a former maintenance barn of the Albia Interurban Railway, which connected this city with two coal-mining communities from 1907 to 1928. The museum's rooms are made to look like yesteryear's businesses and homes (a kitchen features a coal-fired stove), as well as a coal mine containing locally used equipment. Outside is a one-room schoolhouse, the last of more than a hundred once seen in this county.

A block south is the *Monroe County Courthouse*, sitting pretty in the middle of a courthouse square that some say is Iowa's most beautiful. It's hard to argue with that, especially since 92 buildings in the business district alone are on the National Register of Historic Places. Some homes and other structures in and around town have also earned their places on the register. The *Albia Area Chamber of Commerce*, 107 South Clinton Street, (641) 932-5108, has a brochure on this city's architectural wonders.

Return to Highway 5 and continue south of Albia for 10 miles to County Road J18 on the west side of Moravia. Turn left (east) and enter town on North Street. Head for the *Moravia Wabash Depot Museum*, 800 West North Street, (641) 724-3777, free, an early twentieth-century depot with lots of railroad memorabilia and a scale-model train layout. A restored section car and a country church are here too. In July, Moravia hosts its annual *Appanoose County Train Rides*.

Head back west on North Street, cross Highway 5, and take J18 west for 2 miles to County Road J5T. Turn left and head straight south for 4 miles to the dam forming *Lake Rathbun.* Iowa's second largest lake, Rathbun has been nicknamed "Iowa's Ocean." At the south end of the dam that J5T crosses is the *Rathbun Lake Information Center*, (641) 647-2464, which, like so much else here, is administered by the U.S. Army Corps of Engineers. The center has displays about the region's wildlife and its coal-mining history. Around the 11,000-acre lake, which is part of the Chariton River, are lots of boat ramps, five campgrounds, three beaches, and plenty of trails. Popular with sailboat and windsurfing enthusiasts, water skiers, and motorboaters, the lake is also popular with those who love to angle for its largemouth bass, channel catfish, walleye, freshwater drum, and carp.

On the north side of the dam is *Rathbun Marina*, 21646 Moravia Place, (641) 741-3212, which has boat rentals, a restaurant with a lakeside patio, a campground, a convenience store, and an inn where all the rooms have a lake view. Below the dam is the *Rathbun Fish Hatchery*, 15053 Hatchery Point, (641) 647-2406, free. A state facility with 20 outside ponds, 40 indoor tanks, an information center, aquariums, and an elevated walkway through the hatchery building, the hatchery produces around 35 million walleye fry, 5 million saugeye, 400,000 catfish, 60,000 walleye fingerlings, and 15,000 largemouth bass each year.

On the lake's north side, by the way, is *Honey Creek State Park*, (641) 724-3739, an 828-acre park with 155 campsites, 94 with electricity, picnic areas, hiking, interpretive trails, a boat ramp, and swimming.

At the south end of the dam, stay on J5T as it swings to the east and soon meets Highway 5. Turn right (south) and drive to Centerville, about 7 miles from the dam. At Van Buren Street, turn right (west) and drive three long blocks to the courthouse square. Centerville is another community known for having a fantastic town square—this one is so large that eight other blocks line its perimeter. And this one, too, has local supporters who say it's the best in the state . . . so you decide for yourself. In the middle of it all sits the *Appanoose County Courthouse*, which was built in 1904 to replace a brick, two-story, octagonal one that was pretty well wrecked by fireworks during the Fourth of July celebration in 1881. Right after the turn of the century, new sidewalks and streetlights were added to the business district, adding more charm to the 116 buildings there which are on the National Register of Historic Places.

From the square, head south one block on Washington Street to Maple Street. You will be right at the *Historical and Coal Mining Museum*, 100 West Maple, (641) 856-8040, admission, a former post office built in 1903, which has exhibits about the county's early days of settlement, the Mormon Trail, and a replica of a coal mine.

On Maple, go left (east) two blocks to Drake Street and turn right (south). You'll be entering a posh neighborhood known as the Gold Coast some years ago. One mansion you can visit is *Bradley Hall*, 519 Drake Street, (641) 856-5345 and (800) 596-5448, which is now a business called the Shoppes at Bradley Hall. When it was built in 1909, this 10,000-square-foot, tan brick home was *the* place in Centerville and now it's where you can look at and buy antiques, hand-

made items, clothing, gourmet foods, candy, and more. In the ballroom on the third floor, it's Christmas on a year-round basis, and in the carriage house, you'll find patio and outdoor furniture.

Another elegant home, although privately owned, that you can see from the street, is the *Drake Mansion*, 707 Drake Street, which was built by Governor Francis Drake as a wedding gift for his daughter. Also, a block north of the courthouse square is a pretty, Georgian mansion with a portico; it houses the *Columns*, 107 East Washington Street, (641) 437-1178, which sells Amish furniture, jewelry, clocks, books, and special gifts.

Head east on Highway 2 from Centerville for about 9 miles to County Road T61; turn left and cruise north for about 17 miles to Blakesburg, passing through Unionville on the way. At Blakesburg, continue north on T61 (this may not be Iowa's longest county road, but it sure seems like it) for 13 more miles to State Highway 137. Note that a 9-mile stretch of T61, from County Road T7J to Highway 137, is the westernmost segment of the *Woodlands Scenic Byway*, which runs to the Villages of Van Buren County to the east (see Tour 26 for more information).

Quick Trip Option 2: Just a few miles east of Blakesburg on County Road H47 is the *Airpower Museum*. (See Tour 26 for additional information on the museum.)

Turn right (east), cross the Des Moines River, and enter Eddyville, less than 1 mile away. There, turn left onto U.S. Highway 63, a four-lane highway, and follow that north to Oskaloosa, 10 miles away. As the highway curves to bypass "Osky" to the west, go straight into the center of town on Market Street. Along the way you'll pass the west side of a nice downtown square occupied by trees, an octagonal gazebo, and a statue of Mahaska. In an arrangement that's unusual in Iowa, the *Mahaska County Courthouse* is across the street to the east of the square and, sadly, nearly hidden by trees from those traveling on Market Street, the town's main north-south thoroughfare.

Oskaloosa was named after an Indian Creek woman said to be the wife of Osceola, the Seminole who fought for his home in Florida (and who had no ties with Iowa that anyone knows about). More is known about Mahaska, however. An Ioway whose name was also given as Mewhu-she-kaw, which meant "White Cloud," he was

Unlike most other Iowa courthouses, the Mahaska County Courthouse is not situated right on the townsquare.

born near the Iowa River in the mid-1780s and then lived in this area for the rest of his life. A warrior who fought mostly against the Osage to avenge his father's death, Mahaska spent time in a Saint Louis prison for killing a French trader. He escaped and returned to his homeland here. Sensing the relentless, westward movement of European-Americans, he urged his fellow Ioway to be peaceful. When some Ioway were charged with murder, he helped track them down and put them in prison. One of the killers later escaped, made his way back here, and killed Mahaska in 1834.

The bronze statue of Mahaska was made in 1908 by Sherry Edmundson Fry in Europe, where it won the Prix de Rome that year before being shipped to Oskaloosa to be mounted on its pedestal a year later.

From downtown Oskaloosa, drive north on Market for a little more than 1 mile and keep to the right (northeast) at Glendale

The Ioway

The first written record of the Ioway occurred when remarks about them were penned in French journals in Montreal in 1757, although this isn't to say the Ioway lived here at that time. They are thought to have originated around the Great Lakes years earlier and then moved westward into what is now Iowa, where they met French explorers in the late seventeenth century. Even though their name is pronounced "i-o-way," the region where they lived was soon named after them as "i-o-wah" and it's been that way ever since. Also, the Ioway called themselves Bah-kho-je which means "gray snow," possibly a reference to their lodges which, in the winter, were covered with snow made gray by their fires. It's said that Ioway was actually a name bestowed on them by the French but some believe that, in the Sioux language that the Ioway spoke, Ayuhwa means "sleepy ones" or "yawners."

Because of pressure exerted on them by the Americans in the first half of the nineteenth century, the Ioway left where they had lived for many years and are now on reservations in Oklahoma, Nebraska, and Kansas. It is not known if any Ioway live in the state named after them.

Road, which is also County Road T65; go 2 miles. You'll come to the *Nelson Pioneer Farm*, 2294 Oxford Avenue, (641) 672-2989, admission. Started by Daniel Nelson in 1844, this farm remained in his family until 1958, when it became a place to educate visitors about the early farming practices in Iowa. The original log cabin is here along with the Nelson family's first frame house, summer kitchen, barn, and meat house, and they have been joined by other buildings moved to the site, including two post offices, a blacksmith shop, an 1861 school, and a country store. The only mule cemetery known to exist in Iowa is here too, containing the remains of Becky and Jennie, who served in the Civil War before finishing their days at this farm.

Return to Market Street in Oskaloosa and turn right (west) at the intersection with A Avenue West, which is also State Highway 92. Drive to Highway 163 on the west edge of town, turn right, and return to Pella, 17 miles to the northwest. On the south edge of Pella, turn right (north) on South Clark Street, go less than 1 mile to Oskaloosa Street and turn left (west). After a few blocks, turn right (north) on Main and proceed to the Central Park area, where you began this tour.

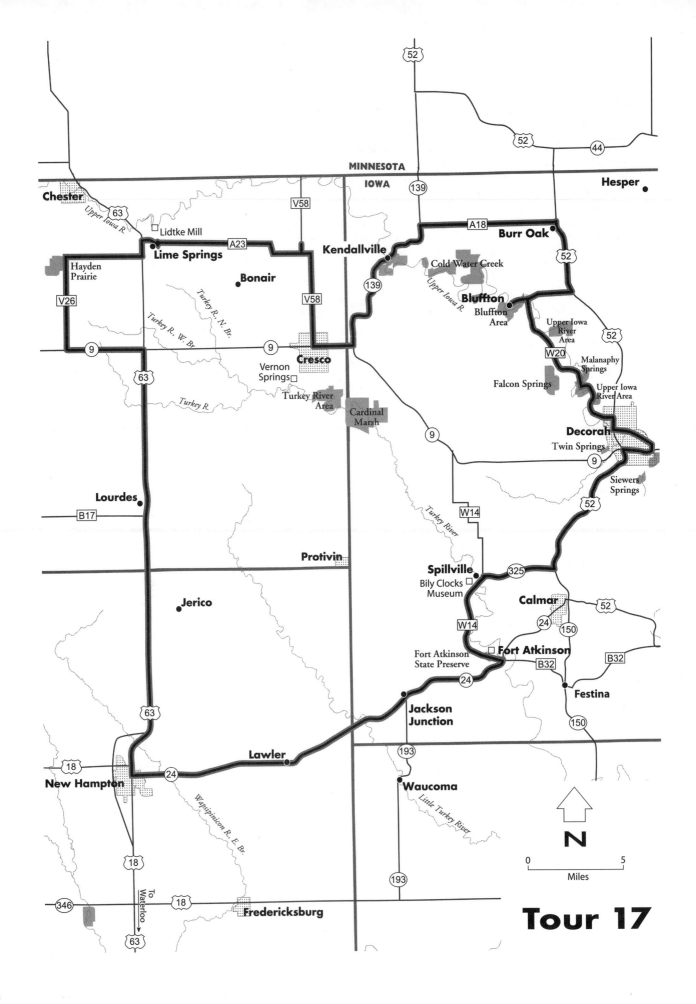

MINNESOTA
IOWA

Hesper

Chester

Upper Iowa R.

63

Lidtke Mill

V58

A18

Burr Oak

52

A23

Lime Springs

Kendallville

Cold Water Creek

139

Hayden
Prairie

Bonair

Bluffton

52

V26

Turkey R. N. Br.

V58

139

Bluffton
Area

Upper Iowa R.

Upper Iowa
River
Area

52

9

Cresco

9

W20

Malanaphy
Springs

Turkey R. W. Br.

Falcon Springs

Upper Iowa
River Area

63

Vernon
Springs

Turkey R.

Turkey River
Area

Cardinal
Marsh

Decorah

Twin Springs

9

52

Siewers
Springs

Lourdes

B17

9

Turkey River

W14

52

Protivin

Spillville

325

Bily Clocks
Museum

Calmar

52

Jerico

W14

24

150

B32

Fort Atkinson
State Preserve

Fort Atkinson

B32

Festina

24

150

Jackson
Junction

63

193

18

Lawler

24

18

New Hampton

Waucoma

Wapsipinicon R. E. Br.

Little Turkey River

N

0   5
Miles

346

To
Waterloo

18

Fredericksburg

193

63

Tour 17

Tour 17
Little Switzerland

Decorah—Bluffton—Burr Oak—Kendallville—Cresco—Lime Springs—New Hampton—Fort Atkinson—Spillville—Decorah

Distance: approximately 135 miles

This tour first wanders through a region of Iowa called Little Switzerland by some because of its hilly topography and then out onto the adjacent plains for a while. Along the way are collections of unique items amassed by past and present residents of the area, homes that are magnificent and humble, tall rocky cliffs, cool springs, rambling rivers, a large rock that some thought was a town, a fort built to protect Indians, and museums that reveal a lot, from the history of immigrants to the most beautiful way to see time tick away.

To start this tour in Decorah, go east on State Highway 9 from its intersection with U.S. Highway 52 just southwest of town. Less than a half mile from the intersection, turn left (northeast) onto Short Street. After crossing three streets and turning toward the north, it joins and becomes Mechanic Street. In about five blocks, turn right (east) onto West Broadway. At the far end of the block is *Porter House*, 401 West Broadway, (563) 382-8465, admission. Once the home of Adelbert Porter, a collector of butterflies, moths, and insects, stamps and first-day covers, rocks, and minerals, this Italianate mansion now displays those collections for visitors. Note how Porter worked the rocks and minerals he collected into the rock, wall he spent six years erecting around the mansion. In the wall, are agate, petrified wood, rose quartz, crystal, jasper, onyx, and amethyst.

From Porter House, go north on River Street for two blocks and turn left (west) on West Water Street, the downtown's main thoroughfare. In a couple blocks you will see what looks like an elegant, three-story, Italianate, brick hotel. Well, that's what it was when built in 1877 but now it's *Vesterheim Norwegian-American Museum*, 520 West Water Street, (563) 382-9681, admission, the nation's oldest and largest museum that teaches about America's Norwegian immigrants. Vesterheim, which means "western house" in Norwegian, displays traditional clothing, folk arts, and various equipment of the Norwegians who settled here in the nineteenth century. There's even a 25-foot sailboat that

brought two Norwegians across the Atlantic to America, and its mast is extended to its full height inside the museum. The third floor holds revolving exhibits, showing different items from the permanent collection with themes that

A former hotel now serves as the Vesterheim Norwegian-American Museum in Decorah.

relate to the Norwegian settlers and their descendants. Behind the museum are historical buildings that include a nineteenth-century farmhouse and gristmill from Valdrez, Norway, where a number of immigrants came from, log homes of some of the early Norwegian settlers, and a four-story limestone mill.

During the summer, the staff hosts workshops that last from one to five days on ethnic crafts such as rosemaling, wood carving, ship carving, spoon carving, Danish needlework, and Norwegian cooking. The museum has a gift shop and carries folk art supplies in its *Westby-Torgeson Education Center*, 502 West Water Street. By the way, Decorah celebrates its Scandinavian heritage the last full weekend of July with *Nordic Fest*, which highlights ethnic crafts, art, food, music, and dancing.

On the same block as the museum is the *Dayton House Cafe*, 516 West Water Street, (563) 382-9683. If you were here in years past, you'll surely remember its Norwegian dishes; well, some Norwegian dishes are still served, but the new owner-chef is more into haute cuisine, which many locals are raving about.

Two blocks east of the café is the *Decorah Chamber of Commerce*, 300 West Water Street, (563) 382-3990 and (800) 463-4692, which has tourism information about the city and Winneshiek County.

Three more blocks to the east is one of Decorah's best surprises, *Hotel Winneshiek*, 104 East Water, (563) 382-4164 and (800) 998-4164. Built in 1905 as a luxury hotel, the Winneshiek, thanks to a lot of careful attention, is still a splendid hotel that will bowl you over the moment you walk inside its octagonal, wood-paneled, three-story lobby where a cherry wood grand staircase goes up to the third level. And that scene, which few hotels anywhere can match, is just the beginning. Sure, by now you're wondering, "What's a hotel as grand as this doing in a medium-size town in northeast Iowa?" Well, it's apparent that whatever the Winnishiek is doing, it's doing it well, and for more proof of that, either stay in one of its very well-appointed rooms or have a meal in its *Victorian Rose Restaurant* at the rear of the first floor. You'll be glad you did.

Trout Farming

A couple miles south of the city is the Decorah Fish Hatchery, 2321 Siewers Spring Road, (563) 382-8324. Created in the 1930s, it raises rainbow and brown trout in waters from Siewers Spring, Iowa's second largest spring, and stocks state waterways with approximately 120,000 of them each year. A gazebo with maps and other information and signs on the property help visitors understand the operations. To reach the hatchery, go to the southeast edge of Decorah on State Highway 9, turn south onto Trout Run Road, and go until you reach the hatchery.

Now, in your car, go two more blocks east on East Water Street and turn left (north) onto Riverside Avenue. Follow the road as it curves to the east four blocks later to become Winnishiek Avenue. After five blocks, bear left (northeast) and take the 5th Street Bridge across the Upper Iowa River. Just past the river, turn left (west) onto Ice Cave Road. After about a quarter mile is the turnoff to Ice Cave, but you should ignore it nowadays because it is basically sealed off—this is mentioned in case you're thinking about checking it out. Snuggled into a limestone bluff, the cave contains crumbly rock, and things were getting dangerous. Also, ice forms in the spring and lasts until summer, and the wet and sometimes icy floor of the cave made footing treacherous. Even though you may have been here in the past when things were less hazardous, don't plan to stop now.

About a quarter mile west of Ice Cave is a more accommodating place to visit, *Dunning's Spring*, (563) 382-4158, free, a nice park where spring waters ramble down through large and small blocks of limestone, forming Iowa's highest waterfall (well, some call it a waterfall). On a warm day, it's quite refreshing to walk in the spring's cool waters, although you should be careful on the rocks, which can be slippery. And now for an important warning: do not even think of climbing the rocky cliffs alongside the stream—they're proven killers. For a safer way to see more of this pretty canyon, take the footbridge across the stream and use a boardwalk there to reach the upper end of the stream.

From Dunning's Spring, head west on Ice Cave Road to where it comes to a T intersection with College Drive. Turn right (northwest) and go about three quarters of a mile to Pole Line Road, passing along the campus of Luther College. Turn left (west) on Pole Line Road. After it crosses U.S. Highway 52 in less than a half mile, it becomes County Road W20. Go for 3 more miles. As the road curves back and forth on its way northwest through densely wooded hills, you'll arrive at the entrance to *Malanaphy Springs State Preserve*, (563) 534-7145, where a dirt road leads to a parking area; note that the short road can be impassable after heavy rains. A quarter-mile footpath takes you from the parking lot to a shaded slope where spring waters gush from among the rocks and tumble down into the Upper Iowa River, which courses through the preserve.

Return to County W20 and continue driving northwest for about 6 miles. You'll come to Bluffton Bridge, which crosses the Upper Iowa. To view a great scene, look upriver to your right where buff-colored bluffs rise as high as 400 feet over the river.

Cross the bridge, turn to the left (south) on Village Road and drive a short distance to Bluffton. This small community is the home of some outfitters who can set you up for a paddling trip down the Upper Iowa (see the sidebar on the Upper Iowa River for more information). On the last full weekend of each July, Bluffton hosts *Lite Up the Bluff*, an outdoor concert that has featured many of the largest names in country music. Nearby is *Bluffton Fir Stand State Preserve*, a grove of rare balsam fir trees.

In the middle of Bluffton, take Bluffton Hill Road north about a half mile to County W20. Turn right (east) and go back to Bluffton Bridge. Just past the bridge, turn off W20 to the left (north) and only a moment later on this curving road, turn left at the next fork onto Hitching Post Road, and take that straight east for 2 miles to Highway 52. Turn left (north) onto 52 and proceed for 3.5 miles directly into Burr Oak. This tiny community offers a big attraction: the *Laura Ingalls Wilder Park and Museum*, 3603 236th Avenue, (563) 735-5916, admission. The only site in Iowa linked with Wilder, who authored several *Little House* books, this simple-looking, white-frame, one-and-a-half-story building was an 11-room hotel that was managed by her father when she was nine years old, in 1876. At that time, Burr Oak was a busy stop on a wagon trail that went through the town, and on some days up to 200 people would pass through the community.

Although Wilder eventually wrote about every place she lived in, including this one, for some reason her publisher never printed her recollections about Burr Oak or the Little Hotel of the Hills, leading some of her fans to regard Burr Oak as the missing link in her writings. This hotel is the sole place where Wilder lived that remains on its original site.

From Burr Oak, head west on County Road A18 for 8 miles to State Highway 139.

Quick Trip Option 1: Five miles west of Burr Oak on A18, turn left at 288th Avenue. Go 1.5 miles south to Cold Water Creek Road, turn left (east), and go a half mile to *Cold Water Creek Wilderness Area*. Turn north, and descend a steep, rocky road to a small parking area in *Cold Water Spring State Preserve*, (563) 382-4895. The rest of the trip is on foot: hike a half mile through a very pretty area of rocky bluffs and woods to the bottom of a spectacular 150-foot-high cliff where the waters of Cold Water Spring gush out. By the way, wear waterproof shoes or boots.

In 1967, cavers dove into the spring and discovered a cave system that's been mapped at least 16 miles long. The cave is ranked as the 33rd-longest in the nation; it's also the most extensive cave system in Iowa. The original en-

Some Places That Can Grow on You

North of Decorah on U.S. Highway 52 are two wonderful places to visit if you're into growing plants.

About 3 miles north of Pole Line Road on 52 is the turnoff to *Seed Savers Heritage Farm*, 3076 North Winn Road, (563) 382-5990, admission—watch for a sign on the right (east) at County Road W34. Not the usual Iowa farm with livestock and crops, this is the headquarters of Seed Savers Exchange, which produces many heirloom vegetable, fruit, flower, and herb seeds, representing plants, including prairie plants, that are no longer commonly grown. These include Bird Egg bean, Moon and Stars watermelon, Brandywine tomatoes, and a few more varieties of plants . . . say a thousand or so. The apple orchard alone has at least 800 types of apples.

Return to Highway 52 from Seed Savers and go north once more, almost to the community of Burr Oak. This time watch for a blue sign that points the way to a gravel road on the left (west). This leads to *Willowglen Nursery*, 3512 Lost Mile Road, (563) 735-5570, free. The specialties here are perennial plants, including some that are hard to find nowadays. The owners also have lots of information on such things as designs for gardens of all types and instructions for making garden ornaments out of natural materials, including willow.

trance is now covered by a gate; although there are other ways in, they are for professional cavers. Still, the preserve is a very pretty place to visit. Return to A18 and turn left (west) to continue to Highway 139.

At Highway 139, turn left (south) and go about 2 miles into Kendallville. This bump in the road has a park offering a good access point for paddlers on the Upper Iowa River. Also in town is a paddling outfitter (see sidebar).

Continue south on Highway 139 from Kendallville for 7 miles to State Highway 9.

The Upper Iowa River

Many people who have paddled and floated on Iowa's rivers consider the Upper Iowa to be the state's premier waterway for such ventures. Try it and you'll soon agree, no matter how you travel—by canoe, tube, or kayak. In a region unlike most of the state, this river curves and bends its way around small meadows and pine-capped, rocky escarpments that loom above the waters and in general takes you away from everything. Although it's possible to put in at Lime Springs (which we'll visit in a few moments by car), most folks put in at Kendallville or, 16 miles away, at Bluffton and then pull out at one of the access points in Decorah, about 14 miles below Bluffton. By the way, between Kendallville and Bluffton is a massive rock formation called Chimney Rock, which stands about 300 feet tall and is 50 feet in diameter.

While many love to travel the river between Kendallville and Decorah, many knowledgeable anglers consider the area below the lower dam, about 10 miles northeast of Decorah, as the state's best fishing spot. In this remote area live channel catfish, walleye, northern pike, sauger, smallmouth bass, rock bass, and, occasionally, trout; the last three are also found in the river between Kendallville and Decorah.

Area outfitters include: *Chimney Rock Campground and Canoe Rental*, Bluffton, 3312 Chimney Rock Road, (563) 735-5786 and (877) 787-CAMP; *Hruska's Canoe Rental and Campground; Kendallville and Bluffton*, 3233 347th Street, (563) 547-4566; *Randy's Bluffton Store, Campground, Canoe Livery*, Bluffton, 2619 West Ravine Road, (563) 735-5738.

Turn right (east) and drive 2 miles into Cresco. As you drive through town on 2nd Avenue, note the antique stores along the highway (there are others off the highway too) as well as *Pine Needles Quilt Shop*, 105 2nd Avenue SW, (563) 547-1212, which has a following far beyond Cresco because of its supplies, patterns, and more.

A few more blocks down the street from there is *Bethany Housewares*, 423 2nd Avenue SW, (563) 547-5873. Should you think this is just another store where you can buy items to use around the house—wrong! This is where they're *made* and they aren't your run-of-the-mill pots, pans, and cooking tools. Remember the Scandinavian foods in Decorah? Well, if you want to try making some of those yourself, step into the retail store of this manufacturing plant and choose what you need from among the many items made here, such as turning sticks, grills, and rolling pins used to make lefse (a flat potato bread), plette pans to make Swedish pancakes, *aebleskiver* pans for Danish apple dumplings, and krumkake bakers. Non-Scandinavian items made and sold here include cannoli form sets, tortilla presses, and lattice pasta rollers. And then there are the everyday items: bagel holders, apple corers, donut makers, and more. Naturally, what are all those kitchen tools worth unless you have some cookbooks? Plenty of those are here too.

At Beadle Park, which is across Highway 9 from Pine Needles Quilt Shop at North Elm Street, is the *Howard County Log Cabin Museum*, (563) 547-3444 and (800) 373-6293, free. Built in 1854, this cabin was used for 110 years and is furnished with early items. Nearby historic locomotives and train cars are open to the public. Just west of the park, at 3rd Street West and 1st Avenue West, a farmers' market featuring produce raised by area Amish and Mennonite families and others is held every Tuesday and Friday, 2–5:30 p.m. during the growing season.

The park is also connected to two trails. To the east, *Prairie Farmer Recreational Trail*, which has a packed-cinder surface, rolls for 19 miles southeast to an old depot in Calmar. To the west runs *Prairie Springs Recreational Trail*, a paved, 2-mile-long path, which leads to *Vernon Springs*, a pretty park with a small lake (actually, a dammed portion of the Turkey River) that supports fishing and small watercraft; a campground is expected to be developed in the future.

The park is also the headquarters of the Howard County Conservation Board, 11562 Valley Avenue, (563) 547-3634, which has a nature center with displays about the county's wetlands, prairies, and woodlands. Of particular interest are the mural along the staircase that shows the transition between the county's ecosystems and a live honeybee exhibit. To reach the park by car, turn south onto 3rd Street West at Highway 9, go to 4th Street SW; turn right and follow the brown county signs, which will lead you onto Vernon Road and then to the park in about a mile.

It should be noted that Howard County is Iowa's snowmobile capital and on the last full weekend in January, the local *Driftrunners Snowmobile Club*, the oldest in Iowa, hosts Snowfest, the state's premier snowmobile rally. Members of the club also maintain more than 350 miles of snowmobile trails that lace this area and link more than a dozen communities when the snow falls. And on the last weekend of August (unless that falls on the Labor Day weekend), downtown Cresco hosts its Agfest, which some people like to visit in conjunction with a similar festival held the same weekend in Postville (see Tour 18) about 40 miles to the southeast.

In 2004, it's expected that the Howard County Historical Society will build a museum near the fairgrounds that are alongside Highway 9 on the west end of town—so keep an eye out for this development.

From the center of Cresco, drive north on 3rd Street West and head out of town on what becomes County Road V58. You should be aware that many Amish and Mennonite families live in the area north and west of Cresco, so drive carefully because you may happen upon horse-drawn vehicles on the roads at times. Also respect the Amish desire not to be photographed.

At County Road A23, 5 miles north of Cresco, turn left (west), but still follow V58 when it turns north again in about a half mile. Continue for 2 miles. You'll come upon *Golden Ridge Honey Farm*, 23226 20th Street,

Cresco's Famous Names

Norman Borlaug was born in Cresco in 1914 and later became a geneticist and plant pathologist who studied wheat. He developed strains of wheat that could be planted in parts of the world where it could not be grown before. Because of these efforts to eliminate world hunger, Dr. Borlaug was awarded the Nobel Peace Prize in 1970.

Born in Cresco in 1904, Ellen Church became a registered nurse and, in California, took flying lessons. Upon being rejected as a pilot by Boeing Air Transport (predecessor of United Airlines), she pitched the airline the idea of using nurses on its passenger planes, an idea that resulted in her becoming the first airline stewardess. Her initial flight was with 15 passengers from Oakland, California, to Chicago in May 1930. Called Sky Girls for a while, the early stewardesses (now called flight attendants) had to, in addition to aiding passengers, carry baggage, and help move, fuel, and maintain the aircraft. They also had to be single, weigh less than 115 pounds, be at most five-feet, four-inches tall and be younger than 25 years old. Their initial pay was $125 a month.

After only 18 months on the job, Church gave up her duties because of an injury suffered in a car accident. She returned to nursing and then joined the Army in World War II, serving with distinction in North Africa, Sicily, and Normandy as she evacuated wounded soldiers from those areas.

Church died after a horse-riding accident in Indiana in 1965. The airfield on the southwest side of Cresco is named in her memory.

(563) 547-4222, which processes the honey from 1,200 area beehives and then packages it for statewide distribution through groceries; visitors are welcome at the gift shop, which has bear-shaped plastic bottles of liquid honey. Nearby is *Golden Ridge Cheese* (no phone), an Amish-owned and -managed facility that makes triple-cream bleu cheese, which restaurants in Chicago and New York order—and here's your chance to have it as fresh as can be!

Return to County Road A23, turn right (west), and roll for about 8.5 miles into Lime Springs. Turn right (north) at Miller Street and go 1 mile to the Upper Iowa River. Here sits the picturesque *Lidtke Mill*, (563) 566-2827, admission, near a 10-acre park where you can fish, canoe, and camp. In 1857, the first sawmill on the premises was built and three years later it was altered to grind wheat. That burned in 1894, and Lidtke Mill was built on the same spot, with an electric dynamo added in 1915. Although pretty year-round, the mill is open only on weekend afternoons during the summer.

From the mill, return to Lime Springs and turn right (west) at Jackson Street. Drive about 5.5 miles, with the last half mile on gravel, to *Hayden Prairie*. At 240 acres, Hayden Prairie is the largest remnant of tall-grass prairie in eastern Iowa and has both mesic (black soil) prairie that supports big bluestem, Indian grass, and northern dropseed and wet prairie, which is characterized by the presence of bluejoint and slough grass. Among the flowers are shooting star, which has white and lavender petals that look like they're the flames of a shooting star being blown back as it streaks across the sky, and prairie smoke, a small plant with feathery plumes.

Head south from Hayden Prairie on County Road V26 for 5 miles to State Highway 9; turn left (east) and go for 4.5 miles to U.S. Highway 63. Turn right (south) and cruise for 23 miles to New Hampton.

As you approach New Hampton, you'll be on the new four-lane section of Highway 63. Take the exit south into town and turn left (east) at Main Street, which, to the east, is also State Highway 24. Go a short distance to Water Street. Near the intersection of Main and Water is the *Carnegie Cultural Center*, 7 North Water, (641) 394-2354, free. A former library, the center hosts events, permanent displays, and rotating exhibits. One exhibit highlighted the baseball teams that played in Chickasaw County in the twentieth century. In the Railroad Room on the lower floor are original railroad artifacts, photo displays about the county's depots, railroad architecture, and local

Saint Peter's Rock

About 6 miles north of New Hampton and 3.5 miles west of Highway 63 on a gravel road is Saint Peter's Rock. Measuring about 20 by 25 feet and standing around 17 feet above ground, this chunk of granite from northern Wisconsin was deposited here when the last glacier in this area melted some 8,000 years ago. Visible for miles, this rock is connected with one of Iowa's bigger frauds.

In 1857, New York lawyer J. T. Donovan concocted a scheme to sell property in the town of Saint Peter, Iowa to unsuspecting individuals back east. The town existed only in his imagination. He even went so far as to show investors pictures of buildings that actually existed in Saint Peter—Saint Peter, Minnesota, although he didn't tell anyone that. Along the way, he took in $7,000. His scheme was uncovered when some of his investors traveled to Iowa and, instead of finding a town, saw nothing more than this large rock.

employees, and a large, working train layout of Chickasaw County showing the railroad lines, farms, and communities during three time periods. There's also a 1/12-scale steam locomotive once used in carnivals. Also on the floor is Virgil's Tractors, a collection of model tractors, and Jerry's World, a cityscape of buildings made of different small building blocks manufactured over the last half century.

Upstairs is the Natvig Brothers Circus, a large, colorful, scale model in which all the people and animals were hand carved and placed in hand-assembled settings by local Richard Natvig, who still adds to the display now and then. There's another exhibit you have to see to believe (you'll catch the pun in a moment)—a collection of various eyeglasses assembled by Winfred E. "Doc" Tunnell, a local optometrist. Among them are sunglasses dating back to the Revolutionary War, driving goggles from the early days of automobiles, eye shields made of ivory by Eskimos, monocles, and a pair of hoity-toity opera glasses made in 1930. Collections of dolls and cast-iron toys are also here.

Head east on Highway 24 for 20 miles, passing through Lawlor and Jackson Junction to Fort Atkinson. In the center of town, turn left (west) at Main Street and follow it a few blocks to *Fort Atkinson State Preserve*, (563) 425-4161, free. Basically a state historic park, this fort is the only one of its kind; that is, it was built to protect one group of Indians from another. What had happened was that the federal government wanted to create a buffer between the Sioux, to the north, and their enemies, the Sauk-and-Fox alliance, to the south. So a 40-mile-wide neutral zone was created, and into it were moved the Winnebago from Wisconsin because the authorities thought the Winnebago got along with the other Indians. Not so—and Fort Atkinson had to be built in 1840 to protect 2,900 Winnebago men, women, and children. When the Winnebago were moved to Minnesota in 1848, the troops left a year later. Some of the limestone buildings have been reconstructed and traces of

The ruins of one building and the re-creation of another are among the things to see at Fort Atkinson State Preserve; the original structures were built in 1840.

other buildings can still be seen. A museum is located in the stone barracks, a two-story building that included the chapel and hospital. On the last full weekend of each September, memories of the past come alive during the *Fort Atkinson Rendezvous*, an event well attended by reenactors.

Quick Trip Option: About 4 miles southeast of Fort Atkinson, near tiny Festina, is the *Chapel of Saint Anthony of Padua*, free. Called the world's smallest cathedral by some, this 14-by-20-foot limestone church with four pews was built by one of Napoleon's soldiers, Johann Gaertner, in 1886 as a gesture of thanks for surviving the battles in which he had fought in Europe. Gaertner, who was 92 when he built the chapel, died the next year, and his final resting place is marked by a boulder behind the church. From Main Street, head south a short distance on Highway 24 to County Road B32. Turn left (east) and about 4 miles away you'll come to State Highway 150. Turn right (south) and immediately watch for signs for the church.

From Fort Atkinson (the park that is), head west on Main, which becomes County Road W14 out of town, and take it west, then north, for 5 miles to Spillville. This town is as rich with Czech heritage as Decorah is with Norwegian history. As soon as you enter town on Main Street, there's no missing *Bily Clocks Museum*, 323 Main Street, (563) 562-3569, admission, not with a huge clock standing outside the red brick building. Carved and built between 1913 and 1958 by brothers Frank and Joseph Bily (pronounced Bee-lee), who were lifelong bachelors, the 40, highly ornate, wooden clocks in the museum were made when the brothers weren't farming near town. Made of butternut, walnut, oak, and maple, these fantastic creations range in size and shape from a violin-shaped clock honoring the great Czech composer Antonin Dvorak (more about him in a moment) to an eight-foot-tall, 500-pound behemoth that shows a parade of the 12 apostles when it chimes. Another clock, made in 1928, honors Charles Lindbergh's solo flight across the Atlantic. There's also one that shows the history of the American pioneer, which some say Henry Ford offered to buy for $1 million in the 1940s. The Bilys never sold any of their clocks, preferring to keep them as a collection in Spillville.

Besides the clock made by the Bilys to honor him, Dvorak has other connections with Spillville. In the summer of 1893, he and his family stayed on the second floor of the museum building while he worked on the scores for his *New World Symphony and American Quartette*. He also took walks along the Turkey River, which flows through town, walks that later inspired him to write *Humoresque*. The room where the Dvoraks lived has information about his stay.

Behind the museum is the two-room *Bouska Schoolhouse*. Made of logs in 1854, this cabin housed a teacher and family in one room while the other served as the classroom.

Farther north on Main is the town square. Turn left (west) there and up the hill on Church Street you'll come to the striking *Saint Wenceslaus Church*. Made of limestone and bearing a red-tile roof, it was made in 1860 for the Czechs who lived in the region; Dvorak often played its Pfeffer pipe organ when he was here. One interesting aspect of this church is visible only if you walk inside: it has no central aisle—that's right, the long pews lay between aisles that run along the side walls. In the church's cemetery are cast-iron grave markers made in the nineteenth century.

Return to Main Street, go south and just past the Bily Clock Museum, turn left (east) onto State Highway 325. Drive for 4 miles to U.S. Highway 52. Turn left (north) and cruise back for about 7 miles to Decorah. Okay, you may think you're done with this tour, but there's one more place to visit.

From the intersection of Highway 52 and Highway 9 on the southwest edge of Deco-

Ornate clocks made in the first half of the twentieth century by brothers Frank and Joseph Bily are displayed at the Bily Clocks Museum in Spillville.

rah (where we began many miles ago), go north on 52 less than a half mile and turn right into *Phelps Park*. Park your vehicle and take to the *Oneota Trail*, part of a 15-mile trail system that wanders through this area along the Upper Iowa River. About 300 yards from the trailhead is something that's rarely seen and a sign points it out for you—an algific cave or an algific slope. Don't expect a big cave you can walk into. No, an algific cave is a series of interconnected, underground passageways that have very small openings in the ground, usually on the north slope of a hill. From deep underground where air stays cool year-round, each opening breathes a chilly breath, if you will, that supports a micro-ecosystem of plants that cannot survive anywhere else, even just a few inches away in warmer air. So look at these fragile, rare little plants all you want but please leave them alone. Although this particular one is marked, algific caves are found throughout this hilly region of Iowa, which is laced with all sorts of caves.

Okay, *now* you're finished with this tour.

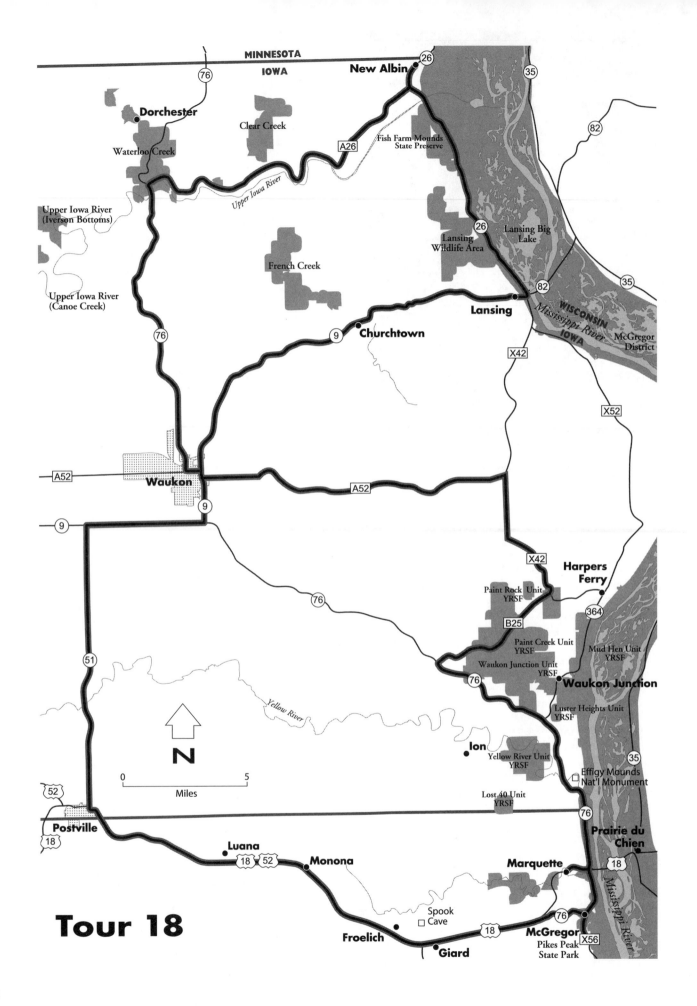

Tour 18

Tour 18
Iowa's Northeast Corner— Where Everything Rambles

McGregor—Marquette—Lansing—New Albin—Waukon—Postville—Monona—Froelich—McGregor

Distance: approximately 125 miles

If there's a tour in this book that's basically a driving tour, in the sense of driving just to enjoy the scenery without stopping too many places, this is the one. That's because in the northeast corner of Iowa, you're in the midst of what's called the Driftless Area, a region that was somehow missed by all the glaciers that ground down and nearly flattened much of the Upper Midwest. Here, just like the rambling waterways, the roads twist and turn, rise and fall as they cross a countryside of tree-laden hills, open meadows, farm fields that are tucked into wherever they can fit, and valleys narrow and wide. Attractions here are spread out but they're still very good and very surprising in some cases.

This tour begins in McGregor alongside the Mississippi River. At the T intersection of Main Street and Buell Avenue, go southeast on County Road X56 for about 1.5 miles. You'll immediately leave town and begin to roll up into the hills. By the way, don't worry about seeing McGregor; we'll be back.

You'll find yourself at the entrance to *Pikes Peak State Park*, 15316 Great River Road, (563) 873-2341. Park and get out for a nice walk along the tops of the hills that overlook the broad valley of the Mississippi River—there are few views in Iowa like this. Two observation platforms project over the edges of the bluffs, which rise up to 500 feet above the river. To the north, is the bridge linking Wisconsin and Iowa; to the south, the confluence of the Mississippi and Wisconsin Rivers. It was in this area that Jacques Marquette and Louis Joliet became the first European-Americans to see the Mississippi River when they paddled their way out of the Wisconsin River on June 17, 1673.

The morning sun shines through autumn-colored trees at Pikes Peak State Park, which overlooks the meandering channels of the Mississippi River near McGregor.

A trail from the larger observation deck leads north into a ravine where a thin but nice waterfall, *Bridal Veil Falls*, drops down a U-shaped canyon; there are many steps along the way, which has a boardwalk. Other trails lead throughout the 970-acre park, going to an old quarry, traversing wooded hillsides, and passing burial mounds, many in the shape of animals, left hundreds of years ago by prehistoric Indians. The park also has 76 campsites, 60 with electricity.

Some readers may wonder, "What's a park in Iowa doing with the name Pikes Peak, especially when a large, prominent mountain in the Colorado Rockies has the same name and is much more famous?" Well, the same Pike, Lieutenant Zebulon Pike of the U.S. Army, was traveling up the Mississippi in 1805 at the same time that Captains Meriwether Lewis and William Clark were leading their expedition to the Pacific Ocean. Pike's mission was to lead 20 men to find the headwaters of the Mississippi River (which they failed to do) and, along the way, reconnoiter sites for forts in what was then a part of the newly acquired Louisiana Purchase. One spot Pike picked was here and it became known as Pikes Peak. However no fort was built here; instead the army constructed one where Prairie du Chien, Wisconsin, is now.

The interior of the River Junction Trading Company in McGregor is an actual store that has outfitted television and motion picture productions, as well as individuals interested in the lore of the Wild (and tame) West.

Not until 1806, when Pike went west with another expedition, did he see the big mountain on the front range of the Rocky Mountains that is now named for him—the *second* Pikes Peak.

From the park, return to McGregor and park somewhere along Main Street. This

charming town began as a ferry landing that Alexander McGregor created in 1837. The charm is immediately evident in the stately old brick buildings of the small business district—a great place to take to your feet.

One very interesting place that should not be missed, although it is a business and not a tourist attraction, is *River Junction Trading Company*, 312 Main Street, (563) 873-2387. Just stepping into the store may make you wonder if you have passed through a time portal and dropped back into the late nineteenth century. Opened in 1973, this business handles and produces items related to the Old West. Want a vest that will make you look like an old-time riverboat gambler? It's here. The same goes for everyday shirts worn by men back then as well as skirts worn by the women. Military-style blouses worn by army officers such as General George Custer are here too, along with saddlebags, gun belts, authentic-looking guns that fire only blanks, spurs, chaps, tipis, ladies shoes, long johns, longhorns, and more. If you want something more authentic than what you see here, you will have to steal it from some museum.

Take your time and walk along the other stores that line Main Street on the way to the river: antique stores, bookshops, gift stores, and more. Along the way is the *McGregor Historical Museum*, 234 Main Street (no phone), and across the street, the *Alexander Hotel*, 213 Main, (563) 873-3838, which was built in 1899 and has a café, pub, and dining room on its main floor and guest rooms upstairs. Also in the area is the *McGregor-Marquette Chamber of Commerce*, 146 Main, (563) 873-2186 and (800) 896-0910, which has information about the region's attractions, restaurants, and lodgings.

Head north out of town on Main Street, which is also State Highway 76. The road runs on a shelf of land between the Mississippi on one side and steep limestone bluffs on the other. At this point, Highway 76 is part of the *Great River Road*, a network of highways and roads that run the length of the Mississippi River from its mouth at the Gulf of Mexico to its source near Lake Itasca in Minnesota (see Tour 19).

About an eighth of a mile out of McGregor is *Boatels*, 400 Business Highway 18 North, (563) 873-3718 and (800) 747-2628. The second oldest boat rental firm in the nation, Boatels can put you in fishing boats, pontoon boats, and houseboats that carry up to 12 people.

A bit farther up the road, where the bluff on the west side ends, is the *Isle of Capri Casino*, 101 Antimonopoly, (563) 873-3531 and (800) 4-YOU-BET. On shore is a 25-room hotel that hugs a cliff and a pavilion with a buffet and showroom, and on the riverboat itself is the casino with slot machines and table games.

Continue north on Highway 76 for about

1 mile to Marquette. There, you'll pass under the large bridge that spans the Mississippi and carries U.S. Highway 18 east into Prairie du Chien, Wisconsin, the largest community in these parts.

Quick Trip Option 1: Before we go any farther in Iowa, you should consider a short jaunt across the Mississippi into Prairie du Chien on the Wisconsin side. The first thing to know is that the name is pronounced "prairie-due-shane," some variations on the last syllable being "-shin" and "-sheen"—take your choice. However you say it though, it comes from the French phrase meaning "prairie of Dog," referring to an Indian named Dog who lived in the region years ago.

To orient yourself· and obtain information about local attractions, visit the *Prairie du Chien Chamber of Commerce*, 211 South Main, (608) 326-8555 and (800) PDC-1673, which is a triangular-shaped building attended by five flags at the east end of the bridge.

In town is the *Fort Crawford Museum*, 7117 South Beaumont Road, (608) 326-6960, admission, a historical museum that teaches about the history of the region, which was contested ground between the Americans and British during the War of 1812. North of the bridge and alongside the river is *Villa Louis State Historical Park*, Villa Louis Road and Bolvin Street, (608) 326-2721, admission. Built in 1870 by the son of a local entrepreneur, the beautiful "villa loo-ee" has furniture and other items that belonged to its original owner's family. Near the villa is a replica of a blockhouse used during the War of 1812. About three quarters of a mile east of the mansion on Wisconsin Highway 35 is *Cannery Row*, 300 North Marquette, (608) 326-6518, a former pickle processing plant that's now selling antiques, candles, pottery, imported rugs, and fudge.

Just north of town is an outlet store of wilderness outfitter *Cabela's*, 1601 North Wisconsin, (608) 326-5600.

Continue north out of Marquette on Highway 76 for about 3 miles. The highway once again becomes a two-lane road between the Mississippi and some bluffs. After crossing the Yellow River and when the highway curves to the left, you'll be at the entrance to *Effigy Mounds National Monument*, 151 Highway 76, (563) 873-3491, admission. Rebuilt not all that long ago, the visitor center gives a good overview about the burial and ceremonial mounds constructed along the river valley by members of different Indian cultures between 450 BC and AD 1250. Just outside the center, to the south and accessible by a boardwalk, are four of the mounds.

Visiting the rest of the 195 mounds here, however, is going to take some effort. As you drove up the highway, do you remember seeing a large hill ahead of you when you turned past

the Yellow River? The bluff that rises near the visitor center? Well, that bluff is what's called the North Unit and it's what you have to go up on a zigzag trail that never seems to end (actually, the ascent takes most people about 10 minutes—it just seems longer). Once past the switchbacks, walking becomes much easier and up there you can see mounds of different sorts. Most of those in the North Unit are dome shaped and they are called conicals. Some others are raised lines; those are linear mounds. And a few are shaped like animals; these are the effigy mounds. Near the edge of the bluff are overlooks of the Mississippi.

Now for some good news and some bad news. The good is that the South Unit, which is just south of the Yellow River bridge on Highway 76, has more mounds of all shapes and sizes; and best of all, it has the greatest collection of the preserve's 31 effigy mounds, which are in the shape of flying birds and the profiles of bears. Some of the bear mounds measure up to three feet high and a hundred feet long, and a line of 10 of them, called the Marching Bears, is atop a bluff here along with three bird mounds. Now for the bad news: these effigies are near the end of a two-mile hike, so gear up for a one-way walk of about 45 minutes and bring water because none is available in the South Unit. On hot, humid days, bring insect repellent too.

Continue north, then northwest, on Highway 76 for 10 miles to County Road B25; turn right (northeast) and go for about 2.5 miles to the entrance to *Yellow River State Forest*. Heavily wooded, this 8,504-acre preserve, 729 State Forest Road, (563) 586-2254, is popular with those who like to hike, ride horses, camp, cross-country ski, ride snowmobiles, and fish, especially for trout in two streams here. Actually, the forest is composed of several units, some adjacent to each other, some off by themselves. The one to concentrate on is *Paint Creek Unit*, on County Road B25; the headquarters is located here, along with the major campgrounds, which have 168 campsites and include three equestrian campgrounds. Also at this site, 25 miles of trails wander amid bluffs, rocky outcroppings, and steep wooded slopes. Besides wildlife like one can expect to see often in other parts of Iowa, the Yellow River is home to beaver, mink, and bald eagles. If you want to wander on the various auto trails and hiking trails, get a map at the headquarters before you head out.

Quick Trip Option 2: About 5.5 miles past Effigy Mounds on Highway 76, watch for County Road X36 on the left (south) side of the road. Turn here and go about 2 miles to Old Mission Drive, which you should take. This leads to *Ion Exchange*, 1878 Old Mission Drive, (563) 535-7231 and (800) 291-2143, where you can shop for the seeds of various wildflowers, grasses, and other native plants (including some you might think don't exist anymore) that are prepared here. You can also stay in one of the facility's cabins, some of which overlook the Yellow River and offer a hideaway in a part of Iowa unlike the rest of the state.

From Paint Creek Unit, continue going northeast on B25 for 3.5 miles to County Road X42. Along the way you'll pass through the forest's *Paint Rock Unit* (notice the difference in the name), another area of narrow valleys and rugged limestone and sandstone hills covered with oak, elm, hickory, and black locust trees. This unit earns its name from a prominent rock at the end of a large ridge on the left (north) side of the road; a landmark in years past, the limestone rock bears petroglyphs painted by prehistoric Indians although they are so difficult to reach that they are inaccessible for the average person. Trust the adventurists who have been there; the petroglyphs do exist.

Turn left (west) onto X42 and drive for less than 6 miles to County Road A52. Turn left (west) and proceed for about 14 miles to Waukon. A part of the *Driftless Area Scenic Byway*, A52 is marked by distinctive brown, green, blue, and white signs. Although Waukon is the approximate midway point of the tour, it wouldn't hurt to check in at *Allamakee County Economic Development and Tourism Commission*, 101 West Main, (563) 568-2624, to see what's

ahead. There are some other neat places in town to visit but we'll check on those a bit later.

At the intersection with State Highway 9 in the center of Waukon, turn right. Head north, then northeast for about 6 miles to the *Landmark Inn.* Now a private residence, the initial part of this two-story, white-frame building was built as a home in 1851; the rear section, added later, was at various times a hotel, a brewery, a post office, a tearoom, a bar, a restaurant, and a store. Out back is a two-story stone fort, often called the Gun Tower or Gun House, which was built in 1853. A blue historical sign in the front provides information about the structures.

Continue northeast on Highway 9 for another 8 miles to Lansing.

Quick Trip Option 3: If you don't want to cut back and forth across the countryside on the way to Lansing as we've done, there's a more direct way from Effigy Mounds to Lansing. About 3 miles past Effigy Mounds, turn right (northeast) onto State Highway 364, which leads to Harpers Ferry, a town that lies alongside the Mississippi River. Continue through town and on the far side, the road becomes County Road X52. This follows the river for a few miles and then cuts inland to go to Lansing, about 14 miles from Harpers Ferry. This way, you'll see more of the Mississippi but miss some of the splendidly varied topography of Yellow River State Forest.

Upon entering Lansing, turn left (north) at 6th Street and follow that a short distance to the top of Mount Hosmer. This 25-acre park is one of the best overlooks of the Upper Mississippi River Valley, about three miles wide at this point, and from here you can see Iowa, Minnesota, and Wisconsin. In May 1851, the steamboat *Senator* stopped here and one of its passengers was 21-year-old Harriet Hosmer. Upon learning that there was time to go ashore and climb the hill, Hosmer challenged a male companion to race up the hill; she won . . . and the 450-foot-tall hill was named in her honor. Hosmer later became a celebrated sculptor and painter.

Return to Lansing and turn left at Highway 9, which is also Main Street. As you continue east on Main, you'll have a view that few other towns in Iowa have—the Mississippi River laid out before you at the bottom of the street.

Close to the river is the *Museum of River History*, 61 Front Street, (563) 538-4641, free, which tells the story of this part of the big river, particularly the story of the fishing and clamming industries as well as that of the period when pearl buttons were made out of clam shells here. Not far away is *S&S Rentals, Inc.*, 990 Front Street, (563) 538-4454 and (800) 728-0131, where you can rent a houseboat to explore the Mississippi

Lansing sits alongside the Mississippi and at the base of Mount Hosmer, which was named for a woman who raced to its peak in 1851.

on your own on a relaxing venture. If you want, you can pull into one of the marinas along the river or simply beach the houseboat on the sandy shore of one of the many islands in the river for an unforgettable overnight stay. If you're not up for a long trip on the river, check with *Mississippi River Cruises*, (563) 586-2179, which offers guided tours of the backwaters of the mighty river; call for reservations.

If you want to paddle the backwaters of the Mississippi here, turnouts along the bridge to Wisconsin provide access points for launching canoes and other kinds of small craft. The area is part of the huge *Upper Mississippi River National Wildlife and Fish Refuge* (headquarters on Business Highway 18 north of McGregor, (563) 873-3423). It provides copious opportunities for viewing a myriad of wildlife, including beaver, fox, muskrat, and otter, not to mention at least 228 types of birds, other mammals, and about three dozen kinds of reptiles and amphibians.

Finally, if you get hungry in Lansing, good things have been said about *Milty's*, 200 Main Street, (563) 538-4585, and *Clancy's*, 100 Main Street, (563) 538-4104, which is near the river.

From Main Street, turn left (north) on State Highway 26 and drive about 7 miles to *Fish Farm Mounds*. Here is a group of 30 or so conical mounds, which are far easier to visit than those at Effigy Mounds. In case you wonder about the name, this state preserve was once part of a farm owned by the Fish family. Incidentally, Highway 26 is another part of the Great River Road.

Continue north on Highway 26 for 2 more miles, crossing the Upper Iowa River and entering New Albin. The town is tucked away in the far, far northeastern corner of the state. On the state border is an iron post erected in 1849 to mark the border with the then newly established territory of Minnesota.

Double back down Highway 26 about 1.5 miles from New Albin and turn right (west) at County Road A26. Drive for 16 miles to State Highway 76. The route, another leg of the Driftless Area Scenic Byway, is about as different from most of Iowa's straight-as-an-arrow roads as you can get. Bending and twisting and looping alongside the Upper Iowa River, this is a ride to savor.

Quick Trip Option 4: There are long barns, tall barns, short barns, and even some round barns but not many 12-sided barns. About 1.5 miles after starting on A26, detour onto County Road A11 on your right (north). This quickly leads to the privately owned Reburn Barn, which was built in 1914 for the original owner's dairy operations.

At State Highway 76, turn left (south) and

proceed into Waukon again, about 13 miles away. After entering town from the northwest on 9th Street NW, proceed to Main Street. Turn left (east) to go to Allamakee Street in the center of town. Nearby, you'll find the *Allamakee County Historical Museum*, 107 Allamakee Street, (563) 568-2954, admission. The building holding the museum was built in 1861 in the midst of a 25-year-long struggle to create a county seat. Finally, after 10 elections, at least two raids on county records, and the construction of two county courthouses—this one and another near Lansing—this building officially became the county courthouse in 1866. In 1941, a new courthouse was built in Waukon, and this building was taken over by the county historical society, which has maintained the courtroom as it had been designed and added displays about Indian artifacts, timepieces, and other collections. Outside is the 1872 log cabin made by immigrant Syver Gjefle.

While in town, visit *Driftaway Tours*, 106 East Main, (563) 568-2051 and (800) 643-9229, to learn about seeing northeast Iowa in some rather different ways: hot-air balloon rides, airboat tours on the region's rivers, fishing on the Mississippi, watching bald eagles in the winter, and more. While you can stop in for information, call ahead for reservations.

Head south on Allamakee Street, which is also State Highway 9/76, until Highway 9 turns to the right (west) less than 2 miles out of town. You should do likewise and then, after 5 miles, turn left (south) onto State Highway 51. Take that for 11 miles to Postville. For many years, Postville was very much like many other communities in the Upper Midwest; most of its residents were Christian and Caucasian. In the late 1980s, Orthodox Jews from New York came to town to open a kosher meat-packing plant—in a facility that had been closed—to control the processing of meat they sold in East Coast markets. Later, many Hispanics arrived to work in another meat-packing plant in the area. At last count, new residents from as many as 27 countries have swelled the population considerably and have turned Postville into quite an international community.

This rapid change has brought the town attention, and many residents feel that reports about the discord in the town are not entirely accurate. Instead, they prefer to focus on the positive changes that have taken place. Nowadays, besides the German and Norwegian accents that have filtered down through the generations, expect to hear English tinged with Spanish, Hebrew, Russian, and Ukrainian accents, among others.

After arriving via North Lawler Street near the center of town, turn right (west) on Greene Street and immediately park near the *Postville Visitor Center*. Located at 111 West Greene Street, (563) 864-3440, this is a good place to begin to understand what's been going on here. Note the sign on the door: "Let Us Take You Around the World in a Day"—that sums up modern Postville. Evidence of the town's international flavor can be found just a few doors west. *Jacob's Table* and *Jacob's Market*, both at 121 West Greene, (563) 864-7087, are the only kosher restaurant and grocery for miles around. And as a matter of fact, owner Shulamis Jenkelowitz caters meals for various occasions as far away as Milwaukee, a four-hour drive. Walk a block to the south on Lawler Street and you'll find *Sabor Latino*, 142 South Lawler Street, (563) 864-3810, another combination grocery-restaurant which features great Mexican meals and foods.

Postville celebrates its many and various cultures with *A Taste of Postville*, a food festival usually held on the last Sunday of each August (unless it's on Labor Day weekend). Some people love to visit this festival and then go west about 40 miles to visit Cresco and take part in that town's annual Agfest which is held the same weekend (see Tour 17).

John Mott, A Nobel Man

An early example of Postville's spirit of tolerance and acceptance, John R. Mott, son of the town's first mayor, won the 1946 Nobel Peace Prize at the age of 81 for working to form ecumenical movements across the world. Creating the Council of World Churches in 1948 as a forum for the people of various religions to work together on social problems, Mott also helped found the World Student Christian Association and the Student Volunteer Movement for Foreign Missions, a division of the YMCA and YWCA. He was called the father of the ecumenical movement.

Go south on Lawler a few blocks to where U.S. Highway 18/52 turns left (east). Take this about 9 miles to Monona. At the west end of town, turn left onto 120th Street, which later becomes Iowa Street, and proceed about 1 mile to Egbert Sreet. Turn right. On the west side of the city park is the *Monona Historical Museum*, 210 South Egbert Street, (563) 539-8083, which has many artifacts related to the city's history and what's believed to be the world's largest collection of wooden chains. More than 400 types, sizes, and styles of hand-carved chains are here, made of at least 85 kinds of wood and ranging from those made from round toothpicks to some about 20 feet

long. Other carved items include animals, religious symbols, and farm scenes of the early twentieth century. The museum is open on summer Sunday afternoons.

From the museum, go south to Chestnut Street, turn right (west), and go one block to Main Street. Turn left (south) and drive about 1 mile to U.S. Highway 18/52. There, turn left (east) and after about 4 miles, you'll come to County Road X32 and a sign that points the way to the Froelich. Turn left (north) and then immediately turn right (east) on Froelich Lane, which parallels Highway 18/52; drive for about a half mile. Here are the few buildings that make up the tiny community of Froelich. Among them are those of the *Froelich General Store and Tractor Museum*, 24283 Froelich Road, (563) 536-2841, donation. The main structure here is Burlingame's General Store, which was also a freight depot and post office. When built in 1891, its wooden sides were lined with metal sheets to ward off sparks from passing steam locomotives. Items from the past are on the shelves and in barrels, just as they were back when. Replicas of some items are for sale.

Inside the store is a display about John Froelich. No, the town wasn't named after him but after his dad, Henry. Still, John did something that turned the world of agriculture around. In 1892, Froelich, who had 18 patents, and William Mann fastened a gas-powered, one-cylinder engine to the frame of a steam traction machine and, after several tries, got the engine to sputter to life and the world's first gas-powered tractor was on its way. After a local trial run, the men took it to Langford, South Dakota, where it threshed 72,000 bushels of wheat in 52 days that fall, in temperatures that ranged from minus 3 to 100 degrees, proving far superior to the big, heavy, lumbering steam-powered tractors of the day.

Froelich later moved his operations to Waterloo where, in 1918, his firm was bought by John Deere, based in Moline, Illinois, which has since made the descendants of the Froelich's tractors. The site has a three-quarter scale working model of Froelich's first tractor, which looks very ungainly as far as tractors go—the radiator is in the back, the driver stands up front (no seats then) turning a vertical steering wheel, the wheels are made of steel and, right behind the driver, a flywheel spins in the open. If OSHA had existed then, this machine might have been its worst nightmare. Generating 16 horsepower, the tractor had a top speed of 3.5 mph. All in all, the site is impressive and plans are to continue to improve it.

Back on Highway 18/52, continue east past where Highway 52 splits off to the right (south). After about a half mile, turn left (north) on Spook Cave Road. Turn left and

A half-size replica of the world's first gas-powered tractor is at the Froelich Historic Site between McGregor and Monona.

drive less than 2 miles to *Spook Cave,* **13299 Spook Cave Road, (563) 873-2144.** Eerie sounds from a small hole in the ground, located at the base of a bluff near Bloody Run Creek, caused locals of years ago to wonder about who, or what, was making those noises; after the hole was enlarged, it became quite an attraction. Hour-long boat rides now take visitors through this lighted cave. People who come here should bring a light jacket—it's 47 degrees in the cave year-round. The site has a swimming beach, picnic facilities, a rental cabin, and a campground.

Return to Highway 18, turn left and go east for 4 miles to State Highway 76. Turn right (south) and cruise for 3 miles into the center of McGregor, the end of this tour.

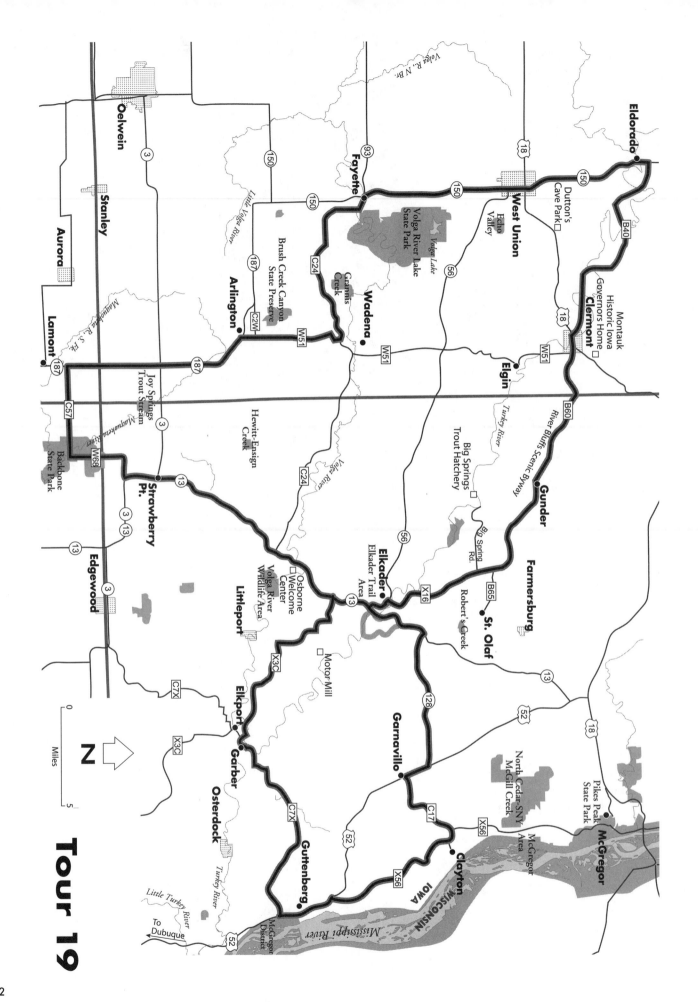

Tour 19

Tour 19
The Mississippi River, Hills, and Plains

Guttenberg—Clermont—Eldorado—West Union—Arlington—Backbone State Park—Strawberry Point—Elkader—Guttenberg

Distance: approximately 135 miles

If you want your fill of hills, this tour should do it for you. Well, there is one short, flat area but otherwise your visit is going to be this way and that, following wriggling streams, encountering exposed limestone bluffs, dropping through wooded valleys, and rising over hills crowned by fields. Along the way are tows and riverboats on the Mississippi, a rare life mask of Abraham Lincoln before he grew his beard, canoes on the Volga River, a rocky backbone in Iowa's first state park, and a visitor center that's also a mini-zoo of animals with ties to Iowa. Ready for some ups and downs in your life? Then let's take to some of Iowa's best-loved hills.

The best place to begin this tour is on U.S. Highway 52, just south of Guttenberg. Along the way into town on the down slope of a hill you will come to a turnout on the right (east), which leads to an overlook that provides a great view of the broad valley of the Mississippi River (the town is hard to see because of trees).

Continue north down the hill into Guttenberg. The town of more than 2,000 residents lies on a shelf of land with bluffs behind it to the west and the Mississippi River lapping at its eastern edge. Originally called Prairie La Porte (Door to the Prairie) by French explorers who passed this way in 1673, this area was later heavily settled by German immigrants who renamed the community in 1851 after Johanes Gutenberg, inventor of movable type. A reproduction of one of his bibles is at the city library, 602 South 2nd Street.

Yes, it's true, Guttenberg, the city, does not match the spelling of the famous printer's name but these Iowans aren't alone. The only other town in America named for him—in New Jersey—is also spelled Guttenberg.

As you enter Guttenberg's south end, turn right (east) at Koerner Street and go a few blocks to South River Park Drive. Turn left (north). Along South River Park Drive are nicely maintained limestone and brick buildings built as early as 1845. The ones on the left side of the street are businesses, shops, and restaurants. On the right are three large buildings that functioned over the years as everything from factories where buttons were punched out of clamshells fished from the riverbed to grain warehouses. Set in two-mile-long Ingleside Park, which fronts the river and makes for a nice stroll, these buildings still serve various purposes. The southernmost one houses *The Landing*, 701 South River Park Drive, (563) 252-1615, an inn with suites, rooms, and balconies; out back are docks and boat rentals. The middle warehouse now holds a hair and tanning salon, as well as *Clayton Ridge Farms Meat Market* and *Picket Fence Café*, 531 South River Park Drive, (563) 252-3820. *Café Mississippi*, 431 South River Park Drive, (563) 252-4505, currently occupies the northern warehouse, which was once owned by the family of Ulysses S. Grant.

Near the warehouses on the waterfront is the *State Aquarium and Hatchery*, 331 South River Park Drive, (563) 252-1156, free. Operated by the Iowa Department of Natural Resources, the building's several aquariums hold fish commonly found in the Mississippi River and the trout streams of northeast Iowa.

Also in Ingleside Park is the *Lockmaster's Heritage House Museum*, Lock and Dam Lane, (563) 252-1531, free, summer afternoons. One of

Cliffs and colorful hills line the Mississippi near Guttenburg.

the last remaining such structures on the Mississippi, the house is furnished with items that were in use when it held the families of the men who were in charge of the nearby lock and dam, which was built in the 1930s. Photos of that era also are in the museum.

Of course, by now no one has missed seeing *Lock and Dam Number 10*, which is operated by the U.S. Army Corps of Engineers. Adjacent to a dam that creates a pool on the Mississippi, Lock 10 is where commercial and pleasure boats are raised and dropped a difference of about six feet on their way between the upper and lower sections of the river near the dam. The site averages about 7,000 lockages a year with the commercial traffic averaging about 14 million tons of cargo annually. Although the lock is 600 feet long, it cannot accommodate an entire tow consisting of a tug and 15 barges; to transit the lock, a tug pushes in the first three ranks of barges, which are locked through and pulled ahead on the other side by cables, then the tug and two sets of barges are locked through and the different sections of the tow are lashed together again. The entire process for such a tow takes around 90 minutes. A free observation post at the site is open April through November.

North of the lock, Ingleside Park is a nice green space with shelters, benches, picnic facilities, and shade trees.

Continue north on River Park Drive, which eventually merges with and becomes North 1st Street in a few blocks. Less than two blocks north of that merger, turn left on Broadway and go to North 4th Street, where you turn right (north). Proceed two blocks to Kosciusko Street and turn left (west). When Kosciusko meets Bluff Street, turn right (north). Bluff then proceeds out of town as County Road X56, which is a segment of the *Great River Road*.

Take X56 about 7 miles until County Road C17 joins it from the right (east). Keep going north for a short distance as the road curves to the left, and then X56 goes off to the right. Ignore that and continue west on C17, which rolls through some heavily wooded hills. After about 5 miles from the X56/C17 junction, enter Garnavillo and meet Highway 52 again.

Turn right (north) on Highway 52 and go for about 1 mile to State Highway 128. Turn left (west) and drive for about 8 miles to State Highway 13. All along the way, you'll pass through some pleasant, rolling countryside.

At Highway 13, turn left (south) and, after a few curves and 1.5 miles, go to High Street NE on the north side of Elkader. Turn right (west) and head out of town. Don't worry about seeing Elkader right now . . . we'll be back to take in more of the town on our return.

About a half mile from Highway 13, turn right (north) at County Road X16, which is also called Gunder Road. About 4 miles out of Elkader, watch for Big Spring Road and turn left (west). Follow the brown signs that lead west to *Big Spring Trout Hatchery*, 16212 Big Spring Road, (563) 245-2446, free. Rainbow, brown, and brook trout are raised at this state facility, which is situated on Iowa's largest spring, and you can explore the place on your own or take a guided tour. You can also fish in the nearby Turkey River and should you not have a license, don't worry; you can buy one at the hatchery.

Return to County X16 and continue north a short distance past County Road B65, which goes east to the tiny community of Saint Olaf (Saint Olaf, Iowa that is, not the more famous Saint Olaf College in Minnesota . . . you haven't gone that far!). Just after B65, X16 turns west and becomes County Road B60. You don't have to do a thing other than follow the road, which is a leg of the *River Bluffs Scenic Byway*, a wandering set of roads that dipsy-doodle through the hills of northeast Iowa. The road cuts through heavy woods and rolling hills blanketed with crops, skirts streams, passes rocky cuts, and rolls through some quaint communities that, because of the geography, seem unaffected by the outside world.

After the road makes that big turn to the west, travel for less than 15 miles to Clermont. Along the way, you'll pass through some of Iowa's more beautiful landscapes on a nice curvy highway (yes, take that as a warning not to speed here—just enjoy the drive).

After entering Clermont on Stone Street, go to Mill Street, which is also U.S. Highway 18, turn right (northeast), and head out of town for about 1 mile. As you round a hill and ascend it, you will come upon the entrance to *Montauk*, Highway 18 East, (563) 423-7173, free. Home of Iowa's 12th governor, William Larrabee, the 14-room mansion is unique among historical homes because all the furnishings here were used by the family from 1874 on, and are not merely approximations of the original items. That's because the last of the governor's daughters kept the place as it was until she died at the age of 96, and it became a state historical site.

Inside the parlor are rotating bookcases designed by Larrabee—be sure to ask about his unique way of signing his books. In the study are a rare life mask of Abraham Lincoln before he grew his beard and a patent Wooten desk that opens its massive wings to become a miniature office. Down the hall, a mechanical bird from the 1904 Saint Louis World's Fair still sings.

Outside, surrounded by 100,000 pine trees planted on the site's 46 acres, is a host of statues of men who were famous in Larrabee's day such as Ulysses S. Grant, William Tecumseh Sherman, and David Farragut.

Return to Clermont and, about halfway through town, turn left (southeast) onto North Street; go one block to Larrabee Street. There, you'll see the *Larrabee School*. Built in 1912, it's the only school in Iowa completely donated to a community by a family; now it houses the Clermont Historical Society and has artifacts related to the region's history. A block to the southwest, at the corner of Larrabee and McGregor Streets, is the *Union Sunday School*. Since it was built as a church in 1858, it's been used by Methodist, Catholic, Presbyterian, and Lutheran congregations before it became a nondenominational Sunday school; it holds the nation's largest pneumatic Kimball organ. Built in 1896, the Kimball is played in concert on the last Sunday of each month in April, June through October, and then on the second Sunday in December.

Return to Mill Street and turn left (southwest). As you turn, look across the street to see the *Clermont Opera House*, which was built in 1912. A block down Mill Street and on the right

is a complex of historical buildings that include the *Riegel Blacksmith Shop*, which was used from 1931 until the early 1980s, an 1852 stone jail, and, near the Turkey River, an old power plant. Among the items in the complex is the 1966 John Deere self-propelled lawn mower used in the movie *The Straight Story*, which was based on the true story of Alvin Straight, who traveled 240 miles in 1994 on a similar mower from Laurens, Iowa, to Mount Zion, Wisconsin, to see his ailing brother. At the age of 73, Straight, who had no driver's license, traveled six weeks at a top speed of five miles an hour. The 1999 movie was filmed in Clermont, Laurens, West Bend, and Lansing, and starred Richard Farnsworth, who was nominated for an Academy Award for his portrayal of Straight.

Just across the Turkey River is Riverside Park where some people cool off in the river and not far away is a good place to put in a canoe.

Head southwest from Clermont on Highway 18 for a very short distance to County Road B40; turn right (west). Now, settle down for a nice drive through the hilly countryside on another part of the River Bluffs Scenic Byway, as winding B40 crosses the meandering Turkey River no less than six times in a 13-mile stretch.

Drive for 13 miles to State Highway 150, where you turn left (south). Proceed a short distance to Eldorado. On your way into town, you'll cross the Turkey yet again. After passing through tiny Eldorado, you'll ascend a hill. If you're careful about oncoming traffic, you can pull off to the left (east) side of the road and look back for one of Iowa's nicer views—of the Turkey River and Eldorado lying below. Just beyond the overlook and on the right (west) side of the highway is *Goeken County Park*, (563) 426-5740, which also has a panoramic view of the region.

Continue south on Highway 150 for 6 miles to West Union. In a few minutes, you'll find yourself suddenly leaving the hills and entering the plains that stretch across much of Iowa.

Quick Trip Option 1: Head east from West Union on U.S. Highway 18 and 2 miles later, turn left (north) onto a county road where a sign points the way to *Dutton's Cave Park* (563) 422-5146, which is administered by the Fayette County Conservation Board. About half a mile from Highway 18, you will be presented a choice: go left to the campground or turn right for the picnic areas. Unless you plan to camp, turn right and follow the signs into the park. You'll end up parking in a flat, grassy valley that lies nestled between wooded hills. Follow the footpath to the rear of the picnic area and beyond . . . it leads into a rocky canyon where spring waters trickle out from the side walls to drop into a stream. The trail can be slippery in a few places so be careful. The cave itself isn't much, but the park provides a nice experience and is a great place to shoot photographs.

From West Union, continue south on Highway 150 for about 4 miles; watch for signs pointing the way to the *Volga State Recreation Area*, (563) 425-4161, on the left (east). At 5,420 acres, it's one of Iowa's largest public properties and has rugged hills, dense woods, and some open prairie. At least 32 primitive campsites are among its rumpled hills, which are laced with 30 miles of mountain biking, hiking, and equestrian trails; an equestrian camping area has water available. The 135-acre Frog Hollow Lake is at the northern end of the preserve and its fish include bluegill, largemouth bass, and channel catfish. Through the preserve runs the Volga River, which is quite popular with canoeists who like to put in at the west end of the park and leave the river at the preserve's east side. Fishing enthusiasts like to try their hooks at catching the smallmouth bass, rock bass, channel catfish, and white suckers that live in the river.

Return to Highway 150 and continue south for 4 miles to Fayette. At the intersection with State Highway 93 in town, turn left (east) onto West Water Street and go about six blocks to Washington Street. **Turn right (south), drive seven blocks to County Road C24, and turn left (east).** At the southeast edge of town, C24 turns to the south and then runs straight east again for a mile or so before running into hills where it dips, sways, and turns as it goes generally to the east.

Go about 10 miles on C24 to County Road W51. Turn right (south) and proceed for about 5 miles to County Road C2W. Turn right (west) and, after a mile, turn right again (north) to head toward *Brush Creek Canyon State Preserve*, (563) 425-4161. Although there is no camping in this 217-acre preserve, the rugged hills along this gorge near Brush Creek are excellent for hiking. The north and east sides of the slopes, some of which are as high as 150 feet, are often shady, cool, and covered with moss and ferns while the south and west faces are drier, sunnier, and warmer. In all, at least 270 plant species have been seen here, ranging from woodland wildflowers to trees, along with 75 species of birds, including some that prefer large expanses of woods, such as ovenbird, yellow-throated vireo, American redstart, and Louisiana waterthrush. In the center of the preserve, one large rock formation once called Chimney Rock has a small prairie atop it.

Return to W51 and continue for about a half mile to Arlington and State Highway 187. Turn left and drive southeast, then south, for about 10 miles to County Road C57. Turn left (east) and cruise for 4.5 miles straight into *Backbone State Park*. The oldest state park in Iowa, Backbone, (563) 924-2527, was named after a ridge of rugged rock that looks like the large, exposed, lumpy backbone of some otherworld creature. As at many of Iowa's other state parks, you can pitch a tent or park an RV at one of the 127 campsites here, but Backbone also has year-round and seasonal cabins; call (563) 933-4225 for information on those. All of the cabins are very nice and very popular, so much so that you might want to hit the phones on January 2nd to reserve one for a week during the following summer (when a minimum week-long stay is required to reserve a cabin). Note that if a cabin has not been rented by the Wednesday of an open week, it can be leased for two-night stays.

Okay, now that you're in this pretty, wooded, 1,780-acre park, you're wondering what to do, right? Do you really need something to entertain you? For openers, lay back and read the book you always wanted to read. Wade through the shallows of the Maquoketa River, which meanders through the park and is little more than ankle deep most of the time. Hike the backbone. Swim in the lake. Rent a boat, a canoe, a kayak or a surf-bike. Fish the trout streams. Picnic. Rappel the 80-foot-high cliffs.

The Maquoketa River winds through rocky formations at Backbone State Park.

Visit the park museum to learn how the Civilian Conservation Corps constructed the park's buildings in the 1930s.

From the north part of Backbone, head north on County Road W68, which turns east to meet State Highway 3 in 2 miles. Follow that north for another 1.5 miles to Strawberry Point. If you're camping in the state park and need food or firewood, you'll find those items in this pleasantly named town of about 1,200. You'll also find *Wilder Memorial Museum*, 123 West Mission Street, (563) 933-4615, admission. Although a variety of items are displayed here, the main collection has more than 800 heirloom dolls and doll furniture, some of which dates back to around 1700. While in town, also check out City Hall to see the world's largest strawberry, a red, concrete tribute to the town's namesake.

Head north from Strawberry Point on State Highway 13 to Elkader, 14 miles away. Along the way, be sure to stop at the *Osborne Conservation and Nature Center,* (563) 245-1516, free, which is 10 miles north of Strawberry Point. Also an Iowa Welcome Center, it's like many of the others in that it has brochures and lots of information about the region. Yet it's very unique because it has three miles of trails that course through 300 acres of heavy woods. A self-guided tour takes you through a pioneer village with historical buildings such as a false-front hotel, an 1840s-era log cabin, a general store, and a depot. There's also a live animal exhibit with species that have lived or live in Iowa, including black bear, coyote, wolf, wild turkey, white-tailed deer, cougar, and bobcat. Colorful flower gardens, prairie exhibits, and a gift shop are here too.

From the nature center, continue on Highway 13 to State Highway 56 just south of Elkader; turn left (northwest) and proceed into the center of town. Nestled into the hills lining the Turkey River, this picturesque community is dominated by the 142-foot-tall spire of *Saint Joseph's Catholic Church,* which almost serves as an exclamation point above the town. At the corner of Bridge and High Streets, is the *Carter House Museum,* (563) 278-2700, admission. Built as a mansion in 1850, this museum has collections of military artifacts, nineteenth-century clothing, pharmacy items, and more.

If you have parked at the museum, just leave your car there and take to foot to visit some other places in town. Take the *Keystone Bridge* across the Turkey River and you're walking on the longest bridge of its type—436 feet—west of the Mississippi. But if you really want an idea of what the bridge looks like when you're not on it, go into the nearby *Keystone Restaurant,* 107 South Main Street, (563) 245-1992, which has outdoor seating that overlooks the bridge and the river.

The Osborne Conservation and Nature Center near Elkader is also a welcome center that features a collection of animals and a historic village.

Not far from the restaurant is the *Elkader River Walk*, a walkway that follows the Turkey River to south of the city where it connects with *Pony Hollow Trail*, part of a 4-mile-long trail system.

Quick Trip Option 2: In Elkader, take Bridge Street northeast out of town and cross State Highway 13, where Bridge becomes Grape Road (and its surface changes to gravel). About 3 miles down this meandering road is Galaxy Road and you should turn right (south) there. Don't worry about the dead-end sign because in 3 miles, that's where you want to be . . . at the Turkey River and the *Motor Mill*, (563) 245-1516. An impressive six-story limestone building constructed in 1855, it's said to be Iowa's largest mill. Although the 80-foot-tall mill is not open to the public, its grounds are, and they're a nice place to visit and picnic.

What's in a Name

Strawberry Point earned its name from early travelers who loved the wild strawberries that grew in this area. On the second weekend of each June the town celebrates with Strawberry Days and serves up free ice cream with, what else . . . strawberries.

From Elkader, take Bridge Street northeast to Highway 13 and turn right (south). Take that for about 3.5 miles to County Road X3C. Turn left (east). Once more you're on a leg of the River Bluffs Scenic Byway. There's nothing to do on this road but drive and enjoy the scenery of this hilly area, so have at it.

Cruise about 10.5 miles to County Road C7X. Turn left (east) at the intersection on the east edge of the small community of Elkport and drive past its twin, the equally small Garber, only a quarter mile away. Drive for less than 11 miles to the south edge of Guttenberg where we began this tour.

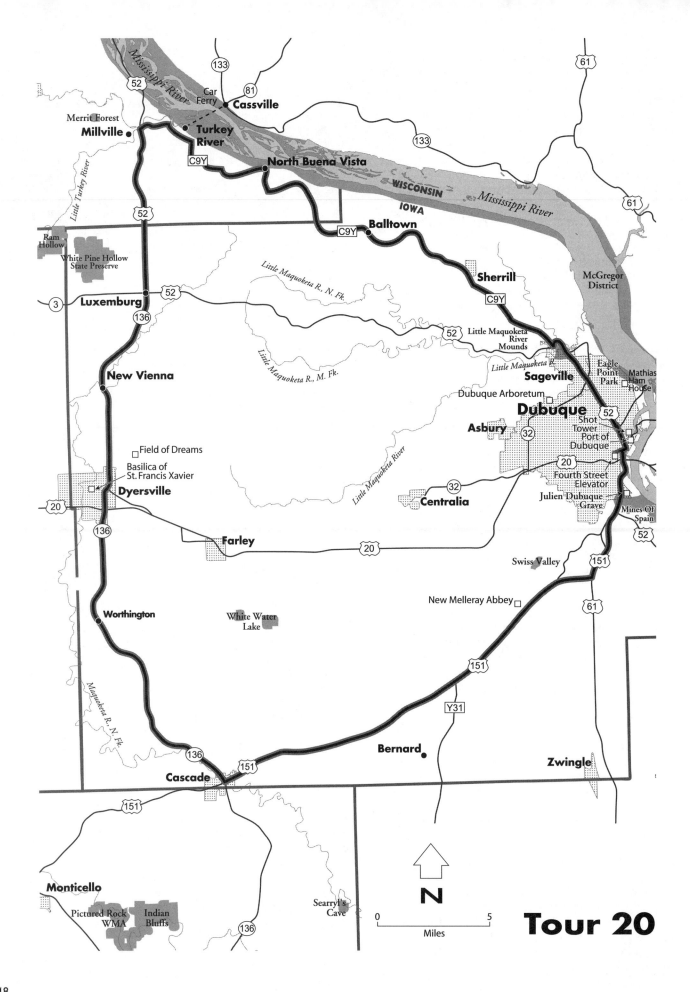

Tour 20

Tour 20
Dubuque County—
Where Modern Iowa Began

Dubuque—Balltown—Luxemburg—New Vienna—Dyersville—Cascade—Dubuque

Distance: approximately 75 miles

Although Europeans are believed to have first set foot on Iowa soil much further south along the Mississippi River, the area around Dubuque is where the first European-American, specifically a French-Canadian, moved into Iowa to work with the Meskwaki who were already here. For a while, this area was the scene of one of the nation's first mineral rushes. It wasn't gold that many people were after but common-as-can-be lead. Still, for several decades, some businessmen shrewdly changed lead into gold by mining it and making it into ammunition.

In this tour are many of Iowa's earliest and prettiest buildings, ranging from mansions, some of which are now B&Bs, to churches that announce the presence of small towns in the country with their lofty spires. And as one might expect near the world's third longest river, a lot of homage and respect is given to the Mississippi River here.

As you approach Dubuque from the south on U.S. Highway 52/151/61 and crest a hill, you'll suddenly view a great panorama of Dubuque and the wide valley of the Mississippi River laid out before you.

Continue down the hill and take the exit that leads to downtown Dubuque, the Civic Center, and Locust Street. Once you have done that, you'll be on Locust Street going north. At West 3rd Street, turn right (east) and go to the intersection with Main Street. There, inside the *Iowa Welcome Center*, 300 Main Street, Suite 100, (563) 556-4372 and (800) 798-4372, is everything you would expect of a welcome center, printed literature and guidance from the staff about what to see in the Dubuque area.

Since you're downtown, you might as well explore it. Within walking distance to the north and south of the welcome center on Main Street are specialty shops, antique stores, fine restaurants, and some art galleries. For more works of art, visit the *Dubuque Museum of Art*, 701 West Locust Street, (563) 557-1851, donation, near the northeast corner of Washington Park, which hosts traveling exhibits in a modern building.

Drive north to 4th Street, turn left (west), and go two blocks to where it ends. (If you're driving a large vehicle like an RV, you might want to turn onto Bluff Street, which is a block west of Locust, and park somewhere along there because there is not much room for an RV to turn around at the end of 4th Street, which all vehicles must do.) At the end of 4th Street and at the bottom of a steep bluff overlooking the city is the *Fenelon Place Elevator*, which is also called the 4th Street Elevator, 512 Fenelon Place, (563) 582-6496, admission. The story goes that to avoid a long carriage ride or walk to reach his bluff-top home from his downtown office at the bottom of the bluff, former mayor and banker J. K. Graves built a personal cable car here in 1882 to transport himself and friends up and down the face of the bluff. Over time the cable cars and tracks have been changed so that two passenger cars that look like they will suffer a head-on collision divert at the last moment to safely pass each other. At the top of the bluff is an overlook that gives a sweeping view of the city and valley. At 296 feet in length, the elevator lifts people 189 feet and is regarded as the world's shortest, steepest scenic railway. At the bottom, stores, an ice cream shop, and more form *Cable Car Square*, and other businesses line nearby Bluff Street. Also at the square, you can catch a one-hour guided tour of Dubuque on the *Trolleys of Dubuque*, (563) 552-2896 and (800) 408-0077, fee.

From Cable Car Square, return to 3rd Street and turn left (east), passing the welcome center and continuing until it ends on the riverfront. This will lead you directly to the *Port of Dubuque*, which is still called the Ice Harbor by many. Much of the Port of Dubuque is newly developed since 2002, including the *Grand Harbor Resort and Waterpark*, 350 Bell Street, (563) 690-4000 and (866) 690-4006, a riverside hotel with 194 rooms and a restaurant where you can sit outside on a plaza overlooking the river. Connected to the hotel is *Huck Finn II*, admission, Iowa's largest themed indoor waterpark. Designed like the inside of an old

Dubuque's Early Years

In the 1780s, French-Canadian fur trader Julien Dubuque came to this region to do business with the Meskwaki who lived here then. However, he noticed that many of the Meskwaki were mining lead, a very lucrative business at the time given the European desire for ammunition, a lot of which, ironically, was used against the Indians. Granted permission by the Meskwaki as well as the Spanish government, which controlled the land then, Dubuque too began mining for lead in what has come to be called the Mines of Spain. When he died in 1810, Dubuque was buried atop a riverside bluff that is now marked by a stone tower, south of the city that bears his name.

The lead business continued for several decades after Dubuque died. In 1856, a shot tower, which still stands, was constructed near the waterfront. Atop the tower were metal plates which had holes of different sizes drilled through them. Molten lead was poured onto the plates and as the liquid lead drizzled through the holes, it formed into perfect spheres which became solid once they hit cool water below. Superior to lead balls made in molds, the musket balls made by the drop process were precise in size for different caliber weapons and were in great demand until lead bullets came into use.

riverboat, the 25,000-square-foot waterpark is where you're going to get wet in several fun ways: on a lazy river, in the kids' pool, by sprays of water located throughout the complex, and on a huge climbing structure with nets, steps, slides, and at the very top an 800-gallon bucket that dumps its wet load on those below four times an hour.

North of the hotel is the *Grand River Center*, (800) 798-4748, a 130,000-square-foot forum and convention facility. To the south are the shore facilities and landing of the *Diamond Jo Casino*, (563) 690-2100, a riverboat with 700 slot machines, video poker, table games, restaurant, and grill. Near that are the landings for the old-fashioned *Spirit of Dubuque* and the sleek, new *Miss Dubuque*, two nongaming cruise boats operated by *Dubuque River Rides*, (563) 583-8093 and (800) 747-8093, admission. The boats take visitors on sightseeing, lunch, dinner, and fall color cruises that last up to four hours. By the way, the Trolleys of Dubuque also pick up passengers here at 12:30 p.m. most days.

Connecting the landings with the resort, convention center, and, farther north, the former *Dubuque Star Brewery* and *Shot Tower*, both of which are being developed, is the *Mississippi River Walk*, a walkway at the river's edge. The River Walk has yet another landing, this one for the big passenger boats such as the *Celebration Belle*, (309) 764-1952 and (800) 297-0034, fee, which takes guests on day-long cruises between here and the Quad Cities and then buses them to their departure points.

An Early Iowan

On January 10, 1833, Susan Ann McCraney was born. Besides being the first European-American born in Dubuque, she may also be the first born in the Iowa territory. Her mother was from Vermont and her father, who mined lead, was from New York.

Walking west of the Diamond Jo Casino, you will come to the *National Mississippi River Museum and Aquarium*, (563) 557-9545 and (800) 226-3369, admission. The museum has been nicely renovated to explain the link between humans and the Mississippi River through the centuries. But the really great item is the new aquarium. From the moment you step in, you know you're not visiting something your grandparents saw years ago with lots of tanks stuck into some walls. No sirree. The first thing you see upon entering is a floor map of the Mississippi from its Minnesota source to its Louisiana mouth, which clearly indicates that this aquarium concerns itself with the entire river, not just the local part. Then you enter a realm of displays showing lively ducks, large and small fish, playful river otters, slow-moving turtles, an ever-waiting alligator, and more, including the realms of backwaters, flooded forests, bayou swamps, and the main channel. One hands-on exhibit lets you fly down the river, using the perspective of an aerial camera that you control. On the second level, you can sit inside sections of a keelboat and a riverboat with projected histories you can choose, or pilot a simulated tow—a set of barges with a tug—at one of three locations on the Mississippi to see how good a river pilot you are.

Connected to the aquarium is the former *Dubuque Depot*, which now serves as a deli. Outside displays include the 1934 *William M. Black*, the last steam-powered dredge, a wetland, a river tug and a children's area where youngsters can maneuver radio-controlled boats. You can easily spend three hours or more here—it's one of the best museums you'll find in the Upper Midwest. By the way, it's possible for groups to spend a night in the crew's quarters on the *William M. Black* and have breakfast the next morning in the galley—call it a boat and breakfast if you like.

The complex also houses the *National Mississippi River Hall of Fame*, which honors Mark Twain, Black Hawk, Karl Bodmer, John James Audubon, Robert Fulton, Diamond Jo Reynolds, and others whose lives have been linked to the great river.

From East 3rd Street, take Bell Street (which the Grand Harbor Resort fronts) and follow that to East 6th Street. Turn left and take that a few blocks to White Street; turn right on White, which is also U.S. Highway 52, and head north. One place to note as you head north is the tall, magnificent high-Victorian-style *Dubuque County Courthouse* between East 7th and 8th Streets. Built in the 1890s, the highly ornate courthouse is topped by the statue of Justice, more than 200 feet above the ground.

At East 16th Street, turn right (east) and drive for a little more than 1 mile, crossing

A couple enjoys the view from an excursion boat on the Mississippi River.

a small channel of the Mississippi. Follow the signs to the *Dubuque Greyhound Park and Casino*, 1855 Greyhound Park Drive, (563) 582-3647 and (800) 373-3647. Greyhound races take place from May through October although simulcast races and slot machines are year-round activities.

Return west across the channel and immediately turn right (north) onto Kerper Boulevard. Follow Kerper, a four-lane highway, for 1.5 miles as it bends around to the northeast and ends at a T intersection with Hawthorne Street. Turn left (northwest), cross the railroad tracks, and at the next intersection turn left (southwest) onto Rhomberg Avenue, watching for signs for the Mathias Ham House and Eagle Point Park.

Go a short distance to Shiras Avenue, turn right (northwest), and in one block you'll come upon the *Mathias Ham House*, 2241 Lincoln Avenue, (563) 583-2812 and (800) 226-3369, admission. Built in 1856, this Italianate mansion with 23 rooms is now a museum. In stark contrast to the elegant house, an 1833 log cabin sits on the nearby grounds.

Dubuque: An Inn Place to Be

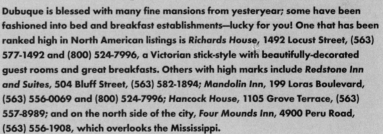

Dubuque is blessed with many fine mansions from yesteryear; some have been fashioned into bed and breakfast establishments—lucky for you! One that has been ranked high in North American listings is *Richards House*, 1492 Locust Street, (563) 577-1492 and (800) 524-7996, a Victorian stick-style with beautifully-decorated guest rooms and great breakfasts. Others with high marks include *Redstone Inn and Suites*, 504 Bluff Street, (563) 582-1894; *Mandolin Inn*, 199 Loras Boulevard, (563) 556-0069 and (800) 524-7996; *Hancock House*, 1105 Grove Terrace, (563) 557-8989; and on the north side of the city, *Four Mounds Inn*, 4900 Peru Road, (563) 556-1908, which overlooks the Mississippi.

Continue northwest up Shiras Avenue to *Eagle Point Park*, (563) 589-4263. Along with the usual park amenities—playground, picnic facilities, and such—the bluff-top park provides an overlook of the Mississippi and directly below, Lock and Dam Number 11.

Return to Rhomberg Avenue, turn right (southwest), and proceed about 1.7 miles to White Street, which is also Highway 52. Turn right (north). After one block, take Highway 52 as it jogs left to join Central Avenue and

The Field of Dreams Movie Site, northwest of Dyersville, was actually a cornfield before it was transformed into a ballfield for the movie *Field of Dreams*.

follow it for about 2 miles to State Highway 32. There are some other sights in Dubuque to see but we'll visit them later.

Quick Trip Option 1: At State Highway 32, which is also called the Northwest Arterial (and which should not be confused with nearby 32nd Street), turn left (west) and go for 1.6 miles, watching for signs to the *Dubuque Arboretum and Botanical Gardens*, 3800 Arboretum Drive, (563) 556-2100, free. You'll arrive at a set of beautiful gardens, all maintained by volunteers (so if you see a weed and really know it's a weed, go ahead and pull it; your efforts will be appreciated). On the grounds are a rose garden, prairie garden, perennials, and an Oriental garden, as well as a gift shop and a colorful and reflective memorial to area veterans. Return to Highway 52 and head north.

From Highway 32, proceed north on Highway 52 for about 1 mile to Rupp Hollow Road. If you're into bicycling or hiking, watch for signs leading to the eastern terminus of *Heritage Trail*, (563) 556-6745, fee paid at self-registration stations. The trail, which has a crushed-limestone surface, leads to Dyersville, about 26 miles to the west, on a former railbed that encounters limestone bluffs, heavily wooded hills, open farm land, old mill towns, mining towns, and river overlooks.

Continue on Highway 52 for less than 1 mile and turn right (north) onto County Road C9Y. Follow the road for about 10 miles to Balltown. For years, this road rambled up and down, twisted, and turned through the hilly countryside north of Dubuque. But the segment between Highway 52 and Balltown was repaved in 2003, the curves straightened a bit, and shoulders were added, making this an easier road to drive. So enjoy the scenery. In Balltown, which has just a handful of houses, is Iowa's oldest existing eating establishment, *Breitbach's Country Dining*, (563) 552-2220, which has been run by the same family for more than a century. The Breitbachs claimed to have served folks from Jesse James to Brooke Shields. The food is good and the desserts, such as the Milky Way pie, are to die for.

A few car lengths past Breitbach's is a turnout where you can park and look over one of the prettier vistas: of farm country below leading to the Mississippi River, more than a mile away, which peeks out from among some of the distant, rolling fields.

From Balltown, continue north on C9Y for 14 miles to a clutch of buildings called Millville and Highway 52 again. This segment of C9Y reverts to its old self–narrow, twisting, turning, and giving quite a rock-and-roll ride as it heads north and east.

Quick Trip Option 2: About 12 miles past Balltown on C9Y is a sign pointing the way down a gravel road to a car ferry, the last one touching Iowa soil. About 2 miles down the gravel road is the *Charlie D,* (608) 725-5180, fee, a ferry that carries everything from bicyclists to semi-truck trailers to Cassville, a pleasant town just across the Mississippi in Wisconsin. The ferry runs from 9 a.m. to 9 p.m., with the last crossing beginning at 8:20 p.m. It operates Wednesday through Sunday between Memorial Day and Labor Day, and Friday through Sunday in May, September, and October.

Once you're in Cassville, visit *Nelson Dewey State Park,* (608) 725-5374, admission, which is just north of town and has some nice overlooks of the wooded hills and bluffs lining the valley of the upper Mississippi. Near the entrance to the park is *Stonefield,* (608) 725-5210, admission, a state historic site made of buildings gathered to create a living-history village of the late nineteenth century.

Return to C9Y via the Charlie D.

Turn left (south) onto Highway 52 and cruise 7 miles to Luxemburg. This is a countryside community that's like many others in this heavily Catholic area in that it's dominated by the presence of the local church, in this case Holy Trinity Church. A memorial in front of city hall from the Grand Duchy of Luxembourg honors the Americans who fought to liberate that country in World War II.

Quick Trip Option 3: Travel 2 miles west on State Highway 3, which intersects Highway 52 in Luxemburg, and then turn north at the sign to *White Pine Hollow,* (563) 586-2254, free. A state preserve named after stands of old white pine among the rocky bluffs, this area has some trails leading through its heavily wooded hills. Some algific slopes can be seen here (see Tour 17 for more on algific slopes), and care should be taken to not disturb the fragile plants near the vents on these slopes. Return to Luxemburg.

In Luxemburg, leave Highway 52 as it turns east and proceed south on State Highway 136 for 5 miles to New Vienna. As you approach town, even at some distance, you'll be able to spot the soaring spire of Saint Boniface Church, which was built in 1887. Once in town, check out *Kerper's Country Store,* (563) 921-2715, which has been in the Kerper family since 1870. Inside, owner Steve Kerper sells wooden duck decoys he has made as well as his home-made baseball bats of all sizes. In 1998, Kerper was one of a select group of Iowans who represented the state in an arts and crafts display at the Smithsonian in Washington, D.C.

Quick Trip Option 4: As you head south out of New Vienna, Highway 136 sways briefly to the southeast and then turns southward again. At that point, turn right onto Vaske Road and about three quarters of a mile west of the intersection, turn left (south) into *New Wine Park,* a small county preserve. If you're here in the fall, this is a great place for finding several types of edible mushrooms.

Continue south on Highway 136 for 4 miles to Dyersville. As you get close to town, you will see not one church spire but a set of twin spires. These belong to the Basilica of Saint Francis Xavier, which we'll visit later.

Also, watch for the sign pointing the way to the *Field of Dreams Movie Site,* 28963 Lansing Road, (563) 875-8404 and (888) 875-8404, free. Follow the sign and subsequent ones along the way. In a few short miles to the east you'll arrive at the location where a movie production company created a baseball diamond out of a cornfield for the 1989 movie *Field of Dreams,* which was based on Ray Kinsella's book *Shoeless Joe.* In a fact-follows-fiction situation, the movie set has continued to draw baseball players young and old, professional and beginner, ever since the movie was made. So grab your mitts, bats, and balls and take to the field for a friendly pick-up game of baseball but be considerate of the nearby private residence. Because the field straddles a property line, a portion of the field is owned by *Left and Center Field of Dreams,* 29001 Lansing Road, (563) 875-7985 and (800) 443-8981, free. Occasionally the owner of this field hosts appearances by the *Ghost Players,* baseball enthusiasts who play in old-fashioned uniforms.

Return to Highway 136 and turn left (south) to enter Dyersville. Just before you cross the tracks, you'll see the west end of Heritage Trail, which runs all the way to a spot just north of Dubuque and which was noted earlier in the tour.

Just after crossing the railroad tracks, turn right (west) onto 2nd Avenue East. In three blocks, turn right (north) at 6th Street NE and then, a block later, turn left (west) onto 1st Avenue East, which is Dyersville's main street. On the way to the basilica is the

Harvested rows of corn create a pattern of lines near Cascade.

Dyer-Botsford Victorian House and Doll Museum, 330 1st Avenue East, (563) 875-2414/2504, admission, which is the 1850 home of the town's founder and houses a collection of at least 1,000 dolls.

Another block to the west is *Evers Toy Store*, 204 1st Avenue East, (563) 876-2438, the first of several toy stores specializing in farm toys that you will find in this community. One of the largest farm toy manufacturers, ERTL, was once located in Dyersville.

Finally, you'll arrive at the *Basilica of Saint Francis Xavier*, which is the 12th of 37 such churches built in the United States and the only one sited on what had been a prairie when it was built in 1889. Each of the twin spires rises 212 feet and is topped by a cross covered with gold leaf. Only the north tower contains bells, all three made in the nineteenth century. Inside, a ceiling painted with the saints of both the Old and New Testa-ments is above the altar, which is flanked by tall stained-glass windows. Nearby is a chair covered by a half-open umbrella, the traditional sign in the Roman Catholic Church of a minor basilica. Guided tours can be arranged by calling the church office.

Return to Highway 136 and head south through town. Along the way are more toy stores, including *H&W Motorsports*, 1317 9th Street SE, (563) 875-7656, and *Racing Champions ERTL*, just south of U.S. Highway 20, (563) 875-5613. Farther south, turn left (east) at the *Country Junction Restaurant*, (563) 875-7055, onto 16th Avenue Court SE. Near the end of the road you will find *Toy Farmer Country Store*, 1161 16th Avenue Court SE, (563) 875-8850; and *Toy Collector Club of America*, 1235 16th Avenue Court SE, (563) 875-9263. Of particular note is the *National Farm Toy Museum*, 1110 16th Avenue Court SE, (563) 875-2727, admission. It has more than

30,000 farm toys, so if you ever played with or collected them years ago, there's a good chance you might see familiar ones here, along with toy fire engines, banks, construction equipment, and more. A film in the museum's theater explains how toys become collectibles.

Return west to Highway 136, turn south, and go for 15 miles to Cascade, passing through Worthington along the way. In Cascade turn left (northeast) onto U.S. Highway 151. Cascade was named after a ten-foot drop in the North Fork of the Maquoketa River that which flows through town.

About 13 miles from Cascade on Highway 151, turn left (west) at County Road D41; drive for less than 2 miles to the *New Melleray Abbey,* **(563) 588-2319.** The monastery is not in the tourism business, but the brothers do welcome visitors to attend their services and visit their gift shop. Besides selling honey, religious items, and furniture made from the trees on their 1,100-acre tree farm, the brothers also make wooden caskets, for which they have been written up in various newspapers, including the *New York Times.* While visiting, be considerate of those brothers who observe vows of silence.

Return to Highway 151 and turn left (northeast). In about 5.5 miles, 151 is joined by U.S. Highway 61. As you continue north to Dubuque, the road is joined by Highway 52 from the right. Turn right onto 52 heading southeast and turn immediately left onto Bellevue Heights Road. That move brings you right to *E. B. Lyons Nature Center,* 8891 Bellevue Heights, (563) 556-0620, admission. Located at the *Mines of Spain,* a 1,380-acre state recreation area named after the location where Julien Dubuque was permitted by the Spanish government to mine for lead, the nature center has bird and butterfly gardens, as well as interior displays related to the area's flora and fauna. Researchers have determined that this region was used up to 8,000 years ago, with evidence left in the form of mounds, stone shelters, camps, and village sites.

Quick Trip Option 5: About 3 miles southeast of where Highway 52 meets Highway 151/61 is *Crystal Lake Cave,* (563) 556-6451, admission. The state's largest show cave, this was discovered in 1868 by miners looking for lead, not natural wonders. The cave contains a small lake and formations called anthodites (also called cave flowers) that are found at only one other cave in the nation. Crystal Lake Cave is a stable 50 degrees year-round so you might want to wear a light jacket or sweater when you visit here.

From the nature center, continue southeast down Highway 52 for about 1 mile to Old Massey Road. Turn left (east), and take that to Mines of Spain Road, and turn left. Now you're deep in the Mines of Spain and passing through woods and prairie. Some small parking areas serve as trailheads for some of the more than 14 miles of trails that lace this area.

About 2 miles from where you left Old Massey Road, you will come to Monument Road on your right. Go up that road to a parking lot that is a short walk to the stone tower covering the grave of Julien Dubuque and overlooking the Mississippi River.

To return to Dubuque from Monument Road, turn right (north) onto Marjo Quarry Road, which runs to the west. Follow this until it turns north to link with Julien Dubuque Drive. Turn left and follow that up a hill to South Grandview Avenue, about 1.5 miles from Monument Road. You can easily drive onto Highway 52/151/61 by turning left onto Grandview Avenue and then immediately right onto the highway, near the spot where we began this tour.

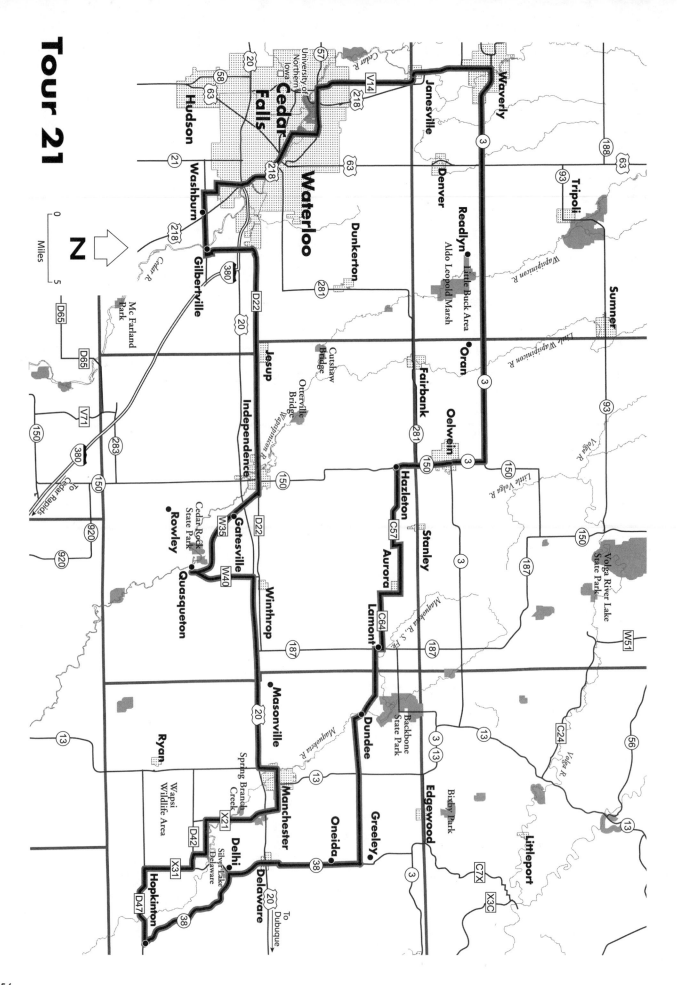

Tour 21

156

Tour 21
The Twin Cities and Plains of Eastern Iowa

Cedar Falls—Waverly—Oelwein—Hazelton—Lamont—Delaware—Hopkinton—Manchester—Quasqueton—Independence—Waterloo—Cedar Falls

Distance: approximately 177 miles

This tour begins by visiting several cultural, historical, and fun places in one of Iowa's larger metropolitan areas that also has ties to our nation's agricultural economy. Along the way between the beginning and end of this tour, however, you get to roll through the countryside that includes a stretch through lands farmed by the Amish and another on one of the state's scenic byways. You also visit communities that, although smaller than the bookends of this tour, have some nice places to visit, including a house that famed architect Frank Lloyd Wright considered to be one of his most complex designs.

This tour begins on the east side of downtown Cedar Falls, at the intersection of U.S. Highway 218 and State Highway 57; take 57, which is also 1st Street, west for less than 1 mile. On the right will be the *Behrens-Rapp Visitor Center*, 1st and Clay Streets, (319) 268-4266 and (800) 845-1955. This classic brick gas station that was built in 1925 now services visitors instead of autos and has plenty of information about the region. If you're visiting the area when this visitor center is closed, the main *Cedar Falls Tourism and Visitor Bureau* is only a few blocks to the south at 217 Washington Street.

While you're at the Behrens-Rapp Visitor Center, you can also visit the nearby *Little Red Schoolhouse Museum*, (319) 266-5149, free, which is just steps away. Built in 1909, it represents the more than 9,000 one-room schools that dotted Iowa years ago and is furnished as many of those schools were.

Just east of the school is the *Broom Factory*, 125 West 1st Street, (319) 268-0877, where great food is served up in a former factory that was built in 1862. The factory first made cornstarch before becoming a broom factory in 1905 and then a business that made pickles too . . . at the same time it still made brooms!

Within walking distance west of the Behrens-Rapp Visitor Center is one of Cedar Falls' more famous landmarks, the round *Ice House Museum*, 1st and Franklin Streets, (319) 266-5149, donation. A hundred feet in diameter with hollow tile walls, this structure housed up to 8,000 tons of ice that was cut and transported from the nearby Cedar River in the winters in the early part of the twentieth century. During the summers, the ice was taken from this well-insulated building and delivered to homes throughout the community. Now a museum, it has displays about the ice industry as well as the settlement of the valley of the Cedar River.

Now, walk back east to Main Street and enter downtown Cedar Falls. If you're up for pedaling rather than walking, visit *Bike Tech*, 112 Main Street, (319) 266-5979, which rents bicycles and gives information on the 30-plus miles of trails that lace the metro area and connect to the *Cedar Valley Nature Trail* that runs to Cedar Rapids.

Across the street is the *Oster Regent Theater*, 103 Main, (319) 277-5283, a nicely restored theater that hosts the Cedar Falls Community Theater, which produces everything from musicals and comedies to dramas. A few doors down is Fiber Arts Studio, 111 Main, (329) 266-7815, which is heavily involved in the arts of spinning, weaving, dying, and production of handmade rugs, baskets, and paper.

A block south is the *Iowa Band Museum*, 203 Main, (329) 266-1253, donation. Located in the state's last band hall—and one that was called one of the finest in the nation by none other than John Philip Sousa—this unique museum is also the home of the state's oldest municipal band, the Cedar Falls Marching Band, which began tooting its horns in 1891. On display are band instruments that include tenor, bass, and baritone saxophones, trombones, a

A New Visitor's Center

Beginning in the fall of 2004, the new office of the Cedar Falls Tourism and Visitor Bureau will be located on the southern edge of the city. To reach the office, leave U.S. Highway 20 at Exit 224 and go north on Hudson Road. The offices will be on the east side of Hudson Road and overlooking Prairie Lakes. The phone numbers will stay the same, and the Behrens-Rapp Visitor Center in downtown Cedar Rapids will remain open.

If you visit the bureau in its new location, then take in the University of Northern Iowa first (its attractions are described later in the tour) and continue north into downtown to see the city's other points of interest.

giant sarrusophone, and sousaphones (nick-named rain catchers). Uniforms are there too, along with the rules that band members had to adhere to years ago. The band performs free concerts at nearby *Overman Park* every Tuesday evening in June and July.

If you want to take a break from walking, head to Washington Street, a block west of Main, where you'll find *Trails End Lodge*, 122 Washington, (319) 277-6400 and (888) 577-1161. There you can inquire about getting set up for a canoe trip on the Cedar River. Now think about it, how many other downtown hotels have you visited offer to put you into a canoe? Now, that's service!

A couple blocks west of Washington Street is Overman Park and across the street to the south from there is *Victorian Home and Carriage House Museum*, 308 West 3rd Street, (319) 266-5149, donation, a pretty Italianate home built in the 1860s with 18-inch-thick walls and a cupola above. Most of the house is decorated with furnishings from the 1880s although the basement holds something that's delightfully out of context with the rest of the house—a 12-by-26-foot, O-gauge train layout. Designed by William Lenoir, who made more than 250 scratch-built scale locomotives, the set shows off his skills in designing other train cars, including some showing dinner service on the tables.

Outside the home on Saturday mornings, a farmers market, (319) 277-1745, is the place to pick up fresh fruit and vegetables from May through October.

One more block west is the *George Wyth Home*, 303 Franklin, (319) 277-8817, donation. Designed as a wood frame house and later fronted with brick, the home has an interior that was recently refurbished in the art deco style popular in the 1920s. The house has self-guided tours on the first two floors. On the third floor is the *Viking Pump Museum*, which traces the history of pumps from the days they were wooden contraptions to the ones that were manufactured by the former owner of the home, George Wyth.

Okay, now it's time to get in the car again— after all, this is a book of auto tours. Return to Main Street and head south about 1.5 miles from downtown. At Seerley Boulevard, turn right (west). In a short distance is the *James and Meryl Hearst Center for the Arts*, 304 West Seerley Boulevard, (319) 273-8641, free, which features works by past and present regional artists such as Grant Wood, Marjorie Nuhn, John Page, and Gary Kelley and hosts traveling exhibits. For all purposes, the art center at first looks like a large, tan-colored brick house, although at second look it's apparent that its backside has been enlarged considerably. Out back is the Woodland Sculpture Garden where a variety of sculptures are set amid the trees, bushes, and flower beds.

Go west on Seerley for about a half mile to the T intersection with College Street and the campus of the *University of Northern Iowa*. Begun in 1876 as one of three state universities, it has an enrollment of nearly 14,000 students.

Turn left to follow College Street to the south; turn right (west) onto University Avenue and then turn right again (north) at Hudson Road to enter the main part of the campus. A short distance up Hudson and on the left is *University Museum*, 3219 Hudson Road, (319) 273-2188, free, which has exhibits about the natural and human history of the world and the region; it has about 114,000 artifacts. Still farther up Hudson and on the right is the 5,300-square-foot *UNI Gallery of Art*, which is in the Kamerick Art Building, Hudson Road and West 27th Street, (319) 273-6134, free. The gallery shows works from its permanent collection of regionally and nationally known artists and presents temporary exhibits as well.

In case you wonder what the big domed building is across Hudson Road from the Kamerick, that's the *UNI-Dome*. Built in 1976 with an air-supported roof, it was converted to a fixed-roof structure in 1998 and, able to hold 16,400 people, is the home of the university's athletic teams and serves as the site of many concerts and other events. Kurt Warner, who was born in Burlington and raised in Cedar Rapids, played for the UNI football team and later directed the Saint Louis Rams to a victory in the 2000 Super Bowl.

Return to 1st and Franklin Streets the way you came and follow Franklin north out of town, where it becomes County Road V14. "Wait a moment," you're wondering . . . "what

From Pumps (Shoes) to Pumps (Water)

When George Wyth was a shoe salesman in the early twentieth century, he formed a company in 1911 with Dr. W. L. Hearst, machinist P. C. Peterson, and Jens Nielsen to manufacture an internal pump designed by Nielsen to remove water from a quarry he developed in Cedar Falls. Because three of the men were of Danish descent, they called their venture the Viking Pump Company and Wyth was its first president. That year, with just two employees working in a 40-by-60-foot building, Viking sold 50 pumps for $2,000 total. Now, the company's manufacturing plant in the city's industrial park occupies 405,000 square feet and is engaged in making pumps of all sorts for a worldwide market, including those used on fire trucks; it also makes clamps, rescue equipment, and color formulation equipment.

about seeing some places in Waterloo?" Well, that will come a bit later when you return to the metro area, so hang on.

About 4.5 miles out of Cedar Falls is *Antique Acres*, 7610 Waverly Road, (319) 987-2380, a collection of antique farm equipment ranging back to steam-powered tractors and the earliest gas-powered ones. The gear ranges from a small, 4-horsepower, Litchfield six-cycle engine to one of the larger traction engines ever made, the 140-horsepower Reeve steam plow, and another steam engine that produces 400 horsepower. Besides its Old Time Power Show, which is held the weekend before Labor Day, the museum hosts other special shows and tractor pulls throughout its season which is 8 to 5 daily, May through October. A modern campground is also on the site.

Continue on V14 for 3 miles to Janesville, latch onto Highway 218, a four-lane highway, and take it north to the very next exit. Leave Highway 218 (also called the Avenue of the Saints there) and enter Waverly from the south on 4th Street SW, a total of 4 miles from Janesville. Go to West Bremer Avenue in the heart of town. On the northwest corner of West Bremer and 4th Street SW is The *Waverly House–Bremer County Historical Society Museum*, 402 West Bremer Avenue, (319) 352-2072, admission. Housed in a former inn built of local wood and brick, the museum displays artifacts from the earliest days of European-American settlement.

A few blocks west is the *Schield International Museum*, 805 West Bremer Avenue, (319) 352-4040, free. The museum has items gathered from 70 countries visited by Marjorie and Vern Schield, who made his fortune with his brother, Wilbur, in designing and building truck-mounted power excavators. Along with numerous small items, the museum has an early crane made by Schield, a hollowed-out log canoe he once used, a Model T, and a diesel tractor. The building also houses the headquarters of *Self-Help International*, a foundation started in 1959 by Vern to help small farmers and families around the world to help themselves. Originally the foundation supplied training as well as equipment such as small tractors, sewing machines, and windmills to 43 countries. However, its emphasis has changed in recent years to training farmers in other nations, most recently Ghana and Nicaragua in particular, in applying technology to their production methods.

On the west edge of town is the *Waverly Sale Barn*, (319) 352-2804, home of the Waverly Midwest Horse Sale. Held twice a year, this sale is the biggest of the biggest—draft horses, that is. Huge 2,000-pound-plus horses are sold and bought here by such diverse visitors as Disney, Budweiser, Amish farmers, carriage drivers, and those who are simply in love with these gentle Clydesdales, Percherons, Belgians, Fjords, and Haflingers. Other items sold during the big sales include wagons, buggies, saddles, horse-drawn equipment, and more.

Return east on Bremer Avenue to 1st Street NW and turn left (north). Shortly, you'll come upon a city park that fronts the Cedar River. In the park is a trailhead for the 7.5-mile-long *Waverly Rail Trail*, which starts by crossing the river on a 500-foot-long bridge here and then goes east. It's expected that the trail will grow and connect to nearby communities in the future.

Return to Bremer Avenue, which is also State Highway 3, turn left (east), and proceed about 28 straight-as-an-arrow miles to the junction with State Highway 150. Turn right (south) on what is now Highway 3/150 and follow that for 3 miles into Oelwein. At Charles Street in the center of town, turn right (west) and go a couple of blocks. There, the *Hub City Heritage Railway Museum*, 26 2nd Avenue, (319) 283-2861, occupies a former railroad express building and yard office. Nearby are renovated engines and cabooses.

Also in town is the *Oelwein Area Historical Society Museum*, 900 block of 2nd Avenue SE, (319) 283-2984, admission, which has displays of period rooms, schools, medical equipment, and a large Delft collection.

Continue south on Highway 150 (Highway 3 turned east in Oelwein) for 4 miles to Hazelton. You're now entering Amish territory so be aware that you may come upon their slow-moving, horse-drawn vehicles on the various roads and highways. Also, be respectful of their desire to not be photographed.

At Hazelton, turn left (east) at County Road C57. About 6 miles later, at the T intersection with County Road C33, turn left and drive a half mile north to where C57 continues to the east. Follow that for 4 miles to Aurora, then turn right (south). You will come upon the *Richardson-Jakway House*, 2791 136th Street, (319) 636-2617, free. Built as a stagecoach relay station in 1851, the house was also a post office and an overnight inn. To tour here, call at least three days in advance.

From Aurora, go south 1 mile and turn left (east) onto County Road C64. Follow that for 5 miles to State Highway 187 at the edge of Lamont; turn right (south). On 187 is *Bossen Implement*, 300 Washburn, (563) 924-2880, a farm implement dealer—of sorts. This one is unusual in that it deals with farm toys, not the big, huffing and puffing rigs used in the fields. The business began as a hobby in the 1980s and now the store carries farm toys covering everything from Avery to Zetor, both used and new. At least 15 manufacturers are represented here, ranging from those made in England, Germany, and the Czech Republic to Iowa-made brands such as ERTL, Spec Cast, and Scale Models. By the way, call these toys if you want—and some are—but many are collectors' items, special editions, custom-made miniatures, and precision replicas with some working components; these aren't the type that are usually seen in sandboxes.

Immediately south of town, turn left (east) onto a continuation of County Road C64 and take that for 4 miles to the southeast and the town of Dundee; turn to the left onto County Road W69 and go 1 mile north of town. There you will find the *Red Barn Model Railroad Museum*, 1388 132nd Street, (563) 924-2482, admission, a collection of model railroads and full-size railroad artifacts. The mod-

els include HO- and O-gauge layouts with cars and engines made by American Flyer and Lionel, some dating to the early twentieth century.

Return to Dundee and continue east on C64 for about 11 miles to State Highway 38, crossing State Highway 13 along the way. Turn right (south) on Highway 38 and roll for 6 miles to Delaware. From there, continue for 3 miles to Delhi and then another 8 miles to Hopkinton. Starting about 5 miles below Delhi, the Maquoketa River parallels your route the rest of the way to Hopkinton.

In Hopkinton, follow 38 as it jogs to the east. In town, on the left (north) is the campus of the former Lenox College that now forms the nine-building complex of the *Delaware County Historical Museum*, (319) 926-2639, admission. The college was actually called Bowen Collegiate Institute when it opened in the fall of 1859 and soon after became the first Presbyterian college in Iowa. In 1863, in response to Abraham Lincoln's call for volunteers to fight for the Union, the Reverend J. M. McKean, president of the col-

The living room of Cedar Rock includes furniture, curtains, and tableware designed by Frank Lloyd Wright to conform to his plans of the house.

lege, and all but two of the 32 male students (one was too young and the other too ill) joined the Union ranks with 70 others from the town. Records show that 27 failed to come home at war's end although the monument at the campus still records only 24 names for some reason.

In 1864, the college was renamed for New Yorker James Lenox who donated money to the institution. In the 1920s, Lenox became a junior college and finally closed its doors in 1944.

Turn back up Highway 38 to return to the west end of town and turn left (southwest) at Marion Street, which becomes County Road D47. Outside of town, the road, which is another segment of the scenic byway, rolls through some pretty countryside.

When you meet County Road X31 in about 5 miles, continue to follow the scenic byway signs and turn right (north). After 3.2 miles, turn left (west) onto County Road D42 and, 1 mile later, turn right (north) onto County Road X29 that leads into the *Turtle Creek Recreation Area*, (563) 927-3410. This preserve sits at an impoundment of the Maquoketa River, called Hartwick Lake, and has a boat ramp, RV campsites with electricity, picnic facilities, and fishing.

Following the scenic byway signs, you soon come to County Road X21 where you turn right (north) and proceed for about 5 miles to Manchester. Along the way, X21 meets County Road D5X, which is also Jefferson Road. Turn left (west) and the road magically becomes Bailey Drive as it enters town.

Quick Trip Option 1: When you reach the intersection of X21 and D5X, turn right (east) (instead of west) onto a gravel road. About 1 mile away, turn south on 205th Avenue, a dead end that leads to *Manchester State Trout Hatchery*, 22693 205th Avenue, (563) 927-3276, free, where you can see trout being raised on guided tours set up by appointment and fish for them in nearby Spring Branch Creek. Up to half a million fingerling rainbow trout, brown trout, and brook trout are raised here each year before being transferred to other fish farms, where they mature until they are a catchable size and then released into Iowa waterways.

At the intersection of Bailey Drive and East Main Street, turn left (west) onto Main, which is soon joined by State Highway 13. Head to the west edge of town to where 13 turns left (south) and follow it a short distance to U.S. Highway 20. Turn right and drive west for 14 miles to County Road W40. Turn left and take that for 5 miles to Quasqueton. In town, just before crossing the Wapsipinicon River, the road jogs to the right (southwest); just after crossing the

The buildings of the Bowen Collegiate Institute, which opened in 1859, now form the campus of the Delaware County Historical Museum in Hopkinton.

Wapsi, as it's known locally, pull into the city park near the dam and leave your vehicle. Now, slowly walk among the rocks below the dam and look carefully. Soon you will find the fossilized remains of creatures that lived here millions of years ago when this area was a shallow, warm-water sea in the Devonian Age. If you take any of the fossils, do so just for your personal use.

Go back north through Quasqueton on W40 and at the intersection with County Road W35, take W35 to the left for less than 2 miles north and west. You'll arrive at the entrance to *Cedar Rock State Park*, 2611 Quasqueton Diagonal Boulevard, (319) 934-3542, free. Those of you who don't know about this site may be excused for thinking that this is about some sort of rock. But it's actually a vacation home once owned by Lowell and Agnes Walter and designed by Frank Lloyd Wright. Completed in 1950, the house is one of 19 structures in the world that Wright signed with specially fired tiles bearing his initials because he considered it to be one of his most complete designs. Besides designing the home, Wright took a hand in the creation of the furniture, drapery, and carpeting, and in the selection of the china and silverware. He even shortened the legs of the baby grand piano. Outside, he designed path lights made of plow disks, a fire ring, and a boathouse/guesthouse that fronts the Wapsipinicon. Visitors arrive at a small information center, designed similarly to the house, and then proceed to the house, which is located among trees down a short drive.

The Name Game
Originally called Burrington, Manchester was renamed for Manchester, England, in 1858 to avoid confusion with Burlington, Iowa, which was already established.

A small version of the Statue of Liberty overlooks the Cedar River and downtown Waterloo.

Return to W35, turn left (northwest), and drive to County Road D22, less than 7 miles away. Turn left (west) and, after 2 miles, enter Independence on 1st Street. At 5th Avenue, which is also State Highway 150, turn right (north) and go about 10 blocks. After you cross the railroad tracks, visit the restored *Illinois Central Railroad Depot,* where the *Buchanon County Tourism Bureau,* (319) 334-3439, has information on area attractions and can guide you to local and Amish businesses if you're seeking finely crafted furniture, quilts, and other handmade items.

Return south on 5th Avenue to 1st Street again, turn right, and go a few blocks west. Just across the Wapsi is the *Wapsipinicon Mill,* 100 1st Street West, (319) 334-4182, free. One of the largest mills in Iowa, it was built in 1867 to process wool; in its later years it ground feed and generated electricity. A museum on the mill's second and third floors has burr stones, grain bins, pulley systems, and other pieces of mill machinery set out for display. A number of Amish set up shop at the mill to sell their fresh-baked goods on Fridays and Saturdays.

From Independence, continue west for 8 miles to Jesup on County Road D22. After about 8 more miles, the road veers to the southwest to enter Raymond. At 3rd Street, turn left (south) onto County Road V49, cross Interstate 380, and go for about 3 miles.

As you come into Gilbertville on 1st Street, turn right (west) onto East Washburn Road, also County Road D38 and drive for about 3 miles to Washburn. Continue west for 2.5 miles to Hess Road; turn right (north) and go for 1 mile to East Orange Road. Turn left (west). Very shortly you'll arrive at *Cedar Valley Arboretum and Botanic Gardens,* 1927 East Orange Road, (319) 226-4966, free. This 74-acre site features at least ten gardens, including the Community Garden where people tend 10-by-10-foot display beds of their own design, and the Enabling Garden which is designed with the physically handicapped in mind. Trial gardens and a Children's Pond are also on the grounds.

Return to Hess Road and continue north for about three quarters of a mile to Shaulis Road. At the intersection is *Lost Island Theme Park*, 2225 East Shaulis Road, (319) 234-3210, admission. With seven waterslides, the waterpark is a quick way to slip-slide away a warm day although you can also enjoy the wave pool and a lazy river, putt around two 18-hole goofy-golf courses, and take to the curves on the go-cart track. The park added a café recently to supplement its concession stand.

Go east on Shaulis Road and after 1 mile, turn onto Highway 218 heading north. In a few minutes this road whisks you into downtown Waterloo where you exit to the right onto Washington Street, which is parallel to Highway 218. Turn left (southwest) at West 4th Street and go two blocks to South Street. Turn right and pull into the parking lot of the *Grout Museum of History and Science and Planetarium*, 503 South Street, (319) 234-6357, admission. Beginning with a couple of thousand items collected by early Waterloo resident William Grout, the museum bearing his name now has more than 75,000 items that are used in exhibits about the natural and cultural histories of the region. Life-size dioramas include a cabin, tool shed, general store, and carpenter's shop; other exhibits relate to the plants, animals, and geology of this part of Iowa. For something out of this world, you can watch the shows in the museum's planetarium or, in the evening, use museum's telescopes during special programs.

North of the museum, in Washington Park, is a small Japanese garden and just beyond that is *Renssalear-Russell House*, 520 West 3rd Street, (319) 233-0262, admission. Built in 1861, this house was used by four generations of one family and is one of the oldest homes in Waterloo.

Next to the house is the *Bluedorn Science Imaginarium*, 322 Washington, (319) 233-8708, admission. The Bluedorn is a hands-on place for everyone with daily scientific demonstrations that involve the physics of light, electricity, sound, and other forms of energy.

Note: each of these attractions has its own admission rates but a package deal that covers the Grout Museum, Renssalear-Russell House, and the Bluedorn is available at a discount price at any of the sites.

Drive northeast from Washington Park on West Park Avenue and a few blocks later, turn left onto Commercial Street. For a look at fine arts in Waterloo, take in the *Waterloo Center for the Arts*, 225 Commercial, (319) 291-4490, free, overlooking the Cedar River. Works by Grant Wood are here along with those representing the largest collection of Haitian art in the nation as well as other pieces of art by Midwestern and African-American artists. The Junior Art Gallery in the building appeals to youngsters with its depictions of ancient cave art, an Athens market, and a Chinese home.

Quick Trip Option 2: Waterloo is home to four industrial plants that comprise the *John Deere Tractor Works*, (319) 292-7801. All can be toured for free, although visitors must be over 12 years of age to go on the tours and reservations are required. The locations of these plants range from the metro's southwest to northeast sides. At these plants, visitors can watch all facets of assembling tractors from casting parts and building engines and drivetrains to the final assembly of all sizes of tractors. Some people particularly like the *John Deere Tractor Assembly Operations*, at 3500 East Donald Street, where the company's largest tractors are assembled and visitors ride trams across the large assembly plant.

For more information about Waterloo's attractions, visit the *Waterloo Convention and Visitors Bureau*, 313 East 5th Street, (391) 233-8350 and (800) 728-8431, east of the Cedar River.

Return to Highway 218 and take it for about 4 miles northwest to the junction with State Highway 57 in Cedar Falls, where this tour began. But to help you wind down from the trip, be sure to make one more stop, this one at nearby *George Wyth State Park*, (319) 232-5505. Set alongside the Cedar River, the 1,200-acre park has 66 campsites (46 with electricity), trails, fishing, swimming, picnic facilities, boat ramps, a 240-acre lake, and concessions. It's a pleasant way to wrap up any tour.

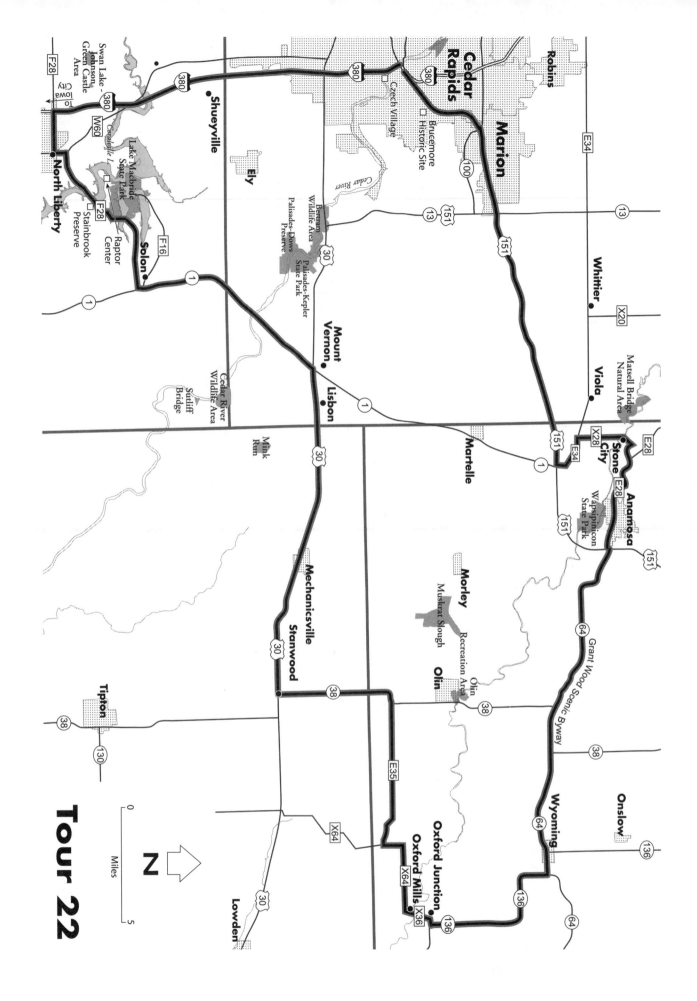

Tour 22
Grant Wood Country

Cedar Rapids—Marion—Stone City—Anamosa—Wyoming—Stanwood—Mount Vernon—Coralville Lake—
North Liberty—Cedar Rapids

Distance: approximately 120 miles

This tour takes you through Iowa's second-largest city and then into small towns and the countryside. Each of those elements played a role in the life of one of America's greatest painters, Grant Wood, who captured them in his paintings, sketches, and drawings. Not only is his inspiration still here but so is the largest collection of his works; it's ironic in a way that the region that so heavily influenced him is now so heavily influenced by his fame. However, others who have played major roles in Iowa are noted here too: the Czechs, Slovaks, African-Americans, and Native Americans, in collections and museums that tell of their lives. Other museums cover the histories of motorcycles and the state penal system. On the natural side, this region is rich with rivers, ravines, steep bluffs, woodlands, and geological wonders of the past, including regions where glaciers once ground their way across this part of the world thousands of years ago.

This tour begins at the junction of 33rd Street SW and I-380 (Exit 17). Go east a short distance to J Street SW and turn left (north). Then turn left again (west) onto Classic Car Court. At the far end of the street, tucked close to I-380 is *Duffy's Collectible Cars*, 250 Classic Car Court, (319) 364-7000, admission, where you can look (but no drooling please) at some fantastically restored cars. And no, this is not a museum but rather an actual show room where, if you really, really, want one of these cars, it's yours if you have the money. Because of the sales, you have a pretty good chance of seeing a different array of beautiful cars every time you visit.

Return to J Street SW, turn left (north), and go to 16th Avenue SW; turn right (east) and go a few blocks. As the avenue jogs to the left, you'll end up in the middle of the *Czech Village*, 700 block of 16th Avenue SW, (319) 362-2846, a region that was settled heavily years ago by Czechs and Slovaks. A real community and not a living history attraction, the neighborhood nevertheless attracts tourists with businesses that are related to its Czechoslovakian heritage, including the *Sykora Bakery*, 73 16th Avenue SW, (319)

364-5271, and *Zindricks Czech Restaurant*, 86 16th Avenue SW, (319) 365-5257. There's also the *Czech Feather and Down Co.*, 72 16th Avenue SW, (319) 364-0952, which began in 1885 and still makes feather-filled comforters, pillows, and beds, including beds for pets!

On a traffic island in the avenue is a European-style town clock and at the end of the block is a large, brick tower that's part of the *National Czech and Slovak Museum and Library*, 30 16th Avenue SW, (319) 362-8600, admission, the large tan building near the tower. Of course, a clue that you are at the museum are the three flags bearing the red, white, and blue of the United States, and of the Czech and Slovak Republics, in different patterns of course. The museum has permanent and traveling exhibits about Czech and Slovak cultures, histories, clothing, music, politics, language, and folk arts as well as about the histories of their people who immigrated to the United States, mostly from 1848 to 1920. The museum is proud to have an original statue of Tomas Masaryk, the first president of Czechoslovakia, which was hidden for years from the Nazis and then the Soviets before

The National Czech and Slovak Museum and Library in Cedar Rapids houses an impressive collection of exhibits and research material relating to the history and culture of the Czech and Slovak people.

surfacing after that country became two free republics in 1993.

Although the museum's address is on 16th Avenue SW, it actually fronts A Street SW. Across that street is the *Round House,* where a farmers market is held in the summer on Wednesday evenings and Saturday mornings.

From the museum's entrance, which is near 15th Avenue SW, drive down 15th Avenue to C Street SW and turn right (north). Drive one block to 12th Avenue SW (that's right, one block, not three—welcome to Cedar Rapids where streets twist and turn now and then). Cross the Cedar River. On your left (north) is a new museum about another part of American society, the *African-American Historical Museum and Cultural Center of Iowa,* 55 12th Avenue SE, (319) 862-2101, admission. Opened in 2003, the museum contains exhibits about ancestral homes in Africa and the roles blacks have played in American and Iowa history. The Nikee Museum Store features African and American-made gifts.

Grant Wood

Grant Wood was born near Anamosa, just east of Cedar Rapids, in 1891. Although he studied in Minneapolis, Chicago, and Europe, he returned to Iowa and lived in Cedar Rapids for several years. He was already fairly well-known by the time one of his paintings, a simplistic arrangement of a farmer and his daughter (posed by Wood's sister and dentist) in front of a small house and called *American Gothic,* won a competition in 1930; it was purchased for $300 by the Chicago Art Institute which still has the painting. After that, Wood's reputation soared but he remained down to earth, teaching summer art classes in nearby Stone City and continuing to work in his Cedar Rapids studio. Wood died in 1942 and was buried in Anamosa's Riverside Cemetery.

At 2nd Street SE, just beyond the African-American Museum, turn left (north). Now go to 2nd Avenue SE and turn left onto this one-way street. Go west for one block to 1st Street SE, turn right (north), and then turn right again (east) a block later at 1st Avenue. There you will find the *Cedar Rapids Convention and Visitor Bureau,* 119 1st Avenue SE, (319) 398-5009 and (800) 735-5557, on the right (south) side of the street. Brochures, pamphlets, listings of events, and so forth are here so pick up what you need to learn more about this area. In particular, make sure you get *Grant Wood Neighborhood Self-Guided Tour and Cedar Rapids Historic Downtown Walking Tour and Art Guide,* which marks the locations of about 20 public sculptures in the downtown area.

West of the CVB and alongside the river on a plaza is the *Tree of Five Seasons,* a 60-foot-tall stainless-steel sculpture of the city's logo. At the base of the sculpture, which marks where the first cabin was built in these parts in 1837, an audio kiosk tells about the region's history.

Do you have your walking shoes on? You should, because once you have your car parked, it's easier to walk around here on some days than to drive.

Walk along the Riverfront Park to 2nd Avenue SE and cross the bridge to Mays Island in the middle of the Cedar River. The large building that's ahead of you on the right (north) is the *City Hall and Veteran's Memorial.* At the entry is a bronze sculpture honoring those who fought at Iwo Jima and, just inside the doors, in a big lobby, is a large stained glass window entitled *Veterans of All Wars* that was designed by Grant Wood in 1928. By the way, with a courthouse also on the island, which resembles a battleship moored by bridges when viewed from the air, Cedar Rapids is one of the few cities with its municipal offices on their own island.

Return to 1st Street SE and turn right (south) (this is easy to do if you're walking; if you're in a car, you're going to have to drive around some because 2nd Avenue SE is a westbound, one-way street). Within two blocks you will come to the *Science Station and McLeod/Busse IMAX Dome Theater,* 427 1st Street SE, (319) 366-0698, admission. In a former fire station, the Science Station was the first attraction here and has three floors of hands-on exhibits that concentrate on all facets of physics such as light, sound, electrical energy, and more. Demonstrations are held in the center six to eight times a day. The IMAX theater features 70mm movies on a screen several stories tall.

Walk back north on 1st Street SE to 3rd Avenue SE and turn right. Walk two blocks and cross the railroad tracks to come to the *Cedar Rapids Museum of Art,* 410 3rd Avenue SE, (319) 366-7503, admission. Located mostly in a modern structure that's connected by an airy, glass atrium to a former Carnegie Library, the museum has 17 galleries and 5,000 pieces in its permanent collection. Besides hosting traveling exhibits, it has the world's largest collection of Grant Wood's works: at least 16 paintings and about 200 smaller works. Thirty to 40 are on display at any one time. Among his works are *Woman With Plant, December Afternoon, Old Stone Barn, Indian Creek-Summer, Young Corn,* and *The Hired Girl.* The museum also owns works of other artists, including sculptor Malvina Hoffman, print maker Mauricio Lasansky, and Marvin Cone, a contemporary and friend of Wood's, along with other regionalists of the 1930s and 1940s.

A few blocks from the museum, *Grant Wood's Studio* is scheduled to open in late 2004. Located on the second floor of a brick garage, Wood built the 1,400-square-foot studio and living quarters to have a European flavor. It was here from 1924 to 1934 that he created some of his most famous paintings, including *American Gothic*. For more information on the studio, contact the art museum, which owns it, or check the Web site (www.grantwoodstudio.org).

Four blocks northeast of the art museum, *The History Center*, 615 1st Avenue, (319) 362-1501, admission, looks somewhat unfinished on the outside but that's because history is never finished. Inside, exhibits relate to the history of the city and the region, and the star of the show is Time Quest, a computer-generated, simulated ride that you steer through early-twentieth-century Cedar Rapids. For a slight additional charge, you guide your "vehicle" through the streets of yesteryear, visiting buildings that have long since disappeared. People on the streets nod as you pass with the sounds of train whistles and horse hooves in your ears. Want to learn more about a particular building? Well, pull up to it and if someone on the sidewalk doesn't start speaking about it, the doors open and you will see a short show about it. An innovative exhibit, Time Quest has been studied by other places, including the Smithsonian, as a means to travel through time.

Okay, you have traveled about as far as you easily can by foot and it's now time to hop into your vehicle. Head northeast up 1st Avenue (which is also Business Highway 151) to 19th Street SE and watch for the signs guiding you to *Brucemore*. This brick 21-room Queen Anne mansion, 2160 Linden Drive SE, (319) 362-7375, admission, was built in 1886 by the young widow of a packing plant owner. The next owner renovated it in 1907 and Grant Wood made a cement mural for a second-floor sleeping porch in 1925. The majority of the house shows the elegant lifestyle of the city's upper class in the early twentieth century but the real delight of Brucemore is in its basement: the Tahitian Room and Grizzly Bar. Together, these rooms resemble a South Pacific getaway with island furniture and a metal roof with palm fronds hanging over the edges. When the tour guide flips a switch, the sound of rain hitting the metal roof resonates throughout the room and it's not a recording. It's real water falling from pipes onto the metal roof above! Brucemore is open daily year-round.

Return to 1st Avenue from Brucemore, turn right, and head northeast for about 3.5 miles to downtown Marion, where the road becomes 7th Avenue.

Quick Trip Option 1: From downtown Cedar Rapids, make your way to I-380 and head north to the 42nd Street NE Exit. Turn left (west) onto 42nd Street NE. Drive 2.8 miles to Seminole Valley Road NE and turn left. Soon, you'll see a turnoff on the left (east) to *Ushers Ferry Historic Village*, 5925 Seminole Valley Trail NE, (319) 286-

Time Quest, a full-sensory visit to the early days of Cedar Rapids, is found at The History Center.

5763, admission. This living history project is a collection of more than 30 homes, shops, businesses, offices, and churches, all representing a nineteenth-century community. Visitors can assist with some chores or sip sarsaparilla in the Corner Place Saloon. Ushers Village hosts reenactments, musical presentations, craft shows, and special events.

Just outside Ushers Ferry Village is *Seminole Valley Farm*, 1400 Seminole Valley Road, (319) 378-9240, admission, which shows what a mid-nineteenth-century Iowa farm was like. The big, inviting farmhouse has braided rugs laid on wood floors, a family sitting room, and a big iron stove in the kitchen, among the other amenities of that era. Other buildings at this farmstead include a summer kitchen, smokehouse, and barn along with a visitor center and gardens.

At 10th Street at the downtown park in Marion, turn left (north). In two blocks you will be at *Granger House*, 970 10th Street, (319) 377-6672, admission. Although modest compared to Brucemore, its original owner was still fairly well-to-do with a large yard and a brick carriage house out back. It's worth a stop.

Return to 7th Avenue, turn left (east), and go a little more than 2 miles to where you meet regular Highway 151. Continue east on that for 12 miles to State Highway 1. Turn left (north) and immediately after that turn left (west) onto County Road E34, following the signs to Stone City. The road rolls up and down some hills. When you come down one where you see a light-colored stone church on the right and a sign Stone City ahead of you, pull over onto the shoulder for a moment. Does the scene look vaguely familiar? It might because this area is near the viewpoint used by Grant Wood for his painting *Stone City, Iowa*, and the scene is almost as rural as when he painted the work in 1930.

As you resume heading down the hill, notice the large drive on your left. That leads to a large three-story barn that serves as the center of the *Grant Wood Festival*, (319) 462-4267, held on the second Sunday in June; besides featuring the works of artists from near and far, the festival usually has some of Wood's works on display in the barn.

On the right side of the drive is a replica of the house seen in Wood's most well-known painting, *American Gothic*; the real house is in Eldon, southeast of Ottumwa (see Tour 26).

At the bottom of the hill below the stone church, follow X28 by turning to the right. Right after crossing the Wapsipinicon River, you might notice the quarry on the left; that's the namesake of the city and the source of cream-colored rocks seen on buildings for miles around. The large stone building on the right (south), just past the bridge, was once a general store but it's now a private residence.

Continue on X28 as it curves to the north and mounts a hill. At the T intersection with County Road E28, turn right on it and go about 4 miles to Anamosa. As you enter town on Cherry Street, watch for South Elm Street and turn right (south) there. In just a few blocks, Elm crosses the Wapsipinicon River and, right after that, turn left (east) into *Wapsipincon State Park*, (319) 462-2761. Just inside the entrance the park drive splits; take the left fork and drive along the Wapsi, as many locals call the river. Eventually the road turns away from the river and goes up into the wooded hills, which contain picnic facilities, a boat ramp, boats for rent, 30 campsites, of which half have electricity, and a nine-hole golf course maintained by the *Wapsipinicon Golf Club*, (319) 462-3930. Multi-use trails lead throughout park, including those that run alongside Dutch Creek and to Ice Cave and Horsethief's Cave.

Leave the park and return via Elm Street to where you entered Anamosa and turn right (east) on what is now Main Street. In a couple of blocks, just after you pass the Jones County Courthouse on the left (north), turn left (north) on the street just beyond it, North High Street. Once you pass the courthouse, you may think you have come upon a tremendously large stone castle transplanted from somewhere in Europe. If you think you can't wait to get in there to see things, well, hold your horses—you need to be convicted of a felony to be admitted. This is the *Anamosa State Penitentiary*, the state's largest and second-oldest prison, which was built by inmates beginning in 1873.

Nevertheless, there is something you can see here so drive past the imposing and impressive prison administration building and, just past the north wall of the prison, turn left at the sign pointing the way to the *Anamosa Penitentiary Museum*, North High Street, (319) 462-4101, admission (which means money this time, not a felony conviction). Set outside the high walls, the museum is in a former cheese factory run by inmates in the 1930s and—don't snicker—one year one of their cheeses was ranked second-best in the nation. Inside are guard and prisoner uniforms, locks, keys, shackles, items used by prisoners trying to escape, newspaper accounts of prison activities, nightsticks, and more that reveal the interesting history of this prison. Also on hand is a replica of one of the four-by-eight-foot, original cells . . . shut yourself in awhile and wonder how you would like being in there for one long day after another, perhaps for life. There is also a gift shop.

Return to Main Street and continue east a short distance. In the downtown is the *Grant Wood Tourism Center and Art Gallery*, 124 East Main Street, (319) 462-4267, free. Inside are panels that Wood, who was born in Anamosa, painted for the Chieftain Hotel in Council Bluffs, prints of his works, and books and other memorabilia about him. Besides prints of his most famous work, *American Gothic*, which may be the second-most famous painting of all time behind Leonardo da Vinci's *Mona Lisa*, the gallery has a number of parodies that have been made of it. Open daily, the gallery also has a gift shop.

Park your car for a spell and walk east from the tourism center a short distance. As you cross Huber Street, you might want to hum "Born to be Wild" because you're about to enter that wood-faced building on the corner—the *National Motorcycle Museum and Hall of Fame*, 200 East Main Street, (319) 462-3925, admission. Formerly in Sturgis, South Dakota, the museum tells all about motorcycles—their history, manufacturers, engines, styles, tires, clothing worn by motorcyclists, and more. The original Captain America bike is here, its red, white, and blue gas tank signed by Peter Fonda who starred with it in the movie *Easy Rider*. A 1947 Indian Chief chopper that actor Steve McQueen used to ride into the desert is here too. So is a 1918 Harley-Davidson with a sidecar, still bearing its blackish-green original paint, quite a contrast to an immaculate, showroom-condition 1934 BSA, also with a sidecar.

Not far from the earliest motorcycles (which look like glorified bicycles), a 1904 Rambler, a 1910 Marsh Metz, and a 1911 Pierce with a leather drive belt, sit a 1942 Indian Scout Army and a 1942 Indian Military, both olive drab, no-nonsense bikes used by army messengers in WWII. Among the other motorcycles are those made by Vincent, Triumph, Suzuki, Honda, Bultaco, Zundapp, and there's even a 1968 Sears

Allstate Street Bike. A 1928 Harley-Davidson Peashooter Pup sits near an original billboard that touts the fun of owning one. Downstairs is a replica of a section of a board track with four racers on it, recounting the days when some motorcyclists raced on tracks made of wood planks.

Saddle up on Main Street again and head east on what is now State Highway 64, passing the junction with Highway 151 just east of town. Highway 64 is a leg of the Grant Wood Scenic Byway, which passes through some of the countryside where the artist lived and which inspired many of his works.

Quick Trip Option 2: If you haven't had your fill of motorcycles, about a mile north of town on Highway 151 is *J&P Cycles*, 13225 Circle Drive, (319) 462-4817, which is the nation's largest after-market store for Harley-Davidson parts. With warehouses covering 100,000 square feet, J&P sells parts at its counters and through its Web site and publishes a catalog of more than 800 pages that show the more than 25,000 parts and accessories it carries.

Now, it's just driving for the enjoyment of heading out into the countryside. Continue east on Highway 64 for 15 miles to Wyoming, where you turn right (south) onto State Highway 136 at the east end of town. Take that for 7 miles to Oxford Junction until 136 turns left (east) at Main Street. However, continue going south to the very next street on your right (west), County Road X64. Turn right and follow the road as it curves to the south and enters Oxford Mills after 1 mile. Continue on X64 for another 4 miles as it turns west, then south to meet County Road E53. Turn right (west) and about 7 miles later, at State Highway 38, turn left (south) for a 5.3-mile drive to Stanwood. There, turn right onto U.S. Highway 30 and drive to Mount Vernon, 15 miles west.

Quick Trip Option 3: When you reach State Highway 1, continue to the west for 3.5 miles on Highway 30 and turn into *Palisades-Kepler State Park*, 700 Kepler Drive, (319) 895-6039, on the left (south) side of the highway. Located along the Cedar River, this 840-acre park has six miles of trails that ramble up the bluffs, down the ravines, and through the woods. Prehistoric burial mounds are evidence that this area has been used for a long time; in the early part of the twentieth century, the park was a favorite retreat of poet Carl Sandburg as well as many other people. Of the 76 campsites, 45 have electricity, and four rustic cabins can be used from around May through October. The park also has picnic facilities and a boat ramp

Anamosa

Early citizens of the area first called their city Buffalo Forks, then Darmouth, and next Lexington. However, because there was already a Lexington, Iowa, the post office nixed that name. About the same time, an Indian man and his daughter, who was called Ana-mo-sah, visited a local inn; the locals, liking her name, chose it for their town, making Anamosa the only city in the nation with that name.

on the river that has various fish, including bluegill, bass, and channel catfish.

At State Highway 1 in Mount Vernon, turn left and go 9 miles south to Solon. There, turn right (west) at County Road F16 and drive 4 miles to *Lake Macbride State Park*, (319) 624-2200, which has two units. Located on the shores of Lake Macbride, an 812-acre lake stocked with channel catfish, bluegill, muskie, crappie, walleye, and Kentucky spotted bass, the 2,180-acre park has picnic areas, a beach, boat ramps at both Lake Macbride and Coralville Lake, and multi-use trails, including one connecting the park to Solon. Rentals of pontoon boats, motorboats, paddleboats, and canoes are available; call (319) 624-2315. The park's northern unit has 40 campsites with electricity and 20 more without, while the southern unit (see the next paragraph) has 60 primitive sites.

Return to Solon and continue south on Highway 1 to the edge of town. Turn right (west) at East 5th Street. After about 2.2 miles, the highway curves to the southwest, becoming County Road F28; about a half mile after that turn is the entrance to the south unit of Lake Macbride State Park. Stay on F28 and travel a causeway that spans part of Lake Macbride. Three quarters of a mile later, at the sign to the *Macbride Nature Recreation Area*, turn right (west). This preserve has primitive campsites, picnic areas, and hiking trails as well as trails used in the winter for cross-country skiing. Also here is the *Macbride Raptor Project*, (319) 398-5495, donation, which is 2 miles from the preserve's entrance. This is where birds of prey that have been injured are rehabilitated for release back to the wild. Around 20 raptors are permanent residents due to their injuries and can be seen at the center; these include bald and golden eagles along with hawks and owls.

Return to F28 and turn right, first going south, then southwest. In a little more than a half mile after leaving the preserve is a road on the left that leads to *Sugar Bottom Campground*, (319) 338-3543, less than 2 miles away. Managed by the U.S. Army Corps of Engineers, which created Coralville Lake by damming a portion of the Iowa River, Sugar Bot-

Colorful motorcycles from the past and present are on display at the National Motorcycle Museum and Hall of Fame in Anamosa.

tom has campsites with and without electricity, multi-use trails (including an equestrian trail), a beach, and a series of off-road mountain bike trails that range from novice to expert.

A bit farther down F28 is the *Merrill A. Stainbrook Geological Preserve*, (319) 335-9293. Park alongside the road, cross a footbridge, and follow the path near the sign on the left (south) side of the road. It will lead you to rocks where you can see grooves ground into them by glaciers long ago, a rare sight in Iowa. If you look closely at some other rocks in the area, you can see the fossilized remains of shellfish and colonial corals (some a few feet across) that lived here when this was part of a shallow warm-water sea about 375 million years ago.

On F28, continue southwest on the bridge across Coralville Lake. Right after crossing the lake, look for Rice Ridge Lane NE, which is on the left (south); take that a short distance through a small, rural residential area to the end. Park at the end of the

road and take to the trail there that leads to *Old State Quarry Preserve*, (319) 335-9293. Just one of the quarries that supplied stone for the construction of the original state capitol in Iowa City as well as for the base of the capitol in Des Moines, you can still see drill marks left by the stone workers years ago. Because of all the hardwoods here, the preserve is exceptionally pretty during the fall.

Return to F28 and continue southwest for about 2 miles to North Liberty. Follow F28 as it turns right (west) at Penn Street and take that for about 2.5 miles to I-380.

Quick Trip Option 4: On Penn Street in North Liberty, turn right (north) onto County Road W60, which crosses I-380 about 4 miles later. A quarter mile after that, cross the Iowa River, and at the very next road, turn right (east). You cross I-380 again and then the road begins to curve to the north. During that curve, you will come upon the *Curtis Hill Indian Museum*, 1612 NE

Curtis Bridge Road, (319) 848-4323, the largest private collection of Native American artifacts in the state. The collection, which you must call first to see, has pieces of pottery dating back to 700 AD, 500-year-old sandals, more than 100 pipes, 20,000 points and spears, 500 axes, and more, all gathered from sites across North America. Return to the tour by continuing up NE Curtis Bridge Road to County Road F12, 3 miles to the north; turn left (west) and upon meeting I-380 1 mile later, turn right (north).

From F28, proceed north on I-380 for 13 miles to the junction with 33rd Street in Cedar Rapids, thus finishing this tour.

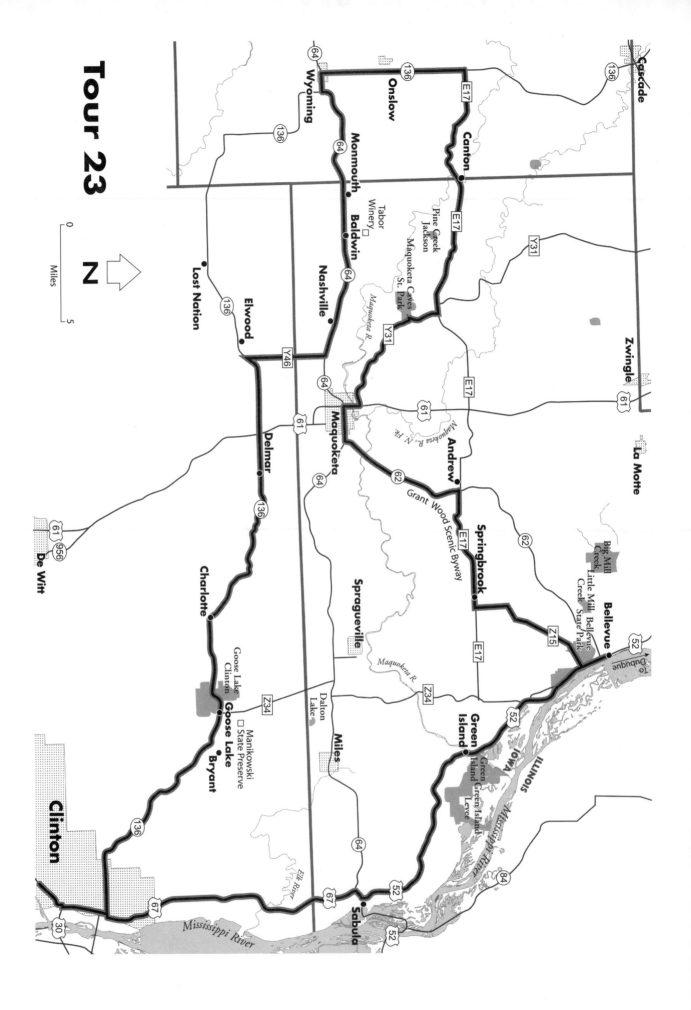

Tour 23

N

Miles
0
5

Tour 23
The Rolling Hills of East Central Iowa

Clinton—Sabula—Bellevue—Maquoketa Caves—Wyoming—Clinton

Distance: approximately 140 miles

Starting in a town once called New York that lay not along the Hudson River but the Mississippi, this tour proceeds through two other riverside communities, one an island city and the other a place where citizens waged a war against a gang of criminals years ago. From there you turn inland, rambling across hills and valleys that influenced one of the world's great painters. As you go, you'll take in cool caves, a vineyard, a garden made just for butterflies (and those who like to watch them), art galleries, the state's largest antiques dealer, historic inns, and one of three drive-in theaters remaining in Iowa. So, without further ado, let's go!

This tour starts on the southwest side of Clinton, at the junction of U.S. Highway 30 and U.S. Highway 67. Follow the combined highway as it curves to the northeast, parallel to a set of railroad tracks and the Mississippi River. Right after the highway turns due north as you approach downtown, turn left (west) onto 8th Avenue South. Go one block and turn left again to go south on South 4th Street. Near the end of the block on the right (west) is *Smith Brothers Hardware Store*, 1016 South 4th Street, (563) 242-0327. Not a museum but a real hardware store, it could be viewed as a museum of sorts considering that the building was built in 1874 and the business itself dates back to 1933. So consider this a living history experience that's great to visit.

Continue south on South 4th Street back to Highway 30 again and turn left, which will once more have you heading north toward downtown on South 3rd Street. Go a short distance to 7th Avenue South, turn right for one block, then left (north again) on South 2nd Street. At the intersection of South 2nd Street and 5th Avenue South, to your front left, you will see the former *Van Allen Department Store*, 200 5th Avenue South, which is now occupied by a pharmacy and other businesses on the main floor, and living units upstairs. Designed by the prominent architect Louis Sullivan and completed in 1915, this four-story brick building is

said to be among Sullivan's finest works.

Across 5th Avenue South is the *River Arts Center*, 229 5th Avenue South (563) 243-3300, free. Works of regional artists are displayed in this finely renovated building, which also sells artworks and homemade candy in the gift shop.

From the art center on 5th Avenue South, drive east to South 1st Street, turn right (south). One block away is the *Clinton County Historical Society Museum*, 601 South 1st Street, (563) 242-1201, donation. In an 1858 building that was once a commission house where riverboats were outfitted, the museum still shows off the original wood floors along with displays related to the region, including a human-powered fire engine.

Origin of the Name

Originally called New York, Clinton was renamed for DeWitt Clinton, a governor of New York in the nineteenth century.

Turn left (east) at 6th Avenue South and drive onto the levee along the Mississippi River. At the top of the levee, which protects the city from severe flooding, the road turns north. Here you'll find yourself in *Riverview Park*, which parallels the river for 14 blocks. Near the river are three small lighthouses that are nice touches to the riverfront, although they were constructed in the 1930s and never really were functional for the riverboats of the past. The park has a bandshell, an aquatic center, a playground, and some railroad cars. Further north, grounded in the levee and not in the water, is a former coal-fired towboat that's now the *Clinton Area Showboat Theater*, Showboat Landing, (563) 242-6760, which has a 250-seat theater. Next to it, and in the water, is the *Mississippi Belle II*, Showboat Landing, (563) 243-9000 and (800) 457-9975, a casino with slots and table games.

Continuing north along the river, you will see the *Alliant Energy Field*, the new name for *Riverview Stadium*, a lovely, art deco, 1930s-era baseball stadium that's home for the *Clinton*

A lighthouse looks out across the Mississippi River at Clinton.

LumberKings, (563) 242-0727, a Class A farm team for the Montreal Expos. The park is also the southern trailhead for the *Riverview Park Recreational Trail*, (563) 243-1260, a paved, hike-bike-skate trail that runs up the west bank of the river to Eagle Point Park about 5 miles to the north. Every July 4th, Riverview Park hosts the state's largest Independence Day celebration, *Clinton Riverboat Days*.

Quick Trip Option: While near downtown Clinton, head west on 2nd Avenue South until you reach South 14th Street, where you should turn left (south). Immediately on your right (west) is *Bickelhaupt Arboretum*, 340 South 14th Street, (563) 242-4771, free. More than 1,500 trees, bushes, and flowers make this a pretty place, along with a rose garden, stream, herb gardens, wildflower gardens, and rare conifers. An education center is on the grounds.

Continue on Riverview Drive to the north end of Riverview Park, where the road curves to the left (west) to become 6th Avenue North. When you meet North 2nd Street (which is also U.S. Highway 67), turn right (north). In the very next block is the *Clinton County Courthouse*, 612 North 2nd Street, a red sandstone building with a tall central clock tower. This is important to note because, over the years, some people traveling through town have thought that Clinton High School, 600 South 4th Street, is the courthouse; it's certainly imposing enough to be one.

Head north on Highway 67, which jogs back to North 3rd Street at Main Avenue, for about 3.5 miles to *Eagle Point Park*. As the highway leaves town and curves to the left, watch for the sign pointing the way to the park on the right, which is perched high atop a bluff overlooking the valley of the Mississippi River and Lock and Dam Number 13 below. The park has a 35-foot-high, castlelike stone tower and a neat stone pedestrian bridge along with picnic facilities and trails.

Continue north on Highway 67 for 12 miles to State Highway 64. Highway 67 is part of the famed Great River Road, a series of roads and highways that run along the entire length of the Mississippi River from its Minnesota source to its delta in Louisiana.

Turn right (east) onto Highway 64 and go less than a half mile to where U.S. Highway 52 begins to run to the north. There, you'll arrive at the *Jackson County Welcome Center*, 60488 Highway 64, (800) 342-1837. Housed in a replica of a one-room schoolhouse, the center has information about this part of eastern Iowa you might find useful and is open daily, year-round.

Just beyond the center across a causeway to the east is Iowa's one and only community sitting on an island—Sabula. It's a very laid-back community so drive around it to take in its mellow, backwater character.

From the welcome center, head north on Highway 52, the next leg of the Great River Road. Take that north for 20 miles to *Bellevue State Park*. The park, (563) 872-4019, has two parts. The first road you meet leads to the campgrounds, so unless you're interested in camping there, keep going north to the second unit and turn in there. Just inside the entrance, the road forks.

Go to the right and you'll end up in the fabulous and famous *Garden Sanctuary for Butterflies*. A large place with three dozen types of plants that grow throughout the grounds and attract about 60 species of butterflies large and small, the garden is wonderful to walk through and enjoy these light airy creatures that flutter around you. It's great for photographing them too. Near the garden is the *South Bluff Nature Center*, which details the natural history of the region.

If you turn left at the fork near the north entrance, you will ascend a winding road that leads to an overlook above nearby Bellevue and the river valley. A short trail leads along the edge of the bluff and passes three burial mounds that are believed to have been built between 700 and 1,000 years ago.

Return to Highway 52 and head north into Bellevue. As you drive on the bridge that crosses Mill Creek, drive slowly if you can and look to your left to take in the sight of the beautiful, red, six-story *Potter's Mill*, 300 Potter Drive, (563) 872-3838. Built in 1843 atop a stone foundation to serve as a gristmill, Potter's is Iowa's oldest mill and was used in that capacity until 1969. At one time, it produced 1,200 bushels of flour a day. Now a bed and breakfast, Potter's also serves lunches, suppers and Sunday brunch.

A bit farther north in town is the *Young Historical Museum*, 406 North Riverview, (563) 872-5830 and (800) 653-2211, on the west side of the highway. A red-roofed, limestone house, the Young has period furnishings and collections of china and Parian Ware, a type of porcelain, usually marble white, popular in the nineteenth century.

On the north edge of town is *Spring Side Inn*, 300 Ensign Road, (563) 872-5452, which sits upon a short bluff to the left (west) of the highway. Another B&B, this limestone building was built in 1850 and once hosted none other than Abraham Lincoln.

Return south on Highway 52 to just south of the north entrance to Bellevue State Park. Turn right (west) onto County Road Z15. This is the eastern start of the *Grant Wood Scenic Byway*, a system of roads that wander from here to Anamosa, taking in many of the landscapes that influenced artist Grant Wood (see Tour 22). Actually, all the roads on this tour could qualify to be part of the byway because they twist and turn past bucolic scenes that no doubt were the basis for many of Wood's paintings. Take some time to examine some of the landscapes, using your imagination to create tufted balls out of the trees, like Wood did, and noting how the lines of crops uniformly roll up and down the hills where fence posts march across the slopes, outlining boundaries. Those familiar with Grant's works will soon recognize scenes similar to his paintings, particularly *Plowing, New Sundown, Black Barns, Young Corn, Arbor Day, Farm Landscape*, and others.

Take County Z15 southwest for 6.5 miles through rolling fields and woods to Springbrook. Turn right (west) at County Road E17, which takes you another 6.5 miles to State Highway 62 in Andrew. There, turn left (south) and drive 6 miles to the east edge of Maquoketa and State Highway 64.

Turn left (east) onto 64 and in a short distance you'll find Costello's *Old Mill Gallery*. Maquoketa is blessed with two excellent fine-art

Potter's Mill has been a landmark in Bellevue ever since it was built in 1843.

galleries, and this, 22095 Highway 64, (563) 652-5971, is one of them. In the old two-story stone Oakland Mill, which dates back to 1867 and was once a barn, is the home, studio, and gallery of Patrick Costello, who is known for his oils and watercolors.

The Bellevue War

Although it's peaceful now, in the early part of the nineteenth century, Bellevue was anything but that. Most of its citizens were law-abiding folks but a hotel in Bellevue run by William W. Brown was thought to be the hangout for killers, livestock rustlers, thieves, forgers, counterfeiters, and others who spread fear for miles up and down the Mississippi valley. Brown claimed that he was not involved with those who frequented his establishment, but things reached a boiling point when a number of those men tried to murder a townsman who had killed a man plundering his house. On April 1, 1840, Brown's hotel was surrounded by nearly 40 armed citizens as he was served with a warrant for his arrest. A shot rang out and then a hail of bullets flashed between about two dozen outlaws in the hotel and the town's citizens. When the battle was over, Brown and two other outlaws lay dead; so did four of the townspeople. Some outlaws escaped but those who were caught had their fate decided by a vote of beans; instead of being hung, they were whipped and sent down river in a boat. Called "The Bellevue War," it was one of the most talked-about gunfights for years and continues to stir up debates about whether the citizens who attacked Brown's hotel were acting within the law or enforcing mob justice.

Return west on Highway 64 and then go north again on State Highway 62 a very short distance to the county fairgrounds on the left (west). There you'll find the *Jackson County Historical Society*, 1212 East Quarry Street, (563) 652-5020, free. With more than 22,000 square feet of display space, the museum has vintage clothing, antique toys, and other items gathered from around the county to show to visitors. A machine shed shelters large agricultural equipment, including an 1830 McCormick reaper, tractors of the past, buggies, wagons, and more.

Return to Highway 64, turn right (west), and enter Maquoketa on East Platt Street. Go about 1.25 miles to the downtown area and turn left (south) on Olive Street. At the end of the first block is the town's second noteworthy art emporium, *Old City Hall Gallery*, 121 South Olive, (563) 652-3405, on the left. There, you'll find the works of two artists whose works are on permanent display, along with works of other artists shown in temporary exhibits. The permanent artists (who actually split their time between here and New York City) are Rose Frantzen, a widely known artist who creates lively, colorful, and wildly imaginative paintings, and her husband, Chuck Morris, who is known for integrating portraits of people into their own drawings and paintings.

Bear of a Name

Maquoketa, the only community in the nation with that name, was originally called Springfield until 1853 when its present name came into use. It comes from the Meskwaki and Sauk phrase for the region, "there are bears."

From Olive Street, go one block west to Main Street and turn right (north), continuing past the intersection with Platt Street. Watch on the left for *Decker Hotel*, 128 North Main, (563) 652-6854, a beautifully restored, three-story brick hotel built in 1875 that hosts overnight visitors and offers great meals in its classy restaurant. Another place to consider staying in town is *Squiers Manor B&B*, 418 West Pleasant Street, (563) 652-6961, an 1860s Victorian mansion with some fantastic rooms, including a three-level loft room atop the house. The owners also own the state's largest antique store, so you can expect to see plenty of very fine antiques. To find that store, which covers 30,000 square feet and is called *Banowetz Antiques Mall*, 122 McKinsey Drive, (563) 652-2359, go to the west edge of town on West Platt Street; the mall will be on the right (north) before you reach U.S. Highway 61.

A few blocks past the Decker Hotel on Main Street, keep to the left, turning onto Hurstville Road, which runs to the north-west. Immediately you will come to the *Hurstville Lime Kilns*, a free historic site you can visit at anytime. In these kilns, now a series of large ruins, limestone was reduced to lime; when they were in full operation in the 1890s, 1,000 barrels of lime a day were produced. When portland cement became more commonly used for making concrete, the need for lime tapered off and the flames in the kilns finally flickered out in the 1930s.

From the Hurstville Lime Kilns, continue on the road a short distance to 63rd Street. Turn left (west), cross U.S. Highway 61, and cruise west on what is now County Road Y31 for about 6 miles to *Maquoketa Caves State Park*. This is another leg of the Grant Wood Scenic Byway, which winds through some hilly countryside.

Like many other state parks in Iowa, 323-acre *Maquoketa Caves*, (563) 652-5833, offers camping, picnic facilities, and so on, but what makes it stand out from the rest are its 14 caves. The largest is Dancehall Cave, where a stream runs alongside the paved, lit walkway that runs for 1,100 feet between three immense openings. Outside Dancehall's north entrance is a natural bridge. Trails running north and south from Dancehall and through a shaded valley lined with limestone bluffs pass several other caves, some reached by boardwalks. Some can be entered easily, some require crawling. Some are shallow, others deep. None, though, require spelunking skills, although you should watch out for your head because there are plenty of opportunities here to knock your noggin. A 17-ton balanced rock is near Dancehall, which was first seen by settlers in the 1830s.

The park has 29 campsites, 17 with electricity.

Return to Y31 from the state park and turn left (north). Upon meeting County Road E17, turn left (west). Although you're no longer on the Grant Wood Scenic Byway when you get on E17, you will feel like you still are, because the scenery is much the same in this very pretty part of eastern Iowa. Because of the hills and curves from now on, passing zones are few so don't get into a rush.

After traveling E17 for about 15 miles, turn left (south) at State Highway 136 and cruise for 8 miles to Wyoming. That's a town in Iowa, not the state—you haven't gone that far. Along the way you'll roll up and down hills and pass fields where the shocks of dry corn stalks painted by Grant have been replaced by rolls of hay. Often they're scattered across the fields like accent marks; sometimes they're end-on-end like giant inchworms.

In Wyoming, turn left (east) onto State Highway 64. As you head east on another leg of the byway, watch the left side of the road for a barn with "It's a Girl" painted on one side. If you want to stop to congratulate the parents, well, you're a mite late because the sign has been there for years; but it's still something that brings a smile to the faces of those who drive by here. Fields, cattle, silos, barns, country cemeteries, and more come and go as you continue on.

Seven miles past Wyoming, continue through Monmouth; and 2 miles after that, in Baldwin, turn left (north) at Main Street, which is also County Road Y34. Go 1 mile north to 67th Street and then turn left (west). In another mile you will come upon *Tabor Home Vineyards and Winery*, 3570 67th Street, (877) 673-3131. In 1997, Paul Tabor and his family opened this winery, using grapes they have grown here, primarily Marechal Foch and some La Crosse grapes, on land settled by their ancestors in the 1860s. At present, the Tabors produce at least 16 types of award-winning wines amid the hills of Jackson County.

Return to Baldwin and continue going east on Highway 64. When you reach County Road Y46 and the turnoff to the Maquoketa Airport about 6 miles after leaving Baldwin, turn right. Traveling south on Y46, you will descend a long slope into the farm fields that fill the valley of Prairie Creek and then climb into the hills south of there.

Four miles later, at State Highway 136—yup, the same one as before—turn left. (By the way, even though you're turning east, the traffic sign will read Highway 136 South.) After 4 miles, as you approach U.S. Highway 61, look to your right at 220th Street. There you will see something rarely seen anymore in the nation. The *61 Drive-In Theater*, (563) 674-4367, just a half mile down the lane, is one of three left in Iowa. Built in 1952, the 61 is where families and friends gather on warm nights to watch movies from their cars or as they lay on blankets on the grassy slopes.

Continue east on Highway 136 for 3 miles past Highway 61 to Delmar, then another 9 miles to Charlotte. If you truly enjoy twisting roads, this entire stretch is for you, but be aware that if you're driving, you won't have much time for sightseeing because you had better watch the road. If you really want to enjoy this part of Highway 136, take it easy, say around 45 miles an hour; because of the scenery, it's certainly a worthwhile road to take.

From Charlotte, continue east for 5 miles to the town of Goose Lake and County Road Z34. Turn left (north) and drive three quarters of a mile to 137th Street and turn right (east). A quarter mile later, turn into the

An arched rock in Maquoketa Caves State Park was once part of a cave millions of years ago.

parking area of *Manikowski Prairie State Preserve*, (563) 847-7202, free. Unlike most other prairies in Iowa where the plants grow on the plains, this 46-acre preserve contains plants growing from soil that has made its way into cracks in the underlying rock, making this the largest limestone prairie in Iowa. Thousands of years ago, when glaciers were melting, these low-lying rocks were part of the bluffs on the west side of the ancient valley of the Mississippi River, which is now about nine miles away. Here, you'll find at least 40 types of plants growing from the rocky ground, including yellow coneflower, shooting stars, mountain mint, rockcress, and indigo bush, and with all these blooming wildflowers, it's no wonder you can also find various butterflies here, including the Ottoe skipper, columbine duskywing, zabulon skipper, and wild indigo duskywing.

Return to Goose Lake and turn left onto Highway 136, which angles to the southeast as it leaves town. A little less than 10 miles from Goose Lake, the highway turns due east and runs for 4 more miles before it enters Clinton as Main Street and meets Highway 67 on the north side of town, ending this tour.

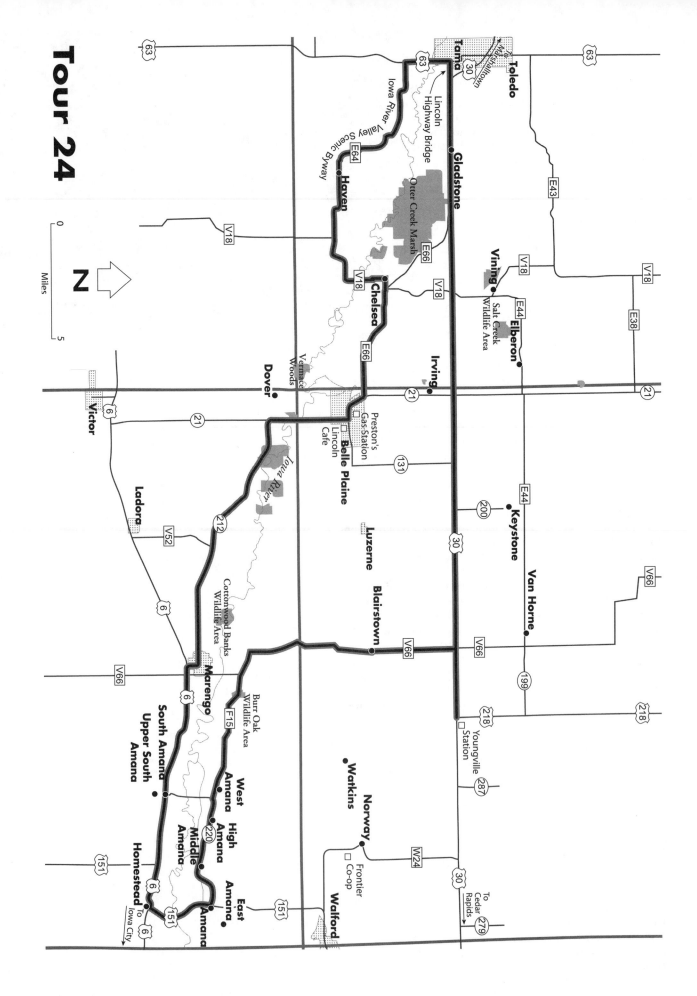

Tour 24

Tour 24
The Amana Colonies and the Iowa River Valley

Amana—Middle Amana—High Amana—West Amana—Blairstown—Tama—Chelsea—Belle Plaine—Marengo—South Amana—Homestead—Amana

Distance: approximately 103 miles

This chapter starts and ends in the Amana Colonies with a drive through the countryside in between. In the Amanas, life flows considerably slower than in the rest of the state. Let other places have garish signs and all-night stores, but in these rural communities, shortly after five o'clock in the afternoon, you can begin to hear the crickets and passing cars are just an occasional noise in the evening hours. To the north and west of the Amanas, a group of seven small communities, you get to ramble across the pretty landscapes of east central Iowa, take in parts of a historic highway that was the first to cross the nation, travel on one of the state's scenic byways along the Iowa River, learn about two famous writers and visit two towns that have had some interesting episodes with water in past years.

This tour begins just north of Amana on U.S. Highway 151. As you approach town, turn right (west) at C Street and follow the road through a curve to the *Amana Colonies Welcome Center*, 39 38th Avenue, (319) 622-7622 and (800) 579-2294. This is the place to pick up information about what's where in the colonies and when things are happening too. The building also houses the theater where the *Old Creamery Theater Company*, (800) 352-6262, admission, presents its productions from March through December. Nearby is a trailhead for the *Kolonieweg (Colony Way) Recreational Trail*, a paved, 3.1-mile-long, hike-bike-skate trail that rounds a small lake and passes through farmland. Bikes can be rented at the *Amana Colonies Outdoor Convention Facility and RV Park* near the Welcome Center.

Before going any further with advice about what to see here, some words about the Amana Colonies. Their beginning goes back to 1714 when dissatisfied members of the Lutheran Church in southern Germany broke away to form their own church, called the Community of True Inspiration. The new church believed that God worked by inspiring some individuals directly, as happened with the Old Testament prophets. To escape persecution in Germany, the church's members, who called themselves Inspi-

rationalists, immigrated to the United States in the 1840s, first to Buffalo, New York and then to the valley of the Iowa River northwest of Iowa City a decade later.

By 1855, they had set up the first of what would be seven villages and called it Amana, which comes from the Book of Solomon in the Bible and means "believe faithfully." A year later, West Amana was built about 7 miles to the west, and South Amana, 2 miles south of there. Mills were constructed in Amana, connecting the small communities economically to the outside world, and three more communities were built over the next few years—Middle Amana, High Amana, and East Amana. When the railroad came to nearby Homestead in 1860, the Inspirationalists purchased that entire town so they could ship and receive goods. Soon Homestead was the seventh and last of what came to be called the Amana Colonies; almost all are gathered around a large central area containing farm fields, a mill pond created in the 1860s to supply power to the mills, and the Iowa River.

The Inspirationalists established the Amana Society, a communal fellowship not to be confused with twentieth-century communes or communism, which owned about 26,000 acres. Everyone worked for the Society and the Society worked for everyone. Adults had tasks, such as working in the fields, at shops, in the kitchens, and in the woolen, flour, and calico mills. In return, the Society provided shelter for everyone and supplied food that was cooked in communal kitchens, one per village. Each village had its own businesses, church, and school. A credit system was established to buy items in the stores that were not furnished by the Society. By no means were the Amanas a tight commune; members could leave if they wanted and they could own personal items. At their peak population, the villages together had 1,813 residents.

In the 1930s, communalism was dropped and people began to work for wages. Still, the church remained the mainstay of the residents as it does today. However, the economics of the colonies have changed greatly and now they have a large focus on tourism and on the appliances made by Amana Corporation, now a division of

Maytag, another Iowa firm. Tourism mostly affects Amana, sometimes called Main Amana, and to a lesser degree, Middle Amana, High Amana, West Amana, South Amana, and Homestead. East Amana and an area called Upper South Amana, which is not a true colony, have no ties with tourism. Also, "Little Amana" is the name lent to a modern grouping of hotels, restaurants, and shops at Exit 225 on I-80, directly south of the colonies; however, it has never been considered as one of the Amana Colonies.

Occasionally some people confuse the Amanas with the Amish and while the names are similar, the people are not. In the Amana Colonies, visitors are welcome to photograph whatever they want, and residents use electricity and modern conveniences (after all, they do make electric appliances at the Amana Corporation) and drive their own cars. In their shops and restaurants, they use a credit system, mercifully in the form of Visa, MasterCard, Discover, etc. With a year-round population of about 1,700 people now, the Amana Colonies are a unique blend of the past and present, and a touch of Europe in the middle of America.

A winery and candy shop now occupy this historic building in Amana.

Now, let's get on with this tour.

Upon leaving the Welcome Center, go south to 220th Trail (also called State Highway 220) and turn left (east). Pass through the intersection with Highway 151 and continue into Amana, the largest of the colonies. Find a place to park and take to your feet . . . you'll see a lot more that way; besides, Amana is not so big that you can't walk across it easily. Stop first at the *Museum of Amana History*, 4310 220th Trail, (319) 622-3567, admission, which is at the junction of 220th Trail and 44th Avenue. The museum consists of three buildings

at this site, including a former communal kitchen that later became a private residence, a wash house, and a school. All hold exhibits that tell the history of the Amanas. By the way, the price of your admission here allows you to visit other museums of the Amana Heritage Society in the other villages; these include the *Amana Community Church* in Homestead, the *Communal Agriculture Museum* in South Amana, and the *Communal Kitchen and Coopershop Museum* in Middle Amana. The Museum of Amana History is open mid-April through mid-November while the others are open from May through October.

All around Amana are a number of businesses in trim wooden buildings that offer a lot—quilts, toys, brooms, baskets, lace, knick-knacks, antiques, candles, fresh pastries and breads, clocks, meats, gifts, and . . . and . . . and . . .

Restaurants abound too, and all serve family-style meals where you get a never-ending stream of side dishes in addition to your entree; basically the rule is, if you empty a bowl, it's going to be replaced by another round of that food. No one, that is no one, walks away from the colonies wanting more food. Take your choice in Amana— the *Ronneberg, Ox Yoke, Amana Barn,* and *Kolony Inn*—you'll be taken care of right nicely.

And then there's that other thing that the Amanas are known for—wine. Do you see those wooden trellises on many of the buildings? They were built years ago to support grapevines, and the Amanas still have a rich heritage of producing their own wines. You should be able to find what you want here in the way of vino—in Amana alone you will find the *Weinkellar, Ackerman Winery, Old Wine Cellar Winery, Sandstone Winery, Village Vintner, Village Winery,* and the *Grape Vine Winery*. In case you want something different, the *Amana Coffee and Tea Company* is in town too.

After it travels a short distance to the east of the museum, 47th Avenue splits off to the right from 220th Trail, leading directly to the *Amana Woolen Mill*, (319) 622-3432 and (800) 222-6430, the only woolen mill in the state. The showroom has quality blankets, coats, and more, made of wool and other fabrics. Displays in other areas show how the mill operated in the past and you can watch workers making various cloth items, including dolls and yarn angels. A walk along the outside of the mill takes you to the millrace that was built years ago to furnish the water that powered the mill's machines.

Across the street is *Millstream Brewing Company*, (319) 622-3672, the state's oldest microbrewery, which makes premium beers, cream soda, and root beer. In 2003, its Schild Brau Amber won a bronze medal from the North American Brewers Association, while its Old-Time Root Beer earned a silver medal in the World Beer Championships.

North of the mill is the *Amana Furniture*

Shop, (319) 622-3291, where chairs, desks, tables and more are handmade from oak, walnut, cherry, and other woods. There's a clock gallery too. Free tours of the work areas are given Monday through Saturday.

Drive west from Amana for 2 miles on 220th Trail to Middle Amana. Along the way you'll pass Lily Lake, which served as a millpond years ago, as well as the big manufacturing plant on the left side of the road where Amana appliances are made. Although Raytheon made the first microwave oven in 1947—it was five-and-a-half feet tall, weighed 750 pounds and cost $3,000—it wasn't until 1967 that the first countertop version, called the Radarange and costing $495, was built for the general public by Amana! More than nine out of 10 American homes have a microwave oven now.

Quick Trip Option 1: At the intersection of Highway 151 and 220th Trail in Amana, turn left and immediately pull into the parking lot of the Amana Handimart. Park at the far end and walk past the pines just beyond the parking lot. There you will find one of the relatively obscure cemeteries that are here and there in the Amanas. Note how all the headstones are the same size: Inspirationalists believe that everyone comes into the world alike and they should go out the same way.

At 26th Avenue in Middle Amana, turn right (north), go two blocks, and turn left (west) at J Street. There you will find the *Communal Kitchen and Coopershop Museum.* The 1863 kitchen is the last complete communal kitchen left in the Amanas and its huge brick hearth, dry sink, and kitchen tools are still there. The dining room has its long wooden tables set with china and silverware. Across the street, it's as if the cooper—the man who made barrels and other containers—just stepped out for a moment.

For a real taste of what was produced in the kitchens, walk west of the communal kitchen to *Hahn Bakery*, (319) 622-3439, the only hearth oven still working in the colonies. The door opens at 7:30 a.m., and if you really want the delicious breads, coffeecakes, and streusels baked in the brick oven, be there promptly.

Return to 220th Trail and head west once more for 2 miles to High Amana. Turn right (north) on 13th Avenue and then, after one block, turn right on G Street. There, you'll come upon the *Old Fashioned High Amana Store*, one of the older buildings in the colonies. Closed for a while, it reopened in 2003 to the delight of many people and you can once more walk its wooden floors and see what's in the old display cases.

A block west on G Street is the *Amana Arts*

Youngville Station, a former stop on the old Lincoln Highway north of the Amana Colonies, has been partially restored; it now houses a museum and is open for some meals.

Guild Center, (319) 622-3678, where residents and visitors alike create works of art, sometimes on their own, sometimes in week-long workshops held each summer.

Return to 220th Trail and head west once more, this time to West Amana, the second oldest colony. Turn right (northwest) onto 8th Avenue. Although it could virtually be a museum, the *Broom and Basket Shop*, (319) 622-3315, is actually a business where you can watch brooms of all sizes and shapes being made. Woven baskets are also sold here. Nearby is an outlet for *Schanz Furniture*, which made and displays the state's largest rocking chair here. It's so big that two adults can sit side by side and feel pint-sized again.

A block west of the broom shop is the *Michele Maring Miller Studio Gallery*, (319) 622-6330. In the former West Amana Church, it has paintings of the Amanas of yesteryear.

Leave West Amana by going to its west end and turning left (south) onto 4th Avenue, then right (west) on County Road F15. This leads through some pretty, rolling scenery on the north side of the Iowa River and west of the Amanas.

About 6 miles beyond West Amana, F15 joins County Road V66 for 1 mile before V66 turns to the right (north). Follow it for a little more than 5 miles to Blairstown. There, continue going north on V66 for 4 more miles to U.S. Highway 30. Turn right (east) and go for 3 miles to U.S. Highway 218. On the northwest corner of the intersection is *Youngville Station*, (319) 472-5545. A two-story, Tudor-style building, it was said to be the largest gas station on the Lincoln Highway in the 1920s. Yes, at this moment you are on a stretch of that famous highway, which has been replaced mostly by Highway 30 in Iowa. Abandoned for some years, Youngville Station, which had a cafe and served as a bus stop for years, has recently been renovated and regained much of its former glory. At present its cafe is open for lunch on Tuesday and Thursday, and coffee and rolls are served there on Saturday morning; those who volunteer here hope to have it open longer as time goes on. A part of the building houses a Lincoln Highway museum, which has among other items a top-loading pop machine—remember those? Outside, three camper cabins that were originally used by travelers on the old highway are being restored. The station is also the scene of a farmers market, 3:30–6:00 p.m. every Friday, where you can buy fresh produce and baked goods during the growing season.

Quick Trip Option 2: From Youngville Station, head east on Highway 30 for 6 miles and turn right at County Road W24. Drive 5 miles south to Norway and turn left at the convenience store; head a quarter mile southeast of town on Euclid Avenue to *Frontier Natural Products Co-op*, 3021 78th Avenue, (800) 669-3275. Since it started in 1976 in a cabin, Frontier has grown into the world's largest supplier of organic herbs and spices and now occupies an 85,000-square-foot facility from which it operates a mail-order business. Frontier raises and processes natural products, including oils, mineral baths, lotions, clay powders, massage and body oils, teas, flours, pasta, soups, beans, and many, many more items. If you call ahead, you can get a tour of this facility

From Youngville Station, head west on Highway 30 for 29 miles to Tama. As you approach the town's east end, you will see *King Tower Café*, 1710 East 5th Street, (641) 484-5970, on your right. An original landmark on the Lincoln Highway, the café was ahead of its time because it was open 24 hours a day and air-conditioned; and it's still in operation after all these years!

Just west of the café is a small park near what may be the most unique bridge on the Lincoln Highway. Built in 1915, this could have been like so many other bridges on the Lincoln Highway, but residents of Tama wanted something different in their community so they pitched in some extra money and had the side railings of the bridge fashioned to read, "LINCOLN HIGHWAY." Like the café, the bridge is still open, which means it's used by traffic (remember that in case you want to photograph it . . . and keep your body intact).

Continue into Tama on East 5th Street until you reach State Street, which is also U.S. Highway 63, a half mile to the west; turn left (south). By the way, Tama is one half of Iowa's Twin Towns—Tama and Toledo. About the same size as Tama, Toledo is just north of its sister city and has the county courthouse and the *Tama County Historical Museum* (see Tour 13 for more information).

Tama features the only bridge railing in the nation bearing the words "Lincoln Highway."

Just south of town, cross the Iowa River, then go a little more than 1 mile beyond to County Road E64. Turn left. You'll be heading east on the *Iowa River Valley Scenic Byway* that runs through the pretty valley of the Iowa River back to the Amana Colonies, passing woods and fields along the way, although for a while the route swings a few miles south of the river. About 2 miles after you pass the very small community of Haven on E64, watch on the left (north) for signs at Q Avenue pointing the way to *Central Iowa Outfitters*, 3752 Q Avenue, (641) 489-2869, fee, a ranch where you can shift from your mechanical horsepower to the real thing in the shape of horses and mules. Rides from a half day to an entire week are available and the folks here can even meet you at a state or county park if you want to ride somewhere other than the ranch. Call in advance to set up your rides.

About 11 miles after leaving Highway 63 and swinging generally to the south and east, E64 is met by County Road V18; take V18 for about 4.5 zigzagging miles to Chelsea, just north of the Iowa River. Well, let's put it this way: you'll be coming into what might be called Chelsea I, because after being flooded by Otter Creek and the Iowa River in 1918, 1944, 1969, and 1993, and suffering minor floods in between those major ones, a number of residents took up a government offer to relocate just to the east on higher ground—call this Chelsea II if you want. Some deep feelings still exist between those who chose to move and those who remain in the original town.

When you arrive in Chelsea on Station Street, turn right (east) onto Irish Street. This is an odd name considering the number of Czechs who settled in this area. Anyway, here you have rejoined the Lincoln Highway. Now you may have thought you were on the Lincoln Highway as you traveled Highway 30 from Youngville Station to Tama awhile ago—and you were. However, for its first few years, the Lincoln Highway came about four miles south so traffic could detour around a number of ridges, called the Bohemian Hills, that were just too steep for the low-powered vehicles of the early twentieth century. Eventually the hills were shaved down, and the Lincoln Highway was routed straight between Cedar Rapids and Tama, the route now used by Highway 30.

In Chelsea, Irish Street is soon joined by County Road E66. Continue east on that for about 6 miles to State Highway 21. Turn right (southeast) and drive less than 1 mile to Belle Plaine, where the road straightens out to the east as 13th Street. In town, which once billed itself as the Lincoln Highway's midway point between Chicago and Omaha, watch

along the left (north) side of 13th Street for *Preston's Gas Station*, (319) 434-6458, free, which is actually two buildings, a gas station and a garage. It's unlikely that many other buildings exist that hold up as many metal advertising, highway, and road signs as these two, so you should be able to recognize Preston's Station pretty fast. No longer an operating service station, Preston's is still a great place to visit and see relics, large and small, associated with the lifespan of this gas station and the Lincoln Highway.

Go two blocks east of the Preston Gas Station on 13th Street to the intersection with 6th Avenue. There, you see three more buildings associated with the Lincoln Highway: the *Herring Hotel*, which is now an apartment building called the Graham House; *Lincoln Café*, which is the oldest restaurant on the highway in Iowa; and the Sankot Garage, which opened in 1914 and is still run by the Sankot family.

Continue east on 13th for another block, turn right (south) at 7th Avenue, and then to the left (east) a block later at Main Street, which is also called 12th Street. Proceed for two blocks to 9th Avenue. Just after making the turn onto 12th Street you will see the *King Theater*, which opened in 1930 and, like the Sankot Garage, is still operated by the same family that originated it. On the southwest corner of 12th Street and 9th Avenue is the *Guthrie Building*, the only structure to survive a fire that practically wiped out downtown Belle Plaine in 1894 and destroyed 80 businesses. Keep an eye on the southeast corner where the Belle Plaine Historical Society is building its museum.

Turn right (south) on 9th Avenue and drive four more blocks to the *Frank Zalesky home*, 802 9th Avenue. Now a private residence, this is where Czech philosopher Ladimir Klacel lived the last months of his life, although some believe he stayed in the carriage house on the property. Klacel was born as Frantisek Matous Klacel on April 7, 1808 in Ceska Trebova in the Austrian-Hungarian Empire; a section of the present-day Czech Republic. Ordained as a Roman Catholic priest, Klacel also was a professor of philosophy and became well known for penning poems as well as philosophical and scientific papers. However, when he began writing that rational thought was the true belief, he ran afoul of the church's doctrines and was dismissed from his position in 1844. Four years later, he quit the church and founded a paper so he could express his opinions. Attracted by religious freedom in the United States, he immigrated to this country in 1869 and tried, but failed, to set up communes of free thinkers. After living in various cities, Klacel moved to Iowa City where he edited the *Slovan Amerikansky*, a newspaper for the Bohemian Freethinkers, based in Chicago. Finally, in ill health, he came to the Belle Plaine home of Frank Zalesky, one of his admirers; it was here that he died on March 17, 1882. When he was buried in Oak Hill Cemetery just east of town, a train brought many of his followers from Chicago for the funeral service. Besides a monument at the Belle Plaine

A Home-Grown Artist

Born in Belle Plaine in 1893, painter Earl Moran started out illustrating men's fashions but shifted to female subjects. From around the 1930s to the late 1950s, Moran was one of the nation's best-known pin-up artists. Among his models were Jayne Mansfield and his favorite, young Norma Jean Dougherty, who later became Marilyn Monroe.

cemetery, another honoring Klacel stands in the Bohemian National Cemetery in Chicago.

At 8th Street, turn right (west) and note, a block later at 8th Avenue, the plaque that tells about the *Jumbo Well*. In August 1886, men began digging an artesian well here to provide the city with drinking water and fire protection. When their well was 193 feet deep, they soon found what they were after and much more. A gusher, spewing about 3,000 gallons of water a minute into the town, shot a spray more than 50 feet into the air. At its peak (no pun intended), the impromptu fountain was producing about nine million gallons of water a day. Not until October 1887 were the waters of what was called "The Jumbo Well" and the "Eighth Wonder

Nancy Drew's Original Author

On the way to Marengo on Highway 212, you pass County Road V52, which leads 4 miles south to Ladora, where Mildred Wirt Benson was born in 1905.

Often called Millie by those who knew her, Benson started her career as a writer when her first article was published in 1914. Thirteen years later, she became the first female at the University of Iowa to earn a master's degree in journalism. While working on that degree, she approached the Stratemeyer Syndicate, publisher of children's books such as the Hardy Boys, Tom Swift, Penny Parker, and the Bobbsey Twins, to ask about writing stories for it. She was hired to write a book entitled *The Secret of the Old Clock*, in which the main character was a young detective named Nancy Drew. Benson wrote 23 of the first 25 Nancy Drew mysteries under the pen name of Carolyn Keene and was paid $125 for each one. Benson went on with a career in journalism that ended at the *Toledo (Ohio) Blade* on May 29, 2003, when she fell ill at her desk and died later that day.

Because Stratemeyer kept its authors nameless, Benson's secret identity was not known until 1980 when a court case revealed her name and she became a celebrity for starting the series that has sold millions of Nancy Drew books in 17 languages. Wanting to infuse her character with a tomboy spirit, Benson drew a lot from her own early years, including the times when she jumped off bridges into the Iowa River. Later in life, she learned to fly at the age of 59 and often traveled to Central America. The Underwood Standard No. 5 typewriter Benson used to write her Nancy Drew stories was acquired by the Smithsonian in 1992.

of the World" finally contained. Ironically, a fire swept downtown Belle Plaine just seven years later, devastating the small community.

Each September, Belle Plaine celebrates its gusher, which brought national attention to the town, with Jumbo Well Days. However, the fire is not honored in any way. By the way, rolle-bolle, a sport popular with Belgians (many of whom settled here), is played during the festival. What's rolle-bolle? Imagine a disk (the bolle) about six inches in diameter and up to three inches thick in the middle; now roll the bolle toward a stake and the closer you get to the stake, the more points your team earns. That's about the best that can be written about the game without resorting to lots of instructions in Dutch, French, or German, the official languages of Belgium.

Continue west on 8th Street for one more block and turn left (south) at 7th Avenue, which is also State Highway 21. You're still on the Iowa River Valley Scenic Byway, in case you want to know.

About 4 miles south of town, turn left (east) along with the byway onto State Highway 212, which rambles for 12 miles alongside the Iowa River to Marengo. The county seat of Iowa County, Marengo was named after an Italian town where Napoleon Bonaparte's French forces defeated an Austrian army on June 14, 1800. Sometime later, Napoleon named a gray Arabian horse after his victory, and his steed Marengo carried him through several other battles. At Napoleon's defeat at Waterloo in 1815, the horse was captured by the British and taken to England, where it died in 1832.

Follow Highway 212 through Marengo to U.S. Highway 6 on the south side of town; turn left (east) and go 6 miles to South Amana. Upon meeting State Highway 220 there, turn left, go north two blocks and turn right (east). This brings you immediately to two museums, both in barns. The one to the east is the *Communal Agriculture Museum*. Built of native timber around 1860 to shelter cattle the barn now shelters exhibits and implements used during the early days of the colonies' settlement. A short walk away is the *South Amana Barn Museum*, (319) 622-3058. Inside are at least 175 hand-carved and hand-assembled, 1/12-scale wooden structures made by Henry Moore, whose son John carries on the tradition. While most of the miniatures represent buildings found in the Amanas, several are of other buildings Henry saw while traveling across Iowa.

Return to Highway 6. Just before you turn left to go east on the highway, note the building housing *Fern Hills Gifts and Quilts*; years ago it was a general store and is said to have been robbed by Jesse James. As you head out of town, you might want to think about stopping to ooh and aah over the fine furniture made at the Krauss Furniture Shop and the *Schanz Furniture and Refinishing Shop.*

Head east on Highway 6 and join U.S. Highway 151 in 3 miles, then continue on to Homestead in another 2 miles. Despite being the only colony without the name Amana somewhere in it, Homestead is just as Amana-ish as the others.

Turn right (east) at V Street in Homestead. Immediately on the left is *Ehrle Brothers Winery* and then you'll see the *Homestead Meat Shop and Smokehouse,* (319) 622-7586 and (800) 373-6328, a place that's impossible to leave with-

Amana Amenities

A number of bed and breakfasts and a motel are in the Amana Colonies and the best way to learn about the lodgings (or anything else in the Amanas) is to visit or contact one of the two Amana Welcome Centers. One, mentioned at the beginning of this chapter, is at Amana; the other, (319) 668-9545, is at Little Amana, Highway 151 and I-80.

out at least sampling some meats, if not buying some to take home.

Across the street to the south is the *Amana Communal Church,* another part of the Amana Historical Society. In this hall that's void of almost everything but a simple cloth-covered table, a wooden chair, and wood-backed benches, Inspirationalists worshipped for 60 years; no musical instruments were used. Services were held twice on Sunday—attendance was once mandatory—and prayer meetings were held daily. Communion was celebrated every other year. The Inspirationalists believed that God had just two commandments—to love God and love each other.

Down the street are *Zuber's Restaurant,* a gallery, and some inns.

Head west on V Street to return to Highway 6/151. Turn right (north) and immediately turn left (west). This leads to the trailhead of the *Amana Colonies Nature Trail,* which is actually a series of trails that range between 1 and 3.2 miles in length. Along three of the trails are three burial mounds left by prehistoric Indians, perhaps 1,000 years ago. At the end of the longest trail, which overlooks the Iowa River, it's possible to see a stone dam, thought to have been built about 250 years ago by Indians to guide fish into a trap where they were caught and then put into a small holding pond; the dam is best seen when the water is low.

Return to Highway 6/151 and head north 3 miles to Amana, completing your tour.

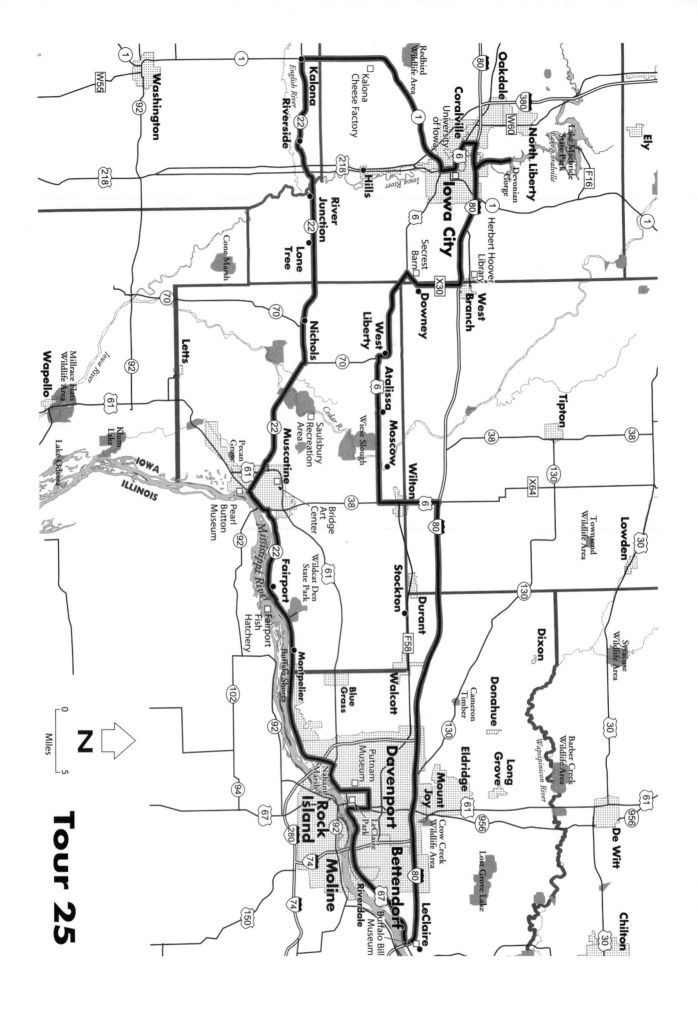

Tour 25

N
Miles
0
5

Tour 25
City Folks, Country Folk, and One Big River

LeClaire—Wilton—West Branch—Coralville—Iowa City—Kalona—Muscatine—Davenport—
Bettendorf—LeClaire

Distance: approximately 165 miles

Welcome to the longest tour in the book—not by miles but by places to see! The tour starts alongside the Mississippi River near the Quad Cities, the label that's often applied to the metro area of Davenport and Bettendorf, Iowa and Moline and Rock Island, Illinois; the tour ends there sometime later. But in between visiting the sites in the Quad Cities area, oh what a great variety of places you will see—one of the oldest soda fountains in the nation; museums about the arts, sciences, and natural history; homes of the rich and famous; an old mill and the old capitol; unusual buildings; fun places for families to play; fossils that are millions of years old; the largest Amish community west of the Mississippi River; and the boats that ply her waters.

This tour begins at the Mississippi Valley Welcome Center at LeClaire, just northeast of the Quad Cites at the easternmost Exit on I-80 in Iowa. To get to the center, 900 Eagle Ridge Road, (563) 322-3911, ext. 120, and (800) 747-7800, ext. 120, leave I-80 at Exit 306 and go north on U.S. Highway 67. In what looks like a large hilltop house that was once owned by a steamboat captain, the welcome center overlooks the Mississippi and has the usual assortment of brochures, pamphlets and booklets about Iowa, particularly the eastern region. Even though you won't be in the Quad Cities until later in this tour, pick up brochures about the attractions and other places in that metro area now. The center also has displays about the early history of the region and a gift shop featuring Iowa-made items. Open daily, year-round, the center is also a stop on the *Great River Birding Trail*; for more information about that, pick up one of the Audubon maps at the center.

On Highway 67 turn left (north) and go a short distance into LeClaire. As you enter town, along the river on the right is the *Buffalo Bill Museum/The Lone Star Museum*, 200 North River Drive, (563) 289-5580/4989, admission. As you might guess, the museum has a relationship with William F. "Buffalo Bill" Cody, the legendary western scout who was born northwest of town on February 26, 1846 and lived

here until he was 8 years old when his family moved to Kansas. At the age of 14, he became a rider for the Pony Express and went on to be a buffalo hunter and scout for the Army, for which he was awarded the Medal of Honor in 1872. Later he created a Wild West show that traveled the world, bringing scenes of the American West to countless people. (Note: if you want to see the *Buffalo Bill Cody Homestead*, museum personnel can direct you there. The limestone farmhouse, built by Cody's father in 1847, is about 13 miles northwest of LeClaire.)

Dry-docked outside the museum is the last steam-powered tug that operated on the Mississippi, the *Lone Star*, which can be toured. Plans are underway by the museum to finance an addition and house the *Lone Star* in a weatherproof building.

Practically right next to the museum is *River Cruises*, at the foot of Wisconsin Street, (815) 777-1600 and (800) 331-1467, fee. Between Memorial Day and mid-October, River Cruises offers round-trip passage to Galena, Illinois, complete with meals, on-shore lodging, and entertainment. The two-day cruises on the riverboat *Twilight*, which passes through the locks at Clinton and Bellevue, are narrated.

Making the World a Safer Place

In the 1940s, at the University of Minnesota, LeClaire native James Ryan invented the first of the black boxes to record flight data about airplanes. Designed to survive severe impact and fire, the black boxes have grown in their capacity to record dozens of types of information about aircraft maneuvers and are actually painted orange to increase their visibility. In addition to his work on black boxes, Ryan helped develop safety standards for automobiles and was largely responsible for the use of seat belts, padded steering wheels, and padded dashboards. Highway deaths have dropped from about 5.5 deaths per million miles in 1966 to 1.5 at the end of the century, and some attribute that drop to Ryan's inventiveness.

Quick Trip Option 1: About 7 miles north of LeClaire is the *Amazing Maize Maze*, 28322 Great River Road, Princeton, (563) 278-9999, admission. With a maze made out of corn and patterns that change each year, this is where you can truly get lost and if you do, a guide who sits in a 24-foot-high tower can give hints on how to rejoin the rest of the human race. Mini-mazes and a petting zoo are there for the younger ones.

Return to I-80 and head west for the longest stretch of four-lane traveling in this guide, all the way to Exit 271, 35 miles away at U.S. Highway 6. Go south on 6 for 4 miles to Wilton. Along the way, if the day is hot and you're looking for a way to cool off, leave I-80 at Exit 292 and turn to the north on State Highway 130. Just past the intersection is *Wacky Waters Adventure Park*, 8228 North Fairmount, (563) 388-9910, admission. This summertime water park has water slides, a wave pool, bumper boats, and a pirate ship. On shore are go-carts and miniature golf.

Quick Trip Option 2: This trip is certainly not quicker than the longer interstate route, but it is an option if you want to get off the four-lane fast track for a while. From I-80, turn south onto I-280 at Exit 290. Then leave I-280 immediately at the first exit and go west on County Road F58. Follow that for 21 miles to Wilton, passing through the small communities of Walcott, Stockton, and Durant.

From Highway 6 at Exit 271, turn left (east) to enter Wilton on 5th Street and go about 1 mile to Cedar Street in its small downtown. Turn right (south) and proceed to the *Wilton Candy Kitchen* on the east side of the street. There, in a two-story wood-frame building that was built in 1856, you'll find one of the country's oldest soda fountains, 310 Cedar Street, (563) 732-2278. It's been in the same family since Gus Nopoulos bought the place in 1910. Now, his son, George (who had his first job winding up a Victrola at the age of four for his father), runs the business with his wife, Thelma. Together, they make homemade sauces and ice cream and then combine them to make all sorts of scrumptious, tasty, chilly treats that sometimes include locally grown berries. If you're wondering about the name Candy Kitchen, the family did make candy here until the sugar shortages in World War II, but don't worry, there's still plenty here for your sweet tooth. A small museum is in the back room of the soda fountain. As George and Thelma put it, if the lights are on, the place is open.

About a block south of the Candy Kitchen is the refurbished 1898 *Chicago Rock Island and Pacific Railroad Depot* that houses a museum and has a caboose on the premises. Both are open on weekend afternoons between Memorial and Labor Days. If you want to see them at other times, find Thelma at the Candy Kitchen and she'll help you.

Head back west on 5th Street and return to Highway 6. Turn left (south) and drive for 13 miles as Highway 6 turns to the right (west) and passes through Atalissa and then West Liberty. Continue on Highway 6 as it jogs briefly north and then resumes its way west for about 6 miles to County Road X30, which leads to Downey; go past that (it's just being used here as a landmark). Very soon, Highway 6 angles to the northwest and when it cuts to the west again, 1.5 miles later, turn right (north) onto Oasis Road, a gravel road. Go 1 mile and turn right (east) onto Osage Street, another gravel road. Continue for 1 more mile. On the left, you'll find the *Secrest Barn*, 5750 Osage Street, Downey, (319) 337-2544, donation, reservations required. This octagonal red wooden barn, which stands 75 feet at its cupola, once held 200 tons of hay in its loft, along with machinery and nearly 50 horses and cattle on the main floor. With its rafters visible, it's easy to see the precise handiwork of master builder George Frank Longerbeam, particularly in the barn's unique laminated roofing and a Gothic-style roof. He designed the structure for Joshua and Esther Secrest in 1883. The Secrests fattened tens of thousands of head of sheep and cattle purchased in New Mexico and Colorado before shipping them farther east to market.

Continue east on Osage Street and follow it as it curves north into Downey and becomes Adams Street. At the first street you meet, Cedar, turn right and drive three blocks east to County Road X30. Turn left (north) and proceed up X30 for 4 miles, crossing I-80 and entering West Branch. You can either follow the signs pointing the way to the *Herbert Hoover Presidential Library*, Parkside Drive, (319) 643-5301/2541, admission, or take the next left to the visitor center at the *Herbert Hoover National Historic Site*, admission (same phone numbers). Either way, this is a small site so no matter where you park, you can easily walk to all the places here. Starting your tour at the library gives a good overview of the life of Herbert Hoover, the only Iowan elected to the White House (and the first president born west of the Mississippi). Displays tell of Hoover's early career as a mining engineer and his later efforts to help feed 300 million people in 21 European countries after World War I. Other displays show how he dealt with the early days of radio and aviation as the secretary of commerce and, after his presidency, worked with relieving famine again. His wife, Lou, is also recognized for her work with the Girl Scouts and for creating the first history of the White House. Traveling exhibits visit the library on a regular basis.

A short walk north of the library leads to the small, two-room cottage where Hoover was born in 1874. Near that is a blacksmith shop similar to the one run by his father, a one-room school, and a Quaker meeting house. On a hillside west of the library are the simple graves of President and First Lady Hoover near a grove of trees.

To the north of the grounds is downtown West Branch, which has a few antique stores among its businesses.

Return south to I-80 and head west for 10 miles to Dubuque Street in Iowa City (Exit 244). Turn right and head north on what is also County Road W66. In 3 miles, turn right (east) at West Overlook Road. This is the entrance to a recreational area administered by the U.S. Army Corps of Engineers at *Coralville Lake*, 2850 Prairie du Chien Road NE, (319) 338-3543, a reservoir created on the Iowa River. Here you will find campgrounds, trails, a visitor center, picnic areas, boat ramps, beaches, and other places clustered near the lower end of the dam that forms the lake. Fees are charged for boating, camping, and swimming.

Also below the dam is the *Devonian Fossil Gorge* that can be visited throughout the year for free. When heavy rains caused the lake to flood in 1993, the overflow ripped out a 15-foot-deep gorge in what had been the spillway. After the waters subsided, people began finding fossils of all types, such as coral, brachiopods, and crinoids that lived here approximately 375 million years ago. Today, a paved trail with a set of interpretative panels and guideposts leads you through the fossils. You are welcome to leave the path and look at any you find on your own, but no collecting is allowed (a rule backed by a very hefty fine). The best time to look for fossils is in the early morning or late afternoon when the slanted light of the low-lying sun picks out details of the fossilized remains in the rocks.

Return south to I-80, turn west, and go a little more than 1 mile to the very next off-ramp at 1st Avenue (Exit 242). You're now in Coralville, Iowa City's twin to the west.

Turn left (south) onto 1st Avenue and drive less than 1 mile south to 5th Street. Turn right (west). A few blocks west on 5th is the *Heritage Museum of Johnson County*, 310 5th Street, Coralville, (319) 351-5738, free. Housed in a prim-looking, two-story brick school that was built in 1876 and resembles a church, the museum has exhibits that include hands-on displays about the history of the region that held Iowa's first capitol.

Return to 1st Avenue and turn right (south). In a strip mall on the right (west) is the *Iowa City/Coralville Area Convention and Visitor Bureau*, 408 1st Avenue, (319) 337-6592 and (800) 283-6592. Like all visitor centers, this one has lots of information about attractions, lodgings, and places to eat, which are plentiful in this metro area that's heavily influenced by the presence of the University of Iowa.

A boat kicks up a wake on Coralville Lake north of Iowa City.

Go south a short distance to where 1st Avenue meets U.S. Highway 6 and turn left (east). You're now in Iowa City again.

Less than a mile east of 1st Avenue, turn left (north) onto Rocky Shore Drive that, a few blocks later, turns to the right (east) to become West Park Road. In six blocks, turn right (south) onto North Riverside Drive. As you head south, you'll pass *Hancher Auditorium*, (319) 335-1160 and (800) HANCHER, site of large concerts and performances, and then the *Museum of Art*, 150 North Riverside Drive, (319) 335-1727, free. With the state's largest collection of African art, the museum has many other works and hosts many visiting exhibits. The museum is open daily, year-round except on major holidays.

Continue south on North Riverside Drive a very short distance until you meet Highway 6 again; keep to the left. After bypassing the Iowa Avenue intersection (primarily because its low, 10-foot, 5-inch underpass might affect tall vehicles), proceed to the second intersection, at Burlington Street. Turn left (east), cross the Iowa River, and in four blocks, turn left (north) onto Clinton Street. Because you're near the main campus of the University of Iowa, parking will be at a premium. Therefore, when you find a parking space, be satisfied with it and plan to walk awhile—you won't have far to walk, by the way. Note that there is a parking ramp at Burlington and Clinton, at the south end of an urban shopping mall, the *Old Capitol Town Center*.

Once you're afoot, go to the *Old Iowa Capitol*, bounded by Washington, Clinton, Jefferson, and Madison Streets, (319) 335-0548, free, which was built in 1840. Housing the executive, legislative, and

The Old Iowa Capitol in Iowa City was the center of the state's government until 1857.

judicial branches of the government under one roof, this building served as the capitol of the Iowa Territory until 1846 and then as the state capitol until 1857 when the government shifted to Des Moines. Upon entry, the first thing that catches everyone's eye is the elegant, wooden, spiral staircase that extends first one way and then another as it connects the upper and lower floors. On the first floor are the governor's office, with spittoons made of fired clay; the treasurer's office that still has a copy of the 1851 *Code of Iowa* among its books; the auditor's office where the state map shows only 21 counties (the rest of the state, which now has 99 counties, was not yet settled); and the chambers of the state supreme court where the judges sat on a raised platform. Upstairs are the senate chambers, shown as a lecture hall, which it was when this building was used by the university for many years, and the chambers of the house of representatives, with just 26 chairs and a 29-star flag. In November 2001, the old capitol suf-

fered a fire that demolished its tower, and other parts of the building were also damaged by fire, smoke, and water. However, extensive restoration efforts are making the building as good as new.

Walk out the front of the old capitol and turn to your left to enter *Macbride Hall*, one of the many buildings belonging to the university. In there you will find the three galleries of the *Museum of Natural History*, (319) 335-0480, free: Mammal Hall, Iowa Hall, and Bird Hall. In the last is a renowned seaside diorama of the birds that made their home on Laysan Island, one of the remote Hawaiian Islands. Another exhibit takes you through 500 million years of Iowa history (in considerably less time, fortunately), starting when this was an ancient sea where one of the strange-looking inhabitants was the fearsome Dunkleosteus, which had a toothy maw twice as wide as that of a great white shark. Two hundred million years later—but just a few steps for visitors—is a peat swamp that will, in millions of years, become the coalfields that were heavily mined in Iowa until around World War II. As you continue walking through time, you'll come upon another diorama where you're atop a bluff on a June day in 1673 where, with some Native American mannequins, you overlook the confluence of the Mississippi and Wisconsin Rivers and see small canoes in the distance bringing the first Europeans to what would someday be called Iowa. These displays and more make Macbride Hall a good place to spend a few hours for anyone of any age at anytime.

When you leave Macbride, cross Clinton Street and go one block east to Dubuque Street. Turn right (south) into the downtown area where you will find one of the best bookstores in the nation, *Prairie Lights Books*, 15 South Dubuque, (319) 337-2681. An independent bookstore, Prairie Lights has more than three floors filled with books that can delight children or make a professor ponder. It also has a 1,100-square-foot coffeehouse that hosts authors who present readings of their writing, just as Carl Sandburg, e.e. cummings, and Robert Frost did here years ago.

South of the bookstore is the *Pedestrian Plaza*, a nice space occupied by trees, sculptures, a playground for children, fountains, benches for watching the world go by, and food vendors who sell everything from grilled cheese and hot dogs to espresso and gyros.

Three blocks west of the plaza is one of the better food cooperatives found anywhere, *Pioneer Food Co-op*, 22 South Van Buren, (319) 338-9441. Since 1970 the co-op has sold natural foods, including fruits, vegetables, meats, cheeses, wine, beer, baked goods, and chocolates.

It's time to hop in your vehicle once more, so return to Burlington Street and continue east. Two blocks away, at South Dodge

Street, turn right (south). In five blocks, after crossing some railroad tracks, South Dodge Street comes to a T intersection with Kirkwood Avenue. Take a left (east) turn and then immediately turn right (south) into the grounds of *Plum Grove Historic Home*, 1030 Carroll Street, (319) 351-5738, free. Built in 1844, it was the home of the governor of the Iowa Territory, Robert Lucas. Now, this brick, seven-room Greek Revival house has been furnished much as it was when the governor and his wife lived there.

Return to Kirkwood Avenue and go west to the end of the street, eight blocks away. Turn right (north) at South Dubuque Street and one block afterwards turn left (west) onto East Benton. After a few blocks, cross the Iowa River and return once again to Highway 6 (which is also South Riverside Drive). Turn left (south) and go to the next major intersection, where 6 goes left (east). You, however, will turn right on State Highway 1. The road angles to the southwest for the first 10 miles, then turns straight south. Travel another 3.2 miles to the intersection with County Road 67. Here, you'll find the *Kalona Cheese Factory*, 2206 540th Avenue SW, (319) 656-2776, which sells its homemade white cheddar cheese along with sausages, crackers, breads, and other cheeses.

By the way—and this is a very important by-the-way—you are in the largest Amish-Mennonite community west of the Mississippi. Because of their beliefs, many Amish do not use motorized vehicles, preferring horses instead. That means you may come upon some of their slow-moving wagons, buggies, and carriages so use caution when driving here.

Continue for another 4 miles to the west side of Kalona, go past E Avenue, the main east-west route through town (which is also State Highway 22), and turn left (east) at B Avenue. After one long block, you'll be in downtown Kalona where there are a number of businesses that include gift shops, quilting stores, and antique merchants. Just past the telephone company is the *Kalona Chamber of Commerce*, which operates Kalona By-Ways Tour, 514 B Avenue, (319) 656-2660, fee. Visitors are given 90-minute tours in minibuses of the town and the surrounding region, which was settled by the Amish in the 1840s, about three decades before the town itself was founded. The tours may include stops at the Kalona Cheese Factory, Amish stores, and an Amish farmers market.

As you make your way around here on the tour or on your own, you'll notice that the Amish live at a much slower pace than many other people. They use pins, hooks, and eyes instead of buttons to fasten their clothes. Although married men have beards, they don't

have mustaches and don't wear neckties. Women wear white prayer caps and black bonnets. Boys have wide-brimmed hats, like their fathers. Instead of gasoline-powered engines, horses pull farm implements in the fields and carriages on the roads. Rather than having churches, the Amish meet in their homes for religious services with men sitting separately from the women.

Most of all, respect the desire of the Amish to not be photographed.

Not All Amish Are Alike

Old Order Amish do not use telephones, electricity, or any modern conveniences. New Order Amish use rubber tires on their farm equipment and buggies. Beachy Amish use electricity, phones, drive vehicles, and use modern equipment.

From the chamber office on B Avenue, turn north on 6th Street and make your way to D Avenue, two blocks away. Turn right (east) and go to the *Kalona Historical Village*, 715 D Avenue, (319) 656-3232, admission. Here, a modern visitor center sits amid a number of buildings built many years ago, including a country church, a two-story wooden depot built in 1879, a schoolhouse, a post office, a buggy shop, an Amish house, and a country store. Inside the visitor center is the *Kalona Quilt and Textile Museum*, covering items made from the 1840s to the middle of the twentieth century, which may help explain why Kalona is called the Quilt Capital of Iowa. Also in the center is the extensive Reif Mineral and Rock Collection, which contains countless gems and rocks from across the world.

The historical village also has the Mennonite Museum and Archives, which tells the history of the Amish and Mennonite communities and is a genealogical repository.

Head east on State Highway 22 and go for 7 miles to Riverside. As you pass through town, you may remember (especially if you're a *Star Trek* fan) that James T. Kirk will be born here on March 22, 2228, and eventually become captain of the *Starship Enterprise*. A 20-foot-long model of its counterpart, the *USS Riverside*, is in Legion Park on the east side of town, and on the last Saturday of every June (that's right, June, not March), Riverside celebrates his coming birth with a parade that attracts Klingons, Vulcans, and people wearing Starfleet uniforms.

Continue east on Highway 22, crossing U.S. Highway 218 and passing through Lone Tree and Nichols, to end up on the west side of Muscatine, 26 miles after Highway 218.

Quick Trip Option 3: About 6 miles after Nichols is the Cedar River and 3 miles beyond that, where Highway 22 begins to run straight east, watch for Keokuk Avenue on your left (north). Take that paved road for 1.5 miles, jog a short distance to the right (east) and then resume going north once more for another 1.8 miles, again on Keokuk Avenue, to Saulsbury Road, which is paved. Turn left (northwest) and you will enter the *Saulsbury Bridge Recreation Area*, 2007 Saulsbury Road, (563) 264-5922. This 675-acre county preserve along the Cedar River has three campgrounds with modern and primitive sites, fishing in the river and nearby Chicken Creek, boat ramps, athletic fields, canoe shuttle service, picnic facilities, hiking and equestrian trails, and a nature center.

What's in a Name?

Muscatine began as a trading post in the 1830s and, as happened in those days, had its first name, Bloomington, nixed by the post office since another town already had that name. Citizens then chose Muscatine, which has two possible origins—either the Native Americans who were called Mascoutin or for the name the Indians had given to a nearby island.

As you approach Muscatine, Highway 22 joins the U.S. Highway 61 beltway around the city, but you should go ahead on what is now Cedar Street, which runs due east here just past the beltway. Here, you'll see the new *Muscatine County Environmental Discovery Park*, (563) 264-5922, free, an 80-acre park that is opening in late 2004 with 2 miles of trails wandering through woods and fields. Discovery Park will also have a learning center with hands-on activities involving the region's plants, trees, and animals, two ponds, a wetland area, two spring-fed streams, and an arboretum.

From the park, continue east on Cedar Street as it angles to the southeast about a

Doing Business in Muscatine

Though one of Iowa's medium-sized cities, with a population of 22,697, Muscatine has a far-reaching influence through some of its companies. Stanley Consultants is the largest engineering-architecture firm in Iowa and designs projects in the states and overseas; its Stanley Foundation is dedicated to working for world peace and social justice. HON Industries is the nation's third-largest manufacturer of office furniture and is ranked by *Industry Week* magazine as one of the nation's 100 best-managed companies; its All-Steel division developed the lateral file cabinets found in many offices today. Bandag has 45 percent of the world market for recapping truck tires, selling at least 18 million retreads in 2001. GPC/Kent Feeds manufactures the world's first cattle feed made of high-quality protein with no fillers added. Since 1976, Musco Lighting has designed, manufactured, and installed specialty lighting at athletic events throughout the world, including Super Bowls, the Olympics, Pam Am Games, and NASCAR races, and aided in the lighting of movies such as *Titanic*, *Field of Dreams*, and *Pearl Harbor*. Also in Muscatine is the site of the first expansion beyond Pittsburgh, Pennsylvania, by the H. J. Heinz Company. The plant here makes all the Green, Purple, Kicker, and Mystery ketchups for the company along with soups and sauces.

half mile later. About 1.5 miles after leaving the park, turn left (northeast) at Parham Street and, two streets after that, turn right on Mulberry Avenue. As you drive southeast on Mulberry, watch on the right side for the elegant Edwardian mansion that now houses the *Muscatine Art Center*, 1314 Mulberry Avenue, (563) 263-8282. Works by French impressionists Renoir, Degas, Chagall, and others are here; but the main thing to see is the Great River Collection, which includes prints, drawings, paintings, photographs, and more that illustrate the entire Mississippi River. The permanent collection also contains works by Grant Wood and Georgia O'Keefe, oriental rugs, paperweights, and American pottery. A contemporary gallery hosts traveling exhibits, and outside are a sculpture court and a Japanese tea garden.

You can continue southeast on Mulberry until you're in downtown Muscatine near the Mississippi River or you can return to Cedar Street and go downtown that way. In either case, at West 2nd Street, turn right (southwest), go three or so blocks, and look for the *Pearl Button Museum*, 117 West 2nd Street, (563) 263-1052, donation. In the late nineteenth century, John Boepple immigrated to this area from Germany where he had made a living making buttons from animal horn. Once here, he explored the possibility of using the shells of freshwater mussels for the same purpose, for in this area of the Mississippi there were plenty of mussels. In 1887, Boepple opened the first pearl button factory here and, by 1900, more than 3,500 people in 43 area factories were producing iridescent buttons, earrings, cufflinks, and fine jewelry, including pendants, necklaces, and bracelets. It's no small wonder that Muscatine has been called the Pearl Button Capitol of the World and the Pearl of the Mississippi.

Near the museum and the library are a number of antique stores and specialty shops featuring handcrafted items in a downtown that has been improving its looks over the last few years.

Quick Trip Option 4: If you head south on Mississippi Drive, which is also U.S. Business Highway 61 and State Highway 92, you will join Grandview Drive as it rounds a riverside bluff and, south of town, enters a wide floodplain of the Mississippi. It is here that the famous Muscatine watermelons are grown along with a variety of other fresh produce, including tomatoes, potatoes, cantaloupe, and sweet corn, and—luckily for you—sold at roadside stands here along with handmade crafts.

From the Pearl Button Museum on 2nd Street, return to Cedar Street and turn right (southeast), cross the train tracks below Mississippi Drive, and go to the area along

the Mississippi River. You will end up at Muscatine's constantly improving riverside, which includes plans for a visitor and community center. Here you'll find a marina with slips and services for pleasure craft and houseboats, along with a park where you can just relax by watching the Mississippi and its boats roll by.

Leave the riverside area by going out the same way you entered—on Cedar Street. Turn right (northeast) onto East 2nd Street, which is also U.S. Business Highway 61. Go about 1 mile to where the highway turns north as it ascends a hill. About a half mile afterward, turn right (east) onto State Highway 22, which is also Washington Street. At the second street on your left (north), you can turn onto Park Avenue to visit *Weed Park.* Named after benefactor Dr. James Weed, the park is loaded with rose gardens, stone benches, a gazebo, a lagoon, ancient burial mounds, a panoramic overlook of the Mississippi, athletic fields, and a new indoor-outdoor aquatic center.

Continue east on Highway 22, which is a segment of the Great River Road, for about 9 miles. If you're interested in camping alongside the Mississippi River, when you're about 6 miles from Muscatine, watch for the sign that points to the right (south) to the *Fairport Recreation Area*, (563) 263-3197, a campground where 42 modern campsites face the river.

About 1.5 miles past the Fairport Recreation Area is the *Fairport Fish Hatchery*, 3390 Highway 22 West, (563) 263-5062, which welcomes visitors. More than 3 million bass, bluegill, walleye, and other fish are raised in 18 earthen ponds each year and then distributed across the state. Begun by the U.S. Fish and Wildlife Service in 1914, the Fairport hatchery has been operated by Iowa's Department of Natural Resources since 1973.

About 1.5 miles past the hatchery, watch for signs pointing the way to *Wildcat Den State Park*, 1884 Wildcat Den Road, (563) 263-4337, which is about a mile north of Highway 22. The park has dense, forested, and hilly landscapes, a playground, and 28 primitive campsites that are near Wildcat Den Cave. The thing to see in this park is the picturesque Pine Creek Grist Mill, built in 1848, and the nearby Melpine Schoolhouse. Hiking and mountain biking trails that traverse through the park lead you to places with colorful names that include Devil's Punch Bowl, Fat Man's Squeeze, and Steamboat Rock.

Return to Highway 22 and continue east for about 13.5 miles to the southwest side of the Quad Cities. After passing under I-280, go to the first street on the right (south), Wapello Avenue, and turn right. This leads to *Nahant Marsh*, a 513-acre cattail marsh and sedge meadow alongside the Mississippi River.

The Pine Creek Grist Mill is located at Wildcat Den State Park between Muscatine and the Quad Cities.

Once practically polluted, the marsh has been making a comeback with the aid of many citizens. The Nahant Marsh Educational Field Station teaches visitors about the importance of wetlands and a boardwalk leads through the area.

Go back to Highway 22 and turn right (east). After 1 mile, the highway joins Highway 61, which enters Davenport as River Drive. Take that for 2 miles and turn right (south) into Credit Island Park. The park has plenty of places to stroll, play, or just nap along the river, but what really makes it stand out from other parks are a number of statues arranged to represent the figures of Georges Seurat's famous painting *A Sunday Afternoon on the Island of La Grand Jatte.* If you have a camera, here's a very direct way to involve yourself in the fine arts by getting into the scene.

Return to River Drive and continue to the east. After less than 1 mile, turn left onto Division Street and take it for another 1 mile as it heads north to 12th Street. On your left at that point are the *Putnam Museum of History and Natural Science* and *IMAX Theater*, 1717 West 12th Street, (563) 324-1933, admission. Opened in 1867 as one of the first museums west of the Mississippi, the Putnam is the Quad Cities' largest museum and is very modern with a variety of permanent and visiting exhibits in its galleries. One gallery that shows the ecosystems of the Mississippi River valley allows visitors to walk through a cave and visit the river's fishy inhabitants in an aquarium. Another gallery tells of the land's inhabitants from prehistoric days to now. The Hall of Mammals displays mounted animals in natural-looking settings, and the Asian-Egyptian Gallery has relics ranging from a 3,000-year-old mummy to those that belonged to warrior societies in Japan. The museum, which has a gift shop, is open until 5 p.m. daily, year-round, although the IMAX Theater has evening shows. Next door is *the Davenport Museum of Art*, 1737 West 12th Street, (563) 326-7804, admission. Its permanent collection includes works by European masters, one of the first collections of Haitian art in the United States, a number of paintings representing Mexico's colonial period, and a number of American artists ranging from Andy Warhol and other pop artists to American regionalists, including Grant Wood whose only self-portrait hangs here.

Just west of the museums is *Fejervary Park*

Museums on the Move

A project called River Renaissance, which will significantly upgrade various aspects of Davenport's riverfront, is also going to affect the Davenport Museum of Art and the Putnam Museum. One element in the new riverfront is the building of the $113.5-million Figge Arts Center in which the Davenport Museum of Art will be relocated during the summer of 2005. Moving into the 70,000-square-foot Figge will be a welcome change for the art museum, which has been able to exhibit only a small portion of its 3,500-piece permanent collection at any one time in recent years because of the collection's growth.

When the present art museum vacates its present quarters on West 12th Street, the Putnam will then expand into that space, utilizing it for more exhibits.

and Children's Zoo, 1800 West 12th Street, (563) 326-7812, admission. This family aquatic park has a zero-depth entry for youngsters as well as a sandlot. The zoo features animals of North America, including elk, cougar, buffalo, wolves, hawks, bobcat, prairie dogs, and more. A petting area has calves, deer, pigs, pygmy goats, and other small animals that appreciate attention as well as being fed by visitors.

Return to Division Street and turn left (north). Go six blocks, turn right (east) on West Locust, and go another 1.5 miles to Brady Street, which is also U.S. Highway 61. Turn left on Brady, a one-way street, and go north four blocks. Turn left (west) onto Central Park Avenue and park on the north side of *Vander Veer Botanical Center and Park*, **(563) 326-7818.** Bounded by Central Park Avenue, Brady, Harrison, and West Lombard Streets, the park is one of many scattered throughout the metro area, but it has its own unique elements: a glass palm house that serves as a botanical center (admission), rose and hosta gardens, a small lake, and a set of three lifelike statues of children at play.

On the west side of Vander Veer Park, take Harrison Street south all the way to 2nd Street. where you turn right (west) and

drive four blocks to the *German American Heritage Center*. The facility, 712 West 2nd Street, (563) 322-8844, admission, is located in the former Germania Haus, which was built in 1868 to temporarily house German immigrants before they settled elsewhere. The four-story center tells the stories of Germans who settled this region during the nineteenth century through documents and exhibits.

At the east end of the German American Heritage Center is North Gaines Street. Head south on that, crossing River Drive and entering LeClaire Park near the Mississippi River. Just as you enter the park, you'll spot *John O'Donnell Stadium*, 209 South Gaines, (563) 324-3000, admission, the home of the *Quad City River Bandits*, a Class A farm team of the Minnesota Twins. Built in 1931, this intimate, brick-walled stadium received a $10 million makeover prior to the 2004 season that included the addition of luxury suites, the creation of a berm beyond the outfield, flood protection, and improved seating and visibility, as well as a new field.

At the river, Gaines Street comes to a T intersection with Biederdecke Drive; turn left (east) and continue through LeClaire Park along the river. After passing Ripley Street, you will come upon the *Union Station Welcome Center*. The facility, 102 South Harrison Street, (563) 322-3911, is a former railroad station that now houses a branch of the *Quad Cities Convention and Visitors Bureau*, (800) 747-7800. If you want to know what's where around here, this is the place to ask all of your questions, get directions, and learn practically anything that there is to know about Davenport, Bettendorf, Rock Island, and Moline.

At the river in the park is the *Rhythm City Casino*, West River Drive, (563) 328-8000 and (800) 262-8711, a 24-hour gambling boat with three decks of slots and gaming tables as well as live entertainment, a buffet, and a 1950s-style diner.

On the north side of River Drive, between Harrison and Main Streets across from LeClaire Park, is the future site of the *Figge Arts Center*, part of Davenport's $300 million River Renaissance initiative (see sidebar). Sitting atop a parking garage that will also act as a floodwall, the Figge's first floor will be 12 feet above River Drive. The four-story building will have 13,000 square feet of gallery space, five art studios, a 180-seat auditorium, a media center, a gift shop, a full-service restaurant, and on top of it all, the glass-walled Winter Garden will provide a view across the Quad Cities and the Mississippi.

One block away on Main will be another component of the River Renaissance, *River Music Experience*, 131 West 2nd Street. Housed in the lower three floors of the historic Redstone Building, which was also known as Petersen's Department Store, the multi-use complex will have restaurants, nightclubs, and performance spaces that include a courtyard. The building will allow people to enjoy the Quad Cities' rich musical heritage on a year-round basis instead of just during its well-known summertime celebrations that include the Mississippi Valley Blues Festival, Quad Cities Jazz Festival, and the Bix Beiderbecke Memorial Jazz Festival. The River Music Experience will also be an entry to the new River Music Skybridge, a cable-stayed pedestrian bridge allowing safe passage above busy River Drive and the nearby railroad tracks to LeClaire Park and providing an excellent view of the Mississippi.

Head east again on River Drive (which is now U.S. Highway 67) for about 2 miles to Mound Street and the *Village of East Davenport.* This is a collection of businesses, stores, shops, boutiques, galleries, and restaurants set in an area that was once a separate community from Davenport.

Just south of the village and across River Drive is Lindsay Park, one of the parks that line the Mississippi in the cities; a number of geometrical sculptures here constitute what is known as Architectural Park. A landing for the

"Bix"

Just say "Bix" to most jazz aficionados and they'll know you're talking about Leon "Bix" Beiderdecke, who was born in Davenport in 1903. At the age of 18, he went to Illinois and, rather than attend formal studies at Lake Forest Academy, took to the jazz he heard being played in nearby Chicago. Bix, who had learned to play piano when he was three years old and cornet when he was 14, began playing gigs in Chicago and on Lake Michigan excursion boats before joining the Wolverines, who played in the Midwest before landing in New York City in 1924. Bix left the group soon after and played with other bands and musicians, including Benny Goodman, Red Nichols, and Paul Whiteman, until his death by pneumonia in 1931. He was also an accomplished pianist and composer who was influenced by the classical music of Debussy. Named to the International Jazz Hall of Fame, Bix has been the subject of at least five books, three movies, a symphony, and performances at Carnegie Hall.

Channel Cat Water Taxi, (309) 788-3360, fee, is here too. You can catch this taxi-boat, which is just what its name says it is, and make your way between this park, Bettendorf's Leach Park, and, across the river, Moline's John Deere Commons and Ben Butterworth Parkway. Another landing is scheduled to open in 2004 at Parakeet Island, a new amusement park in Moline.

Quick Trip Option 5: "Quick Trip" may be a misnomer here because you'll need to set aside a

Davenport is a vibrant city alongside the Mississippi River.

good amount of time if you want to give the Illinois side of the Quad Cities its proper due. Below, you'll find a listing of what you can see there.

Be aware that there's a city called Rock Island and an island of the same name that is occupied by a federal arsenal; sometimes locals call it Arsenal Island. On the island, which is accessible only from its Moline entrance, you'll find:

Rock Island Arsenal Museum, (309) 782-5021, free, a collection of American and foreign small arms, including those that have been developed here. A nearby park displays U.S. and foreign artillery pieces and armored vehicles.

National Cemetery, the final resting place for many American military men and women.

Confederate Cemetery, holding the remains of Confederate soldiers who died while being held in a prison camp here during the Civil War.

Colonel Davenport Home, built in 1833 by George Davenport, who founded the city and was then murdered here by river pirates on July 4, 1845.

Quarters 1, although it cannot be toured and can be seen only as you drive by it on the way to the Colonel Davenport Home, this cream-colored home with a tower is the second-largest home owned by the U.S. government; only the White House is larger.

Lock and Dam 15 Visitor Center, (309) 794-5338 and (800) 645-0248, free, perhaps the best place on the Mississippi to learn what locks and dams are all about. Once you view the displays, you can walk outside and watch tows and other boats pass through the locks. Note how the nearby combination railroad-vehicle bridge pivots to permit large boats go up and down the river.

Fort Armstrong, a replica of a blockhouse of the fort that was built here in 1816. At the end of the Black Hawk War in September 1832, peace treaties were signed here between the Americans and the Sauk, Fox, and Winnebago. The fort was abandoned in 1832.

In the city of Rock Island, you'll find:

Quad City Botanical Center, 2525 4th Avenue, (309) 794-0991, admission, a 70-foot-tall center where everyone is under a glass ceiling. The center has gardens with plants from throughout the world, including a rain forest and a tropical Sun Garden.

Quad Cities Art Center, 1715 2nd Avenue, (309) 793-1213, the largest fine-arts center in the Quad Cities with works by local artists.

The District, an urban neighborhood near the art center with restaurants, pubs, coffee shops, art galleries, boutiques, specialty stores, and live theater.

Jumer's Casino Rock Island, 18th Street, (309) 792-4200 and (800) 477-7747, a riverboat casino.

Black Hawk State Historic Site, 1510 46th Avenue, (309) 788-0177, free, a state park featuring the John Hauberg Indian Museum, (309) 788-9536, donations, which has artifacts of the Sauk and Fox who occupied this land in what was once North America's largest Indian settlement, Saukenauk Village. Artifacts from the family of Black Hawk are here too.

Whitewater Junction, 18th Avenue and 17th Street, (309) 732-7437, admission, a new aquatic park with a railroad theme at Longview Park, which has a zero-depth water play area, a lap pool, slides, a water geyser, a teacup fountain, tumble buckets, and concessions.

Moline has the following attractions:

Naibi Zoo, 13010 Naibi Zoo Road, Coal Valley, (309) 799-5107, admission, with more than 900 animals representing 160 species from throughout the world.

Deere-Wiman House, 817 11th Avenue, (309) 765-7970, donation, the 15,000-square-foot mansion of Charles Deere, son of John Deere (the home of John Deere, at 1217 11th Avenue, is being restored and is expected to be opened for visitors soon).

Butterworth Center, 1105 8th Street, (309) 765-7970, donation, an 1892 mansion near the Deere-Wiman House, built by Charles Deere for his daughter and son-in-law. Fantastic gardens.

John Deere Commons, 1400 River Drive, (309) 765-1000, free, a complex of buildings that basically form a large museum and visitor center related to John Deere, one of the most well-known names in farm implements. John Deere Pavilion displays classics from the past as well as the latest designs off the production line. John Deere Store has practically everything that bears the John Deere logo such as caps, shirts, toys, and more. In John Deere Collector's Corner, workers restore vintage John Deere tractors, and the place looks like a 1950s-era dealership.

Celebration Belle, 2501 River Drive, (309) 764-1952 and (800) 297-0034, fee, a non-gaming riverboat that has local excursions as well as lunch, brunch, dinner, and dance cruises. It also cruises every Monday to Dubuque, with a return trip by bus that same day.

Adventure Quest of the Quad Cities, 3501 27th Street North, Rapids City, Illinois, (309) 523-3629, admission. East of the Quad Cities near the junction of Interstates 80 and 88, this new 56-acre recreation area has hayrack and train rides, inflatable games, mountain boards, summer sleds, panning for gems, a corn maze, picnic facilities, and a gift shop. Animals such as deer, wild turkey, pheasant, and quail roam its woods and prairie.

Parakeet Island, 5420 River Drive, (309) 736-9099, admission, another new recreation park featuring sand volleyball, indoor and outdoor miniature golf courses, a raceway with electric go-carts, pool, gift shop, café, and snack bar, all with a tropical island theme.

For more information about sites in Illinois, contact the Quad Cities Convention and Visitors Bureau, (800) 747-7800.

From Mound Street in Davenport, go east on River Drive for 1 mile and enter Bettendorf, where the road becomes State Street (but is still Highway 67). Another park in which you can relax and watch the river traffic is *Leach Park*, which is near the Interstate 74 bridge. A short distance beyond *Leach Park* is the *Isle of Capri Casino*, 1777 Isle Parkway, (563) 359-7280 and (800) 724-5825, a gambling boat with table games, slot machines, and regular cruises.

Continue east on State Street a short distance to 18th Street. Turn left (north) and, after less than 1.5 miles, cross Middle Road. About a half mile farther north is the *Family Museum of Arts and Sciences*. Formerly the Children's Museum, this facility, 2900 Learning Campus Drive, (563) 344-4106, admission, is still very much a hands-on place for kids (adults can join in too). They can make clouds, drive a combine, dance in a shadowbox, make music, play with water, and, outside, enjoy the playground and a children's garden.

Return south to Middle Road, turn left (east), and proceed less than 1 mile to Devil's Glen Road. Turn right (south), drive 1.5 miles back to State Street, and turn left. Cruise northeast on what is still Highway 67 for about 7.5 miles to the Mississippi Valley Welcome Center, just north of the intersection with I-80 in LeClaire where we began this tour.

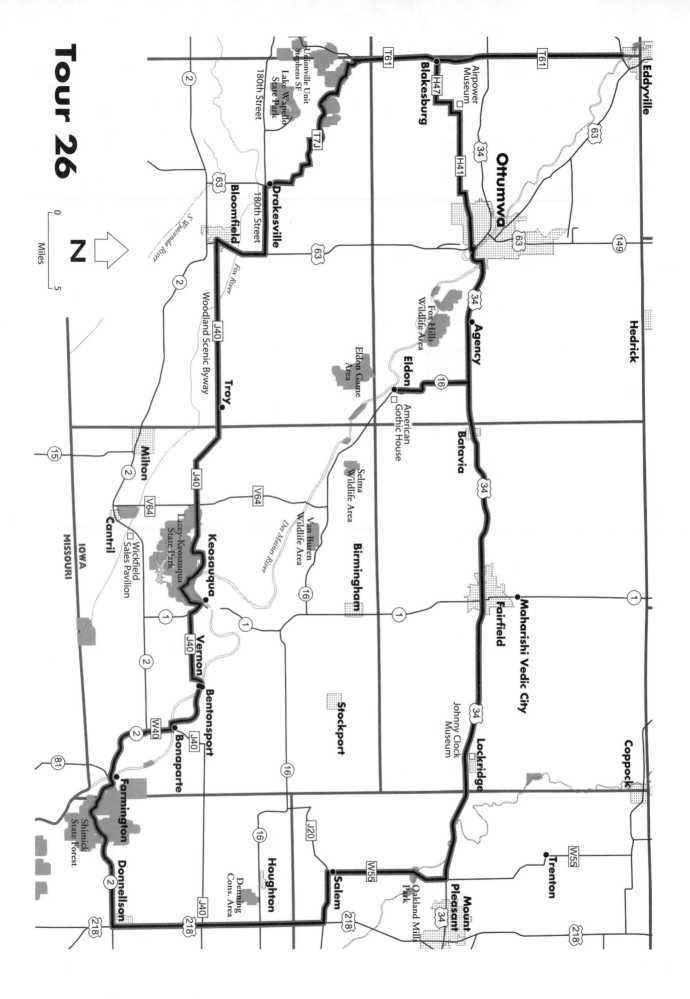

Tour 26

N

0 Miles 5

Tour 26
Among Iowa's Oldest and Newest Cities—and Everything in Between

Ottumwa—Blakesburg—Bloomfield—Drakesville—Keosauqua—Bentonsport—Bonaparte—
Donnellson—Lockridge—Fairfield—Eldon—Ottumwa

Distance: approximately 175 miles

Just like it flows through Iowa, the Des Moines River courses through several tours in this book and makes another appearance in this tour, touching several communities as it winds its way through the southeast part of the state. Besides encountering the river several times in this tour, you will come upon some of the rarest aircraft in the world, walk through some of the oldest buildings west of the Mississippi River, travel a scenic byway from beginning to end, visit a county without a single stoplight, and kick back in some of Iowa's finest state parks. So let's have at it.

On this tour, you'll get a nice view of the countryside (in this case, the Des Moines River valley) right off the bat. Begin at the north edge of Ottumwa on southbound U.S. Highway 63. As you head south into downtown and approach the river, turn left (southeast) onto West 4th Street. After two blocks, turn right (southwest) at Washington Street, which leads directly to the former Burlington Northern Depot on West Main Street. Well, *former* may be too strong a word since AMTRAK has offices there, along with the *Wapello County Historical Museum*, 210 West Main, (641) 682-8676, admission. Outside, near a fountain and a water trough with lion head spigots, is a Burlington Northern steam locomotive. Inside are many other items related to the history of the county and Ottumwa, including a 1925 America La France fire truck housed in a re-creation of an old fire station, a life-size reconstruction of part of a Sauk and Fox village, geological displays, archeological artifacts, and a scale model of Ottumwa's Coal Palace, an exhibition hall (long since gone) that was constructed and decorated with materials, notably coal, native to this part of Iowa.

Head southeast a few blocks on Main to the *Ottumwa Convention and Visitor Bureau*, 217 East Main, (641) 682-3465 and (800) 564-5274. One brochure at the bureau introduces you to several Ottumwans—all buried at the Ottumwa Cemetery—and the 59 types of trees that surround them. The bureau also has a

walking tour of the downtown area's historic buildings, including the county courthouse, topped by a statue of Chief Wapello.

Chief Wapello

Chief Wapello was born around 1787 near Prairie du Chien, Wisconsin, where his native Fox, or Meskwaki, lived. As time went on, he and his people moved to eastern Iowa; when Wapello learned that his friend, Indian agent General Joseph Street, had established an agency near present-day Ottumwa, he persuaded his people to move there in 1838, creating one of several villages in the area. Although he was a long-time friend of the white settlers, Wapello nevertheless resisted moving again as they continued coming west and encroaching upon Native American land. However, Wapello died in March 1842 before talks were finalized and, only months later, the Meskwaki signed a treaty causing them to move to where Knoxville is today. Two years later, they were completely gone from Iowa, having been moved to Kansas. Wapello was buried 12 miles east of Ottumwa near his friend, General Street, who had died in 1840.

Head west on Main to Market Street, turn left (southwest), and cross the Des Moines River on the Church Street Bridge. On the south side of the river is *The Beach Ottumwa*, 101 Church Street, (641) 682-7873, admission, an aquatic park with slides, wave pool, a four-acre lagoon with kayaks and paddleboats, volleyball courts, and more, making this a good place to cool off on a warm day or, if the weather's chilly, to enjoy its indoor pool. Just outside the entrance to The Beach Ottumwa, a farmers' market is held during the growing season at the nearby municipal parking lot.

South of The Beach Ottumwa and across Cook Avenue is *Ottumwa Park*, (641) 683-0654, quite a recreation complex with winding drives, ponds, picnic facilities, an oxbow lake, ball fields, ball courts, fishing, canoeing, paddleboats, 335 campsites, and two long trails. One leads to Chief Wapello's grave, 12 miles away, and the other goes down the Des Moines River Valley to Eldon.

From Church Street, go about a half mile northwest on Cook Avenue to Wapello Street, at the center of the park's north end. Turn left (southwest) and take that for

Famous Ottumwans

Julius Fecht was one of several cigar manufacturers in Ottumwa during the late nineteenth century when the city was one of the world's cigar capitals. Fecht would ship tobacco from his Cuban plantation under armed guard to Ottumwa, where it was fashioned into cigars.

Author Edna Ferber lived in Ottumwa from 1890 to 1897 as a young girl and may have seen riverboats that inspired her to write the book *Showboat* (1926), which later became a Broadway musical and a movie. Among her other books were two that also become movies: *Cimarron* (1929) and *Giant* (1952). In 1924, her novel *So Big* won a Pulitzer Prize. The *New York Times* wrote that she was the greatest woman novelist of her day.

Floretta Doty McCutcheon, born in 1889 in Ottumwa, was bowling's first female celebrity. Taking up bowling to lose weight, she soon turned professional and in 10 years of touring had 10 perfect 300 games and amassed a 201 average in 8,076 games.

For several months during 1942 and 1943, long before he became president, Richard Nixon was a navy lieutenant handling administrative duties at an air station near Ottumwa where pilots serving in World War II were trained; his wife, Pat, worked a as bank teller in town for about $80 a month, and they rented an apartment in town.

Tom Arnold grew up in Ottumwa and attended Indian Hills Community College before going to Hollywood where he has worked as a writer, producer, comedian, actor, and sportscaster. True to his alma mater, he established a writing scholarship at Indian Hills.

1.5 miles to the T intersection with Mary Street. Turn right (west) and drive for about 8 miles on what becomes County Road H41 right outside of town. You'll arrive at the *Airpower Museum*, 22001 Bluegrass Road, (641) 938-2773, donation. Home of the Antique Airplane Association, the museum has a grass airstrip and feels like a small 1930s airport. In one building are aircraft engines, scale models, propellers, aviation artwork, and displays about the early days of aviation. In the museum's hangars are a number of restored and well-maintained aircraft, most built before 1940, that visitors admire for their beautiful lines. Among the 50 or so antiques, classics, and home-builts are such luminaries as the buglike Welch OW-8, the wedge-shaped Nesmith Cougar, a sleek, red and yellow Ryan STA, and the very sweet Rose Parrakeet A-1, a honey of a biplane if there ever was one.

The museum also has a library dedicated to the 6th Air Force, a nearly overlooked military command that patrolled the Caribbean and Central America during World War II.

Continue west and south on H41 and then H47 until you reach Blakesburg, 4.5 miles away. There, turn left onto County Road

The Airpower Museum in Blakesburg has a number of full-size and scale aircraft from the years preceding World War II.

T61 and head south 4.7 miles to County Road T7J. Turn left (east) there and ramble for 13 miles to 180th Street in Drakesville. Ever since leaving Blakesburg, you've been on the *Woodlands Scenic Byway*, a route that offers stunning views of southeast Iowa's rolling hills and twisting roads all the way to its termination east of Farmington. So enjoy the ride. By the way, Drakesville was named for John Drake, originally of North Carolina and the father of Francis Marion Drake, founder of Drake University in Des Moines.

Quick Trip Option 1: Six miles west of Drakesville on 180th Street is *Lake Wapello State Park*, (641) 722-3371, a 1,150-acre retreat nicknamed "the country club" of Iowa's state parks. That's because it has 89 campsites (half with electricity), miles of trails, 14 seasonal family cabins, swimming, a seasonal restaurant in the renovated, 1930s-era, timber and stone lodge, and a 289-acre lake stocked with bluegill, bass, crappie, and catfish.

From Drakesville, head east on 180th Street for about 4 miles to U.S. Highway 63. Be aware that you're now in a rural Old Order Amish area, where they use slow-moving, horse-drawn vehicles, so drive carefully.

At Highway 63, turn right (south) and take that for 3 miles into Bloomfield, where the road is also Washington Street. Before entering downtown, stop at the *Davis County Welcome Center*. In an original house ordered from a Sears catalog and built in 1910, the welcome center, 301 North Washington, (641) 664-1104, is one of 21 around the state operated by the Iowa Bureau of Tourism. It has literature about the region and a gift shop featuring items made by locals, including the Amish. To visit Amish businesses, use the maps available here to locate them and remember to respect their desire not to be photographed.

Continue on Washington for three blocks to Franklin Street. You'll come upon one of Iowa's best town squares. Here, about 40 businesses encircle the beautiful 1877 *Davis County Courthouse* that features a high clock tower and designed in the French Empire style. If you feel like you have been here before and you really haven't, it may be because you have seen some prints by P. Buckley Moss, who has used Bloomfield as an inspiration for some of her works of art.

From the town square, go east on Franklin a few blocks to the William Findley House, 302 East Franklin, (641) 664-1855/1512. This home, built in 1844, is now the *Davis County Historical Museum*. It features a village of sorts, including a 1902 country church, a livery barn, a log cabin, and a country school that

The Hotel Manning has been welcoming guests ever since it opened in Keosauqua in 1899.

still has a dunce cap that can accommodate practically any size head!

Continue east on Franklin, which becomes County Road J40 as you leave town. By the way, get used to J40—you will be on it awhile, and note that you're still very much in Amish territory.

Take J40 for about 11 miles to Troy, then go another 12 miles to the northwest entrance of *Lacey-Keosauqua State Park*, (319) 293-3501. For starters, just inside the park are 19 burial and ceremonial mounds built by the Woodland Culture People some 2,000 years ago. Created in 1921 and encompassing 1,653 acres, Lacey-Keosauqua is one of the largest and oldest state parks in Iowa and, with all the hills, bluffs, and woods here—as well as the fact that it's near a graceful bend in the Des Moines River—it's a very pretty state park too. Here are 113 campsites, 45 with electricity, a 30-acre lake with fishing, boating, and swimming, a boat ramp, six seasonal cabins, trails that roam everywhere, and

Ely Ford, a shallow, rock-bottomed part of the river that was a crossing for years.

The park is connected by a hike-bike trail with *Lake Sugema*, (319) 293-3589, a 3,000-acre park just south of Lacey-Keosauqua (and accessible by vehicle via State Highway 2), which has a 547-acre lake stocked with largemouth bass, black crappie, bluegill, channel catfish, and saugeye. Two modern, year-round, lake-view log cabins can be rented from *Lacey Trail Cabins*, (319) 293-6454.

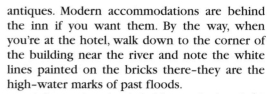

The Villages of Van Buren County

Just after you passed through Troy going east on J40, you entered Van Buren County. While most counties in Iowa usually have one large community, most often the county seat, that's not the case in Van Buren County where all 11 organized communities within the county are rather small. Even the county seat, Keosauqua, has just over 1,000 residents. Realizing sometime ago that there is an advantage to working together, many Van Buren residents pooled their talents and resources into creating The Villages of Van Buren County, an organization that promotes the communities' attractions, restaurants, lodgings, and a way of life that is considerably slower—in a nice, charming way—than that of the rest of the state. After all, how many other counties can brag that they have no fast-food restaurants, no chain hotels, or even a single stoplight?

Quick Trip Option 2: This is for barn lovers. About 3 miles west of Lacey-Keosauqua State Park, at the junction of J40 and County Road V64, turn south on V64 and go for 5.5 miles to State Highway 2. Turn left (east) and as Highway 2 curves to the northeast, watch on the right for 250th Street, a paved road that runs to the east, and turn to the right there. About three quarters of a mile later is the unique *Wickfield Sales Pavilion*, an impressive, three-story, round structure that some call a barn, but it really wasn't. When built in 1918, it was part of the world's largest Hampshire hog farm, which fed up to 1,500 hogs at a time. The first floor was for sales, living quarters were on the second floor, and a poker room and parlor were on the third. Contact (319) 293-3129 and 397-2340 for more information about the pavilion, which is still being restored.

From the east entrance of Lacey-Keosauqua State Park, turn left (north) onto Main Street (which is also County J40), cross the bridge over the Des Moines River, and enter Keosauqua. Immediately afterwards, turn right, pass a small park, and stop at the *Hotel Manning*, 100 Van Buren Street, (319) 293-3232 and (800) 728-2718. Built as an inn in 1899 with locally made brick, the structure holds its original charm and is now a B&B with a two-story porch, a lobby featuring a 16-foot-high ceiling, and a large wooden staircase at the main desk (which has lots of tourism brochures on the region in case you need some information). The 18 rooms upstairs are not roomy by modern standards but they, too, have a charm about them and are furnished with

antiques. Modern accommodations are behind the inn if you want them. By the way, when you're at the hotel, walk down to the corner of the building near the river and note the white lines painted on the bricks there—they are the high-water marks of past floods.

A farmers' market is held near the hotel, 4-8 p.m. on Fridays during the growing season.

Proceed to Dodge Street, two blocks northeast of Van Buren, turn left (northwest), and go a few blocks to the *Van Buren County Courthouse*, 902 4th Street. Almost unaltered since it was built in 1841, this two-story brick building is the oldest courthouse in continuous use west of the Mississippi and the second such oldest courthouse in the nation. On the main floor is the county's tourism office, which has lots of detailed information about the *Villages of Van Buren County*, (319) 293-7111 and (800) TOURVBC. The courtroom, which you can visit when court is not in session, was where Iowa's first capital sentence was handed down in 1845; on April 4, 1846, William McCauley was hung nearby for a double murder.

Continue northwest a few more blocks on Dodge to *Pearson House*, 718 Dodge Street, (319) 293-7111, admission. With a first floor made of stone and the second of brick, this home, now owned by the Van Buren County Historical Society, was a stop on the Underground Railroad before the Civil War. Runaway slaves would use a trap door to reach a hiding place beneath the first floor.

Make your way back through Keosauqua to Main Street (County J40) and follow that out of town for about 1 mile to where J40 turns left (east). Follow that for 5 miles to the point where it turns north, crosses the Des Moines River once more, and enters Bentonsport. In the nineteenth century, this was once a thriving riverboat landing of about 1,000 residents, but the town is considerably smaller now—its population is about 40 people. What remains certainly gives you the comfortable feeling that this is a place where life goes slow, and so should you . . . so walk around awhile. Signs describe most buildings and the few businesses that are here cater to visitors and are near the river. Most prominent is *Mason House*, (319) 592-3133 and (800) 592-3133, an 1846 riverfront inn (the river's oldest) that has rooms in the main house, a general store next door, and an 1852 post office. If you're daring, you can sit in the old-fashioned copper bathtub that swings down from a wall in the inn's keeping room (if you want privacy, ask for a bubble bath).

East of the inn is a cluster of stores where you can enjoy delicious fudge that melts in your mouth, browse through gifts, order a frame, and check out hand-forged iron, hand-made lace, and fibers woven into rugs and lace. A bit farther up along the river are the ruins of old mills, where the locals have made a pretty rose garden. Upon the hill behind town is an 1855 Presbyterian Church that you can visit.

Walking south across the bridge over the Des Moines River, you enter the ghost town of Vernon, where watercolor artist Wendell Mohr, (319) 592-3427, makes his home and studio in a quaint brick schoolhouse built in 1851.

Return to J40 and continue east on it for 4 miles to Bonaparte. With a population of about 450, Bonaparte is the smallest town in the nation to have been named a Main Street Community and was one of only five to receive the Great American Main Street Award in 1996, which is given annually to communities that have shown extraordinary efforts to revitalize their downtown areas. As you enter town, the big mill on the right (south) will undoubtedly grab your attention; it's now a restaurant called *Bonaparte's Retreat*, (319) 592-3339. Although in an out-of-the-way town, the restaurant's great reputation draws people from far away. Hint: ask for the canned beef but you must order it before arriving.

Next door is another mill, now called *Bonaparte Mill Antiques and Collectibles*, (319) 592-3274, and down the way are other buildings of yesteryear, including *Aunty Green Hotel*. Built in 1844, it was the town's first brick building and which now houses the city library and museum. Also in the area is an ongoing archeological dig on the former site of *Bonaparte Pottery*, 411 1st Street, (319) 592-3620, admission, an 1866 business that made all types of containers, brick, and pipe.

At Bonaparte, you leave J40 (finally), cross the river (you know which one by now), and take County Road W40 south for about 2.5 miles to State Highway 2. Follow that east for about 3.5 miles to *Indian Lake Park*, located just before you reach the river (yup, same one). The 117-acre city park, (319) 878-3706, has a 44-acre lake, rental canoes, campsites, two frame cabins, and four more that are renovated construction trailers (don't laugh —they are very nice, inside and out).

Cross the Des Moines River, drive a short distance through Farmington, and then go east for 11 miles to Donnellson. Just past Farmington, the highway curves and twists through the pretty woods of *Shimek State Forest,* (319) 878-3811. This 8,832-acre preserve has trails, including equestrian paths, campsites (none have electricity but two equestrian sites have water), picnic facilities, ponds, and fishing.

At Donnellson, turn left (north) on U.S. Highway 218. Here is the termination of the Woodland

Scenic Byway that you've been on, in the form of several different roads, since Blakesburg.

Quick Trip Option 3: Because this section of Highway 218 is also mentioned in Tour 27, see Quick Trip Option 2 in that tour.

About 15 miles north of Donnellson on Highway 218, turn left (west) at County Road J20 and go to Salem, 3 miles away. As you approach Salem, the road swings to the north, but you should continue straight ahead to the west on Pioneer Avenue. After a half mile, this comes to a T intersection with Main Street (which is also County Road W55). Turn right (north). On the southwest corner of the very next intersection to the north is the *Lewelling Quaker Shrine*, 401 South Main, (319) 258-2541, donation. Built by Henderson Lewelling in the 1840s, the nine-room house was designed with trapdoors, hideaway closets, and other places to hide slaves running away from nearby Missouri, which was a slave state before the Civil War. Lewelling transported some of the runaway slaves to and from the house in wagons carrying fruit and hay.

Continue north on Main Street/W55 out of Salem for 5 miles to the marked turnoff to the *Oakland Mills Nature Center*. Sitting on a hill on the right side of the highway, the facility, (319) 986-5067, free, is operated by the Henry County Conservation Board and has mounted animals, interpretative displays about the regional wildlife, trees, waterways, and plants, and hands-on activities.

Just below the nature center on W55 and straddling the Skunk River is *Oakland Mills Park* (same phone number). Sited where a hydroelectric plant operated for about 40 years until the 1960s, the park has fishing access to the river, picnic facilities, and a pedestrian bridge across the river. A viewing scope is available for watching wildlife along the river, including the bald eagles that frequent the area in the winter. Campsites are on both sides of the river: on the south bank is a modern campground with 24 electrical sites and 11 primitive units; north of the river are primitive campgrounds, a playground, and an observation tower.

Used as the backdrop by Grant Wood for his painting American Gothic, this small home is on the east side of Eldon.

Continue north on W55 for 1.5 miles to U.S. Highway 34. Turn left (west), go about 7 miles, then turn right (north) on County Road W40 (which is also Center Street). Take that for less than a half mile to Main Street in Lockridge. Turn left (west) and, a mile later, you will come upon the *Johnny Clock Museum*, 711 West Main (319) 696-3711, admission. Featuring clocks carved by John R. McLain, who learned woodworking on his own, this collection is similar to the Bily Clocks in Spillville (see Tour 17) except Mc-Lain's works are more contemporary and whimsical. Among his creative timepieces are a seven-foot-high depiction of the governor's mansion, Terrace Hill; one in the shape of Woody Woodpecker; a clock showing Disney characters; one that serves as a display case of Coca-Cola; a Memories Clock, which holds items given to McLain by his friends, family, and neighbors; and his Grandmothers Clock, which stands more than seven feet high and has memorabilia related to the woman who gave him his first carving knife years ago. In the Native American Room, furniture made of red oak includes a lamp measuring more than eight feet high and four feet wide and illustrated with carvings of the Indians' way of life, including a buffalo hunt and a ceremonial pipe.

Continue west on Main Street, which is also Old Highway 34, until new Highway 34 curves up to join it. Continue on 34 for about 10 miles to Fairfield. This is the home of the first Carnegie library built west of the Mississippi. It was the first time industrialist and philanthropist Andrew Carnegie funded a library ($30,000 for this one) in a town that did not have a connection with his business, a practice he then continued across the rest of the nation.

Quick Trip Option 4: Those interested in transcendental meditation have long known that Fairfield is the home of the *Maharishi University of Management*. In 2001, several devotees of TM created their own community, Maharishi Verdic City (pronounced "vah-dick"), 2 miles north of Fairfield along State Highway 1. The city, which is Iowa's newest and has its own currency (smartly, though, dollars are still welcome here), is planned with a circular design, and all homes, offices and other buildings face east. Some have golden domes and many of the homes are startling. Future plans call for the creation of Maharishi Veda Land, a theme park. Four-hour tours of the community (admission) are given on Friday and Saturday, beginning at *Raj Ayurveda Health*

Spa, 1734 Jasmine Avenue, (641) 472-9580 and (800) 248-9050, which also offers rejuvenations, or holistic cleansings. By the way, Maharishi is pronounced "ma-har-shi."

From Fairfield, continue west on Highway 34 for 15 miles to State Highway 16. Turn left (south) and proceed for 6 miles to Eldon. Follow the signs to the *American Gothic House*, 301 American Gothic Street, (641) 652-3406, and soon you'll be in front of the five-room home that artist Grant Wood saw when he taught a workshop here in the summer of 1930. He was so taken with its Gothic-style upper front window, a touch of class for such a small rural house, that he worked it into the background of his most famous painting, *American Gothic*, which depicts a farmer and his daughter in the foreground (actually they were Wood's dentist, Byron McKeeby, and the artist's sister, Nan, whose faces Wood painted to mimic the window shape's and length).

Return north to Highway 34 and resume going west for about 11 miles back to Ottumwa. Along the way, at the tiny town of Agency, a sign points the way to the grave of Chief Wapello where a shiny obelisk reflects the colors of the sky.

In Ottumwa, go to U.S. Highway 63, turn right (north), and proceed into the center of town, thus ending this tour.

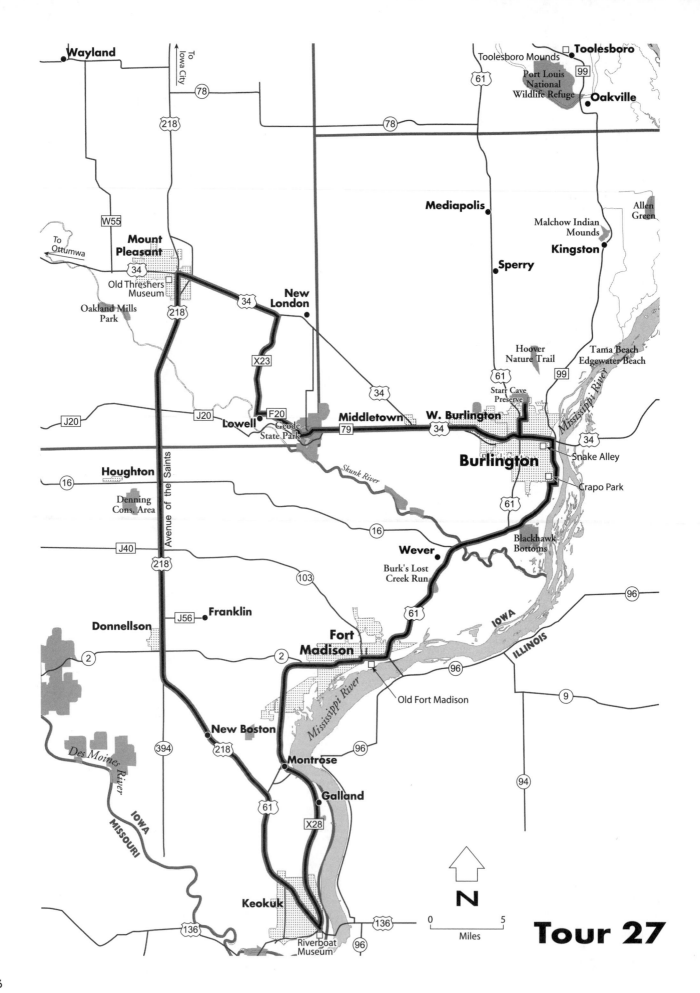

Wayland

To Iowa City

78

Toolesboro Mounds ☐ **Toolesboro**

Port Louis National Wildlife Refuge

61 99

Oakville

78

218

Mediapolis ●

Malchow Indian Mounds

Allen Green

W55

Mount Pleasant

Old Threshers Museum

Oakland Mills Park

34

218

34

New London

X23

Sperry ●

Kingston ●

Hoover Nature Trail

Tama Beach Edgewater Beach

61 99

Mississippi River

J20 J20

Lowell

F20

Middletown

79

Starr Cave Preserve

W. Burlington

34

Geode State Park

34

Houghton

16

Denning Cons. Area

Avenue of the Saints

Skunk River

Burlington

Snake Alley

Crapo Park

61

J40

218

Franklin ●

J56

Donnellson

2

16

103

Wever ●

Burk's Lost Creek Run

61

Blackhawk Bottoms

96

Fort Madison

2

IOWA

ILLINOIS

9

Old Fort Madison

96

New Boston ●

218

394

Des Moines River

IOWA

MISSOURI

Montrose ●

Galland ●

X28

Mississippi River

61

96

94

96

Keokuk

136

Riverboat Museum

136

96

0   5
Miles

N

Tour 27

Tour 27
Rolling Near the Mississippi River in Iowa's Southeast Corner

Burlington—Geode State Park—Mount Pleasant—Keokuk—Fort Madison—Burlington

Distance: approximately 110 miles

The southeast corner of Iowa may be at the bottom of the state but it's certainly tops in areas like history, mansions, and natural wonders, including geodes and fantastic vistas of the nation's mightiest river, the Mississippi. Museums here are loaded with information about the region's residents, all the way from those who built burial and ceremonial mounds more than 2,000 years ago to those who survived the disastrous floods of 1993. Among the people who have lived here are the Illini, Mark Twain, Robert E. Lee, Mrs. John D. Rockefeller, and a set of brothers who developed one of the nation's larger department store chains. Interesting places include the state's first fort, first capitol, a power plant that was once the world's largest, a very snaky street, and the spot where the American flag first flew above Iowa.

Begin this tour in downtown Burlington, at North Main Street going south from U.S. Highway 34. If you approached Burlington on Highway 34 from either the east or west, you had to be impressed. If you arrive from the east, you have to cross the elegant new Great River Bridge rising high above the Mississippi. If you come from the west, you will see the bridge rising ahead of you, its H-shaped tower and cables creating graceful lines against the sky.

On North Main, turn left (east) as soon as you can turn. You will wind up at the *Port of Burlington*, a former riverfront warehouse with several functions. One is housing the city's *Welcome Center*, 400 North Front Street, (319) 752-8731, which has plenty of information about Iowa and this region where there is a lot to see, so study the brochures and pamphlets. Displays discuss the history of Burlington and the Mississippi, and audiotapes are available for visitors to play as they drive around Heritage Hill and West Jefferson Street National Historic Districts, which have more than 200 fantastic homes that may be viewed from the outside. A gift shop has items about Iowa as well as many made in the state.

The port building is also where *Catfish Bend Riverboat Casino*, (319) 372-2946 and (800) 372-2946, a gambling boat, docks from November to April (it's at Fort Madison during the other months when it cruises the river). Able to carry 1,500 passengers, the boat has gaming tables and slots as well as live entertainment, dining, and dancing. Finally, the port building has a nice plaza that overlooks the Mississippi, just yards away, and the $60 million Great River Bridge, the pride of the area.

South of the port building is *Memorial Auditorium*, a sparkling white, Moderne-style building that hosts concerts, conventions, and other events. By the way, if you're here on a hot day and don't mind the kids getting wet . . . or wetting your own toes . . . find the sidewalk-level water fountains near the auditorium they're a delightful, refreshing way to have a cool foot massage.

You can also continue to stroll along the river in the city's Historic Riverwalk.

Famous Burlington Natives

Burlington has been home to many noteworthy people, including Lewella Parsons, an early Hollywood gossip columnist; conservationist Aldo Leopold; astronaut James Kelly; the inventor of nylon, Wallace Carothers; Laura Spelman, a young laundress who worked for rich people and became one herself—Mrs. John D. Rockefeller; and Roy Edward Marquardt, who made everything from rocket nozzles and engines to kidney dialysis machines.

Go about four blocks west on Columbia Street, which is almost directly behind the Port of Burlington, and drive up the hill there. On the way, you will see *Phelps House Museum*, 521 Columbia, (319) 753-2449, admission, an 1851 mansion that had an Italianate tower added two decades later. Inside are furnishings of well-to-do families from the nineteenth century—marble fireplaces, furniture of mahogany and walnut, and parquet floors. On the third floor, things change radically with displays of medical items used when the house was a hospital for five years.

Just a hop, skip, and a wow next to Phelps House is Burlington's most famous landmark, *Snake Alley*, Columbia and 6th Streets, (319) 752-6365 and (800) 82-RIVER, free. This twisting road is only a block long, from Columbia Street South to Washington Street, but it has a drop of

A driver slowly negotiates the many curves of Snake Alley in Burlington.

58 feet. In 1894, an engineer, an architect, and a contractor came up with an ingenious way of permitting horse-drawn vehicles to go down the south face of this hill. Knowing a straight road was a sure way to put carts on top of the horses by the time they arrived at the bottom, the men created a twisting-and-turning solution—a street with five half curves and two quarter curves that make a safer ride although it still tests one's anxieties—try it and see. It's a one-way, going down, thank goodness.

Other Burlington Sites

As you went up Columbia, you might have noticed a marker at 3rd Street noting that the site was the location of the second capitol of the Wisconsin Territory from 1837 to 1838, and the first capitol of the Iowa Territory from 1838 to 1840 when the government shifted to Iowa City.

Nearby is the renovated *Burlington Free Public Library*, 4th Street and Columbia, (319) 753-1647, an architectural gem showing touches of Italian Villa, Renaissance Revival, and Georgian Revival styles. Belonging to Iowa's oldest public library association, which began in 1868, the 1898 building holds a nice art collection.

In May 1839, the *Burlington Patriot* newspaper began publication; now called the *Hawkeye*, it's the state's oldest newspaper.

Down on Washington Street, go a few buildings to the right to visit *Arts for Living Center*, 7th and Washington Streets, (319) 754-8059, free, a former church that shows the works of local artists.

Quick Trip Option 1: Take Main Street to the north of downtown where it quickly changes to Bluff Road and then Des Moines Avenue, all of which are also County Road 99. Head 12 miles north to *Kingston*; 1.2 miles past that town is a small parking area and a sign on the left (west) for *Malchow Mounds State Preserve*, (319) 523-8319, free. A short but hard trail leads up to 60 burial and ceremonial mounds believed to have been built between 100 BC and AD 300. Items found at this site, once occupied by the Middle Woodland people, have included those from as far away as Yellowstone National Park, the Appalachian Mountains, the eastern seaboard, and the Gulf of Mexico, illustrating how extensive trading was between the prehistoric Indians years ago.

Twelve more miles up 99 is *Toolesboro* and just beyond this small community is *Toolesboro Mounds State Preserve*, (319) 523-8381, free. Much easier to visit than the Malchow Mounds, these seven conical mounds are believed by some to be where French explorers Louis Joliet and Jacques Marquette first met with the Illini who were living here in 1673. (Others believe that research in the 1990s indicates the meeting occurred on the southern banks of the Des Moines River, northeast of Keokuk but in what is now Missouri. Still, considering the Frenchmen took eight days to get from the mouth of the Wisconsin River to the place where they met the Illini, it's conceivable that they stayed somewhere in Iowa in those eight days.) An information center has displays about the prehistoric Indians who also lived here.

Return to Highway 34 and head west for 2.5 miles to U.S. Highway 61. Turn right (north) and, after about 1 mile, turn right (east) at Sunnyside Avenue. After a half mile, turn left (north) onto Irish Ridge Road and, in another half mile, turn to the left (west) to *Starr's Cave and Preserve*, 11627 Starr's Cave Road, (319) 753-5808, free. Here, a large, mill-like structure holds a nice nature center, and trails lead through the heavily wooded grounds that are bisected by Flint Creek. If the water's low, you can wade to more trails that lead to Starr's Cave; mercifully, a set of steps have been erected to the cave, which is high on a limestone bluff. Visitors can't venture very far into the cave because its walls get narrow very fast, but there's a nice view from the entrance. Also, study the walls of the cave for fossilized crinoids; they have been here for eons.

If the creek is high, you can go north of the preserve's entrance on Irish Ridge Road to find another access; park near the signs that point the way to the cave.

Return to Highway 34 and continue going west for 6 miles to Middletown. Along the way, you will pass the massive locomotive repair shops of the Burlington Northern Santa Fe Railroad and a short time later, the U.S. Army Ammunitions Plant.

At Middletown, as Highway 34 angles to the northwest, go straight west on County Road 79. After 6 miles you'll run arrive at *Geode State Park.* At 1,641 acres, Geode, (319) 392-4601, is one of Iowa's larger state parks and has 186 campsites, about half of which have electricity, lots of trails, swimming, a boat ramp, and boat rentals. Named after the state rock, Geode State Park has a display of the hollow limestone rocks with quartz interiors at the main campground.

Make your way around the south end of the park's 200-acre lake and leave by the park's west entrance. Take County Road F20 to Lowell, less than 2 miles away, and turn right (north) onto County Road X23. Take this for 7 miles to Highway 34, then go left (west) for 9 miles to Mount Pleasant. A few blocks after you pass U.S. Highway 218 at that city's eastern edge, turn left at the signs pointing the way to the Midwest *Old Threshers Heritage Museum,* 405 East Threshers Road, (319) 385-8937, admission. If you love old tractors and have never been here, congratulations, you've reached heaven. It's filled with steam- and gas-powered tractors, stationary engines, and antique farm implements pulled by tractors and horses. There's also an operating carousel and electric trolleys.

A part of the complex is the *Theater Museum of Repertoire Americana,* (319) 385-9432 and (888) 826-6622, admission, a collection of items used in theaters of the past, including back drops, painted stage curtains, scripts, playbills, and musical scores, some dating back to the 1850s.

Return to Highway 34, which is also called Washington Street here, turn left (west), and proceed just beyond the town square to the *Van Allen House Heritage Center.* A welcome center and the home where scientist James Van Allen grew up, the facility, 502 West Washington, (319) 385-2460 and (800) 421-4282, free, has tourism literature about the area as well as displays about Van Allen, whose equipment on America's early satellites made possible detected the radiation belts that surround the earth.

Head back east on Washington Street to Highway 218, turn right, and head south for 24 miles to the place where the highway veers to the southeast. Drive another 15 miles to downtown Keokuk and Main Street. After you enter Iowa's southeastern-most city, it may seem like quite a trip to reach the downtown area near the Mississippi River. Just past 4th Street, visit the *Keokuk Area Convention and Tourism Bureau,* 329 Main, (319) 524-5599 and (800) 383-1219, which has information about what's in this historic community. Be sure to pick up the brochure *On the Avenue* for use later on.

Quick Trip Option 2: On the way south on Highway 218, about 8 miles south of Mount Pleasant, turn left (east) at County Road J56. Less than 3 miles away, upon entering Franklin, go two blocks past the city park and turn right (south) on 3rd Street. At the end of that street, in three blocks, is the *Christian Herschler Historic District Winery and Stagecoach Stop,* 3rd and Green Streets, (319) 835-9432. Built in the 1860s as a stagecoach stop, the building still has original murals that you can view. Meats, cheeses, crackers, and wines are made right here.

From the visitor bureau on Main Street, drive southeast toward the bridge over the Mississippi River but, at the very last moment, turn right (southwest) at South 1st Street. After one block, turn left (southeast) onto Johnson Street, which takes you down to the river. Here, you'll see the *George M. Verity Riverboat Museum* in Victory Park, (319) 524-4765 and (800) 383-1219, admission. Landlocked now, this 1927 paddlewheel boat, which was once called the *SS Thorpe* and was the first steamboat to take barges from Saint Louis to Saint Paul, worked on the river until 1960. Now it's full of artifacts and displays about what it was like to work and live on the Mississippi.

It's possible to watch huge tows passing through the locks on the Mississippi at Keokuk.

Just north of the bridge is a turnout near what had been the old bridge crossing the Mississippi; now it's a nice observation deck to view boats passing through *Lock and Dam Number 19,* below. With a length of 1,200 feet, it's one of the longest locks on the upper Mississippi and can accommodate an entire tow: 15 barges and a tug. As for the power plant at the dam, it was the world's largest electric generating plant when built in 1913; now it's the largest privately owned plant on the Mississippi and still uses all of its original 15 turbines. The observation platform is a good place to watch bald eagles when they congregate here in the winter to snatch fish from the open waters below the dam; the third weekend of January is celebrated as *Bald Eagle Appreciation Days*.

Iowa, High and Low

Keokuk has the lowest elevation of anyplace in Iowa, 480 feet above sea level and 1,190 feet below Iowa's highest point near Sibley.

From the observation platform north of Main Street, drive northwest up nearby Blondeau Street and go to North 5th Street; turn right (northeast) and drive a couple of blocks. You'll arrive at the *Miller House Museum*, 318 North 5th Street, (319) 524-5599 and (800) 383-1219, admission, home of Samuel F. Miller, who was appointed to the U.S. Supreme Court by Abraham Lincoln in 1862 and served there until 1890.

Continue northeast on 5th for a few blocks to where it turns into Grand Avenue. Follow Grand as it overlooks the Mississippi River on the right. Remember the *On the Avenue* brochure you got awhile ago? Well, open it now as a guide while you drive slowly along Grand Avenue, admiring the big, luxurious homes that have been built here over the years. One home, at 925 Grand, belonged to Howard Hughes, Sr., father of the reclusive billionaire. Two others are B&Bs so if you want to stay in one of these mansions, here's your chance; they are the *Grand Anne*, 816 Grand, (319) 524-6310 and (800) 524-6130; and River's Edge, 611 Grand, (319) 524-1700 and (888) 581-3343.

Continue north up Grand Avenue a short distance to Rand Park. Here stands a statue of Chief Keokuk overlooking the Mississippi below. No one knows why the town is named after him, and it's also not known if he was really a chief. In fact, he may never have been here for all anyone knows. He was said to have one-quarter French and three-quarter Indian ancestry and his last name may have been LaMotte—and there is a town by that name in Dubuque County.

On the last full weekend of each April, Rand Park serves as the battlefield for Civil War buffs who reenact the *Battle of Pea Ridge*, a Missouri fight won by General Samuel Curtis, a former mayor of Keokuk. During the two-day event, a battle is presented each day featuring infantry firing muskets, galloping cavalry, and thundering artillery. Visitors can take in the soldiers' camps, dance at an elaborate military ball, attend a memorial service at the National Cemetery at 1701 J Street, (319) 524-5193, listen to military concerts, watch a women's style show from the 1860s, and perhaps meet Abraham Lincoln and his First Lady. Earning Iowa's Tourism Event of the Year at least four times, the reenactment has also been named among the top 100 events in the nation by the American Bus Association.

A historical note: during the Civil War, Keokuk had seven hospitals. Its National Cemetery was the first west of the Mississippi and is the only one in Iowa.

Stay on Grand Avenue going north, which eventually becomes County Road X28, and take that for about 5.5 miles to Galland. Part of the *Great River Road*, one of two national scenic byways in Iowa, the road stays close to the river and a railroad track much of the way. Galland is where a replica of Iowa's first school, *Galland School*, stands, barely bigger than a one-car garage.

Brushes with Fame

Samuel Clemens, known also as Mark Twain, lived in Keokuk from 1855 to late 1856, working for his brother, Orion, a printer. Besides selling his first article to the local *Saturday Post*, 20-year-old Clemens made his first public speech ever in Keokuk on January 17, 1856 at a printer's banquet and was listed in the city directory as "Clemens, Samuel L., Antiquarian, 52 Main street, bds at Ivins House."

Another Keokuk resident who made news was John W. "Bud" Fowler who was known earlier as John W. Walker. In 1878 he became the first African-American to play professional baseball with the Lynn (Massachusetts) Live Oaks and in 1885 played here with the Western League Keokuks in a variety of positions but most often at second base. Fowler is said to have invented shin guards, to protect his legs from the spikes of white baseball players. Regarding the Keokuks, they played in the National Association of Professional Baseball Teams with teams from Saint Louis, Chicago, New York, Boston, and Philadelphia.

In the 1830s, a young army engineer, Lieutenant Robert E. Lee, led a party of surveyors to study the Mississippi rapids that were notoriously known as the Des Moines Rapids and designed a waterway through them. He also suggested that the rapids were an excellent potential source of hydro-energy. The rapids have since been covered by the portion of the river behind the dam, which is 32 feet higher than the lower part. By the way, Lee County is named after William Elliot Lee, a New York financier, not Robert E. Lee.

In 1856, brothers Lipman, Samuel, and Marcus Younker, who had all just arrived from Poland, opened a dry goods store at 82 Main Street. In 1874, their younger brother, Herman, opened a store in Des Moines, where the entire operations shifted six years later. Today, Younkers, Inc. has 50 stores in six Midwestern states.

Continue on X28 for 3 more miles to Montrose, where you turn left (west) on State Highway 404, go 1 mile to U.S. Highway 61, and turn right (north). Drive for 13 miles to downtown Fort Madison. Along the way, the highway is joined by State Highway 2 and turns to the east.

Turn right at 10th Street toward two nicely restored depots. The first one you encounter is the former Burlington Northern Depot, now the *Fort Madison Art Center,* 804 10th Street, (319) 372-3996, free. Along with jewelry, pottery, photographs, and paintings by about 40 local artists, the center hosts exhibits by other artists known regionally and nationally.

Across the tracks to the south is the *North Lee County Historical Center*, 10th Street, (319) 372-7661, admission. In the former Santa Fe Depot, which was built in 1909, the museum has displays related to the region's railroad history, the Civil War, and the town as it grew from a solitary outpost in the wilderness to a thriving community. This is also where you can learn about Sheaffer pens, which are made at the company's headquarters less than a mile away (the headquarters has no tours or displays), the Santa Fe Railroad, and the nearby penitentiary. One display in particular is an eye-opener: it represents a room in a house that was visited by the famous floods of 1993—the ooze looks so real that you expect to slip at any moment. While here, pick up the brochure *Driving Tour of Victorian Homes* and check out nearly 90 historical houses around town.

The next destination, *Riverview Park*, is nearby, but the best way to get there is to return to Highway 61 (also known as H Street in town), and drive a short distance to the east rather than trying to walk through an area that's busy with train traffic. Upon entering the park, which fronts the Mississippi, you'll be right at *Old Fort Madison*, (319) 372-6318, admission. A re-creation of the fort built here in 1808 by the American army, the modern counterpart is staffed with reenactors who play their parts as soldiers, officers, cooks, and others. You enter through a trading post called the Factory and pass into the fort where the log structures look as though the troops departed just moments before. Inside are barracks, officer's quarters and offices, kitchens, dining rooms, and more, all outfitted as they were nearly two centuries ago.

The real fort was actually upriver by a few hundred yards—its site is marked by a sole chimney on the south side of the highway near the Sheaffer Pen company. Aiding the British during the War of 1812, some Sauk, Fox, and Winnebago (not all were unfriendly to the Americans, by the way) attacked the fort in September 1812 and then withdrew. But the next summer, the Indians

Old Fort Madison is a re-creation of the original fort that was located near here during the War of 1812.

were back and, worried about holding the fort, the commander ordered his men to abandon it. So, one night in September 1813 the soldiers set the fort on fire and made their way to boats they had secreted on the riverbank to escape safely down the Mississippi.

The replica's buildings were made by inmates of the nearby penitentiary.

Near the old fort is the landing for *Catfish Bend Riverboat Casino*, 902 Riverview Drive, (319) 372-2946 and (800) 372-2946, which operates here between May and October when not at Burlington.

Return to Highway 61 and turn right, which will take you out of town in a northeasterly direction. Right past Riverview Park is the city's *Welcome Center*, 1st and H Streets, (319) 372-8648, at the foot of the *Santa Fe Swing Bridge*. After looking at the brochures and getting any additional information you want, check out the bridge. It's the world's longest double-deck swing bridge. On top is a road for motorized vehicles and below, train tracks; a 525-foot-long portion of the bridge rotates to permit large vessels to pass by on the Mississippi River.

Up the highway a bit as it curves to the northeast is the Iowa State Penitentiary, which opened in 1839—before Iowa was a state! If you want to see what life is like in a prison—without committing a felony—visit the Anamosa State Penitentiary Museum in Anamosa (in Tour 22).

A Two-Seat County

Because residents of Keokuk and Fort Madison could not agree on which city should be the seat of Lee County, the state legislature made each city a county seat. As a result, Lee County is the only one in the state with two county seats, and thus two county courthouses too. The sheriff's office, though, is diplomatically located between those two cities, in Montrose.

Continue northeast up Highway 61 for about 9 miles to the Skunk River. About 3 miles after that, when the road curves to the north, turn onto County Road X62, which is the former Highway 61. This leads directly into southern Burlington and becomes a street that changes names several times along the way—Summer Street, Fort Madison Road, and, once in town, Madison Avenue.

As you enter town on Madison Avenue, turn right (east) into Crapo Park. Wind your way east through the park (pronounced "cray-poe"), which is filled with flower gardens, open lawns, trees, play areas, and more. At the east end of the park, across South Main Street, is the *Hawkeye Log Cabin*, (319) 753-2449, admission, a reconstruction that gives the traveler an idea of what an early settler's home was like.

On August 23, 1805, Lieutenant Zebulon Pike walked up from the Mississippi to a spot along the nearby bluff and planted a flagstaff. It was the first time the American flag flew in what was to become Iowa.

Go north on South Main Street directly to downtown and Highway 34, finishing this tour of southeast Iowa.

MORE
GREAT TITLES
FROM TRAILS BOOKS & PRAIRIE OAK PRESS

Activity Guides

Great Cross-Country Ski Trails: Wisconsin, Minnesota, Michigan & Ontario,
Wm. Chad McGrath

Great Minnesota Walks: 49 Strolls, Rambles, Hikes, and Treks,
Wm. Chad McGrath

Great Wisconsin Walks: 45 Strolls, Rambles, Hikes, and Treks,
Wm. Chad McGrath

Paddling Illinois: 64 Great Trips by Canoe and Kayak, Mike Svob

Paddling Southern Wisconsin: 82 Great Trips by Canoe and Kayak,
Mike Svob

Paddling Northern Wisconsin: 82 Great Trips by Canoe and Kayak,
Mike Svob

**Wisconsin Underground: A Guide to Caves, Mines, and Tunnels in
and around the Badger State,** Doris Green

**Minnesota Underground & the Best of the Black Hills: A Guide to
Mines, Sinks, Caves, and Disappearing Streams,** Doris Green

Travel Guides

Great Little Museums of the Midwest, Christine des Garennes

Great Minnesota Weekend Adventures, Beth Gauper

The Great Wisconsin Touring Book: 30 Spectacular Auto Tours,
Gary Knowles

Tastes of Minnesota: A Food Lover's Tour, Donna Tabbert Long

Wisconsin Lighthouses: A Photographic and Historical Guide,
Ken and Barb Wardius

Wisconsin Waterfalls, Patrick Lisi

Wisconsin Family Weekends: 20 Fun Trips for You and the Kids,
Susan Lampert Smith

County Parks of Wisconsin, Revised Edition, Jeannette and Chet Bell

Up North Wisconsin: A Region for All Seasons, Sharyn Alden

Great Wisconsin Taverns: 101 Distinctive Badger Bars, Dennis Boyer

Great Weekend Adventures, the Editors of Wisconsin Trails

Eating Well in Wisconsin, Jerry Minnich

Acorn Guide to Northwest Wisconsin, Tim Bewer

Nature Essays

Wild Wisconsin Notebook, James Buchholz

Trout Friends, Bill Stokes

Northern Passages: Reflections from Lake Superior Country,
Michael Van Stappen

River Stories: Growing Up on the Wisconsin, Delores Chamberlain